YOUNG RADICALS

Also by Kenneth Keniston

The Uncommitted

Young Radicals

Notes on Committed Youth

Kenneth Keniston

Harcourt Brace Jovanovich, Inc., New York

A
Harvest
Book

ISBN 0-15-665508-X

Library of Congress Catalog Card Number: 68–23578

Printed in the United States of America

G.6.70

FOR ELLEN

Acknowledgments

In many respects, this study is a collective work. Much of the book consists of quotations from the leaders of Vietnam Summer, most of whom read an earlier, much shorter draft of this manuscript. Many sent detailed comments that improved not only the substance of this book, but its style, grammar, and even spelling. Some of these comments have been included as quotations in the present text, while others led to major revisions of the manuscript. My principal co-authors must remain nameless here; but my debt to them is overwhelming, and it is more than perfunctory to remark that the errors that remain are literally my own.

In addition, many others read and commented upon the earlier draft of this book. I have profited from, used, and shamelessly exploited their help. Among those to whom I am indebted are Gar Alperovitz, Philip Altbach, Earl Brown, Kai Erikson, Richard Flacks, Christopher Jencks, Joseph Katz, Andrew Kopkind, Richard Peterson, Nevitt Sanford, Brewster Smith, and Michael Walzer. I am more than ever indebted to my friend and colleague Robert J. Lifton. His comments, more than anyone else's, helped me clarify and formulate these observations on young radicals and their historical position. To Hiram Haydn I am grateful not only for his perceptive advice, but for his understanding of my eagerness to see this account of the leaders of Vietnam Summer 1967 published before the summer of 1968.

Aspects of this study were discussed at the meeting of the Group for the Study of Psychohistorical Process at Wellfleet, Massachusetts, in August, 1967. I am grateful to the members of that group, in particular to Erik Erikson, Robert J. Lifton, Frederick Wyatt, and Robert Coles, for their lucid and helpful comments. Discussion of a paper on "Psychological Issues in the Development of Young Radicals," presented at the annual meeting of the Academy for Psychoanalysis in December 1967, helped me sharpen further my thinking. Portions of this book were presented as lectures at Trinity College, Hartford, Connecticut, in February, 1967.

To the Foundations Fund for Research in Psychiatry, I am indebted for their prompt response for an "emergency" grant at a time when the topic, methods, and goals of this study were completely undefined. Mrs. Sylvia Rifkin and Mrs. Mary Dixon typed the research interviews and several drafts of the manuscript with extraordinary skill, intelligence, and patience.

My wife, Ellen Uviller Keniston, first encouraged me to undertake this study despite my own misgivings; her intuition added enormously to my understanding both of these young radicals and of my own involvement with them; she endured my many physical and psychological absences made necessary by this study. Her largely unacknowledged help makes me the more regretful that so few of those I studied were women, for I suspect it is as true for many radicals as it is for me that women are crucial to the work of men.

K. K.

New Haven, Connecticut
January, 1968

Contents

Introduction: Vietnam Summer and the New Left 3

What was Vietnam Summer? 4
The course of this study 8
Vietnam Summer leaders and the New Left 13

1. The radical commitment 20

As seen in interviews 21
On being a radical 25
The openness of the future 36

2. Personal roots: struggle and specialness 44

Two inadequate hypotheses 45
In the beginning 48
Maternal love and pressure 51
The split in the image of the father 55
The principled parents 60
The experience of struggle 67
The early sense of specialness 70
Childhood and politics 74

3. Personal roots: turmoil, success, and the end of the line 77

Turmoil-filled adolescence 78
The resumption of success 86

Portents of radicalism 92
Nearing the end of the line 98
Adolescence and politics 101

4. *Becoming a radical* 106

Continuity and change 111
The "naturalness" of commitment 120
The confrontation with inequity 125
The shock of confrontation 126
The failure of the system 127
The radical reinterpretation 129
Outrage, deprivation, and guilt 131
Activation and engagement 133
The extension of responsibility 134
The finding of models 135
The issue of effectiveness 140
Engagement with the Movement 143

5. *The tensions of Movement work* 147

Encapsulation and solidarity 150
Participation and power 160
Process and program 173
Cultural and political revolution 182
Group tension and personal change 190

6. *The continuation of change* 193

Weariness, rage, and resistance 194
Persistence and reward 204
The continuation of change 216
Accident, obedience, and history 225

7. *Change, affluence, and violence* 229

Change and the credibility gap 231
The advent of automatic affluence 239
Violence: sadism and cataclysm 247

8. *Youth and history* 257

"Young radical": a temporary identity 259
Youth as a stage of life 264

The post-modern style 272
Fluidity, flux, change, movement 275
Generational identification, inclusion 277
Personalism, participation 279
Ambivalence toward technology 282
Non-violence 285
The search for new forms 285

Appendix A A note on research involvement 291

Appendix B The sources of student dissent 297

Two varieties of dissent 298
The sources of activism 305
The protest-prone personality 306
The protest-promoting institution 310
The protest-prompting cultural climate 314
The protest-producing historical situation 318
The future of student activism 320

Appendix C Alienation in American youth 326

The alienation syndrome 327
The ideology of alienation 329
Alienation as a style of life 330
Alienation and the personal past 332
Alienation in fantasy 335
Hypotheses about the psychological sources of alienation 337
Limitations and implications 338

Reference Notes 343

Bibliography 361

YOUNG RADICALS

Introduction: Vietnam Summer and the New Left

One afternoon in May, 1967, I received a long-distance call asking me to take part in a study of Vietnam Summer. The caller introduced himself as a member of the National Steering Committee of that organization; the summer project, he explained, would attempt to organize new groups to oppose the war in Southeast Asia, and several social scientists and journalists were being invited to study the development and effectiveness of the summer's work. "We hope that we can learn more about ourselves," he said.

Surprised by this call from a person I did not know, inviting me to study an organization that did not exist, I excused myself from any involvement. A busy summer lay ahead: there were deadlines to meet, a book to work on, articles to be finished, and a vacation planned. Much as I would have liked to, I could not see my way to "studying" Vietnam Summer. "We would really like to have you involved with us," he said. "Think it over for a few days."

I did think it over, I rejuggled my summer schedule, and I eventually called back to say I had changed my mind. We made arrangements to meet, and from this meeting there evolved these observations on young radicals. Before presenting the observations in detail, something must be said about Vietnam Summer, about the young radicals on whom my observations are based, and about the nature of my own involvement with them.

What was Vietnam Summer?

Vietnam Summer, as it developed from June to September, 1967, was a large and far-reaching group dedicated to "organizing new constituencies" to oppose American involvement in Southeast Asia. Those who conceived the project were identified with the "New Left," while those who actually led it were "new radicals" who strongly opposed the war in Vietnam, but were equally or more committed to other major changes in American values, institutions, and policies both abroad and at home. Non-doctrinal, and containing within it a great diversity of outlooks, Vietnam Summer generally took the view that "we will work with anyone" willing to organize to oppose the Vietnamese war. The formal statistics of the summer's work were impressive. Over twenty thousand individuals were involved at least part time in Vietnam Summer work. The National Office had on its payroll approximately two hundred workers, most of them paid subsistence or token wages; perhaps five hundred others were involved in more or less full-time organizing work in local communities. In the course of the summer, approximately $500,000 was raised, more than half of it raised in and spent on local projects.

The prime tactic of Vietnam Summer was the "teach-out"—the effort to build local organizations through door-to-door canvassing, often in connection with referendums, petitions, and public-education efforts. It was hoped that such local groups, initially organized around opposition to the war, would eventually evolve into "multi-issue" groups concerned with the whole spectrum of radical objectives from open housing to support for "liberation" movements abroad, from stopping the war in Vietnam to starting an effective attack on poverty. The long-range goal, then, was to begin through the summer's work to politicize new groups in a radical view of society. A great variety of organizing techniques was used: canvassing, circulating referendums and petitions, organizing peace fairs, lectures, films, and discussion groups, preparing and distributing information leaflets and books, supporting draft counseling and draft resistance.

Anti-war organizing work was aimed at a variety of different "constituencies," for example, middle-class professional groups, working-class groups, labor unions, inner-city Negroes, teachers, housewives, and so on. In some communities, attempts were made to bring pressure on political officeholders and civic leaders; in other areas, the focus was on building local organizations without regard to immediate political impact. The National Office of Vietnam Summer provided speakers, leaflets, work lists, and other materials to local projects. More important, through its field representatives and regional offices, it initiated a number of local efforts, trained local workers, distributed organizing manuals, and provided seed money to sustain new local groups until they could become self-supporting. The National Headquarters tried to keep in regular touch with local projects, area headquarters, and field coordinators through two WATS (Wide Area Telephone Service) lines installed in the National Headquarters and used twenty hours a day throughout the summer. Six issues of seventy-five thousand copies of *Vietnam Summer News* were published; organizing manuals were prepared; press releases, informational booklets, and broadsheets were distributed.

Gauging the "success" of Vietnam Summer is almost impossible. It was the largest organization ever put together by the New Left; it touched the lives of tens and hundreds of thousands of Americans. It obviously "failed" to stop the war in Vietnam, but none of those who planned or led the project expected that it could accomplish that objective. During the summer of 1967, there was some evidence of mounting public opposition to the war in Vietnam. While this sentiment can in no way be directly attributed to the efforts of Vietnam Summer, these efforts were among the many factors that may have helped produce a temporary increase in opposition to American military involvement in Southeast Asia. But the goal of organizing new multi-issue local groups with a radical political perspective proved more difficult to accomplish than many had anticipated. Students were, in general, the most active workers for Vietnam Summer; and with their return to college in the fall of 1967, local groups dependent on their energies tended to dissolve. As one young radical put it after the summer:

> Thirty million Americans may oppose the war, but they are middle-class Americans who are not at all personally affected by it. Vietnam Summer was unable to build the strong community organizations it had aimed for at the outset. This was largely because anti-war organizing proved exceedingly difficult. With the exception of students, the war is not a particularly effective organizing issue among any group of Americans.

If there was any one model for Vietnam Summer, it was the 1964 Freedom Summer in Mississippi. Mississippi Summer has now attained an almost legendary image among New Leftists and veterans of the civil rights struggle. The murder of three civil rights workers at the beginning of the summer of 1964, coupled with the very real dangers of civil rights work in the Deep South, gave to the direct or vicarious participants in Mississippi Summer a special intensity and dedication. Yet the applicability of the "lessons" learned in the South was continually questioned; indeed, it was never agreed just what these lessons were. On the one hand, efforts like Mississippi Summer clearly played a role in the creation of a national mood that led to the passage of important civil rights legislation. On the other hand, Mississippi Summer was, in retrospect, the culmination of the Civil Rights Movement, rather than a step in its development.

After the summer, the Civil Rights Movement began to dissipate, and many of its leaders either dropped out or became increasingly radicalized. Thus, it seemed to some that the "accomplishments" of Mississippi Summer had been ephemeral, and that the publicity and mobilization of national opinion achieved that summer had paradoxically contributed to the undermining of the Civil Rights Movement as a whole.

Furthermore, there are obvious differences between civil rights organizing and peace organizing. Mississippi Summer was largely an attempt to organize Negroes in a state where the caste system was particularly rigid, and where the white "power structure" was almost unanimous in its hostility to civil rights workers. Vietnam Summer was an attempt, largely in white communities, to organize opposition to a war that was already strongly opposed by many million Americans scattered across the country. To many Americans, the moral issues in Mississippi seemed more clear-cut than those of the war in Vietnam. In addition, Mississippi Summer found few allies among influential white Southerners, while Vietnam Summer found many allies among influential Americans who question the war in Southeast Asia. Finally, Vietnam Summer involved strong opposition to the policies of the national government, whereas Mississippi Summer was more nearly an effort to implement these policies. Comparing the effectiveness of the two projects, interpreting the "lessons" to be learned from the first, or deciding whether these lessons were applicable to Vietnam Summer were all difficult and controversial.

Vietnam Summer was a *summer* project: this fact made possible a loose coalition of individuals and groups who held a great variety of views about tactics and goals, a coalition that could not easily have been sustained for more than a summer. Deep in the mythological substratum of American life is the image of the "summer romance," an image of coming together, of intensely passionate love affairs whose inevitable end is commemorated in a series of bittersweet ballads about the "autumn leaves" and "the things we did last summer." The summer is, for Americans, a time when harmonies are possible that cannot be achieved during the workaday year from September to June. Yet it is also a time whose consequences are not expected to last past the first frost. The question "What will become of the summer?" was asked from the first days after Vietnam Summer was conceived until the last telephone wire was disconnected on September 20, 1967. But it was never answered, and perhaps that fact helped make Vietnam

Summer possible. An answer would have committed those who worked for Vietnam Summer to some vision of long-range goals that might have made this coalition impossible.

The course of this study

Vietnam Summer provided the context for these observations on young radicals, but this study was not focused on the effectiveness, organization, or impact of the summer project. Rather, it was centered on a small group of young men and women who worked in the National Office of Vietnam Summer and were directly responsible for the tone and direction of the summer project. This group consisted of approximately a dozen young men and women who had "come up through the Movement," New Leftists with a deep commitment to community organizing and peace work as a part of a broader objective of social change. In their early or middle twenties, these were committed radicals, most of whom had already devoted several years to full-time work in the Movement. Since my own involvement with these young men and women was crucial to whatever I learned about their lives and development, something more must be said about how this study evolved.

In June of 1967, still uncertain of what topic, if any, I could profitably study, I attended the Vietnam Summer Institute in Cleveland. There, three hundred young men and women met to discuss the problems of organizing against the war—a goal that for most of them was but one aspect of the objective of "radically" transforming American society and the world. For several days, I sat in on meetings, talked with experienced organizers and neophytes, and was impressed by the intelligence and dedication of those who were planning the summer.

Largely on the basis of this experience, I gradually developed a plan of research. I would undertake the study of the process of "politicization" as it had occurred in the "leaders" of Vietnam Summer—specifically, in the young men and women who constituted the "political staff" of the National Headquarters of Vietnam Summer in Cambridge, Massachusetts. This topic attracted me because of a long-standing interest in the psychological, social, and historical forces that lead to political action, commitment, and alienation. It was relevant to those I interviewed partly because of their interest in "recruiting"—an interest that involved learning how to identify and "bring along" those who might provide the basis for a politically viable New Left in American society.

A small grant from the Foundations Fund for Research in Psychiatry enabled me to travel often throughout the summer to Cambridge, where my method was to interview those I identified as "leaders" in the National Office. Despite the visible discomfort of many of these young radicals when placed in "leadership roles," it was possible to identify within the National Office a small group of young men and women who together made most of the decisions concerning the over-all tone, policies, and objectives of Vietnam Summer. Nominal power lay with the National Steering Committee, where the National Office staff was represented but outvoted by a group of somewhat older representatives of existing peace organizations, civil rights groups, and "academic radicals." The latter, although but a few years older than the National Office staff, were perceived as of an "older generation," and were viewed with some suspicion by the National Office staff because of their less radical views. But as the summer progressed, effective control of Vietnam Summer was increasingly in the hands of those who worked full time in the National Office.

I approached interviewing with a caution that turned out to be quite unnecessary. Previous experience led me to expect that a psychologist inquiring about the psychological development of young radicals immersed in active organizing work might be seen as threatening, undermining, or potentially "reductive." I expected that my questioning might be interpreted by some as an effort to "explain away" their conscious values, activities, and beliefs. Furthermore, since my own politics are in some ways more "liberal" than theirs, I feared that my lack of political commitment to the New Left might make me appear unreliable or suspect. Recalling the adage of the cultural anthropologist that a primitive tribe should be approached through its chieftains, I therefore discussed my research plans at length with those I took to be central to the National Office, explaining my objectives and seeking their assistance.

These preliminary conversations proved unnecessary. Co-operation was immediately taken for granted, and we turned to discussing specific questions of how individuals become politicized and involved in the Movement. Not only did everyone I approached agree to be interviewed, but, without exception, the staff shared my interest in the origins of their involvement. They often commented that they had given a good deal of thought to the questions that interested me, and would like a chance to talk about them. And although I told all those I interviewed that I would be glad to change the subject if I asked them questions they preferred not to answer, no one ever took me up on this offer. No topic was too personal to be discussed, no matter how obviously painful or difficult. Moreover, despite the fact that I was a stranger to them, they took my discretion and reliability for granted. Nor was there ever any suggestion that my psychological questions might derogate them or their beliefs. On the contrary, they were often more ready than I to seek the roots of their political commitment in their early experiences.

I devoted the first interview, usually lasting one or two hours, to the history of the interviewee's political development. I tried to obtain a picture of each individual's early political activities and beliefs, of his first "political memories," and of the way he had become involved in New Left organizations, looking especially for the point at which he began to think of himself as a "radical." It proved impossible, however, to talk only about "political" matters, for the interviewees often spontaneously brought up the role of family, early conflicts, and non-political events in their political lives.

I generally prefaced the second interview by explaining my own assumption that adult commitments, including political commitments, are influenced by the events of childhood, by important themes in family relationships, and by the attempt to come to terms with one's parents and their traditions. This assumption seemed to correspond to that of these young radicals, and they readily embarked on accounts of their early lives. During the second interview, I often asked directly about childhood events, family relationships, sexual development, and personal fantasies and conflicts. The third interview and any that followed it usually began with my asking the interviewee how he connected the events of his early life to his subsequent political activities and views. From then on, I had no particular plan other than to try to understand this particular individual's development.

The interviews were largely conducted in the library of the Cambridge Friends School, which housed the National Headquarters of Vietnam Summer from June to September, 1967. I tape-recorded the interviews, and undertook to maintain the confidentiality of information obtained from interviews, promising that in any report of my observations, I would not identify specific persons. On two occasions, I was asked to turn off the tape recorder briefly, once because the information discussed might be damaging to another person, and once when the interviewee was talking about an extremely painful episode in his own life. I had expected more objections to the use of the tape recorder than I encountered. In all, I interviewed seventeen individuals in the National Office of Vietnam Summer. These included six young men and women whose involvement was peripheral: they were part-time workers, individuals without previous experience in the New Left, or those who had merely "joined" without being sure of their commitment to the New Left.

The validity of my observations is obviously affected by the amount of time I spent with each interviewee. At the most, I had available to me information based on six or eight hours of interviewing, plus an equal amount of time in which I had been able to observe the interviewee "in action" with his co-workers. At the least, I had spent only one or two hours with the interviewee, and had had little opportunity to observe him in his work. What would have emerged from further contact with these young men and women I do not know. But what they told me usually seemed credible, not especially self-serving or self-justifying, and consistent with their current behavior. As I note below, these young radicals are unusually open and self-aware, willing and able to discuss freely both the intimately personal and the public aspects of their lives. Although further interviewing would have undoubtedly produced an even more complex picture of their development, I believe that my account of their lives in the next chapters is basically accurate.

After the summer was over, but before the interviews were transcribed, I wrote a preliminary and much shorter draft of this book. I distributed this draft to all of those I had interviewed, requesting their reactions, corrections, and criticisms. Their replies ranged from two to forty-five pages, and were of inestimable value in rewriting this draft. During the fall, I also reinterviewed a number of the veterans of Vietnam Summer, both to get their retrospective views on the summer and to continue my inquiry into the roots of their radicalism. Thus, I have remained in touch with all of those about whom this book is written, and I have included in this text many quotations from later interviews and letters written after the summer.

Throughout this book, I consider the special limitations and advantages of the interview method used in studying these young radicals. And in Appendix A, I discuss at greater length several aspects of my personal involvement in this research, which may be germane to placing these observations in better perspective. Here, I will only note that in general I sympathized with most of the objectives of these young radicals, and in particular with their view that ending American involvement in the war in Vietnam was a matter of urgent national importance. I have elsewhere attempted to spell out some of my interpretations of the major sources of inconsistency and tension in American society; and I have argued that "radical" changes in our society are needed. Nevertheless, I sometimes disagreed with the tactics proposed to implement the objectives of the New Left. Furthermore, I began these observations on the "new" radicals with a series of more or less explicit hypotheses concerning their psychological development, as about the differences between "activist" youth like young radicals and "alienated" youth like their hippie contemporaries. Many of these hypotheses proved incorrect, others close to correct. I have included in Appendices B and C two earlier papers that summarize these hypotheses, along with the available literature on student activism and my previous work on culturally alienated students.

Both my expectations about activism and my views about the objectives of the New Left, then, influenced my perception of these individuals and my initial judgment of the importance of what they were attempting to do. As the study progressed, I had to alter many of these expectations and judgments. I was repeatedly surprised by what I found, and I ended with a more positive evaluation of these young radicals than I had begun with. But in no sense is this a value-free or "neutral" study; rather, it is an effort to communicate some of the observations that surprised me and changed my evaluations. Indeed, I doubt that, in the summer of 1967, it would have been possible for most Americans to study young anti-war radicals without some view about the merits of their work that would have affected, pro or con, their judgment of these individuals.

Vietnam Summer leaders and the New Left

Before turning to the personal history of these young radicals, something must be said about their representativeness and their place in the New Left. I have limited this report to observations on "committed radicals," by which I mean individuals who (a) consider themselves "radicals" and/or part of the Movement, and

(b) have spent at least one year during which their primary work involved community organizing, civil rights work, peace work, or some other Movement work. Eleven of those I interviewed met these criteria. One or two had combined a primary orientation to Movement work with college or graduate school, but most had spent long periods in full-time work with the New Left, the average time being two or three years. In addition, I had previously interviewed three young men in connection with other studies who met both these criteria; these three were very similar psychologically to the Vietnam Summer leaders, and they support the generalizations made in the next chapters. The total group on whom these observations are based, then, numbers fourteen.

The age of those interviewed ranged from nineteen to twenty-nine, with an average of twenty-three. All of the radicals were white; three were women. Two came from lower-middle-class families, two from upper-class families, ten from upper-middle-class families; most frequently, their fathers were businessmen, teachers, or professionals. Seven came from Protestant backgrounds, five from Jewish backgrounds, and two from Catholic families. Three came from clearly "radical" families, with parents who had been active in left-wing movements during the 1930's; the parents of most of the remainder were Democrats, often of a "Stevensonian" persuasion. The great majority of their parents at least began college. All of the interviewees had at least begun college, and the colleges they had attended were generally academically excellent, highly selective liberal-arts colleges or private universities. Socio-economically, these young radicals clearly come from relatively privileged and advantaged sectors of American society.

In all these respects, this small group of young committed radical leaders is "representative" of other groups of radicals studied by other researchers in other contexts with other methods. In Appendix B, I summarize a large number of studies of "activists," most of whom belong to New Left groups. Like the leaders of Vietnam Summer, they tend to come from advantaged sectors of American society, to have upper-middle-class, politically liberal, and well-educated parents, and to attend prestigious colleges and universities. Many of my findings about the psychological characteristics of those I interviewed are also reported by other studies that use more statistical methods: *e.g.*, a questioning, independent spirit, freedom to express underlying feelings and impulses, orientation toward principle, outstanding academic performance, and so on. In all these respects, the leaders of Vietnam Summer are "representative" of other young radicals.

But there are other characteristics that clearly distinguish this group. Their average age of twenty-three makes them older than most student radicals; their one or more years of Movement work indicate a greater commitment to radicalism than that likely in those who merely "belong" to New Left groups. Their accounts of their past activities indicate that they have been "leaders" rather than members for some time. Furthermore, the fact that they were willing to work in the National Office of Vietnam Summer says something more about them. Not all young radicals would have been offered or would have accepted leadership positions in this project. Some radicals considered Vietnam Summer too conservative, too "coalitionist," or were opposed to national projects. Other seasoned radicals—for practical, temperamental, or ideological reasons—worked for Vietnam Summer as field workers and regional co-ordinators, and were not available to be interviewed. Although the young radicals who led Vietnam Summer had many vocal doubts about the value of national campaigns, they were willing to test these doubts against the summer's experience. And they had been "chosen" to head Vietnam Summer by members of the National Steering Committee. Thus, judgments about their effectiveness and ability to mount a national project with less than two months' lead time entered into their selection.

The position of these young radicals within the New Left is also important in judging their representativeness. In general, they occupied an ideological position somewhere between the old New Left and the new New Left. That is, they continually fought the "conservatism," "coalitionism," and emphasis on electoral politics of the National Steering Committee. One of the major arguments of the summer, for example, was between the National Office staff, who wanted to support draft resistance, and the National Steering Committee, who did not want Vietnam Summer to be identified with such militant tactics. The National Office staff prevailed. But at the same time, Vietnam Summer was too conservative for some of the most radical members of the New Left. To the most radical, Vietnam Summer was too "bureaucratic," too big, and too moderate. And its primary emphasis was on middle-class organizing, a tactic strongly opposed by the most militant New Leftists.

Yet this characterization does not indicate the enormous range of opinions and political positions *within* the National Office of Vietnam Summer. The groups with which those I interviewed had worked ranged from the American Friends Service Committee, a non-violent and relatively conservative peace organization, to the May Second Movement, an extremely radical group influenced by Chinese Communist doctrines. Between these two extremes were a great variety of other New Left organizations, including Students for a Democratic Society, National Conference for New Politics, the Student Non-violent Coordinating Committee, the Congress of Racial Equality, the Southern Student Organizing Committee, and a number of lesser-known radical groups. Together, these groups cover the entire spectrum of the New Left. Three of those I interviewed were highly sympathetic with the most radical, disruptive, and "insurrectionist" wing of the New Left: all three had misgivings about their participation in Vietnam Summer, and two said they believed that the "failure" of Vietnam Summer would demonstrate to the Movement the correctness of their own more militant views about tactics. Others I interviewed were skeptical of this militant point of view and considered themselves "moderates" within the New Left.

The New Left itself is, of course, not an organization, but a scattered and unco-ordinated group of young Americans who share certain basic criticisms of contemporary life, a common style, and a similar impatience with traditional political institutions. What those within it sometimes call the "Movement for Social Change" is not a movement in the traditional sense, but a series of unco-ordinated groups and individuals who reject the traditional "liberal" approaches to political action, just as they reject the "Old (Marxist) Left," with its doctrinaire views of history, social change, and tactics. It is impossible to characterize in a paragraph or even a chapter the central positions, views, and controversial history of the New Left. Some of the mood, the style, and the outlook of the New Left will emerge as I describe this group of young radicals.

Here it is enough to note that there is agreement within the Movement on only a few basic assumptions. First, it is assumed most major decisions in American society are ultimately determined by the industrial-military combine against whose influence General Eisenhower warned in his last address as President. This "power elite" acts so as to maintain and extend American economic interests abroad (economic imperialism), opposing all left-wing governments that might threaten these interests in the developing nations (anti-Communism). Making the massive efforts required to solve the domestic problems of American society or supporting the forces of independence and self-determination abroad are not on the power elite's agenda. Traditional liberalism has failed not only in its foreign policies, but also in its inability to give power and dignity to the poor, the deprived, and the disadvantaged. And since traditional social and political institutions have proved themselves unwieldy and unresponsive to the needs of the people (especially poor people), new social and political institutions must be created. Such institutions should be local and decentralized; they should aim at enabling all men and women to participate in making the decisions that affect their own lives.

Although the New Left has no clearly defined or agreed-upon political program, radicals share several basic (if often unstated) assumptions about the directions in which society should move. In foreign policy, America should support in every way the forces of independence in the Third World, abandoning anti-Communism in favor of support for "liberation" abroad. Specifically, this means that movements like the National Liberation Front (Vietcong) in Vietnam should be tolerated or supported rather than militarily opposed. Each nation should be allowed to work out its own destinies without American intervention. At home, most radicals would advocate far greater local autonomy in decision-making, especially for the poor. Poverty programs should be vastly extended, and their control should be in the hands of the people whom they affect. All racism and discrimination should be vigorously fought. Most young radicals also advocate some form of socialist control of the economy, although few are interested in the specifics of economic planning, production, and organization. Perhaps most important, new institutions must be created to counter the impersonality, dehumanization, and unresponsiveness of those that currently exist. Indeed, within the New Left there is a certain anarchistic strain that opposes *all* large institutions in favor of small, face-to-face groups. If there is a hidden utopia, it is the utopia of a small group of equals, meeting together in mutual trust and respect to work out their common destiny.

New Leftists do not agree on how these changes in American society are to be achieved. Within the New Left, there are a variety of "tactical" perspectives. A decreasing few favor "electoral" tactics, aimed at electing radical candidates on third-party tickets, or as regular (Democratic) party candidates. Others favor "organizing" tactics. Until 1967–1968, the organizing perspective had much support; this tactic emphasizes the importance of "grass-roots organizing," especially among the poor and disenfranchised, but also among sympathetic middle-class liberals who might be "radicalized." This perspective prevailed in Vietnam Summer: as I have noted, its goal was not only to organize for political action against the war, but also to "politicize" larger and larger groups of people by creating multi-issue groups that would eventually "radicalize" their members. A third tactical perspective emphasizes "resistance," disruption, and even insurrection as the only possible ways of building a radical movement. Its proponents argue that only through "organized confrontations" and "creative disorder" can the facts of American and international life be brought home to a public unwilling to acknowledge these facts. Resistance, too, is increasingly attractive to those who believe that the war in Vietnam is "absolutely" wrong, and that disruptive acts are justified if they will interfere with the war effort. All of these perspectives, ranging from the least to the most radical, were represented among those I interviewed.

The question whether these young radicals were "representative" of the New Left cannot be finally answered. Indeed, I am still not sure how one would go about finding a group of "typical" radicals. For among the prime characteristics of the New Left are variety and change, both of which make representativeness hard to gauge. Since the summer of 1967, both the New Left and these young men and women who consider themselves a part of it have changed, so that no statement of their position, or that of their Movement, can be considered final.

What follows is therefore a description and analysis of what I observed, rather than an attempt to characterize all radicals, or the new radicalism in its entirety. I begin with a summary of the quality of commitment in the group that led Vietnam Summer. I discuss next the personal roots of radicalism and the steps by which these particular young men and women came to think of themselves as radicals. I then turn to the tensions, frustrations, and satisfactions of Movement work as seen through their eyes. Finally, I examine the broader historical context within which they work, and on which they seek to have an effect. I undertook this study with the hope that from this small and accidental group of young men and women, we might learn something about our common predicament.

1 The radical commitment

In the summer of 1967, the young men and women who led Vietnam Summer were still in the midst of their personal and political development. More than most of their contemporaries, they considered their lives and their characters changing and incomplete. Most were still deliberately attempting to change themselves as people, to educate themselves as radicals, and to train themselves for greater political effectiveness. And all convincingly described a trajectory of personal growth whose terminus neither they nor I could foresee.

To speak of "the radical commitment" as seen in these young men and women is therefore to try to describe a process rather than an achievement, an evolving style and orientation rather than a finished identity or fixed ideology. The task of this book is to trace some of the interwoven themes—psychological, social, and historical—that enter into the continuing development of this small group of young radical leaders. But what is to be explained is the process of change itself, rather than a group of finished people or a completed Movement. Indeed, one of the central differences between the new and the old radicalism is the fact that process and motion are the essence of today's Movement, a movement of changing young people who deliberately eschew the often rigid personal and ideological positions of the Old Left.

This chapter is an account of who and where these young radicals were during the summer of 1967. One thing they were, of course, was intensely involved in their work with Vietnam Summer, and, for all, that experience was itself important and formative. The summer project was by far the largest effort ever organized within the New Left; it not only demanded from its leaders a high degree of commitment and the full use of skills previously learned in New Left work, but also the development of new skills and tactics suited for a large-scale co-ordinating organization. More important, it activated and focused the considerable energies of these young men and women on a project that was sufficiently successful to prevent the despairs of earlier organizing efforts, and sufficiently short term to avoid the fragmentations that a more long-range project might have produced.

The lens of interviews conducted during this summer therefore looked out on a group of young men and women employed to their fullest, personally and organizationally mobilized for an intensive and short-term effort, intensely and warmly related to each other, fully activated. Many noted that their mood during the summer was different from that on previous occasions. The intense activity of the summer lightened pre-existing gloom; the need for twelve to sixteen hours a day of focused and engaged work required putting aside long-range questions about the future; and the effort to learn how to run a large-scale organization in a style consistent with the values of the New Left gave these young activists a sense of personal motion and of challenge. Yet interviews conducted during the fall of 1967 indicated that the lens of the summer had not drastically distorted their features. To be sure, in the fall the intensity and focus of the summer project had been lost, but the individuals remained much the same, albeit in different settings.

As seen in interviews

That the young men and women I interviewed were extremely different, one from the other, is not in itself surprising. It is axiomatic that any given external behavior (like working in Vietnam Summer) can spring from diverse motives in distinct types of personality. But the normal expectation of diversity was more than normally fulfilled with these young radicals. Their most striking characteristic as a group was their separate "personhood," their distinctiveness, complexity, and individuality, their colorful, vivid, and expressive manner—in short, the fact that no two were at all alike.

I would have preferred to discuss the life histories of several contrasting individuals at length, thus illustrating concretely their diversity. But I could find no way of doing this without violating the confidentiality I had undertaken to maintain. In the following chapters, I have therefore used the method of a collective biography, emphasizing those issues that recurred most frequently in the lives of these young men and women. To preserve confidentiality, I have had to summarize or abstract many of the most vivid anecdotes and episodes of their lives. And I inevitably treat these young radicals as a more unified and homogeneous "type" than they are, and thus neglect in practice what I can only assert in principle: that a collective account of these young radical leaders omits many of the special themes that contribute to the intense individuality of each, and that one of the most enduring issues for almost all of them was the ambivalent meaning of that sense of "specialness" they had long possessed.

Some of the most striking characteristics of these activists will be difficult to illustrate in the pages that follow, since they cannot be conveyed in quotations from an interview transcript. For example, as I have noted, I had not expected individuals so open, so unthreatened by my interviews, or so willing to discuss not only the public aspects of their lives, but also the sometimes painfully personal and private. Despite all that has been written about the paranoia of the Leftist—old or new—these young men and women were unusually open, trusting, and candid, at least with me. They are unself-consciously at home with psychological questions and explanations, which they "naturally" apply to their own behavior. Although rarely versed in academic psychology, they take for granted an intimate connection between inner life and social action. Only two of those interviewed had been in psychotherapy, but the remainder discussed themselves with the kind of insight that one normally expects to find from those who have had extensive psychotherapy.*

Another quality that cannot be conveyed by interview transcripts is the intensity of feeling they experienced and expressed as they talked about their present and past lives. Talking about an important past event was frequently enough to evoke the emotions that had originally accompanied it. The interviewees expressed joy, sadness, anxiety, fear, love, and hate freely as they recounted their development. Several cried briefly in recalling painful (or in one case joyous) experiences. In previous interviewing experience, I have rarely found such readiness to express feelings in a short series of interviews: it suggests unusual emotional openness, whether based on genuine acceptance of feelings, or on a more ominous lack of self-control. In this case, self-acceptance seemed more explanatory than lack of self-control, for another quality of these young radicals was an unusual intellectual coherence, a high degree of cognitive organization, and a capacity to differentiate the distinct aspects of life. Despite the intensity of their feelings, they were able to keep to the point, or to return to the topic at hand after a lengthy digression. Part of this coherence is a function of high intelligence and unusual verbal fluency; another part seems related to a psychological style that involves the capacity for self-control in the presence of intense feelings.

The most graphic demonstration of this control was their reactions to the frequent interruptions in our interviews. The school library where our interviews were conducted was visible through a

---

* One interviewee, reading an earlier draft of this, wrote, "I tend to agree with your point that Movement people are more open . . . than students in general. . . . On the other hand . . . you were received as you were because you were seen immediately as an honest man with good questions. If you had come on as 'Dr. Keniston, the mind expert,' our tense and fractured group would have affirmed its essential solidarity by running you out before the first day."

glass door from the busy main corridor, and we were often interrupted without warning by telephone calls, by letters to be signed, or by lengthy consultations. The young radicals were almost always able to shift from personal and sometimes emotion-laden topics within the interview to the business that had suddenly intruded. And once this business had been dealt with, they could shift back to the narrative of their personal lives.

Despite the intensity of their feelings, almost none of the young radicals attempted to use the interviews as a means of obtaining explicit help, interpretations, support, or reassurance. In many interviewing situations, a proportion of those interviewed request, implicitly or explicitly, some form of therapy from the interviewer, and often develop complex feelings about him that are "transferences" from important early relationships in their lives. But virtually all of these young men and women accepted the role of "co-researcher," treating me as a colleague in a joint inquiry about their personal and political development, in which they were both personally and vocationally interested. While they discussed their past and present problems freely, they seemed to accept the fact that I was in no position to provide them with any psychological help; the focus in these interviews remained the mutually agreed-upon topic of how they had become radicals.

The following account will minimize or neglect much else that was important to the lives of these radicals in the summer of 1967. For example, I will not discuss at any length how these young radicals interacted with each other, the formal and informal group structures they evolved in Vietnam Summer, or the style they developed during the summer. Here, as in other areas, there were enormous individual differences: in group meetings, for example, some preferred the role of silent listener, limiting themselves to an occasional enigmatic comment; while others were active, forceful, and at times directive. Yet what I observed of them in their work was consistent with what they had told me of themselves in interviews, and indeed suggested an unusual integration of private and public life.

On being a radical

No one can predict—and especially not these young men and women themselves—whether, and in what sense, they will remain "radicals." But during the summer of 1967, as during the months that followed, one of their shared characteristics was their deep sense of commitment to the New Left. For each individual this commitment had its idiosyncratic roots. But beyond these important idiosyncrasies, there runs the theme of a deep, shared engagement with the Movement for Social Change and a continuing effort to reshape themselves so as to be more effective in that Movement.

Any interviewer who in effect asks a group of young men and women "How did you come to be what you are?" almost inevitably elicits answers that somewhat artificially integrate and sum up an ongoing process. Such answers must be seen as provisional and preliminary, as progress (or non-progress) reports, as time-slices across a moving flow. Yet such statements are useful, for in them the crucial themes of past and present life are often interwoven. These themes will recur again and again in later chapters, as I trace the complex development that led these young men and women into the New Left.

One young woman, when I asked her if she had ever considered abandoning her work in the Movement, replied:

> No, I've really been very happy. This is one of the things I feel very positive about. . . . One of the things I've learned in the last two years is that you don't need very much to live on. . . . It gives me a completely different perspective on what it is that I decide to go into. I wouldn't mind having a car, but I would have to learn to drive first. I can think of ways to enjoy a nice way of life, but I don't feel obsessed with it. . . .
>
> I sort of feel myself to be open and I feel very happy. It is like I have built a whole new world. It has been a very good transition. I feel like I have a solid foundation. . . . I just saw a friend of mine

> from ten years ago the other day, and it was very difficult to talk to her. . . . You realize that the people you want to be your friends are people where you don't have to go through the whole process of justifying why you're doing what you're doing. . . . You end up eliminating a lot of your old friends. . . . The kind of people who get involved in the Movement are really people who have a strong need for friendship. . . . I don't feel as politically conscious as maybe I should. Maybe I'm approaching things much more pragmatically. How do you build something? How do you get things done?*

In this statement about herself, she introduces issues that will recur in these interviews: her relationship to middle-class monetary and success values, her feeling of openness to the future, her gradual entry into the Movement and her loss of her past friends, her need for friendship, her sense of ideological inadequacy, and finally—and perhaps most important—the questions with which she approaches her own future and the future of the Movement.

For this young woman, as for all of her fellow workers in Vietnam Summer, personality and politics are impossible to separate. Again and again, they stressed the personal origins of political beliefs, and the effects of political involvement in their personal lives. For many, political involvement had been a major catalyst for personal change:

> It was only when I first began to do my first political activity, which was—I can't remember, a boycott or peace work or something—but I really started to move personally. I started to put my mind to a project, an activity, a way of thinking. I really started to

---

* All of the quotations in the text are from the young radicals I interviewed in Vietnam Summer. I have changed many personal, organizational, and place names. My own comments or amplifications are noted by brackets. I have used ellipses to indicate deletions from the original spoken narratives. Some quotations have been edited to eliminate unnecessary redundancy or to increase clarity. Apart from these minimal changes, they reflect accurately the spoken style of those I interviewed.

> work hard in terms of learning how to do that stuff. . . . I really put my personality into it. That's what I've been doing ever since. I obviously sublimate a lot of stuff into political activity.

Not only does this young radical underline the personal component of his political life, but he clearly indicates that a major part of the meaning of his radical commitment lies in its role in helping to start "to move personally." Another, summarizing his political development, said:

> The politics came after the people. There was always a personal relationship first. And the most important thing of what you were going to do with a person was personal, not political. The political development came from that background, and from the reading I did.

Here again, the inseparability of the personal, especially the interpersonal, and the political is underlined.

As a rule, formal elaborated and dogmatic ideological considerations were seldom discussed in these interviews; they rarely formed a major part of the radical's presentation of himself to me. No doubt, had I been a political scientist inquiring about political philosophy, statements of formal ideology could have been obtained. But to give great emphasis to such statements would, I believe, falsify the personal position of these radicals, which rests on a set of time-honored principles rather than on any elaborately rationalized ideology. One interviewee, for example, volunteered:

> One of the things that makes it difficult for me to trace where I came from is the fact that I don't have an ideology. If I did, if I knew precisely, I mean if I had clear political goals—well, I have something of an analysis of why certain things happen, and why certain things must happen. But it's not very tightly formulated and I'm very flexible about it. If I did have a rigid view, I would be better able to look back and say, "This is where this and that came from." . . . But I think it's better this way. It's more real, it ties in, it forces you to bring yourself together more as a unified thing rather than to say, "Here are my politics, Dr. Keniston, and this is where they came from. Now if you want to talk to me about a

> person, that is something else." But things really are together, and that's real. It's so— Things really *are* together.

And another noted in a similar vein:

> I have never been an ideologue. I always have been a guy who winds up, in terms of ideology, taking it for the excitement of it and really examining it, but I have a lot of difficulty in putting together broad theories. I feel much more humble, I think, than other people do. I think I'm probably wrong about that, but it was always the organizing things that I felt the most at home with. . . .

Formal statements of rationalized philosophy, articulated interpretations of history and political life, and concrete visions of political objectives were almost completely absent in the interviews (and in this respect, as in many others, this is a typically American group). But what did emerge was a strong, if often largely implicit, belief in a set of basic moral principles: justice, decency, equality, responsibility, non-violence, and fairness. The issue of "tactics," too, was often discussed—the utility of demonstrations, community organizing, electoral politics, or "resistance" as instrumentalities for the New Left. But the primary orientation to basic principles, although one of the most important issues in their lives, was so taken for granted by them (and to a large extent at the time by me as well) that it was rarely emphasized in these young radicals' summaries of themselves. And questions about tactics seemed to them so much a pragmatic matter of effectiveness that they did not include them in their self-descriptions.

Convinced that the personal and the political were linked, and emphatically anti-ideological in their ideologies, these young men and women usually emphasized the personal satisfaction they derived from Movement activities. One individual, when asked why he planned to persist as a radical, said:

> Part of it is that it's something that I do well. I wouldn't like to have to get up at 9:00 o'clock every morning and finish work at 5:30 and be under somebody's authority. [Laughs] . . . and then one is contemporary with the mainstreams of society. One feels on top of things.

Another spoke in comparable terms about the "motion in the Movement":

> I've had a lot of help, because you know there's motion in the Movement. There are people doing things, there are things happening, there are all kinds of exciting people. That helps. That helps a lot.

Still another sustaining force for some of these young radicals is the conviction that they are part of a rising tide of radicalism that is increasingly required by modern American society. For example, one young man, after having discussed his own father's growing impatience with American society, said:

> It's happening now on a national basis, some of the people who are old liberals in the analysis of American society are increasingly radical. For example, Gunnar Myrdal, who back in the fifties had a kind of "growing pains" analysis—you know, America is young and is having growing pains—his analysis is different now: something has got to be done. And I found this also among people like my father, intellectual types, that they are getting the same type of response. A lot of people of your generation or my father's generation, and from your discipline, are getting drawn into political activities.

One prime source of satisfaction in the radical's commitment, then, derives from the feeling of contemporaneity, of being in motion with others, and of involvement with a changing, growing tide of radicalism.

For others, the satisfactions of Movement work come partly from a feeling of continuity with the values of the personal and collective past. One young man from a radical family summarized his recent development as follows:

> It just seems to me that what happened was that I saw a different way of relating to people. When I started to look around at things, I felt that political activity was a vehicle for that. But it wasn't until last year that I really started feeling that I've come all the way back round full circle. Politics was no longer a vehicle, but this was *the thing*. And then I said to myself, "My God, it never *was* a vehicle.

This is what you *were*. This is where you're *at*. This is where you've come from. This is how you're made up. And you aren't supposed to be doing anything else. You shouldn't feel badly about not doing this or not doing that. This is what you *are*."

It's just, you know, a nice feeling. It's very, very supportive, both that emotional and intellectual feeling. It helps you on. It's not something that happens once and there's beautiful flowing music. But once you get that feeling, it's there, and when the time comes and you start getting into the dumps, you can say, "Look, this is what you were made to do."

Another young man, this one not from a radical family, described a strong sense of continuity to the basic values of his family:

I had a good solid family, no parental trouble among themselves or with the kids. My old man is very straight with the kids. That's been very important, because it has kept in the back of my mind all the time concepts like responsibility, seriousness: "If you're going to work on this, you can't just do it on weekends." I have this whole complex of ideas about carrying through with what you start, being serious about it, being confident about it. I really never could have come close to just flipping out and becoming totally alienated. . . . It doesn't seem to me that simple. All capitalists don't beat their wives, all workers are not hopeless charlatans. . . . That kind of thing was in the back of my mind, nagging at me: "You're not involved, you're not doing anything." . . .

The values I got from my family, the ones that I've kept, are good. I've pared them and peeled them to fit my own style, but there is a good continuity here. I mean it's a new generation, but there's a lot from my old generation that can't be minimized. Otherwise, I might have flipped out or something like that, or just turned myself off altogether.

This young man, from a relatively apolitical background, links his involvement in the Movement and his escape from "just flipping out and becoming totally alienated" to his continuity with the values of his family.

No summary can characterize the satisfactions of Movement work: for each individual, they are numerous and complex. To return to a central theme in radical development, the crucial sustaining force in the radical commitment is probably an underlying sense of acting on one's basic principles. One individual, for example, who grew up in a religious family, argued that his "basic rhetoric" is a theological one, now translated into secular terms:

> I don't get upset about sexual things, and I don't get upset about religious things. But I feel that honesty, among yourselves, is necessary. I feel that people should fulfill their commitments. I feel that one has to be serious, and able to work hard. . . . I feel those kinds of things. It's not that I'm against pot smoking or having great dances or wasting time or watching television—I love all those things. . . . But my vision had always been that all of a sudden a million people would march on Washington, singing "A Mighty Fortress Is Our God," and the government would come tumbling down. I would feel much more identified with that than if a million people marched on Washington singing "The Internationale." . . .
>
> If I let down all of my defenses, I would wind up being Billy Graham or Elmer Gantry. That would be my first impulse, to say, "That's immoral." My basic rhetoric is a very theological one. . . . Maybe if I were born three or four hundred years earlier, I'd be a preacher. I'd say that the people should reform, that they should stop being sinners, that they should realize that the world has to be built on different foundations—"Tis the final conflict," "Let each man take his place." [Laughs] . . . My initial thing is to get up and preach to people and expect them to follow me. That's where my impulse is, to speak out to the world.

Here the underlying appeal to moral principle is clearly stated: the call to sinners to reform and repent. He went on to note, however, "My problem is that the basic rhetoric is one that's irrelevant. . . . [It] just doesn't work."

Still another, in the course of discussing whether he should buy a friend's Volkswagen microbus, indicated the importance of his underlying moral commitment:

> It may cost me three hundred dollars, and I *had* been going to give that money to a political organization. I may buy it anyway—I think I probably will. It will be nice to have a microbus, and I will

> have a long life to give money away to political organizations.
>
> [K. K.: But it's a conflict for you.] Right. [Pause] But right now, it looks like there aren't many more kinds of possessions I would like to have. I don't believe people should go crazy and work sixteen hours a day because the revolution isn't coming tomorrow. It's wrong not to live until then. But I feel very strongly that people with a lot of money should give it. That comes from the same kind of value—you absolutely must do what's good for everyone, not what's good for yourself. It would be impossible for me to do that. . . . I'm not uncommitted. I have meaning in my life, that's not the problem. I have other problems, but that's not one of them. . . . And that's something (it's certainly true that I got it from my parents) that was very valuable.

In asserting that "you absolutely must do what's good for everyone," and in connecting this value to his parents, this young man affirmed both his moral commitment and his link to his past.

Another aspect of the radical commitment involves a sense of having "grown up" through involvement in the Movement. Many noted how much they had changed, in ways they liked, since their involvement in the New Left:

> I started off being very insecure in terms of what I was thinking and what I was saying. I usually felt I was wrong, and that I should follow other people's directions. But then, over the last years, I have realized that I am usually right. . . . It's not a matter of whether my predictions are right, whether Bobby Kennedy will run or not. . . . But I feel much more secure in myself, and I am much more willing at this point to project my alternatives onto people, and to push them very hard. I am more willing now to have people follow my direction and to take responsibility for it. That means the possibility of failure and getting people angry at you and all kinds of things. That was a very big struggle within myself. . . .

Finally, being committed to the Movement means being involved with other people, not being alone, being part of a meaningful group. The radical, as a member of a small political minority, must continually remind himself and be reminded that he is not alone. One individual, for example, said:

> You get these periodic shots in the arm that are very essential. Just like the parties around here. You'd think that in this place you wouldn't feel isolated. But after you get back to your apartment or to wherever you live, you see how few you are, and it gets to be very discouraging. There are billions of *them* out there, and we can't even move the students, we can't even get ten per cent of the students. But then, you have a party after the meeting on Thursday night, and you get sixty guys who you really like that are radical, and you say, "All right, sixty is enough." You feel reinspired and reinvigorated. It's the same thing with national meetings. You get people together and they give you a shot in the arm. You figure there are some other people around, and you're ready to go back to your own turf and do something yourself.

In raising the issue of helpless isolation ("There are billions of *them* out there"), and then dispelling it by discussing the importance of personal contact with others in the Movement, this young man pointed to a crucial theme in the political lives and personal histories of most of his fellows.

Yet whatever the sense of solidarity in the New Left, membership in a small, fragmented, struggling, and largely unsuccessful radical movement is clearly difficult to sustain. And sustaining most of those I interviewed was their basic feeling of self-respect or adequacy, a feeling they usually traced back to their families. One young woman, when I asked her how she managed to keep going when times were bad, said:

> I don't know. I always had the feeling in the family that I was better than [my siblings]. I was smarter than they were, I didn't have to study as hard, that my mother liked me best. . . . That's a terrible thing to think at times, and I felt guilty about it. And then my mother was very supportive. She was always very supportive, and even though I didn't always trust her, I always fell back to her. If I needed her, she was there. A lot of times I still do that now. . . . And I've been lucky because there has always been somebody there who had said the things that need to be said when I'm in a slump. Those have been my friends and my parents—my mother—even though she has all these bad things, when I'm down in the dumps, she is there, even now. I don't go to her any more, but when I was a kid I always did.

Another, describing himself in general, said:

> I'll tell you this much—I have . . . a funny kind of self-confidence. And what it did was probably to accentuate even more my need for what I'm doing now. That is to say, "See, boob, you can really finish something; you can work on it and you can really see it through." And then you can say, "Well, that's good, let's look at what it was you finished, let's look at the part you played, what you did."

For all of their self-confidence and commitment to radicalism, these young men and women also have abundant self-doubts. Some of these are intimate and personal. One young man, discussing the undesirable aspects of his parents' relationship with each other, said:

> I find that I seem to be duplicating that relationship. I seem to be just moving irrationally into that, using my parents' relationship as a model for my relationship with Judy. In a sense, she puts more value—I do too, but I don't move naturally in that direction—on a *relationship* between people. And I put much more emphasis on the family being an arena from which you go out and do things . . . for instance, my father doesn't do any work around the house, and Judy gets angry at me because I don't take out the garbage or wash the dishes. It's not that I don't think I should, it's just that I've never seen it like that before. . . . That makes me very upset because I consider my father a failure.

This young man's most pressing self-doubts center on his fear of being like his father, a fear that is unusually intense in him, but that has echoes in others with whom he worked.

Others questioned their competence for the work they set out to do. One, discussing the aftereffects of a recent meeting that depressed him, said:

> I began to question a lot in terms of myself, about where I am in the Movement. Every so often that happens. The whole question came up of which tools I have at my disposal to do the job I want to do. Sometimes I feel that they are very very lacking. . . . I feel I should read more, but I feel I have worked so long and I'm so exhausted that I just can't. Or I read something that's non-political. I'm very very shoddy about it. It's very depressing to me, because I

used to like to read like crazy when I was younger and I was in college. But now I don't. . . . I've never read a basic economics book. How about that?

It may be very odd—I say odd because I can't find a better word—I really knew a hell of a lot for an eighteen- or nineteen-year-old kid. . . . In terms of politics, I had been doing a lot of reading. I knew a pretty good deal. The problem is that (this may not be true) I haven't made three years' progress in three years' time in certain areas of knowledge. I have developed very well certain abilities, really pushed them almost to the limit of their development at this stage of my life. Yet there are other things which I need to have as a background. I need things that would give me more perspective to help me analyze what it is I've done and what it is I need to do. I need to know more about economics to know how that functions. I want to do more reading in history . . . for example, labor history. I don't know about that. I think if you have a radical perspective, you really should. I just don't have those things.

But for all of their personal and political self-doubts, and for all of the changes that have occurred in their lives in recent years, the most impressive feature of the radical commitment in these young men and women is the sense of continuity most of them feel with their pasts. One young man, discussing his parents' desire that he return to school, said:

This summer they were talking about "Are you thinking about going back to school? We're proud of you and of what you're doing, and we don't want to push you, but let's sit down and talk about this." And I said, "Hey, great, let's *do* talk about it." I'm looking forward to really trying to explain to them the kinds of things I feel, that I am a very personal embodiment of what they are, what they created in a son, and what they brought me up to be. The thing I want to say to them is, "If you feel you've made a mistake, then tell me so. But *I* feel this is the way you brought me up. This is the way you and all the other influences that you put before me in life, that you provided for me—directly and indirectly—[that you] helped make me." I'd like to sit down and really talk with them.

Here again, two important issues are joined: the inner conflict between the Movement and the Academy, and the view of radicalism as an outgrowth of the core values of the past.

To these young men and women, then, being a radical means many things. It of course means a general commitment to the general goals and tactics of the New Left. But for all, this commitment is more personal and moral than dogmatic or formally ideological; and in telling me, a psychologist, who they were, they invariably underlined the correction between the private and the political in their lives. Being a radical means a commitment to others, to a Movement "in motion," and to some kind of effort to create a viable radicalism in America. The radical commitment rests on a set of basic moral principles and instincts more than on any formal and elaborated philosophy. And these principles were invariably felt to be continuous with the people and the principles of the personal past. Finally, being a radical meant being open to an indeterminate future.

The openness of the future

In late August, 1967, fewer than half of those interviewed in Vietnam Summer knew for sure what they would be doing on September 15. Those who did know were planning to continue or resume their educations, and had no plans beyond the completion of their studies. Indeed, some were not sure that they *would* complete their studies at all. A sense of openness and indeterminacy toward the future characterized them all. They repeatedly insisted that the future must, in some way, involve continuing work with the Movement; but they could never specify precisely how, where, and in what capacity.

One thing, however, was clear: the conventional options open to this group of intellectually able and personally forceful young men and women attracted them little. One young woman, for example, who had recently spent a year in graduate school, said about her future:

> I don't really know what I'm going to do. I feel very open to respond. I've talked to enough people to have a feeling that they just

move through college and graduate school without knowing what is going on, and I don't know how much they profited from the academic work they were doing. I'd like to do something that was at least relevant, to feel that at least I'm learning something. . . .

[She talks about her experiences at graduate school.] It was hard to have to say this again, to say that I still had no one to talk to. There *were* a few people. But I mean, when I became *the* expert on Negro history, it was a very sad state of affairs. There are very few academics who see some kind of relationship to what's happening in the world. I don't want to be a scholar, but at some point, I feel a responsibility to bring education to bear on my world.

I would like to teach people to be people—that is more important than writing a paper. And I got scared when I looked at these kids twenty-eight years old, married with two kids, sitting in the stacks and throwing away time for five or six years. Their thesis is on the Abolitionist Movement, but they have no idea of what has been taking place in America in the past twenty years. They have their deferments, and they read a newspaper once in a while, but they don't really feel concerned. That really frightened me.

The issues mentioned by this young woman recur in the comments of others: academic life is the great temptation, yet is also a symbol of irrelevance and irresponsibility; continuing involvement in the Movement is essential, but precisely how and where the radical commitment can be realized remains unclear. Yet somehow she rejoices in (or at least accepts) the openness of the future.

The tension between academic life and radical work is understandably strong for these intellectually able young men and women. In talking about the future, they almost always discuss academic life in order to reject it. One young radical, asked about his future plans, replied:

It'll be in political organization one way or the other. I don't see myself going into the academic world, although I do a great deal of reading and writing and I think I can operate in that environment okay. . . . But I don't think I would be happy in it. . . . I don't want to take a job . . . where I have to "operate." I mean I want to be part of something where I don't have to worry about what I'm going to say and what I'm going to do, or about whether I have to keep things silent and the rest. . . . I don't enjoy it, it's too manipulative, and it doesn't give me a sense of satisfaction. Or maybe I wouldn't mind doing it, as long as I was part of a primary group that was doing it. But I don't want to be isolated. . . . I just don't like to get the feeling that I'm all alone and I'm doing something to everybody else. I like to have the feeling that there are fifty of us or five hundred or ten thousand that are doing it together. And I want to feel that I have friends and that I'm in a spirit of comradeship with them. . . .

The implicit picture of academic life is clear: it requires "operating," manipulation, and isolation, in contrast to this young man's perception of the New Left.

Another young man was unusual because he hoped to resolve the tension between radicalism and the Academy by combining the two, although his basic commitment is to the Movement.

I don't know what I am going to do. I don't think I want to be a full-time politico . . . and I don't see academics as in the center of things. Especially in this country, the left wing has been very isolated in the academic community. . . . [Also] it is clear that students by themselves can't be a revolutionary, a decisive revolutionary, force. So I guess it's for that same reason that I don't want to be an academic. On the other hand, I don't think I could become a truck driver—I'm too far gone for that. . . . And it's very important for me to live among people I can communicate with. Because, you know, for a long time I was lacking in that. . . . Yet I don't think I would want to do political work full time, because, for one thing, it is always so frustrating and unsuccessful. You know, the revolution isn't going to be here in a few years, and we should all be sane when it happens.

Still another described the conflict between the academic and the political in similar terms, and was also determined to combine the two, at least in the next years:

I still think I eventually want to go to graduate school. But I can see that I'm also becoming increasingly—I'm getting sucked into more full-time political involvement. I'm not sure I want to let that happen. I've done very little reading this summer. . . . For a while earlier this year, I had very little to do with political stuff. I really worked and read. I escaped and got lost in reading, and I enjoyed it

> for a while. And then I started listening to the radio, "Another fifty thousand troops going to Vietnam," and I would say, "What the fuck am I reading this for, I've got to get back into some group." . . . It's not an alternation because it's not one or the other—it's a case of sixty–forty one way or forty–sixty the other. . . . I don't want to neglect my studies and I don't want to neglect my social responsibilities, which means that you get very little sleep.

Another rejected option is immersion in conventional middle-class life. Some young radicals are very explicit about their desire to define an alternative to Establishment America, and about the difficulties they have in doing so. One young woman said, for example:

> One thing that took me a long time to learn is that there are models of marriage and adult life, but that they don't work. . . . My friends have helped, because all of them saw that: it was the same with them. The Movement brought people together who see things not working, and we have many hang-ups in common. Maybe the hang-up is between living and not knowing what you're going to be doing, and knowing but not having it work. Maybe that's what makes it so intense. It keeps you trying to find your way. I think it's highly probable (and then again it's not) that I might end up living like my mother. It could go like that very easily. But on the other hand, the things I see are so cruddy. Every now and then the cruddiness comes through. . . . I don't think I want to live like that, but I don't know of anyone who has found another way yet. I haven't found any other model. . . .

The fear of middle-class life is especially strong in this young woman because of her rejection of the materialism in her mother's life. (But her mother was also an intensely political woman.) Her problem in finding models of adult life is common to many others. She continues:

> There is that whole conflict about being a professional, leading a middle-class life which none of us have been able really to resolve. How do you be an adult in this world? . . . It's very easy to get caught back up in it, especially when you don't know what you're going to be doing over the next years. . . . I don't want to get caught up in that whole professionalism and lose something of what has been built into me. . . . I'm not that secure myself: I'm afraid

I'll fall back. I know the feeling. In a lot of people, especially people that are doing professional organizing work, there is a huge conflict . . . about being middle-class, about having things, and all that means. . . .

But most young radicals feel less acutely endangered by middle-class life than does this young woman. One young man said of his years in secondary school:

One thing I found at school was that I never had much sympathy for executive life or suburban life. It is partly because I read all of the Babbitt books, and secondly because my forte has never been an ability to get along with other people in a "ha-ha" kind of way. I was too impassioned and too angry and too individualistic. I knew I couldn't do it. . . . I would be very unhappy. Second of all, I sort of have the thought that those kinds of pretensions [of upper-middle-class business executives] don't belong in a democracy, that they are completely wrong, and that you shouldn't be associated with them.

One alternative to academic or professional life, of course, for the radical, is organizing work of some kind, whether it be local community organizing or, as is increasingly the case, organizing "resistance" groups concerned with the draft, civil disobedience, or other forms of non-legal political action. One young radical turned toward draft-resistance work after the summer; another said, when I asked her what she thought lay ahead for her:

If we go ahead, we can only go so far. [Laughs] . . . In terms of my own development, I feel that I've developed administrative skills, and I can run an office, I can set up a seminar, I can set up a regional conference with a great deal of ease. But I lack a kind of community experience I need. I would really prefer to do that for awhile. . . . There are probably about ten or fifteen people, maybe more, who have said (maybe who have not said, but are thinking): "We are going to be working in the South for the rest of our lives." And we are beginning to dig in now. . . . There's not a deliberate plan, no one sat down and mapped it out. . . . But it's there, and those are the people that I'm going to be working with for a long time. I'm still very close to them. I consult with them, and don't make plans in isolation.

Several of the Vietnam Summer leaders turned again in the fall to full-time organizing work. But still others undertook to continue their educations in some context where relevance and responsibility could be better combined with learning than—as they saw it—in the typical college or graduate school. Thus, schools with "progressive" curricula and strong work-study programs, institutions like the New School for Social Research or the Institute for Policy Studies, drew several of these radicals. And even the one interviewee enrolled in a graduate program in a conventional university had so arranged his schedule that he almost completely escaped normal course work. In all of their efforts at continuing self-education, these young radicals consciously sought to define some new form of learning in which relevance and theory, action and reflection, could be combined.

Several themes unite these statements about the future. As I have noted, the personal future is open, fluid, undefined, and indeterminate. Immersion into middle-class academic or professional life is clearly rejected, but in its place the young radical often finds it difficult to define clearly an alternative role, way of life, or style. As the young woman quoted above put it, "I haven't found any other model." Yet all of those I interviewed agreed that somehow the future must involve a continuation of Movement work. One said:

> In ten years, I definitely don't want to be away from this. That's the only sure thing I can say. I want to continue to be a part of this. I'm not sure what part or what role I could or should play. This is very important to me, the work, the Movement. What I'm saying is that I really hope it's going to be possible for me to be whatever I want to be when I "grow up" [laughs] without breaking the ties. I want to show that it really can be done, that I don't need to burn all these bridges behind me, as part of my past. So I definitely know that I want to be connected with Movement activities. In what way and what form I don't know, I can't tell. Who knows what the Movement is going to be like in ten years. . . .

Somehow all seemed to manage to tolerate the uncertainty and ambiguity of the future. This is partly because they feel caught up in the "motion in the Movement," and partly because of a more basic self-confidence that assures them that they can respond as needed to whatever is needed in the future. To an unusual degree, selfhood in these young men and women, although highly defined and individualized, is also tied in to a loosely defined Movement for Social Change, integrated in solidarity with small groups of other young radicals to whom they turn for guidance and counsel, and dependent upon a series of social and historical changes that the radical seeks to effect. Who, indeed, "knows what the Movement"—or for that matter American society and the world—"is going to be like in ten years"?

The ability to tolerate indeterminacy, then, is related not only to the self-confidence of these young radicals, but to their sense of involvement in a social, political, and historical process that is itself indeterminate. The result is that these young adults show surprisingly little anxiety and apprehension about what they will do: on the contrary, many have learned to enjoy the openness. Of the future, one said:

> For the first time, I have not felt the need to have something certain there that I could go into, that I could stay with, and say, "I am this-and-this man, I am working for this." Now I welcome the uncertainty. I welcome the choice. I welcome the thinking that that forces. That's one of the things that's really keeping me going now.

This young man, like some of his co-workers, has come to identify in part with the change and process of the Movement and of his surrounding world, rather than with the achievement of clearly defined future goals. Animated in part by a dim and rarely articulated vision of a revolutionary changed world, he is sustained even more by the conviction that what he is doing is right, both psychologically and ethically. From such an inner sense of rightness come self-affirmations like the following:

> I've taken a lot of shit for the work I've done. When I was a kid, there were family problems, and then later, for being involved in Movement things. But I wouldn't trade it. It just seems to me that I have had what I consider great fortune—to grow up with the people

> I grew up with, and the situations I did, with the perceptions I have, and with the feelings that I have. I still feel very proud of the fact that I can cry, that things can really dig me up inside, that I can cry when I'm happy. [He tells about an evening the previous week when he had started out feeling depressed, was with friends he liked, sang, and played the piano.] Afterward, I just went upstairs and my eyes filled up, I felt so good. I felt so turned on and I hadn't touched anything all evening. I got so high, so turned on, just being able to do that—it really digs me, being able to be happy.

It is on personal feelings such as these that the radical commitment is built. Facing a problematic and indeterminate future, members of a small, fragmented, and often confused Movement, tempted by, but determined not to succumb to, the lures of conventional middle-class or academic life, these radicals stand on their own feelings of inner rightness, and in the last analysis identify themselves with that process of social and historical change that their Movement seeks to effect. For all of their many doubts about themselves and their effectiveness, for all their inner conflicts, they express little doubt about their commitment to radicalism:

> When *they* drop out, when *they* wind up being associate professors here and there, I'm going to keep on going. . . .

2 Personal roots: struggle and specialness

In so diverse and individuated a group, it is difficult to isolate common themes of psychological development, the more so as one turns from the present, when these young men and women at least share a commitment to radicalism, to the past, when they shared much less. I found no one theme, issue, event, or relationship that characterized all of those I interviewed; I could find no psychological "type" or set of types into which these young men and women could be fit. Yet as the interviews progressed, certain themes were repeated again and again, and the feeling "I have heard this before" was an initial guide to my later efforts to formulate what these radicals brought in common from their own past.

In the account that follows, I have emphasized the recurrent themes in the past histories of the young men and women who led Vietnam Summer, constructing a schematized picture of the personal roots of the radical commitment. In the search for consistencies in this group, I was guided not only by what they told me, but by comparisons with other groups of young men and women I had interviewed in other contexts: "alienated" and "non-alienated" college students, college dropouts, students who elected to work in developing countries, student drug-users, and so on. These informal comparison groups helped me to distinguish what is "typical" in the lives of other talented young Americans from what seemed especially relevant to the development of these particular young radicals. In the account that follows, I have underlined the themes that seem to distinguish this group from others. But this account should be qualified by a continuing awareness that the search for consistencies neglects the most important consistency, the individuality of those I interviewed.

Two inadequate hypotheses

The study of the personal roots of political convictions is often surrounded with an aura of reductionism. We generally seek the psychological origins of our opponent's views, but assume that the "objective situation" suffices to explain our own. Moreover, it is often assumed that once we have found the personal *roots* of a conviction, commitment, or style of life, we have explained (or explained away) all its *causes,* as if somehow convictions that have psychological roots have no other origins. A search for psychological factors in political conviction often is taken to be inconsistent with an interest in the social, political, and philosophical origins of these beliefs. And finally, a study of the psychology of political beliefs and acts is sometimes confused with a study of their validity, as if political views with personal roots were therefore trivial, emotive, irrelevant, or "only" psychological.

I myself assume that all important political beliefs and acts have psychological roots, as well as social, historical, political, and philosophical ones; that this generalization applies as much to political views I admire as to those I despise; that the study of the psychology of politics is complementary, rather than opposed, to an interest in the sociology, history, and philosophy of these views; and that while the psychological functions and effects of a political commitment may be of interest in judging its validity, such considerations alone are never decisive. The study of the early lives of political actors, then, can best be approached as an investigation of the special sensitivities, values, adaptations, and strengths that the political actor brings from his youth into his political career.

In keeping with their willingness to admit the role of psychological factors in their own lives, most of those I interviewed had developed some theory about the relationship of early experience and later radicalism. Two general hypotheses were continually put forward to explain the personal roots of radicalism: I will call these the "radical-rebel" hypothesis and the "red-diaper-baby" hypothesis. These same two hypotheses, stated in somewhat more scholarly form, are often advanced in more academic accounts of the genesis of radicalism. Both views are widely held, but neither is adequate to account for the actual complexity of these radicals' development. A summary of them, therefore, can stand as an account of what the personal roots of the radical commitment are not.

According to the radical-rebel hypothesis, especially as put forward by those least familiar with New Leftists, the position of today's young radicals reflects a violent rebellion against and hatred of all male, parental, and societal authority. The radical, according to this view, is "displacing" the conflicts of his family onto society and the world, "acting out" intrapsychic conflict in his external behavior. This interpretation of radicalism is generally associated with a psychological critique of it. But this need not be the case: one set of interpreters of young left-wing militants term their militancy "pro-social acting out," acknowledging that, whatever their psychological motives, young activists are also acting to further purposes that are in the long-term interest of society.

A more sophisticated version of the radical-rebel hypothesis was, on occasion, put forward by those sympathetic to, or involved in, the New Left. According to this view, radicals tend to come from families in which they have experienced, perhaps to an unusual degree, the ultimate barrenness, flatness, and emptiness of American middle-class life. While not necessarily "rebels" against their own families, radicals are seen to be in strong reaction to the family milieu from which they come. Specifically, sympathy and even pity toward parents is said to be combined with a major effort to avoid their lives—lives of emptiness, spiritual impoverishment, and quiet desperation. Stated differently, it is the radical's exposure through his own family to the worst aspects of American society—to its enfeebling, unsatisfying, and dehumanizing aspects —which turns him toward the effort to change that society.

A second, sharply contrasting hypothesis was often put forward by individuals active in New Left work. This thesis could be called the "red-diaper-baby" hypothesis, a phrase used within Vietnam Summer to characterize those who came from radical or left-wing families. According to this hypothesis, present-day radicals come largely from politically radical families where, from early childhood on, they have been exposed to radical ideas about social reform, political action, and society. The personal development of the radical is here portrayed as smooth and uninterrupted, as a simple assimilation of parental values of dissent and indignation at modern American society, coupled with a determination to work toward correcting injustices. A number of those interviewed argued that this explanation applied to several other members of the National Office staff, although it did not "exactly" apply to them. Added credibility is given to this hypothesis by the many studies that show that members of the New Left tend to come from families with unusually liberal or left-wing political values.

In fact, neither the radical-rebel nor the red-diaper-baby hypothesis proved adequate when applied to the experience of those I interviewed. Those individuals pointed out as typical red-diaper babies invariably turned out to have undergone an extremely complex development despite their radical background. Conversely, the current political beliefs of those who had at some point rebelled violently against their parents could never be interpreted as a simple reflection of hostility toward fathers, mothers, or parental authority. With this particular group, the prevalence of the red-diaper-baby hypothesis seemed primarily a manifestation of the need for those in the Movement to find historical roots by exaggerating the (very real) familial continuities in their lives.

This need may in turn be paradoxically related to the sense of many young radicals that their own political styles are in some respects very different from those of their parents' generation. The radical-rebel hypothesis, in turn, is inadequate because it sees radicalism as requiring a far more total break with the past than it actually involves. In reviewing the development of these young radicals, I will consider the role of both continuity and change in greater detail. For now, it is enough to note that both of these hypotheses overlook the actual complexity of radicals' development, and both posit either a total break with the past or total acceptance of it, which rarely occurs in human life.

In the beginning

In the course of my interviews with these young radicals, I usually asked them about their first memory. Not all were sure they could "really remember" the scenes they recounted, yet their early memories often have a ring of truth. Such first memories are of special interest in understanding an individual's development, for they often summarize issues of abiding importance in his life.

In answer to my question, one said:

> I remember the end of World War II, and leading a parade of kids around our summer house, me with a potato masher. I *think* I remember that. . . .
>
> And I remember being fearfully scared of—I remember a guy came to our summer house, it must have been '48 or '49—and sold my mother an encyclopedia. He gave my mother the first A of an encyclopedia. She never bought the rest. I remember reading it and seeing a picture of an atomic bomb and a tank going over some rubble. And I think I became hysterical. I screamed and screamed and screamed. I *do* remember that.

In this memory, his rejoicing at the end of the war is followed by his abject terror at the symbols of that war's violence. Another young man, from a left-wing family, recalled the following incident:

The earliest thing that I can remember . . . is a funny incident. It was the Westville Riot in '49 after the Davis concert. My parents were some of the people that organized that concert. And Davis—when it was all over and there was that unbelievable massacre out there with people being beaten unconscious, cars turned over and burned, and the police standing by and watching—Davis was put in the back floor of my parents' car, covered with a blanket and they were immediately followed by cars full of men carrying sticks and bats just in case they ran into any trouble. They ran the gauntlet and brought him to our house.

I was sleeping at the time, but I heard all this commotion and people pouring into the house, and I got up and there were people running around and telephones ringing. My nurse brought me downstairs, and there I was sitting on her shoulder and Rob Davis was there and I guess he was very nervous. So he said, "So this is your son?" And he took me up and he held me there like that [at the end of his arms]—I was an ugly kid, by the way. . . . I was three or four. I started to scream. I didn't know who the hell this character was, and I let him have it. Wham! Bam! I just hit him with all my little four-year-old might.

In this recollection, too, he remembered his own fear and rage against a backdrop of threatening mass violence.

Another young man recalled the birth of his brother:

I remember when my brother was born. . . . I remember the whole thing. . . . Somewhere along the line, in these early months, I can remember getting into his crib, and occupying his place, taking his spot. I damn well knew what I was doing. I remember knowing that I was just pushing that poor fellow out, wanting to get back that attention. And I knew that that was bad, that I should be more magnanimous. I knew it. I was only three. . . .

At any rate, at least while I was a kid, I thought I was getting the raw end of the deal because I really wanted attention from my father. . . . I used to belt [my brother] or something and he'd go off screaming, "He hurt me," and my old man would come in furious and say, "Pick up a club and hit the bully. Take a knife and stab him." He really did. He told my little brother, "Kill him, you know, sneak up behind him when he's not looking." And that would just infuriate me. I'd say, "Man, you guys do that and you're going to be dead." That would infuriate my old man, too. . . . That

> pissed me off, and my old man, too. It really used to piss me off. . . . Eventually we worked it out.

In this recollection, the broader historical scene is absent, but in the foreground is his conscious jealousy, his feeling of displacement, and his murderous rage that he had to share his father with his brother.

Another interviewee recalled the following scene at his grandmother's estate:

> When I was a little boy, I would go down to where my grandmother used to live. When I finished my nap my grandmother would ring the bell and the little Mexican boys would come to play with me. It was really sort of bad. I think even then things struck me that way. Something was going on that wasn't right. . . .
>
> It seemed to me completely obvious that these kids were smarter than I was, they were quicker, they were faster, they were stronger, they knew more about things. And yet, you know, I was the one that lived in a place where there were fans and no flies, and they lived with the flies. And I was clearly destined for something, and they were destined for nothing. . . . Well, I sort of made a pact with these people that when I got to be powerful I might change some things. And I think I pursued that pact pretty consistently for a long time.

He continued his recollections:

> In the first grade, I remember lots of fights with kids. . . . The most coherent memories of that relate to these gangs. . . . The elementary school that I went to, it was always a fight. We went outside and it was the foxes and the hares. . . . If I sat down here, I probably could remember a half-dozen or ten really gruesome fights, really juicy fights.

In these recollections, two crucial themes stand out. First, these earliest memories are to an unusual degree connected to the broader social and historical scene: the end of the war, a well-publicized riot, the interviewee's favored social position. This sensitivity to the social scene recurs throughout these young radicals' lives. Second, the issue of violence, external and internal, runs through these early memories: the outer violence of the atomic bomb, the threatening crowd, or the "gruesome fights" in the schoolyard; the inner violence of fear-filled anger and jealous rage. This issue, too, persists.

Maternal love and pressure

The variety of relationships with parents portrayed by these young men and women is difficult to exaggerate. On one extreme, there were a few, especially from left-wing backgrounds, who described idyllic relationships with both parents: understanding, support, and sympathy were the rule throughout childhood. At the other extreme, there were a smaller number whose development had been marked by unusually violent rebellion against parents, rebellion that they invariably connect to their current involvement in radical politics. But perhaps the most striking feature of these young radicals was their relative detachment, compassion, and ability to view their parents in the "round," as complex and differentiated human beings. And perhaps related to this current sympathy for their parents was a portrait of early family relationships and of family atmosphere most often characterized by parental warmth, closeness, and idealism.*

A great variety of anecdotes, early recollections, and later events suggests an unusually strong tie between these young men and their mothers in the first years of life. Such a close maternal tie is, of course, not unusual amongst young Americans, but in many

* In discussing particular family relationships, I will be referring primarily to the eleven young men I interviewed. Three women are not a sufficient sample for even the most tentative generalizations. Much of what follows, however, could be generally applied to the three young women I interviewed with the proviso that the relationships of men with their fathers were paralleled by those between women with their mothers, just as the relationships of men with their mothers were essentially similar to those of women with their fathers. Nevertheless, my illustrations of *specific* family relationships will be drawn from interviews with the men.

of these young radicals it seems to have been particularly intense. What is most impressive in these early memories is the automatic ubiquity of the mother, that so many specific recollections take her presence for granted, that she was so often there. This close maternal tie seems to have evolved into an unusual responsiveness to the mother's wishes, especially with regard to academic achievement.

The mother's interest in the academic performance of her son is illustrated in a diversity of anecdotes, starting from early life and continuing through college. One young radical remembered how his mother coached him for school:

> From way back, my mother had taught me a little bit of arithmetic and stuff. I had always been ahead in my class. In junior high school, she got a little bit worried because I was learning new things in class instead of going over the things that she had already taught me. . . . Most kids learn things first in class. They may be helped by their parents at home, but it's not really expected that they would have learned *everything* that they come to in class before they get there. . . .

Another recalled how his mother got him into a private school:

> One time, when I was in the eighth grade, I was talking to a kid who lived in a more wealthy part of town. He said, "I'm not going to Oakwood High School, I'm going to a private school." So I went home and told my mother and father, and they said, "Well, if *he* can go to a private school, *you* can go to a private school."
>
> So she calls up on the phone these private schools and says, "My son wants to go to . . ." whatever-the-school-is. So we set up interviews and I was accepted at a number of schools. . . . I never really understood why they accepted me, but they did. I got there, and I was pretty out of my element because everybody was cosmopolitan and had a lot of experience and had gone to boarding school before. . . . I didn't feel any personal desire to go to boarding school.

In some cases the maternal emphasis on grades seems to have been seconded by the father:

> In elementary school and junior high, my marks were too low. You know, we had subscriptions to twenty-five different magazines at one time at home, and I used to read them all. I didn't do any schoolwork. But I knew everything that was going on in the world. I was doing very badly in school. That's what made them get on my back to do homework: "Can we *help* you with your math? Be *glad* to go over it with you." And that kind of thing. And then when I got a little older, I had a conflict with my mother about my not spending enough time at home. . . .

Here, although he initially speaks about both of his parents, he indirectly suggests that his mother was the prime complainer about his grades.

Others make the same point more explicitly:

> She really cared about my grades. But see, as long as I knew I had half of the family [my father] willing to put up with my antics, I didn't mind. And anyway I got good grades. It wasn't too hard to get A's in elementary school, mostly A's through high school. . . . My old man would be the "have you done your homework?" type. He just wanted to make sure I was putting in the hours. And I would say, "Look, I'll handle that. The day I start bringing home a C you can start asking me about my homework."

Given the intensity of maternal pressure for academic performance, it was fortunate, if not accidental, that these young men (and women) complied by doing extremely well in school. They were gifted, if not precocious, from an early age:

> I remember in my first grade in school I didn't do at all well, according to my parents. But starting in the second grade, I had straight A's, and I generally continued that right on through. . . . There was always a lot of pressure on me by my parents to make it perfect: "You have all A's, but one B. What about that B?" . . . The pressure came from both my parents, but my mother, I think, exerted it more on a day-to-day level.

The same pattern usually continued throughout high school and into college. One interviewee had attended one of the most demanding colleges in the country:

> The first quarter I was extremely conscientious, and I got mostly A's on my mid-terms, which really surprised me because I had figured I wouldn't be able to get through with anything higher than a C. Once I figured that out, I leaned back and took it easy. I came out of the year with an A and three B's. It could have been better, I realize that. But they live and let live in college. They didn't demand too much. . . .

One consequence of a close maternal relationship, coupled with intense pressures for academic achievement, was the scholastic accomplishment of these young men and women. But another less obvious consequence seems to have been a certain identification of the academic with maternal pressure and even with the feminine. This identification, too, will recur in their later lives.

Yet for all that these young men (and women) sometimes resented their mothers' pressures, they nevertheless point to their mothers as crucial in the evolution of their basic views on the world. One said:

> One thing that struck me very early in the game, when I would come home from school, say, filled with talk about how good this or that war was, was how negatively she would react. . . . I can remember once when we were in some resort, there was a picture in the newspaper of Henry Wallace with a tomato thrown all over him. I remember bringing that picture in and saying, "Wasn't it great, how they got that Commie." And she really got very angry and said, "It's not like that at all, it's terrible they threw that tomato.". . .
>
> She was one of the few people around who didn't think that Joe McCarthy was wonderful. . . . In one way or another, she has given me an idea of what she thought a man should be. And one of the things was gentle toward women, and brave, and not afraid to fight, and things like that. . . . By fighting, I mean fighting for the right.

And one young woman, with an ambivalence that characterized the three young women's attitudes toward their mothers, said:

> I always thought that she demanded too much of me. She literally demanded that I participate in the work of the house . . . and I was doing many more things than other girls of my age. I resented

> that. She demanded much more of me than I thought other mothers did of their daughters. . . . And sometimes, you know, I regret that my mother made me do this and that.
>
> But later I was kind of glad. By the time I was in college, I felt much more mature—even in high school I felt much more mature—than the other girls I was with. Because I had had much more demanded of me.

The evidence, then, especially for the men, points to a very close relationship with an achievement-demanding mother whose values had a considerable influence on those of her son. However complex their later feelings about their mothers, most of these young radicals looked back gratefully on much of what they had learned from her.

The split in the image of the father

Even more important in the development of these young men, is their intense and highly ambivalent involvement with their fathers. The term "ambivalent" understates the facts, however, for ambivalence toward their father is routine in the development of men. With these New Leftists, ambivalence seemed unusually great: the image of the father, as seen through interviews, was split into two contradictory parts. On the one hand, the father was portrayed as highly ethical, intellectually strong, principled, honest, politically involved, and idealistic. But on the other hand, this same father in other contexts was seen as unsuccessful, acquiescent, weak, or inadequate. This split in the paternal image was found in almost all of the young men I interviewed; a similar split in the image of the mother was apparent in all of the young women.

Most of those interviewed began by speaking very positively of their fathers. One said with obvious pride:

> We have a news clipping at home, about how two guys in a railroad station grabbed an old lady's pocketbook and one of them had a gun. But my father jumped on both of them and held them

down until the cops got there. You know, he's that kind of a guy. He's very impetuous, and he sometimes does foolish things like that.

Another said of his father:

> He was there when you needed him. I could always talk to him a lot better, although I could talk to my mother. But I could talk to him better. And I just got this feeling that no matter what happened, he understood. Maybe that was because of his general sort of quiet, accepting nature.

But this same young man commented at another point in our interviews:

> In terms of handling some of the problems of the family, he keeps busy and reads a lot, but I don't know. . . . I get the impression that as much as he's a progressive guy and doesn't necessarily accept this whole bit about "a man has to be this and a man has to be that," that it still bugs him that my mother is working and making a lot of money. . . . And the problem is that my mother is very dominant, very strong, very quick-tempered, quick to criticize. . . . There was a time when I was *so* uncomfortable in that house, when I was seeing the way she would get irritated and pick on him for little things. Now, I guess, I just learned to accept that.

Despite this young man's very positive view of both his parents, his father's lack of dominance vis-à-vis his mother clearly disturbs him.

Another young man stresses his close relationship with his father from an early age. One of his first recollections was:

> There were only three of us then. We lived in a tiny apartment. My old man was a grad student, and it was very nice. He was completely captivated with the idea of being a father, and he had all kinds of interest in seeing me get educated. All the way through school I had a special pride in my father, because he always taught me differently from the way they taught me in school. . . . I remember when I was in second grade, the second grade teacher said, "The sun is ninety-three million light years away from the earth." I raised my little paw and said, "No, it isn't, it's ninety-three

million miles." You know, she sent me to the principal for insubordination.

But I mean I never wavered, because I knew. I didn't have the slightest doubt in my mind that it was ninety-three million miles, because that is what the old man had taught me. It was great. He taught me how to write, too. So I could write my name before we got to writing and I was conscious of that. I liked to write my name on my little papers. I got berated for that because we hadn't done that yet, we weren't supposed to write our names, and I got marked off for it. You know, kids are perceptive, so it wasn't too hard to figure out that it was the educational system that was fucked up.

Despite the warmth of these early memories, and despite his repeated emphasis on how much he learned from his father, this young man, too, indirectly pointed to his father's acquiescence:

[My mother] has more strength of the two. My old man likes to come home and stay around the house, and doesn't particularly want to fight anybody's battles when he doesn't have to. She was the more ambitious of the two, and that was a bone of contention. He didn't give a shit so long as he was pulling in the scratch. . . . It hurt him, when he realized it was going to take a lot more effort than he was willing to expend to become the world's greatest lawyer. But she wanted him to become the world's greatest lawyer.

Still another interviewee remembered among his most positive memories his early walks with his father, a man who was a radical in his youth:

I used to have these long talks with my father when we went on walks—these strange kinds of long talks. In a way, it was my political education . . . he'd tell me sort of a child's version of working-class history, revolutionary history. I think it went through until I was eight or nine. . . . He would tell me about the origins of money and things like that. . . . He clearly went out of his way to do it.

But the son is extremely conscious of his ambivalence toward his father. Comparing his parents, he noted:

My father, on the other hand, is sort of accommodating. He very readily gives in to her. Although she is not strong, she is willful

. . . [I tend to think] of my father as being non-masculine. And I tend to look in myself for traits of his. That's partly valid and partly not. . . .

Some things about my father I like. Like . . . he did a lot of great things when he was younger. [He discusses several of his father's early accomplishments.] But it's clear that he cannot organize his own life, and that he shouldn't have married my mother. . . . My father is not just gentle and loving, but he's also very weak in an interpersonal sense, though not in an intellectual sense. But he is a very submissive person. I mean he always does whatever she wants. . . .

But he was a good businessman, too, in a funny kind of way. He didn't enjoy it, but the business prospered, and he got lots of customers because he was always honest with them. . . . So when it's a matter of doing something himself, he can go ahead and do it, but if it's a matter of pushing against other people, he can't.

Another young radical was unusual in that he recounted a history of open conflict with his father throughout childhood. But commenting on their fights, he noted:

My father was generally, after a certain point, pretty respectful of me. And strangely enough, although we fought a lot, it was never any kind of destructive fight to the death, even psychologically. For example, he didn't really do everything he could to reassert his dominance. He really left me alone pretty much and respected my independence.

The father's tacit respect for his son was fully reciprocated. In commenting on the sources of his own radicalism, this young man commented:

From my father, I developed a sense that the present system was not legitimate, because he did not believe it was legitimate. . . . There was not that sense of legitimacy about the present system as there is with most upper-middle-class families. It didn't take me a hell of a lot of intellectual effort to see the hypocrisy of the system. . . . [My father] understood very clearly why people were exploited, and that that was terrible. That was one of the worst tragedies that could happen to somebody all of his life.

He also understood that business was a lot of fraud and a lot of bullshit. He was very explicit about that. For example, his attitude toward trade unions was that he had to fight them because what

> they got he didn't get, but basically they were justified and necessary. A lot of it had to do with the fairly honest man who went through the Depression. He had seen real poverty, and had had a sense that there were men as able as he was who didn't make it because of chance and circumstance. He never had a sense of capitalist mission, or competition, and "The most talented are chosen." . . .
>
> For him, life was a game that rewarded him with good things—power, prestige, money, comfort, good food, servants. . . . I respect him, I think, because he is pretty honest. A lot of what I feel happened happened because there weren't a hell of a lot of choices open to him, given the fact that ambition and success had been defined for him in a certain way.

This young radical's basic perceptions of society, then, are fully in accord with those of his father's. Where father and son part company, as the son sees it, is that the father's actions are not based on his perceptions:

> My father, unlike most businessmen—unlike all businessmen I have met—is probably the most sympathetic toward poor people. I mean he really understands the injustices. He has a real understanding for people. With wealthy liberal people, it is so difficult for them to feel that. They have a sense that basically what happens is right. . . . I'm sure my father has a much better understanding of what Stokely Carmichael is about than most people do.
>
> But his point of view would be a very narrow, selfish one. He would say [about the things that my friends and I are doing now]: "That's great, but let it happen after I'm dead. You guys can have your way then, but in the meantime I'm enjoying life."

In most young radicals the positive side of the paternal image is uppermost, and the negative side emerges only later; sometimes only in apologetic asides. Yet whichever side of the ambivalence is most stressed, there almost always seems to be a quite conscious split in the image of the father, involving the picture of him (and by extension his tradition and the older generation) as idealistic, sympathetic, honest, highly principled, warm, and admirable; but on the other hand, as dominated, humiliated, ineffectual, or unwilling to act on his perceptions of the world. These two contrasting images help define one of the basic tensions in these young radicals, the tension between having principles and acting upon them.

To stress this common ambivalence toward the father is, of course, to neglect the many differences in these radicals' relationships with their fathers. The examples I have given point to a continuum of father-son relationships. At one end of this continuum are some, especially those from radical political backgrounds, who convincingly described paternal and familial relationships of unusual warmth, demonstrativeness, openness, and honesty. But no matter how positive the bonds between father and son, the son seems to have been reluctant simply to follow in his father's footsteps. At the other end of the continuum are a small number of New Leftists whose early family environments involved violent conflicts or extraordinary isolation between family members. But those who had most violently rebelled against their fathers nonetheless admired them, or certain aspects of what they stood for. Most fall somewhere between, "basically" admiring their fathers, but also expressing dismay about their ineffectuality.

The principled parents

In describing the family atmosphere and mood, as in characterizing their parents' relationships to each other and to their children, these young radicals again described a great variety of patterns. Especially in families with left-wing outlooks, openness, warmth, and sharing seem to have been the idiom of the parents' relationships with each other and with their sons or daughters. This family atmosphere, and a characteristic filial response to it, is illustrated by the following account:

> There's an awful lot of love in my family. And we talk a lot. I run up huge phone bills. It always blows my father's mind at the end of the month. I've also always been very open with my parents. Even when I was doing things that they might not like, I would tell them and they wouldn't get upset. Like, you know, I'm living here with my girl in Cambridge, and they didn't think it was a good thing beforehand. They said, "At the end of the summer when she's got to

go back to Central College and you've got to go back to Northern College, it'll feel like a separation after a marriage, and you won't be able to do it." . . . But I let them know I was doing it.

His parents' reasons for not approving of his living with his girl are significant: they object not on moral grounds, but because of the anticipated pain of separation.

Another described his parents in similar terms:

> Except for some growing-up-type problems, my parents and I had an unbelievable relationship. I was just marveling at that fact last Friday. I have a girl who lives in New York, and I went down to see her and to do some other stuff, get my teeth cleaned and what have you. She and I went out to a movie and had dinner with my parents. We really had an unbelievable time. A really great evening. All these other kids talk about "my mother this and my father that." A lot of them don't seem to get along with their parents at all. I consider myself very fortunate in being able to.

In contrast to the warmth and affection apparent in these families, another young radical describes a family atmosphere of great distance:

> As I remember, my parents were distant from each other, but very affectionate toward me. Perhaps I shouldn't say affectionate—affectionate implies kissing all the time—but very positive toward me. . . . At very early times, I spent a lot of time with my mother, her strolling me around. My father also used to take me to a lot of ball games and football games. Then sometimes he used to take me out on Saturdays to watch the men work or to help out and carry paint pots and trays. I used to enjoy that an awful lot: it made me feel I was involved with something important, I remember. I remember that when I was younger. But when I was older, at six or seven or eight, somehow I wasn't as close to my parents. . . . I remember—I don't know whether this is true in terms of total time—having to spend a great deal of my time alone.

Describing the same period of his life, he said in another interview:

> My parents never told me what they were thinking about. I never heard a complaint from them; they just worked; they worked damned hard every single day; they never took vacations. And I

never heard them say to me or to each other about how tired they were, or how they were unhappy with their life or with what they were doing. . . . I think they were probably very frustrated very deep inside, but they probably built up enough covering over that so that they don't feel it. They're both people who feel that there is a lot in the world that is hard. One has to be prepared to bear with it and keep going as much as possible. So I never had any kind of close relationship personally with either my mother or my father. . . .

My mother and father never spent very much time making me happy or being concerned with me. I mean they *were* concerned with me, but it wasn't a doting kind of concern. I mean they talked with me, but it wasn't in any significant kind of way to say what I should be doing and what I shouldn't be doing. I always used to play alone, Lincoln logs and castles. And I would draw maps and write stories and write essays and read books.

The unusual isolation within his family is reflected in the special value that this young radical now places on working together with others.

As these examples suggest, the parents' relationship to each other varies greatly from family to family. But as my earlier discussion indicates, in most of these families the mother was the more active and vigorous. With only one or two exceptions, each young man suggested that his father's greatest strength lay outside the family, in his work. The following example is extreme, but the pattern of parental relationships described runs through the lives of most of his fellow workers:

My mother is a much tougher personality than my father. My father gets himself dominated by her pretty thoroughly. She winds up making just about all the decisions. But she doesn't feel very confident of herself either, so that's a strain. She is sort of aggressive but she's very, very scared as well. She doesn't like the fact that she feels that the decisions are all on her, and that he easily passes decisions off on her.

Despite their many differences, virtually all of these families shared a marked concern with the moral dimensions of life, defined not as a narrow restraint of impulses, but as a higher ethical orientation toward personal principle within the family and outside it. Almost without exception, these young radicals had principled parents. Psychologists often distinguish among three general types of discipline: physical punishment (spanking, slapping), deprivation (ostracism, taking away gifts, privileges, and rights), and "psychological methods" (reasoning, explaining, holding up high standards). In terms of this trichotomy, these young radicals were almost invariably disciplined as children by "psychological methods." Yet this term does not do justice to the role of principle and ethical consciousness in their families. In this regard, there was little difference between the men and the women in the group. One young man, in attempting to describe the way his parents "educated" him, put it this way:

> Let me try to make up my own thing to describe it. It is sort of a carrot-before-the-horse thing, but every so often, they would make sure the horse got a bite of the carrot. They would constantly feed you ideas, ways of expressing yourself—not by jamming them down your throat, but by exposing you to them. Instead of just saying, "Look, this is what you can be when you grow up," they would let you take a taste. They would make sure that, even if it was ever so slightly, you just got involved somewhat in these things. Every once in a while, you'd get a bite of the carrot, and it tasted good. They put that together with a very demanding sense of achievement, and for utilization of your talent. . . .
>
> To carry the thing with the carrot further, the carrot is good for you because it's nutritious, and it also tastes good. You should eat it for all those reasons. Not only are these things wonderful experiences, but they are things that you must be doing, morally, politically, personally. So what happened was that I had a weird combination of a personal and intellectual drive to experience. I think that can be traced back very, very far.

In this family, the combination of the enjoyable and the ethical was complete: it made a lasting imprint upon the son.

In many families, the basic orientation to principle was combined with active involvement in the community:

> My parents are both very involved. They are both involved in [a liberal religious organization]. My mother also does charity work. They're very socially conscious and they're both very passionate

people. My father can sit down and watch a movie and cry. He's not ashamed to cry. He's easily moved, and I think I am too. Like when those three guys were killed in Mississippi, I remember how I was really broken up. I think it may be a matter of sensitivity. It is something like sensitivity training, but this is *real* sensitivity training, because that's how it is—you don't have to be trained by some behaviorist in a group. . . .

But neither of them were ever involved [in politics] when they were young to the extent that I am. They were both somewhat aware, but not as active. . . . They are both very, very warm people. Very giving and very free. Like I am told that I was once punished, but I don't remember it. I don't remember *ever* being punished. I remember my father losing his temper with me a lot of times, and my mother took my side. But generally, I was allowed to do what I wanted to. Every once in a while, my mother went into a thing about my health and welfare, and there she always drew the line. But there was never any big conflict in my family.

Another young man, in commenting on his parents' politics, moved quickly to their more basic principles:

They were Stevensonian Democrats. Basically, it's an apolitical family, but my old man is very liberal, always was, always against McCarthy. I mean we were raised, for instance, we were rigorously taught from a very early age to tolerate no sign of racism within the family. I remember distinctly when I was ten, my little brother was a toddler. We went into this department store on Saturday, all of us, and there was this big black lady there, and my little brother was scared shitless. He had never seen anything like that, and he went up to her and said, "Man, you're black," or something like that. My old man practically killed him. He said, "If you ever do that again, it's all over for you." I remember those things. . . .

[We got a lot of the] traditional Christian liberal values. Values like honesty. My old man is the most honest man I've ever met in my life. He's much more honest than I am. He's rigorously honest. But he doesn't fetishize any of it, he's just an extremely moral man. And it's an extremely strong force in the family. . . . He just values those values per se, without putting them into a pinnacle context. . . . Yeah, honesty was big. And my old man was very tolerant. I mean he would never bug me about my grades or anything like that at home.

I have already mentioned the importance of religious upbringing in some of these families. One young woman described her family's religious beliefs:

> I have a feeling that most of it was just a way of life. That's the way I remember it. Maybe later I discovered that people didn't take it seriously, and it appalled me. . . . I took the basic teachings of the church seriously. I never thought a lot about the question of whether there is a God or not. I just thought there's obviously something in the world besides yourself . . . and that all men were brothers: that was very important.

Several of these young radicals grew up in families where left-wing politics were taken for granted. One said:

> You see, I always took for granted my views about society. And when I did political work, I was not expressing those views: I was willing to compromise what I did. Whereas people who had just become political tended to, in their actions, express their new views. I wasn't interested in expressing my views. You see what I mean? [K. K.: You mean these were the views that you had always grown up with?] Right, and therefore I didn't need to express them. Whereas people who were new, they had to express them, they were expecting confrontations, they were saying it isn't important to win.

One young woman described her mother's political involvement as follows:

> My mother was very active in community organizations, in P.-T.A. kinds of things. But she was really quite radical. During McCarthy time, she really got smashed and she quit. . . . In the fifties, I think they had a really rough time. . . . My mother was always on the telephone. There was this staircase going down to the basement, and she would sit on the stair with the door closed, sit for hours on the phone, and come off the phone just absolutely crying. I knew there was a whole lot going on. They never even talked about it, they hardly ever talked about anything political. . . . They had this whole thing about shielding kids from—they never talked about anything. They've never talked about it since, either, even when I asked them. . . .

And one young man, commenting on his mother's family, said:

> I was very proud of the fact of what they had done. You know, for example, the fact that my cousin had been before the McCarthy Committee was almost a red badge of courage.

In these families, as in all others, there were contradictions. Sometimes they revolved around the appearance of democracy. One young woman said:

> It was all, well, it was all *very* democratic. Everybody sat down and made decisions. Only some decisions happened and other decisions didn't happen. [Laughs] Some people could work on making them happen. We talked about a lot of things, we talked about our dreams, and my mother was very progressive. . . . She read Spock all the time. And when she heard about the peace movement, that Dr. Spock is in it, she didn't think it was that bad. . . . When she was young, my mother was active in politics, although she says she was active more than she really was. Probably a lot of what I do now is because of her telling me I should be involved—she never actually *said* I should be involved, but I had a feeling she felt that way.

Another interviewee was unusually explicit about the conflicts between religious and materialistic values within his family:

> It seems to have a lot of tensions in terms of its orientation—what your aspirations are, what they should be or shouldn't be. "It isn't important that you make money, it's important that you be godly. But why don't you go out and make some money?" A whole series of contradictions. In terms of what I should do, what my life should be like. . . .

Yet whatever the contradictions in some of these families, they are less impressive than the consistent orientation to principle. Somehow these parents communicated, often without saying outright, that human behavior was to be judged primarily in terms of general ethical principles; that right conduct was to be deduced from general maxims concerning human kindness, honesty, decency, and responsibility; that what mattered most was the ability to act in conformity with such principles. Whether the principles were religious or secular, the atmosphere within these radicals' families during their early years was one in which ethical principles occupied the highest position. As one put it:

In a very early way, I developed a kind of personal responsibility. I think that all through that— Let's put it this way, in a very personal way, my family experience reinforced a lot of the things I was reading from books and from outside of the family in terms of values, plus the way you deal with people. Well, responsibility to me is a big bit. It's the same kind of thing I feel personally toward people.

My parents have pretty much stuck by me through most everything. It's just that I think that [long pause] it was always there. It was always there, in terms of starting at a very personal level. I'm really glad it started that way. Because if it had been a very harsh ideological upbringing, it would have been different. But it was always expressed in a personal way. Even in terms of political discussions it was always a matter of "When this or this happens politically, this is what happens to *people*," or "This is why *people* suffer here and there."

In the end, what is most impressive about these young radicals' discussions of their parents is the *way* they talked about them. In most individuals, ambivalence is not so conscious: it often emerges only after prolonged interviewing, and sometimes only with the aid of special techniques for eliciting unconscious material. Moreover, many young men and women in their early twenties still find it impossible to present a differentiated portrait of their parents, and much questioning is required before any picture of the parents as people begins to emerge. With these young radicals, however, the ability to differentiate between the parents, and between different aspects of each parent's character and behavior, was highly developed. They seemed unusually able to tolerate ambivalence, to explain parental failure with its probable causes, to combine praise and affection with the recognition of defects. Their life histories indicate this capacity was not achieved without struggle.

The experience of struggle

In discussing the first memories of these young radicals, I emphasized the importance of outer violence and inner fear and anger. Their later childhood memories also contain frequent allusions to the theme of struggle and conflict, and may help explain why early memories involving this theme should be so selectively recalled.

For several, the focus of childhood conflicts was a sibling who deprived the young radical-to-be of an exclusive relationship with his or her parents, as with the young man who crawled into his brother's crib. One referred in retrospect to "the drawing of the factional lines in my family," and made explicit the parallel between familial and political life.

For another, struggle was witnessed in open conflicts within the family:

> I remember my father would get drunk and he would get into a fight with my mother. I took her side, which I guess is not uncommon. I can remember getting slapped once for making fun of my father and getting really mad. . . . I don't know really whether I was mad then. I was probably scared to death. But the memory left me mad. The incident I remember was one of those cruel and pointed little children's jokes: I kept telling my father he was getting drunk, as a joke. Ha-ha. And then he turned around and slugged me.

His experience within the family extended to school, where he conducted his first organizing effort:

> I guess when I was very young, when I was in elementary school, I was a leader, like a real fighter. And even then, I liked social action. Like I tried to organize lots of gangs of all the kids who got picked on, and I would lead them into battle against the bullies. And then, of course, they would all panic and split.

Later, attempting to analyze the personal roots of his radicalism, he explicitly connected family and political struggle:

> I think another very important factor was the fact that in the family life, struggle was taken as something very legitimate, or at least so necessary that it had to become legitimate. I think that's a very important factor for a radical, because even if you believe all of those other things, if you don't believe that struggle is legitimate [pause]. [K. K.: What do you mean by struggle?] Arguing, pushing, examining. And not only that, that people use force and power. You're aware that people use them all the time. . . . It's

very easy for someone from a background like mine to read the works of Mao Tse-tung and to understand what he means. You can beg them to lay off, but the peasants have got to get guns and learn how to use them.

Others pointed to the role in their political development of community conflicts in which their parents were involved:

> What I think made it so clear in my mind, in terms of conflicts and power structure, at an incredibly early age, was the conflict in the town we lived in. . . . The whole crew of us ran into that problem with the local kids. . . .
>
> And although politically and geographically it was all the same town, ethnically and sociologically it was divided. It became very clear to me that there were a lot of issues, that there were certain points of view that people didn't want discussed. There were certain patterns in life that certain people did not want to accept.
>
> I had no politics when I was a kid. I was just an average kid who liked to go to school dances and what have you. But by some quirk of fate I was born into a social grouping that was talking about these issues, that was doing the things that other people didn't want done, expressed, or thought about. It became clear that there was this constant opposition, this constant friction, and that it wasn't all on the level.

In evaluating the impact of family and community conflict upon these young radicals, it should be recalled that despite their intellectual ability and a certain moral precocity these were also children with extremely strong feelings. They did not take defeat lightly, they were intensely involved with their parents and their schools, and they reacted strongly to the events of family and community life. Even in the majority of families where domestic tranquillity was the rule, conflict outside the family often had a profound impact. Being criticized and ostracized by other children for refusing to take part in an air-raid drill was not an event they could lightly slough off or forget. This early experience with conflict served both to accustom these young radicals to it and yet to inoculate them against it, motivating them to struggle to minimize violence.

The early sense of specialness

Another recurrent theme in the interviews was the sense of specialness that in some way characterized their childhoods. The sources of the feeling of being different or unusual varied, but the resulting self-characterization continues to be important throughout their later development.

In one, for example, the sense of being different stemmed from the isolation of his parents:

> I was very isolated, I think, from all the other people around. I'm just not sure to what extent that was semiself-imposed, or semi-externally imposed. Because my political ideas, those of my family, were very different from the people around . . . I was isolated both in school and in the neighborhood. It was both political and personality. . . .
>
> I grew up very sort of estranged from the other people around. My parents were also very, very concerned with intellectual work, and that's not a good way to be in an American community. . . . So that I developed a set of values that was very antagonistic to those of the kids around. You know, that didn't help at all either. Some of these were really good values, but I don't think all of them were, by a long shot. I didn't really get unisolated until I was in high school, late in high school.

Here, his basic allegiance to his family's values contributed to a lasting feeling of difference.

In others, their very capability and precocity distinguished them from their fellows. One, describing himself as a child, said:

> I was a snotty kid. [Laughs] One thing I brought from my family is something that I had to overcome in my work, the "you can be the best" type of attitude: "You can do it the best, therefore you should do it yourself." It took me a long time to really overcome that, and not to be pushy about doing things myself. . . . That was because my parents were just always pushing us, academically and in other ways—specifically academically—to do

better, to do better, better. It was mostly my mother, less my father. . . .

So there was a great deal of self-confidence in terms of your now being able to go out and do the thing, whatever it was. We were all very precocious in many ways, because our parents didn't really keep very many things from us. . . . There wasn't all this "this is adult talk" stuff. Things were just discussed pretty openly.

It took me a great deal of time to learn not to do things myself, but to let other people do them. It took me a hell of a long time, and a hell of a lot of hard experiences. I think that was something that started way back then.

For this young man, the sense of specialness is tied to his self-confidence and his implicit assumption that his family's values were superior to those of the surrounding community.

Another described in himself a strong early identification with revolutionaries:

One very important part of the story, looking at the personal level, is why from an early age I could always identify with the revolutionary. I mean, this is something that really was burned into me. . . .

I can remember in a sort of a Sunday school, the teacher telling us all that God was really wonderful because he always looked after little children. This was after the end of the Second World War. I didn't really think it was. I thought it was a lot of shit. I thought, "She's just lying." . . . And from then on, Bam! Never again! I just didn't believe it. I thought, "Well, God isn't doing me any good. So you know, who is she kidding?" . . .

I would identify in history with aristocrats who had been the people's champion, who had fought for them. And then I would always be very disappointed when some hero I had learned about came out to be a selfish shit. And then also, I obviously thought of myself as an intellectual—not that I had models or anything, or even a vague idea of what that meant. But at least I read in books, and I assumed that people who read books thought. So I read books and I thought. . . . All in all, it was a very provincial background. I really had no idea what people normally thought about. . . .

One young woman described her feelings of difference as a child:

> I didn't like that farm very much. I liked the space, but I never had any nostalgia about it. It was a very hard life. I was very happy to move away to the town. I used to equate living in the city with being more well off financially. . . . The kids I knew in the country couldn't read like I could read. They didn't have the same amount of material things that the kids I went to school with had. So there was that kind of contrast. . . .
>
> I have always liked school, and I think I was happy. But there were many unhappy moments. I did not like the farm. I disliked being different. . . . I tried very hard. I wanted to excel for those reasons. And I made it. I was very popular in high school and in college.

In her life in the country, this young woman felt different from both the other farm children (she read and they did not) and from the children in the city where she attended school (they had material things, she did not).

Finally, the sense of specialness was related to the moral and political precocity of these young men and women. I have already noted their childhood involvement with social and political issues. Many report holding unpopular views in grade school and defending them vigorously, usually with the support of their families. In many cases, these students were the "leaders of the opposition" around issues like local elections and presidential campaigns. This, too, often distinguished them from their classmates.

> In the spring semester, we were doing American history and we got to discussing the Korean War. . . . I said "Why should we just go on one textbook?" The teacher was a good guy and he said, "Yeah, let's discuss that." But there were these five guys who beat up on me after school, because they thought that really wasn't such a good idea. . . .
>
> It scared the shit out of me, I'll tell you that. I'd never been much for fighting before. I was always the one to try to settle fights by talking reasonably. The maid next door always used to say, "Johnnie and Rickie fight so much, but when Bill comes along he always seems to settle things without fighting." I had a long talk with my older brother about this incident, and the result was that I came out feeling that I was right in what I'd done.

As a child, this young man reacted to events and people in the moral and ethical terms taught him by his family, rather than in the terms of the surrounding community or in the impulsive way more common to his contemporaries. These young radicals were concerned with moral issues at an age when most of their classmates were not. And although most had a circle of close friends, these friends were usually others like themselves, intellectually able, active, and vigorous children who knew how to lead in the defense of an unpopular cause.

Yet despite their sense of being different, their intellectual ability and historical precocity, these were not unusually studious, withdrawn, or joyless children. Many were good sand-lot athletes; they had good friends and playmates; and they were the sort of children who were routinely elected president of their grade-school classrooms. A few were solitary and withdrawn, but most described themselves as sociable and outgoing, as making friends readily, and as moving easily in the world of their families and school friends. The childhoods of these young radicals-to-be were neither unusually happy nor unusually unhappy: what distinguished these young men and women, even then, was their talent, their orientation to principle, their sensitivity to conflict and struggle, and their feeling—often based in a correct perception of themselves—that they were in many ways different from their contemporaries.

During childhood, then, a sense of specialness began to develop, a feeling about themselves associated partly with their intellectual superiority, their ability to lead, their capacity to defend right against wrong, and their identification with the principles of their parents. But on the other hand, specialness also contained even in childhood a hint of the possibility of moral wrongness, of potential sinfulness, of dangerous deviation, of personal isolation, and the possibility, at some deep level, of deformity. It is not easy to be special, and it is especially hard to live with the high ethical standards that give one the need to be especially right. With adolescence, the negative pole of the sense of specialness comes to dominate for a time in the form of feelings of special sinfulness, special weakness, and special loneliness.

Childhood and politics

The connection between childhood experience and later political action and belief has been often asserted, but rarely demonstrated or studied systematically. The Jesuits argued many centuries ago that a child's religious fate could be sealed by the time he was six; and Freud later pointed to the same age as the time when the basic patterns of personality are already established. In the preadolescent years, the child develops his basic cognitive and conceptual maps of the world, his fundamental categories of right and wrong, good and evil, legal and illegal. And these early concepts, though they may be modified in later life, never totally disappear. Yet for all of our theoretical reasons for believing that childhood experience may be crucial to later political involvement, the topic has been little studied.

A retrospective study like this, focusing on a small group of unusual individuals, cannot be the basis for generalizations about the relationship of childhood experience and political commitment in *all* men. Not only is the sample small and exceptional, but the method—interviews that rely on what the subject can remember and what the interviewer can infer—has its own limitations. The most obvious of these results from the universal human tendency to cast back over childhood the contours of the present self, creating a consistency that links the individual to his past; in creating these links, the individual may substantially distort what "really" happened. Furthermore, vast selectivity is required to recount in two, four, eight, or even three hundred hours the events of twelve childhood years. Distinguishing clearly what was really crucial and significant at the time from what assumed meaning and importance only later is difficult. In listening to the accounts of these young radicals, I was sometimes aware of a search for roots, a struggle to establish continuity, and a tendency to attribute portent to events that at the time may not have possessed it.

Although the "real" childhood always remains elusive, some of the distortions of memory can be eliminated or at least made plain through the co-operative inquiry of both interviewer and subject. With open and insightful young men and women like these, it is often possible to ask directly whether a given interpretation was apparent at the time, or only later. Most could distinguish between the significance they attributed to an event as children and the implications they see in it now. Furthermore, psychoanalysis has taught us that even the retroactively exaggerated or fabricated event illuminates the ramifications of inner life and permits inferences about intrapsychic development. To be sure, the subject can only tell us what *he* remembers in the context of an interview. It is up to the interviewer, if possible with the subject's help, to try to infer what discrepancy, if any, exists between the adult's recollection of his childhood and what "objectively" happened. When this collaborative inquiry succeeds, both interviewer and subject understand better both what "really" happened and what the subject made of it. And through this process, both move closer to understanding the impact of childhood on later life.

A survey of the childhood experience of one small group of young men and women, then, can tell us something about *one* way childhood experience is related to later political development. The accounts of these young radicals make clear that many of the basic issues that now concern them as political actors first became important to them long before they awoke to full consciousness of the broader political scene. In childhood, for example, "history" did not exist for them as a separate category. But these particular individuals, from an early age, were more attuned to the historical currents in their lives than are most children. Also, from an early age, they began to think of themselves as special and different people; they became sensitive to, and inoculated against, the issue of violence, struggle, and conflict; and they developed an important ambivalence toward their fathers as being on the one hand highly principled, but on the other hand often ineffectual. All of these themes persist and are expressed in their later radical work.

For all that childhood sets the stage for what happens later, it does not rigidly determine it. In retrospect, these young radicals often feel that there was a certain "necessity" in their becoming what they are today. But this judgment must be taken with caution. I doubt that anyone, viewing these young men and women at the end of their childhood, could have predicted that they would all eventually become radicals. It might have been predicted that they would continue to think of themselves as being in some way special or different, that they would seek to lead principled lives in one or another arena, and that they would remain especially sensitive to the issue of violence and struggle. Yet none of this required that they become radicals. For that to happen, much else was needed. In addition to what they brought from childhood, their present political position is built on a complex process of further psychological development. And this further development is determined not only by the legacy of childhood, but by the familial, social, political, and historical actuality in which they lived as adolescents and young adults. Stated differently, post-childhood development was determined not only by what happened within them, but by what happened *to* them, by what was available *for* them, and by what was going on *outside* of them.

All we can say, then, is that childhood creates in each of us psychological configurations that summarize the tensions and joys of our early lives. These configurations are, in one way or another, interwoven into our adult political commitments (or into the fact that we have none). Just as the foundation of a building limits, but does not determine, what can be built upon the site, so the legacy of childhood sets outer limits and establishes enduring sensitivities for later development, but does not dictate it. To understand more of how these young men and women came to be radicals, we must examine what happened during adolescence.

3 Personal roots: turmoil, success, and the end of the line

Adolescence is by definition a period of physical change, and it should also be a time of intellectual and psychological change. The start of adolescence is defined by the bodily changes that move the child toward becoming a sexual adult. And if he is not too severely damaged by his childhood, the adolescent also moves toward a greater maturity of thought and personality. His thinking, formerly tied to the concrete and immediate, is freed, and he becomes capable for the first time of logical and deductive reasoning, of comparing the actual with the ideal, of relating himself to the distant past and to the present, and of understanding his place in society, in history, and in the universe. Given a relatively benign environment and the freedom necessary for adolescent development to occur, the early adolescent begins to reassess himself in relation to his own body's new potential, to his social world, and to his family, gradually moving toward greater psychological autonomy and self-direction.

But beyond these general changes, the particular form of the adolescent experience is affected by what the individual brings with him from childhood by way of special sensitivities and strengths, and by what is available for him and what happens to him in the course of his adolescence. With adolescence, the relevant environment begins to enlarge past the childhood world of family and school, eventually to include the entire social and historical world. Moreover, the relevant environment now comes to include the distant reconstructed past and the imagined future, so that the adolescent increasingly relates himself not only to his immediate world, but to his tradition and to his vision of the future.

The form and quality of the adolescent experience therefore varies enormously, even within middle-class American society. Many, and perhaps most, young men and women pass through adolescence with only minimal external turmoil, and sometimes with very little conscious internal upheaval. Others—the young radicals I interviewed were among them—recall an adolescence that was tumultuous, complex, and full of both inner and outer tensions. As these young radicals described their childhoods, conflict and struggle were largely outside—in their families, in their communities, between their parents and friends. But as they entered adolescence, what was outside began to be experienced inside. "Conflict" now came to mean not what happened in the world, but what happened within one's self. In childhood, their sense of specialness was largely external in origin, a matter of the way they were seen by others; whereas in adolescence, they confronted the question, What does it mean to me to be special? Similarly, in childhood these young men and women lived out in a relatively unquestioning way the principles of their family; but in adolescence, some of these principles became their own and were used against the parents from whom they had been learned. With adolescence, then, their narratives begin to focus more on the inner life.

Turmoil-filled adolescence

With the beginning of adolescence, a drastic reversal in behavior, accompanied by major psychological changes and conflicts, generally occurred. The preadolescent pattern of outgoing activity changed, often in a few months, to a new style of seclusiveness, a feeling of social awkwardness and moral inferiority coupled with intense intellectual concerns and, at times, with extreme religiosity. The outgoing preadolescent became, almost overnight, the shy, awkward, and tormented early adolescent.

The issues to which the turmoil of this period was consciously connected were sex and relationships with peers. One young man described his relationships with his friends in early adolescence:

> I was fairly [pause] removed. I'd just go home after school and read. I had a few close friends, but I was never a big social-type kid. . . . [K. K.: In what way did you feel removed?] Like I couldn't do it. [K. K.: Not that it was beneath you?] No. A lot of times I'd get upset if I wasn't invited to a party or something. It really had meaning to me, but not enough to make me change. I don't know what the formula is, but I know that it hurt me because I wasn't in there pitching socially all the time. Yet it never hurt me enough to change. . . . But then, starting in ninth, tenth, eleventh, and twelfth grades I began to change, because there was this large group of people with the same kind of values. . . .

One young woman described similar feelings in early adolescence:

> I just hated those years. . . . I felt very awkward. It was just awful because you were in that transitional stage, you were very nervous about your relationship with the boys, you felt very awkward and very unsure of yourself. I felt all of that. . . .

Another young radical is now very explicit about his feelings of social inferiority with his former friends:

> I still had friends; I went out visiting. But I was conscious of the fact that I wasn't as I had been before. These parties—there was a kind of very fast-moving crowd by the end of eighth grade. That really aggravated all of this, knowing—not so much being upset because there was a lot going on and I wasn't getting any—but that there were all these things going on, and all my former friends were involved in it, and I was outside of this thing. I didn't know how to relate to it. I was treated by them as being outside of it, and socially I began to feel inferior. That was the most important thing.

In addition to these problems in joining the teen-age culture of their peers, many connected their upset during early adolescence to their sexual feelings. One young man said:

In terms of sexual hang-ups, I think that's probably important, too. I don't know what it means, whether it's stronger in me or whether I was just more conscious of it, but without knowing the name of it, and without knowing it was a widespread thing, I was very conscious of the Oedipal thing. . . . I remember being very conscious of it and very disturbed by it. I don't remember consciously feeling anything in the least bit of antagonism toward my father at all. But I remember having definite fantasies about going to bed with my mother, and being very disturbed about them. . . . I would imagine that kind of thing must have been involved in my —I don't know.

Others mentioned their anxieties about masturbation, about their sexual fantasies, and about their feelings toward girls.

For some, the beginning of adolescence was followed by a great intensification of largely self-generated religious feelings, often despite a relatively non-religious childhood and background.

The religious thing is very important. . . . In eighth grade—that was the worst time. Looking back on it, from the early tenth grade on, I thought, "God, I must have been really miserable then." But the religious thing was very meaningful. . . . [It] got much stronger. I was always interested in it, but—I don't remember if it was in eighth or ninth grade—I got very involved with [a Jewish youth group]. It was a very meaningful thing to me. . . . I used to get this really calm, relaxed feeling after services. It reminds me of talking with my father about a year ago. He said that religious services meant nothing to him, but he liked to go because it made him feel so calm. . . . Anyway, my parents began to worry about me. . . .

That this religiosity was not just a reflection of his parents' values is shown by their alarm.

Another recounted an even more intense religious phase:

Well, I had gone to Sunday school an awful lot, but I never took it very seriously. Then all of a sudden, maybe in eighth grade, I started to take it seriously. It became very grasping, as if there was a force there that wanted to take control of my entire life. Because, for instance, I would pray. Then I would say to myself, "You weren't properly respectful when you prayed and you have to pray again. And again, and again, and again, and again."

> This went on for about two and a half years. For instance, I had to carry a copy of the Bible around with me for a long time. And every evening I would pray very extensively, and also I would have to be rigid. It was all very sexual. I would have to be very rigid in bed at night and not move a muscle. . . . I think it was connected with masturbation.

The facility with which this young man now connects his religious scrupulosity to his anxieties about masturbation is typical of the psychological-mindedness of these young radicals.

Another young man spoke of his intense involvement during early adolescence with his parents' conflicts:

> I guess it was when I was about thirteen. They had a big fight one night, and I got very angry. I told him, "Get the hell out or I'll kill you." And he left, I'm sure for a lot of reasons. And this was one of the maybe two or three times when they considered getting a divorce. . . .
>
> When he left, after about a month, it really became clear to me (at least it seemed to me at the time) that [the rest of the family] did nothing but sit around in the corner and cry most of the time. It must have been two or three months until . . . it sort of seemed to me that the only thing we could do was to try to work out some sort of compromise.

In recalling this event now, he is no longer sure that his father's departure and return was solely his doing; but his involvement in his family's conflict profoundly affected his adolescence.

In early adolescence, too, feelings of loneliness, solitude, and isolation came markedly to the fore. Several young men and women began adolescent diaries, which they kept for many years, prefacing them with such thoughts as "Since I have no one to talk to, I will have to talk to myself." Turning toward themselves rather than toward their peers, these young radicals began a habit of self-analysis that continued in later years. Yet a journal is rarely an adequate companion, and feelings of loneliness were common:

> For a long time, it seemed like, in junior high school I really felt terribly alone. I think that probably I was much stronger in the eyes

> of my classmates than I would have believed myself to be. What they thought didn't rate anything in my book. Deference was paid to me because it was thought that I might go further than those other kids. But I thought about the fact that I was different.

Such feelings of aloneness and difference came up again and again. The more neutral childhood sense of specialness had been transformed into something lonely and largely negative. Some felt that they were especially filled with evil thoughts, others felt unable to relate to their peers, and others even wondered about their sanity and intactness.

Without exception, then, those I interviewed told of intense inner turmoil during the early adolescent years. The conflicts they had portrayed as being largely outside them during childhood were now within them. In the internalization of what had been external, accident and happenstance also played a role: in one case, a catastrophic family illness disrupted the household for three years. Another young radical was expected to assume major responsibilities for the care of a sibling; and in still another case, a young man was intensely involved in family conflicts. But what differentiates their accounts of adolescence from those of childhood is that in childhood the *inner* experience of turmoil was not in the forefront; whereas in reviewing their adolescent years, they now begin to view outer events as the product of their inner lives, rather than vice versa.

Some of the ways in which these radicals reacted to inner and outer turmoil can be inferred from the statements already cited. One reaction was asceticism, rigorous self-discipline, and an effort to deny the flesh. Another was intense and at times scrupulous religiosity, which they often now connect to sexual anxieties. Many also reported an intense preoccupation with intellectual matters in early adolescence. One said, describing eighth grade:

> I became sort of disillusioned with most of the work I was doing. . . . And I started to read. The academic work, I didn't consider it critical. I started reading a great deal, and got involved in reading philosophy and psychology and literature—no political

science, and no economics, nothing like that. . . . I would literally start at one end of the library and just work back and forth and read everything that there was. I didn't study any longer. I just read all day long. I'd read three or four books a day. . . . It was all sort of philosophical, and at fourteen years, I became an existentialist. That was generally what I did for the next three years.

Discussing this period in a later interview, he commented:

> My mind was very sharp during that period. I was just as sharp as a whip. I can understand what monks are now. I just seemed to have felt that my mind was very sharp, very tight, during all of those years, seventh, eighth, and ninth grades.

In connecting the sharpness of his mind to monasticism, he seems to suggest that his voracious intellectuality was connected to his ascetic denial of the flesh. Others also indicated that they now considered their intense intellectual concerns in early adolescence a defense against their inner turmoil.

At the same time, most of them devised stratagems for filling their loneliness with thought. Sometimes these thoughts were ritualistic prayers, sometimes grandiose political and philosophical ideas, at other times elaborate self-analyses. One young man elaborated an extraordinary fantasy world that both countered and complemented the troubles of his daily life:

> I was very rarely that deeply involved [with my family in a day-to-day way]. . . . Most of the other time was in fact spent trying to build a world that was different. . . . Much of what was happening was going on in my mind. I really created a sort of world of my own. . . . It was an almost all-encompassing fantasy world. I created a kingdom where things happened every day. And when not much was happening in the real world, I would just tune in on that. Things were happening there all the time. . . .
>
> Almost everything that happened in the real world was translated into the images of that world. It was a world with a king, with nobility, with peasants, with wars, with beautiful women. . . . In fact, a lot of the problems that I was faced with in daily life would be set in there. And decisions would be made . . . in terms of King Arthur and his Court sitting around figuring what to do with invading Welsh. . . .

> The whole kingdom was me. There were good guys and bad guys. But I had a kind of historian's attitude toward the kingdom. Everybody had his point to make. . . . I would have said that this country, let's say, was controlled by a very puritanical fighting nobility, but that a middle-class revolution was going on. And it would have presented a not inaccurate picture of actually what was going on in my mind. I would have been conscious of that as well.
>
> What I was trying to do was that I had become so rigid in my family, now I was trying to break out. Other parts of my personality, more spontaneous parts, were trying to assert themselves. This was a very tough fight. . . . It was very instrumental, but finally it reached the point where the kingdom, that whole way of life, had to dissolve itself because it was no longer instrumental to live experience twice or three times removed from real life. [That happened] when my life became somewhat richer, when other people became more important.

Two or three years after this upsurge of adolescent turmoil, many of the interviewees entered into a period of rebellion against their parents, usually focused around parental "unfairness" and "injustice." The particular issues at stake in these mid-adolescent rebellions centered largely around the individual's views that his parents attempted to restrict him excessively, did not allow him sufficient freedom to be "himself," tried to control his life, tried to plan his future, and so on. Both the intensity of the rebellion and the feeling of moral outrage and betrayal that accompanied it seem unusual:

> I feel that they were really grossly unjust to me, just *really* insensitive to what kinds of social needs a child has—or that anybody has. They have the same needs, and that's why I have those needs. . . . So we used to have big fights about that.

Another interviewee rebelled at the responsibilities he was expected to take within his family:

> I reacted very violently. . . . I just got furious . . . [my parents and I] had these tremendous shouting matches, just *pure* shouting matches, as to just where responsibility lay. . . . I was

> feeling very rejected and very unattended to. But my parents understood that, they knew it very well. . . .

These incidents illustrate the peculiar quality of adolescent rebellion in many of these radicals: at the very time that they rebelled, they realized that their parents "understood" and "knew" why they were rebelling. Put differently, their rebellion characteristically consisted in using against their parents the parents' own principles, and inspiring *their* guilt.

One young woman, for example, described her mother's reaction after a family crisis during which her mother had neglected her:

> My mother felt very guilty for ignoring me for all that time. And she tried to make it up to me, she tried to give me presents and attention. But by that time I had learned to be independent. . . . So I didn't want her interfering with my life then. I was sixteen and I had been independent since I was thirteen. She didn't have any place in my life any more. I resented her trying to do that again. . . .

In all these rebellions, the issue of parental and filial principle is important. Rebellion characteristically consisted of angry outrage and betrayal upon discovering that the parents themselves did not practice the values they espoused. In particular, these adolescents felt outraged when their parents, who had consistently urged them to be independent, free-thinking, and autonomous, intervened in adolescence to attempt to control their lives.

In addition to the reasons given by these young radicals for their adolescent rebellions, there sometimes seemed to be another, less mentioned, reason. In at least a few of these families, the net weight of the family tradition seemed especially great, and mid-adolescent rebellion seems to have been unconsciously directed less at the real faults of individual parents than at a family legacy or even an honorable tradition, which the individual had to repudiate lest it overwhelm him. For example, one young radical grew up surrounded by a family and family friends whose lives were successfully and happily organized around left-wing politics.

His parents' best friends were Old Leftists whose works he later read; his own best friends were their children. His family, as he judged it both then and now, had a valuable tradition of intellectual and political accomplishment. And his parents appear to have understood him and treated him well throughout his youth. It seems difficult to understand his adolescent rebellion solely in terms of the specifics to which he connects it. Perhaps equally important for him is the fact that this intensely admired family tradition seems to have been overwhelming precisely because he admired it so. It may therefore have required an unusually strong act of repudiation in order for this young man to achieve a separate individuality, a separate identity as a radical.

For a minority of those interviewed, the turmoil of early adolescence led directly to the development of psychological symptoms. Some of these symptoms, had they come to the attention of a psychiatrist at the time, would have seemed relatively ominous. They include, for example, the previously mentioned elaboration of a fantasy world more real and engrossing than the actual world, the emergence of elaborately obsessional fears of sexual intimacy, an abortive suicide gesture, and the development of a transient paranoid view of the world. Most of those interviewed, however, developed no overt symptoms, but described themselves as often unhappy, subjectively isolated, inwardly frustrated and unfulfilled. These symptoms and feelings, and the rebellion against parents that often accompanied them, dissipated slowly as adolescence progressed.

The resumption of success

Merely to discuss the turmoil, the rebellion, and, in some cases, the symptoms of early adolescence would be to overlook the continuing psychological strength shown by these young radicals. Whatever their inner turmoil, in the midst of their rebellions and despite symptoms that would have incapacitated many, these particular young men and women "functioned" extremely well. Even in early adolescence, those with the most intense conflicts often seem to have been strikingly successful despite them. And as adolescence progressed, almost all overcame their earlier feelings of seclusiveness and withdrawal; relationships with the opposite sex were established—slowly and painfully, but surely—and the preadolescent pattern of leadership of peers coupled with academic achievement was almost invariably resumed.

Looking back now on the early adolescent years, most of those I interviewed admitted the anguish, but felt that they had in some way learned or grown as a result of it. One said:

> I felt like I was carrying a considerable burden. But on the other hand, it didn't seem to me at all as much of a burden as it would seem to me now, or to an older person at the time. It seemed perfectly natural. I was old enough, I could do almost everything I wanted to. [Long pause] On the other hand, clearly that way of growing up had its disadvantages. But it had its advantages, too.

And another put it this way:

> For three years, like, maybe it did mess me up an awful lot. But it was a matter of how I dealt with it. And then I came out of it, you know, in the last years of high school and then went on to college. I had gotten a lot of experience and strength and perception from it. So I guess it all depends, I'm sure I can still be very hung up about all that if I look back on it from one point of view. . . . But I usually don't. I don't know why that is. I guess it's the way people are put together.

The events of later adolescence make these retroactive judgments of the "experience and strength and perception" that grew out of earlier turmoil convincing. For in senior high school, and usually continuing on into college, these young radicals describe a pattern of outstanding success and leadership.

Most of those I interviewed tended to minimize or deprecate their actual achievements. One young woman, for example, initially said, "I was very much a typical college student. . . ." But later, in answer to a more specific question, she said:

> I worked on the newspaper. I was chairman of the Social Life Committee, and I was on the Student Council. . . . I got mostly A's.

A similar story of academic and social accomplishment emerged from the narrative of most of her fellow workers in Vietnam Summer. In high school, and even in college, their major energies were most often turned to academic success.

> In the eyes of the high-school administration, the most radical thing I did was that I was the one who led the move to graduate after three years. I went to summer school after my freshman year, I took six majors in my sophomore year and five and a half in my junior year. There were other kids who would take advanced courses in math, English, and science in the eighth grade, and they could graduate in their junior year. About five of them decided to do that.
>
> I caught holy hell from the principal—"See what you have done," and all that. He thought that was really bad, because it was undermining the whole purpose of the honor system. The purpose was to get people to have more experience, more classwork and maturity behind them when they went to college, not to get them to college sooner. . . . I went off to college very, very fast, in order to get in and get going. I thought I was really sure about what I wanted to do. . . . There was huge pressure on me because my brother had goofed off and hadn't done well in college. . . . It might have been a good thing to take a year off then. [K. K.: But that didn't occur to you at the time.] The pressure was on. Boom boom. [K. K.: What pressure?] Just going to college, I don't know. To get away from the folks and school, and having graduated in three years, and all . . .

The pressure on this young man was unusually intense, but others implied a similar parental interest in their academic performance, and almost all reported little difficulty in doing outstanding work in high school and college. Their talents and academic motivations were sometimes rewarded with national scholarships and advanced admission to desired colleges.

But despite academic success, most of these young men and women became increasingly disregardful of formal academic requirements, and more and more dubious about the value of academic performance per se. One young radical said, for example:

> I went through college with a fair amount of ease. I never studied. I could always get by without studying and play around a lot. I didn't take school that seriously. I never thought that you had to study to get a lot out of it. If I had a professor who I didn't like or who I thought was a poor professor, I wouldn't study for him and I would get a C and it wouldn't bother me. But if I had a professor that I liked and thought was a good teacher, then I would work very hard for him. . . . I always felt that the people who really studied hard were kind of dull people. I would see them getting into a box of not being really creative at all. I think they'd just be studying a lot and not learning anything. . . .

Others found they learned most from what they did and read outside of class:

> In my senior year [in high school], I spent a lot of time reading bizarre things—I was just ape-shit on books. . . . I read a lot of French literature. I read St. Augustine, the Modern Library on Santayana. I wanted to drink them all in—poetry, novels, philosophy, a lot in my education that I hadn't been taught. . . .

Like this young man, most young radicals began to scorn the ease with which they could get good grades, and a number decided that classroom work was largely irrelevant to their real education. The conventional intellectual achievement that had been so highly valued by their parents gradually was disparaged; it was replaced by a determination to "learn for myself." This emerging ambivalence toward the "merely academic" is an enduring issue to these young radicals: it is related to the pervasive theme of "specialness" in their lives. For increasingly, these young radicals felt (or realized) that the conventional education that appeared to suit their classmates did not fully meet their needs.

Some of these future radicals were at this stage in their life very far from political commitment. One young man was particularly soured on political life:

My parents had always said, "Look, man, you ought to go in the foreign service. You ought to go into politics. You ought to go into public service." This all weighed on me as a great burden. I felt, "Okay, maybe those people who have gifts do owe them to society. But how can I get involved in any kind of politics in this country? It's ugly, disreputable. No honorable man would be a politician." It may be unfair, but I just said categorically, "You'll never see me in public life."

You know, it was a kind of a shame. Because personalitywise, my gifts were more in that direction than they were in being introspective, or at least in being isolated. [In high school] you have two bags—the politics bag and the artsy-craftsy bag. . . . I thought, "Okay, my bag is going to be literature. I'm going to study literature in college, and maybe I'll write someday."

Looking around at the movements for peace and civil rights, this young man reacted negatively:

I thought, "Oh, boy, here are all those guys with peace hang-ups. They feel guilty about their middle-class existences. They're just getting their hang-ups out on the black people. A bunch of liberals going out with hearts of gold and no sense." There was some element of truth in that, but I made it into a gross generality, which allowed me to dismiss all of it. At the time, though, I recognized that there was some very courageous people involved, and I respected them for doing it.

For almost all, the years of high school and college were years of growth and change. One described the impact of his years in college:

So I went to college, and college meant I was living with people, other people my age. The atmosphere was very liberal . . . but for about a year, I went around being very rigid. . . . I didn't have very many friends other than the political ones. We formed ourselves a little clique. . . . We didn't involve other people in decision-making at all.

But I sort of gradually changed. I made new friends in the second year. I got two new roommates that I was very close to. You know, I made a lot of close friends. That really helped me out a lot. It didn't change my basic politics, but it just helped me personally. I think that you can't have very strong political ideas or do a lot of political things without that interacting with your personality.

For others, personal growth meant establishing relationships with the opposite sex. One young radical, whose earlier adolescence had been particularly filled with anxiety over his relationships with girls, commented that later:

> The girl friends that I went out with were the major relationships that I had. I considered them all very close friends of mine, I loved them all very much. I never went out with somebody, or very rarely, just for a date or two. I would get very involved, and there were lots of problems, but I really valued them as friends. They were major personal influences.

Recognizing that his sister had been exposed to many of the same influences that had inspired his own early adolescent problems about sex, he invited her to visit him and his girl friend:

> I was very happy at the fact that my girl and I at that time were getting along very well. We were sleeping together and had a wonderful equal time. . . . Because that was probably the first relationship that my sister saw where two people really loved each other, also the first physically close relationship that she had ever been close to. . . . I always really made an attempt when I was talking with my sister, a strong attempt, to give her a positive image of personal relationships. I talked with her . . . about sex and people being nice, and how nice it was. . . . I talked about those kinds of things because I realized what kind of an image we had gotten from my parents.

For this young man, the struggle to attain intimate and sexual relationships with the opposite sex was particularly difficult. But others also felt that intimacy with the opposite sex had been a major factor in their growth. One, for example, discussing the disappearance of his earlier psychological problems, commented:

> I think that the reason for [their disappearance] was my increasing capacity to love and become deeply involved in real people. Sexual expression, making love, was very important in breaking down those walls, draining the wells of suspicion and loneliness on which these problems fed.

The outward picture, then, as these young men and women approached adulthood, was one of renewed success in almost every area: academic, interpersonal, organizational.

Portents of radicalism

Despite their outward success, these young radicals were in many ways exceptional young men and women even before they became radicals. Not only were they unusually talented and often considered leaders of their peers, but they also brought from earlier life a sense of their own ultimate differences from others, very high principles, and an unusually strong sense of independence. These qualities anticipate their later radicalism. And even before they began to think of themselves as radicals, these same qualities often brought them into conflict with their environment.

Those who came from politically active families, whether liberal or radical, sometimes began in high school to take minority stands that brought them into conflict with school authorities:

> [In senior high school] we got involved in this newspaper. We called it *The Forest Hills Stinker*. We started distributing this in school. It was a paper where the columns debated issues. We did editorialize, but only in one sense—we always put the good position on the left and the bad position on the right. [Laughs] But that's the only thing we did: there were no editorials in it. We thought it was a pretty good thing.
>
> Well, we got kicked out of school because we refused to stop distributing it on school grounds. . . . The rules were that you had to get permission, so we tried. We went as far as to knuckle under to the system and tried to get permission. But we weren't granted permission and we kept on distributing it anyway. David's mother was on the school board so he didn't get kicked out. Tommy and I both got suspended for—I don't know for how long—a week, something like that. . . .
>
> [K. K.: What did your parents do?] Well, there wasn't much *to* do about it. You just sat it out. They said, "This is your decision, and if you think what you're doing is right, okay." I could afford to sit it out in terms of the schoolwork.

Another tells a comparable story of preradical social action in high school:

> There were thirteen of us, thirteen seniors. We all thought we ought to do something. We wanted to leave some kind of positive legacy, aside from the broken windows. See, it was a school like a lot of other schools in Suburb Town that had an honors program. We had the best teachers and the advanced stuff and we got college credit for stuff in the ninth grade. The other kids were really getting a shitty education. . . .
>
> Anyway, we sat down and wrote up a list of what we thought ought to happen. A free student newspaper, student say in the curriculum. Wow, the reactions to that was amazing! . . . This was after the decision about the prayers and Bible reading in the schools, so one of the things we said was that they should not have benediction at convocations, assemblies, and graduations.
>
> Then the thirteen of us—I was the chairman—and the girl who was president of the Student Council, we took these things to the principal. He acceded to some of our demands, and told us that others were out of his hands and that we had to see the Board of Education. Five of us went to see the Board. Another kid went, too, whose father was on the Board. We thought that would help. [Laughs] We were thinking of it tactically. They agreed to get rid of the convocation and benediction at graduations and assemblies. But they said that they had already invited people for the coming year, so we had to understand that Rabbi Israel and Reverend MacNamara were going to have to be there. . . .
>
> But then we found out the next year, and the year after . . . they still have it. They would tell kids anything to get them out of their office. And the student newspaper is still controlled.

In the next chapter, I will consider in more detail how such experiences of unkept promises by authoritative persons contribute to becoming a radical. Here I should note that one consequence of early political involvement was to interest the future radical in the motivation that underlay his own political commitment:

> I read Eric Hoffer's *The True Believer,* and it didn't ring true to me at all, I couldn't identify with it at all. I couldn't put a lot of the people I knew into that group either. I think I'm being honest with myself when I say that my friends seemed to have my motivations, too.

A similar interest in the sources of political action had developed in others, and the amount of thought and reading they had devoted to this subject was apparent in their conversations with me.

The independence of these young men and women showed itself in their relationships with their peers as well. One young woman, for example, discussed her experiences with cliques of girls in high school and college:

> Like for instance there was a group of seven girls. And I was identified with that. And then I had one very good girl friend in it. The whole structure was very tight. . . . But I made it a point to break out of that group and to establish relationships with other people. I don't know why. I was the only one of the group who did that. . . .
>
> The same thing happened in college. I was again part of a group in college, and out of a silly little incident, which was to me a matter of major integrity, I broke away. . . . [She talks about a fight between two girls.] I refused to participate in the sniping at her. . . . I defended her. And for some reason that was a major incident. . . . I felt very lonely, but it was important to me not to take part in that. I just couldn't do it. But it was, there were hard times.

Despite her loneliness and her emphasis on these being "hard times," she was a recognized student leader on her campus.

The combination of independence, political involvement, and demand for intellectual relevance that was developing in these young men and women sometimes made it hard for more conventional colleges to meet their needs, or, for that matter, to tolerate them. One young man illustrates this conflict in his account of the conservative liberal arts college he first attended:

> When I went out there for an interview, I told them I had been working with SNCC and so on, and they said, "You're just the kind of kid we're looking for." But when I got there, there were very few people like that. Just kids with names like Reichlog and Rolvag. Of course, there were thirty-five kids in the SDS chapter, but they took a lot of finding. . . .
>
> During the year, we got letters sent to us from the president of the school, saying that if we didn't like the school we shouldn't try

> to change it, we should leave. So eleven of us transferred. Six of the eleven had the highest point averages in the school. They were by far the best students in the school, these eleven. And a lot of faculty left too. . . .
>
> And then I knew I didn't want to stay there because when I was a freshman I got into the Hegel seminar, which was only for junior and senior philosophy majors. It was a good course. But I was the only freshman in the course: there were five juniors and five seniors and me. I got one of the two A's in the course. It was absurd, because they were all philosophy majors. I saw that if I stayed there much longer, there wasn't going to be much more stimulation than I had already found.

He eventually transferred to a college with a strong work-study program where he prospered.

Their peers and teachers recognized a "difference" about these young men and women, sometimes responding by electing or appointing them to positions of responsibility, but at other times questioning their reliability, and sometimes even pointing out to them a latent radicalism of which they themselves were not aware at the time:

> One night when I was in college, I had dinner with [a conservative professor] and he proceeded to get quite drunk, and he said, "You know, you're a fucking traitor. You're going to be one of *those* guys. You're going to be a quisling for your own country." I was really stunned. But already, even then, there were differences developing.

What is striking in such accounts is the future radical's sense of astonishment and outrage that he should be considered unreliable or irresponsible by those whom he respected. Some of those I interviewed were considered "radicals" by those who knew them long before they had to come to think of themselves as such.

One young woman, for example, had applied for an overseas job after college:

> The person who was interviewing me said, "This is a job that's open, this is what you must fit into." That bothered me; it bothered me that I had to fit into this slot. And then I went to have a

psychological examination for the whole thing. He was a psychiatrist who was paid by them. And he said, "You would probably not fit very well into the structure of this world, because if you were told to do something you didn't think was the right thing to do, you wouldn't do it. . . . You're too independent to really work under this kind of structure. . . ." What he was really telling me was that I'm not good at taking orders.

That upset me very much, and I went directly to the dean and said what he had told me. She said, "He's probably right, you know. You wouldn't take orders and you might not be comfortable in it." At first, I was incensed, but afterwards I decided that he had probably been right.

Another of those interviewed had applied for a job with the government:

They wouldn't let me in because they said I was "too cosmopolitan." . . . They were basically right; they searched it out. Well, they knew me better than I knew myself. . . . I was trying to get in the door, or, being in the door, trying to bring new ideas into the door with me, trying to get into another room. But I wasn't able to make it. I could never get me in and all my baggage too. [K. K.: What baggage do you mean?] Well, now I'd say that one piece of baggage that I never would have been able to get rid of is that, even when I was very young, I had seen too much poverty and exploitation to really be able to believe that the liberals were right. . . .

In retrospect, this young man understands what his interviewers saw in him; but at the time he was hurt and puzzled.

Despite the many precursors of their later radicalism, it would be wrong to conclude that these young men and women were rebels before they became radicals. Once their early adolescent rebellions against their parents had run their course, most of them "settled down" to a period of several years of success in general conformity to the expectations of their environment. Although they sometimes found themselves in conflict with others, this conflict sprang less from generalized rebellion than from their independence of mind or from principled objection to what they saw happening around them:

> I wasn't really a rebel, I was just stubborn. . . . I'm not, you know, totally alienated. I didn't have a sudden break with my past. But I can see now that even in college I did have certain questions, say, about the value of exams, even about the value of honors I made in college. And I think I had always been doing that, but I never had enough reinforcement, except from some of the faculty. And this now, I think, has changed. . . .

Yet in retrospect, the principals, college presidents, psychiatrists, government interviewers, peers, and professors who described these young men and women as somehow unreliable, as too "cosmopolitan," as troublemakers who should leave college, as "too independent," or even as future "quislings," clearly saw something that was really there. And increasingly, these young radicals-to-be became aware of it themselves. On the surface, they were successful, well-organized students, often leaders of their contemporaries. Their superficial problem was a surfeit of adult options. But subjectively, these options did not seem particularly interesting to them. Indeed, the open avenues toward adult achievement and success were, psychologically, no longer experienced as available at all. What one termed the "Establishment options" attracted them little. It was not that they disparaged technological, academic, or financial success, but that they dimly felt there was something else more important. One young man, describing his thinking in college, said:

> In my confused mind at the time, I said, "I'm not going to relate to machines, I'm not going to relate to books, I'm not going to relate to money. I am going to relate to people, on a very, very personal basis of service." . . . I talked around, I talked to people who I was very close to. . . . The decision was very indicative of the way I was going to move. It wasn't really that professionally calculated. It was almost a process of elimination. The other things didn't matter that much.

Others, increasingly convinced that their formal education was largely irrelevant to their needs, considered dropping out of college. Some left, but others stayed.

> I wasn't sure if I wanted to stay in school or not. But I knew that there was a hell of a lot more reading I had to do in my field. And if I wasn't in some kind of institution, I probably wouldn't do it. I'd probably just get totally involved in politics. So I figured I wanted to go to school and try to combine the two.

Little by little, then, these young men and women began to experience a sense of inner frustration, discontent, and stagnation, coupled with a vague search for alternatives to the futures that lay open before them. They were, as one put it, "nearing the end of the line."

Nearing the end of the line

It would be wrong to overdramatize the "crisis" from which each of these young men and women moved toward the New Left. Indeed, to call it a crisis at all may suggest a degree of agitation and self-consciousness that this period did not possess. What actually seems to have happened was that at some point, usually during or after the college years, these future radicals began to feel they were "wasting" their lives, and that despite outward success, they were in some sense marking time. Many had periods of dejection, discouragement, and "downness," when the world seemed flat, tasteless, and stale. Others seemed to have felt something like shame at the perceived meaninglessness of their lives. And still others came to question their basic abilities:

> [In college] things were a little tougher. I had to face up to that, and that really shook me. I didn't know how to face failure or the threat of failure. I had never been taught about that. . . . I began to question seriously my own abilities. I began to wonder, "Well, where are you really at? Where do your abilities really lie?" . . . I did a lot of soul-searching, and I said to myself, "You are really very immature. . . ."

One young man, for example, became increasingly dissatisfied with the college groups in which he was an acknowledged leader.

He was troubled by the reintensification of old psychological symptoms and became progressively more involved in leadership positions in campus political organizations—an involvement that was accompanied by the diminution and eventual disappearance of his symptoms. Another, headed for the career his parents desired him to enter, began to do poorly in his required courses, and out of the ensuing crisis withdrew from college. His parents reacted strongly:

> They were furious. When I called them, it upset their intellectual values. I called them at home and said, "Look, I'm coming home." They insisted upon coming to see me, but I refused. I said, "Look, I think this is the right thing for me to do. Whatever the reason behind it we can talk about it on the phone, we can talk about it later, but you cannot come up here to see me." So they didn't. I just took a leave of absence. I was in good academic standing. . . . I felt very isolated and I felt very away from things that were morally—I can't even say politically—because I'm not even sure I had any politics then.

This young man's difficulty in describing the precise reasons for his crisis was typical. He can only say that he felt "very away from things that were morally—I can't even say politically . . ." One missing dimension in his life was moral, and its absence is somehow related to his later political involvement. But at the time, and even now, he had difficulty in pinpointing precisely *what* was wrong.

For almost all, the sense of approaching the end of the line was related to similar feelings of vaguely articulated moral irrelevance. These young men and women were not possessed of any sense of destiny. But they retained from earlier life an unusual orientation to moral principle, together with a feeling of their own difference. For them, more than for most of their contemporaries, it was not enough merely to "have principles"; it was necessary to live by their principles. The increasing sense of the inadequacy of their own lives and of the options before them was therefore related to a growing feeling that the direction in which they were moving was ethically inadequate and therefore personally irrelevant. Once again, the issue of principle—and the shame that arose from failing to follow its lead—was crucial.

Beyond these communalities, there were also great differences in the extent of the crisis that readied these young men and women to move toward the New Left. For one or two, the "crisis" was marked by an event or experience that can in retrospect symbolize the dissatisfactions of many months or years. But for most, no single episode can be found that adequately summarizes their growing sense of failure; a sense paradoxical and difficult to understand because of their continuing outward success. A few were aware that something was going wrong with their lives, and self-consciously sought alternatives. Most, however, were not aware, and only in retrospect can describe the increasing sense of emptiness and frustration. Nor did any of these young men and women actually *reach* the end of the line, in the sense that they arrived at a point when they felt they could not go on. Rather, their growing feeling of wasting their lives was increasingly countered by a new involvement with the Movement for Social Change.

In the gradual evolution of a readiness for radicalism, then, many factors were fused with varying weights depending on the individual and his circumstances. Perhaps the continuing sense of specialness made it more psychologically possible for these young men and women to turn toward a movement that represents a special minority of young Americans separated from most of their contemporaries. Clearly, the role of principle, and specifically the shame of an unprincipled life, was important for all. But beyond these consistencies, the sense of nearing the end of the line also reflected different and sometimes opposite things for each person: a fear of becoming too like one's ineffectual father, or a guilt at not implementing the father's principles; the frustration that followed an honest attempt to "join the Establishment," or the psychological impossibility of even getting near it; the sense of the barrenness of middle-class American life as seen in his own family, or the implicit desire to extend to all Americans the warmth and excitement of his own family. What these young radicals shared was merely the growing awareness that their lives were inadequate.

Adolescence and politics

The adolescent experience of the young radicals who led Vietnam Summer is obviously exceptional from many points of view, just as these young radicals differ from those in the conventional political scene in a variety of other ways. Political action for them is not a job but a calling; they strongly resist a "professional" approach to their work; they insist on the importance of personal commitment and conviction; they come from unusual families; their psychological development differs from that of most Americans of comparable talent. Were they to be compared with equally able age-mates planning to make their careers in conventional party politics, these radicals would undoubtedly be more intense, more oriented to principle, less inclined to view their political commitment as a "career."

Any simple comparison between the precursors of politicization in these young radicals and in others is therefore bound to be fallacious. There are many paths to political action, and the path taken by these particular young radicals is unusual: it may be unique to them. But even with all of these qualifications, examination of their experience does permit the development of tentative hypotheses concerning the personal roots of radical commitment, and allows us to delineate at least *one* pathway through adolescence to political action.

Many of the events and feelings in the early adolescences of these young radicals will be well known to anyone familiar with the psychoanalytic literature on adolescence. This literature, strongly influenced by experience with upper-middle-class adolescent patients in Europe, stresses such issues as early adolescent turmoil centered around the onrush of sexuality, the development of defenses of intellectualization and asceticism as a way of warding off uncontrollable instinctual drives, and rebellion against parents as a means of breaking the bonds of childhood dependency. If such accounts are taken as descriptions of "typical" adolescence, then the adolescent experiences of these young radicals are extraordinarily true to the norm.

But as clinicians with experience on both sides of the Atlantic have observed, adolescent development among most middle-class American youths usually takes a different form. The most common adolescent pattern in America involves what Peter Blos terms "uniformism": a turning away from the family toward the peer-group culture, acceptance of its norms as infallible and regulatory, and the use of conformity to peer-group norms as a means of simultaneously regulating one's own impulses and attenuating one's family ties. Erik Erikson's account of typical American adolescence similarly emphasizes the "ego restriction" by which many Americans effectively ward off feelings and personal relationships that might otherwise produce more turmoil and drastic changes in behavior. My experience with American college students supports these observations: most commonly, the problems of early adolescence are dealt with by submersion into the teen-age culture. In many instances, involvement with the peer group helps prevent the "normal" (to the European) turmoil of early adolescence; in some cases, it may also serve to prevent a real adolescence.

Compared to their more "typical" American contemporaries, then, these young radicals seemed to have undergone an unusually "European" adolescence. At the same time, they really did *have* an adolescence, with all of the anguish and the possibilities for growth that this stage entails. I have already noted the individuality of these radicals as young adults. I have also noted that, paradoxically, those who came from what to an outside observer would appear to be the "best" families often underwent a severe struggle to emancipate themselves from these families. It may be that the very closeness, warmth, and encouragement toward independence in some of these families were what made adolescence both possible and necessary. Put differently, many of these families seem to have given their children the strength and the need to challenge, re-examine, and partially reassimilate their parents' values, and eventually to achieve an unusual degree of individuality for themselves. If we consider adolescence not merely as an awkward and painful stage to be outgrown as soon as possible, but as a phase essential to attaining the fullest possible human development, then one characteristic of these young men and women is that they were fortunate enough to possess the familial, personal, and environmental resources to allow them a full adolescence. In this regard, too, they differ from many of their contemporaries.

In discussing the evolution of political and religious ideas, some have argued that adult commitments often grow out of the resolution of "the adolescent crisis." In the turmoil and confusion of adolescence, new instinctual and intellectual forces are released that unbalance the childhood equilibrium of the personality, requiring a new resolution and synthesis that may include, for the first time, "ideological" commitments to politics, world view, and religious belief. A superficial reading of the events of these young radicals' earlier lives may suggest that such an account is applicable to them.

But closer examination of the events I have discussed indicates that their development was actually more complex. These young men and women underwent *two* crises, not one; and the characteristics of these two crises were quite different. The second occurred only after the first was adequately resolved; political commitments grew out of the second and less stormy period of personal reorganization. The first crisis was clearly the major turmoil, guilt, loneliness, anxiety, and misery of early adolescence. It is this stage that is so well described in the European psychoanalytic literature. Yet for most of these young men and women, the storms of early adolescence did *not* lead directly to political commitment, but rather to a resumption of the preadolescent pattern of success, to a reordering and reorganization of the personality, to an impressive, although in retrospect transient, stability, and to the development of a whole repertory of new relationships—to same-sex friends and contemporaries, to the opposite sex, to established authority, to ideas, and so on. This new equilibrium, in most cases, lasted several years, and only gradually outlived its usefulness.

Out of the preliminary equilibrium of late adolescence, then, a second crisis—what I have called the sense of "nearing the end of the line"—gradually evolved. This second crisis, which several called an "identity crisis," differed markedly from the first. It involved far less anxiety and conscious turmoil; it remains more difficult to describe and understand; and it is most easily described in philosophical, ethical, and existential terms. In this second crisis, traces of earlier problems can still be detected: problems of identification, the recurrence of psychological symptoms, irrational behavior, and neurotic anxieties are still apparent. Nevertheless, this second crisis emerges primarily from *the failure of success.* Although the equilibrium established in late adolescence was enough to satisfy the world and to open doors to many good things American society offers its more fortunate adults, there was something about the prospect before them that seemed unsatisfying to these particular young radicals. Faced with the move from late adolescence into the adult roles of the established society, they balked, became mildly depressed, and, without fully understanding at the time what they were doing, gradually became involved in the New Left. In these particular young men and women, the move toward radical politics was not a direct outgrowth of what is ordinarily considered "the adolescent crisis." They had long since resolved their first adolescent crisis in a way that almost everyone but themselves would have judged eminently successful. Commitment to the New Left developed out of a later crisis, one that occurred as entry into the Establishment became more imminent. And this second crisis seems less a part of adolescence itself than a crisis at the threshold between adolescence and conventional adulthood.

The hesitation at the door of adulthood by these young radicals can be judged in two very different ways. On the one hand, reluctance to seize the options before them can be interpreted as a reluctance to "grow up": it would probably be so judged by many Americans. And evidence could be adduced from the material I have presented to support this view: conventional adulthood might mean the loss of that sense of specialness that had been so long with these young men and women; it might mean becoming like the ineffectual side of their fathers, all of whom were in some sense involved in conventional American life. Delaying may therefore represent a childish reluctance to abandon the uncompromising adolescent insistence on purity of principle. But judged from another perspective, their hesitation may reflect strength rather than weakness. These young men and women usually had already "proved" that they could succeed in the terms that American society uses to define success. Most of them had excelled, but had gained scant satisfaction from their own excellence. So judged, their reluctance to take up the jobs, fellowships, offers, and rewards before them might indicate that they were able to demand more, not less, of themselves and of life.

But however we judge the adolescences of these young men and women, it is clear that as they approached adulthood, they were seized with a disquiet that they still find difficult to explain. Whatever its origins, this sense of having tested the psychological possibilities of one way of life and found them wanting was a prelude to their becoming radicals.

4 Becoming a radical

To pick out one period of life as crucial to becoming a radical is largely arbitrary. A review of the major themes in the early lives of these young radical leaders indicates the many precursors to their development as radicals. And the next chapter, dealing with the strains of Movement work, is concerned with the continuing process of radicalization. Yet it is possible, for all of those interviewed, to find a period—often of several years—during which they first came to think of themselves as radicals: when those from liberal backgrounds "woke up" to realize that they were part of the New Left, and when those few from radical backgrounds were first able to accept that tradition as their own. In no instance was radicalization sudden or dramatic; in every case, the process was gradual, unself-conscious, "natural," and at the time largely unexamined. None of these young men and women deliberately set out to *become* radicals; rather, they came to realize, as a result of their activities, that they *were* radicals.

Precisely how long this process had been under way depends on how one defines it. In one sense, it had begun in early childhood, where the underpinnings of a later radical commitment were developed. In another sense, radicalization began with the growing sense of self-dissatisfaction and stagnation that afflicted most of these young men and women as they entered adulthood. Defined in still another way, real radicalization began only when these young men and women awoke to realize that, generally without specifically intending it, they considered themselves radicals or a part of the Movement. And certainly some within the New Left would argue that many of those who led Vietnam Summer were still not "real radicals" at all, because they were insufficiently committed to tactics of resistance and confrontation.

Only by an arbitrary definition, then, can we designate a certain stage as the stage of radicalization. It is not possible to define a sharp beginning or end to this stage; but one can delimit a period of life when the individual did not think of himself as a radical, followed after an interval of months or years by another period when being a radical was a crucial and even central part of his concept of himself. I will call this intervening interval the stage of radicalization. This stage is important, partly because it is so frequently discussed by radicals themselves, by their sympathizers, and by their detractors. How does one recruit new radicals? Or how can the "spread of radicalism" be prevented? Furthermore, the question of radicalization is relevant to the broader question of how individuals previously inactive in political life come to be involved in, to take positions with regard to, and to be actors in the political process.

The topic of radicalization, or, more specifically, the question of how to radicalize others, was frequently discussed within Vietnam Summer, and is obviously a crucial question for the entire New Left. My own interest in this question helps explain the willingness of the leaders of Vietnam Summer to co-operate in this study, for the question seemed vitally relevant to their own continuing work. On long night car rides home from distant meetings, the organizers and office workers of Vietnam Summer sometimes asked each other, "How did you get into this?" and felt closer to each other for the effort to answer. And the more general question, "How can we get *others* into this?" of course underlay the summer's entire effort; how to build the climate, the organization, and the workers who would create the basis for a mass radical movement was continually discussed.

The most common controversy in such discussions was the relative weight of emotion and intellect in radicalization. Some argued that their own involvement in the New Left had been largely the result of feeling, emotion, and passion—indignation, idealism, frustration, and anger. Such individuals saw radicalism as a "gut reaction" that preceded the development of more articulated intellectual positions. Others considered that their entry into the New Left had been more a matter of conscious reflection and thought, primarily the result of an intellectual awareness of the discrepancy between America as it is and America as they believed it should be. Arguments within the National Office about how to recruit new workers into the Movement often became polarized around the issue of feeling versus intellect; discussions of tactics opposed emotional and intellectual appeals to the constituencies to be organized.

What I have already said of the development of these young radicals should make clear the impossibility of choosing between intellect and emotion in the process of their radicalization. Those I interviewed were in many ways an unusually intellectual group, to whom ideas mattered probably more than they do to most of their contemporaries. All had had to fight the tendency to separate intellect from life; and all had worked hard to join knowledge to action. In this sense, their radicalization had important intellectual origins. But at the same time, all brought to their involvement in the Movement strong emotions, powerful fantasies, and intense feelings of indignation, anger, hope and commitment.

Moreover, the psychological diversity of the leaders in Vietnam Summer entailed similar diversity in the relative importance of intellect and feeling in their radicalization. In general, each individual's views about how others became radicalized tended to reflect his own perception of how he himself had become radicalized. One, for example, stressed primarily his "need for intellectual stimulation," and his admiration of the intellectual qualities of those he met in his early days in the Movement. He had been involved in a conventional electoral campaign:

> Bill Westbury came and sort of complimented me for what he felt was a good job that I had played. . . . He said, "SDS is holding a series of seminars this year, and would you like to get involved?" I said, "I would love to," because I really felt the need for intellectual stimulation. . . . At the time, I was for peace, I was for dissent, I was for civil rights, and then sometimes, if the situation presented, I would wind up arguing for socialism. But I would also argue for better Medicare, higher minimum wages, or something like that. I considered myself a sort of liberal. A very militant political liberal. . . .
>
> [He went to a national student radical meeting.] I heard several people whom I was unimpressed with, but it was Clarkson . . . who just overwhelmed me with his mind. He didn't turn me on and say I should become involved or anything like that. I was just impressed with his mind and his grasp of politics. So I decided at that point that I wanted to become part of that. That was what I was going to do, to be a part of, because I could learn a hell of a lot. And they were nice, they were good people. And I had a lot to learn. So what I did for the next year and a half, was just to listen. . . . I didn't say a word, I never even opened my mouth. I took notes, and I'd come back at night and study them and try to remember what was said. I read all the literature. . . .
>
> The thing that I was thinking about was what was I going to do with my life, what kind of job am I going to have? And I wound up feeling that I might want to go to graduate school, but I never applied. . . . I wanted to learn, I wanted to learn how America was organized and I wanted to find out more about myself. I figured that these guys and publications and the books that they read could help me to do that. . . . Another thing I felt was kind of the ideology of the alienated: "The old values have been destroyed; the old structures and institutions of the past no longer fit our needs; therefore we must rebuild." That's how I personally connected into it.

But even this account makes clear how intertwined were his intellectual needs with his personal needs: his admiration for the first radicals because "they were good people," his questions about "what to do with my life," his need to "find out more about myself."

Another interviewee, in contrast, emphasized her primarily emotional reaction to her first meeting with civil rights activists:

> The initial reaction was just a very emotional one. . . . It wasn't at all intellectual with us. In fact, if we had thought about it, we wouldn't have done it. If we had reflected on it, we would have known the consequences. But it's just one of those things you have to do. . . . That emotional reaction was enough to get us started, but when it came to having any organizational skill or any kind of conception of what we wanted to be doing two or three years from now, that flopped miserably. That's when we had to learn politics. . . .

Here, too, any neat distinction between intellectual and emotional reactions falls down. Although she emphasizes her "emotional reaction," she also stresses the more cognitive "organizational skills" and conceptions that she had later to develop.

If it is difficult to define exactly the relative weight of intellect and emotion in the political development of these young radicals, it is even harder to provide any simple formula to explain how and why they became radicals. A majority came from politically involved, liberal, and socially conscious families, though not radical ones; but a few came from relatively apolitical families, and some from families with a strong radical tradition. How far these young men and women had to travel, what they had to overcome or to assimilate from their pasts, which emotional and intellectual resources they could take for granted and which they had to develop—all of these differed from individual to individual. But if the leaders of Vietnam Summer are taken as a group, it is possible to define a process of radicalization that applies, to a greater or lesser degree, to most of them. This process involves psychological continuity—indeed, a return to one's roots—at one level, and psychological change at another; it entails a major confrontation with unwelcome inequities in American society; and it leads to an activation and engagement whereby the individual comes to feel himself personally responsible for effecting radical changes and feels a part of a movement of others similarly committed. The task of this chapter will be to outline this over-all process of radicalization.

Continuity and change

It is usually assumed that those who hold positions considered "extreme" by most, whether on the Right or on the Left, are involved in some strong reaction against their past. The taking of radical positions is thus often interpreted as a way of repudiating important layers of unconscious feeling or fantasy, as an unconscious rejection of parents and family traditions, or as a search for an all-embracing ideology to assist the individual in suppression of his own neurotic difficulties. Studies of the "authoritarian personality" have interpreted fascistic ideology—with its black-and-white view of good and evil, strong and weak, heroes and sinners—as a complex working out and denial of the individual's repressed hostilities toward his own parents. Similarly, other writers have argued that there are many "authoritarians of the Left" whose psychodynamics are similar, and this epithet often has been applied to young radicals. The "true believer" is seen as an inwardly empty man, who seizes dogmatically and rigidly upon a utopian ideology in order to relieve his inner emptiness and/or assuage his guilt about his own privileged position.

While there have been few empirical studies of radicals of the Left, the most common assumption brought to the analysis of radicalization is, as in the radical-rebel theory, an assumption of a profound and usually unconscious discontinuity. According to this view, radicalism serves the psychological function of rejecting some real attribute of the individual, like his wealth or privileged position, or else serves to repudiate crucial individuals in the past, like his father. For example, the mistrust of authority found among radicals of all kinds is said to be based on a rejection of, or intolerance for, the authority of their own fathers.

My observations of this small group of New Left activists do not allow me to test the validity of such generalizations as they apply to the radical Right, to the Communist Left, or even to the New Left in general. But in the group I studied, explanations that posit a basic discontinuity between the young radical and his past or his tradition, or a major suppression of important aspects of his own personality, are not adequate. Equally irrelevant to this group are those explanations of political "extremism" that point to the role of an embracing ideology in allowing the individual to repress or deny his personal problems: in this group, formal ideology is almost completely absent. Missing as well in this group are those precipitate conversions that suggest a sudden reordering of the personality, accompanied by the suppression of what was previously dominant. In all these respects, the young radicals I studied are exceptions to most generalizations about the process of involvement in politics.

In my earlier discussion of the "radical-rebel" and the "red-diaper-baby" hypotheses, I indicated that both continuity and change are present in the development of these young men and women. As I have noted, a psychologist who interviews a group of young men and women about the relationship between their past and present may tend to elicit statements of consistency and continuity. Yet I deliberately attempted to study both continuity and change; indeed, in focusing upon the process of becoming a radical, my questions were intended primarily to evoke statements of what had changed, of how far the individual had come, and of what in his past he had rejected. Since most of this chapter will be devoted to the changes that occurred in the process of radicalization, I will begin by underlining the more important continuities.

In considering the relationship of these radicals to their families, two levels of belief must be distinguished. On the one hand, families have what we can call *core values:* basic assumptions concerning desirable human relationships, feelings, and motives.

Such values—like honesty, deference, success, kindness, achievement, getting one's own way, or humility—are more often implicit and expressed in behavior than formally articulated. On the other hand, families have publicly articulated *formal values,* which include more intellectual policy statements concerning attitudes to the wider society, formal religious conviction, and so on. Among formal values, articulated political beliefs must be included.

Becoming a radical, as seen in this group, involves *no fundamental change in core values.* To be sure, the formal political beliefs of parents and children invariably differ, even in the children of radical families. But each of those interviewed was brought up in a family whose core values are fully congruent with his present radical activities. For example, the great majority of these radicals' parents currently applaud, approve, or accept their activities; and while some are dubious about the *extent* of their son's or daughter's commitment to the Movement, their reservations are most often based on "practical" considerations such as the need to obtain more education before plunging into the political world. Especially for those from radical families, the process of radicalization involves a return to the fundamental values of the family. As one young man from a radical family put it:

> Look, there never were any other values for me to make my own. . . . There were always just clear lines between those values [of the rest of the community] and mine, those of my parents. I could never adopt those, because they were always the things that seemed opposed to me. Even if I had been a political dullard, from a personal, ego point of view, I never could have done that. These are *my* values. In college, I began to claim them as my own. They were no longer my family's, because I had to defend them now on my own.

For this individual, as for those few others who came from clearly left-wing families, the process of radicalization did not involve acquiring new values, but rather an arduous effort to make his family's values his own.

In most of the others, who came from politically liberal but not radical families, the continuity must sometimes be read between the lines, but it is nonetheless there. One young man, for example, dropped out of college and lived for a time in Europe. He described his thinking while in Europe as follows:

> I got really upset about Vietnam in Europe. I followed it in the *Times,* the *Tribune,* and *Le Monde,* and I thought it was for shit. The alienation was really closing in on me. I was seriously thinking of not going back. Or going back and bumping off my B.A. and getting right straight back to Europe and living a Henry Miller–Lawrence Durrell expatriate life. I could get some pad out there in Southern France, there were nice cultural people to talk to, and you could go to see the churches, and go to Greece and smell the lemons. But I just had too much social something in me. I would have missed a lot of things. . . . I wanted to be involved with people, I wanted to be fighting something, and I have a kind of a gut love for the United States. . . .
>
> I thought that if I'm going back to the United States, well, I had this feeling of *responsibility*. And now it seemed to me that there was some alternative. It didn't seem that one had to go into the foreign service or the party structures to be in public life. I thought, "Look, man, there are a lot of kids raising shit about the war and civil rights back there. There is no reason why I shouldn't be doing something about that. That's good, that's healthy. Only in America are people rising up to try to say something about it. They wouldn't do that here in France. . . ." So I decided to go back and do something about that thing that was bugging me, which is the war.

This same individual discussed his father's values as follows:

> My old man is very straight with the kids. That's been very important, because it has kept in the back of my mind all the time concepts like responsibilities, seriousness, "If you're going to work on this, you can't just do it on weekends." I have this whole complex of ideas about carrying through with what you start, being serious about it, being confident about it. I really never could have come close to just flipping out and becoming totally alienated. . . .

For others, the essential continuity was with religious values they had learned at home and in church. One young man, for example, described his first participation in a demonstration as follows:

> One time when I was buying books, I think, up on Central Street, a group of eight or nine people were picketing the local five-and-ten. I joined them for twenty or twenty-five minutes. I always felt that it was important to witness your beliefs in terms of the church. It was never a big deal for me to become involved. It wasn't a major conversion. It seemed to be relatively natural, something that I had never thought about. It was just there.
>
> [K. K.: When you say "witness your beliefs," what were those beliefs?] All people should be equal. And everybody was talking about how Southerners were uncivilized. I mean it wasn't a big deal. . . . Then later there was an announcement on the bulletin board to come to an organizing group called the Student Integrated Housing Committee. So I said, "Well, that should be interesting to go to." And then I said, "But if you really believe in something, you have to spend some time doing it. You've got to stand up for your beliefs."
>
> So I went to the meeting and because I had some experience, and was considered a strong personality on campus at that time, I wound up being a co-chairman of this group of eight. We set out on a campaign to find out whether or not the university discriminated. . . . And we found out that the university did indeed do that. Then we organized a big campaign at the school with three hundred, four hundred, or five hundred kids . . . to get the university to remove housing that discriminated from its list. That was the first organizational thing that I got involved in, really.

One young woman discussed first the influence of her religious upbringing upon her current beliefs, and went on to describe her father's reaction to the Supreme Court decision in 1954 as follows:

> My father, I remember, in 1954 when the Supreme Court decision was made, he was defending the position of the Supreme Court . . . the only thing I remember his saying is that Negroes should be allowed to go to school with whites. The argument came back to him about intermarriage. He said, "If you can educate a Negro, he won't necessarily want to marry a white person." That's what I remember. . . . I have a very deep admiration for my father, by the way. I feel very close to him. . . . [About her

> parents:] Their values are good, decent values. They worked hard all their lives; they never had very much, until now they live a fairly middle-class, solid existence.

Later, she turned to her parents' attitude toward her political involvement:

> Well, they knew I was doing something, and they didn't feel too good about it. But they didn't know how much I was getting involved. So I wrote them a letter, and they were very good. I wrote them a long letter, saying, "Look, these are the things I believe, and probably that's because I have an education, probably it's because of the people I've been with in the last year. I don't expect you to understand this, but I do expect you to keep on loving me." After that there were never any real doubts. That laid it on the table. We never talked much about it face to face except on one occasion. . . . At odd times, I can sense that my mother is maybe kind of proud that I'm doing these things. Although for the life of her, she can't understand why her daughter works for four years to get through college (I had to go on scholarships; they didn't have much money), why I want to work for twenty dollars a week. She still doesn't understand it.

Even in these last two instances, where parental approval is something less than complete, there are important ties between the individual, his family, and the values he learned as a child. And these ties are often illustrated, as above, by the fact (or fantasy) of parental admiration for the radical's activities.

In understanding the continuity of values between these radicals and their backgrounds, it should be recalled that the basic values of the New Left are neither new nor startling. However revolutionary the objectives, however radical the tactics proposed to attain them, the basic values of the young radical are ancient and familiar: the only startling fact is that he takes these values seriously and proposes that American society and the world set about implementing them. Thus, for young men and women like these, who were brought up to believe that prejudice, hatred, and discrimination are wrong, that suffering should be alleviated, that all men should have equal opportunities and an equal say in the decisions affecting their lives, that peace and justice should be sought after, that violence should be minimized, and that men should seek to relate to each other in a human, open, direct, and personal way, the values of the New Left are not at all alien. Also, at the level of even more basic personal values, these young men and women had been brought up to cherish honesty, responsibility, seriousness, and thoughtfulness. Their work in the New Left, far from requiring them to repudiate these values, offered an arena in which they could act on them.

A closely related area of continuity is the basic orientation to principle of these young activists. Despite their many doubts concerning their effectiveness in radical activities, none ever questioned the fundamental rightness of the principles upon which he was acting or the need to act upon them. For example, one individual discussed his doubts as follows:

> It always involves trying to get people to do things that you think it would be good for them to do, and yet they don't think so yet. And I don't have, way down deep inside, I don't have a whole lot of confidence that I can do that. There is a certain amount of tension when I do political work. [K. K.: You mean confidence that you can persuade them, or confidence that you are really right?] Oh no, I always have a lot of confidence that I'm right, but not a whole lot that I can persuade them.

Another interviewee spoke in similar terms of her work:

> There was a period when we thought, "Maybe we're all wrong. Maybe because we put so much personally into it, we can't expect anybody else to pick up on it." We wondered, "What kind of a base is there for this?" [K. K.: Did you ever wonder whether the assumptions on which you became involved were wrong?] No, we never questioned that idea. That's one of the things—you asked me before what kept us going—it never occurred to us to question the basic idea. That point was obvious to us from the beginning. It's obvious to us now. We never questioned that. . . .

Another important continuity is around the issue of specialness. I have discussed the sense of these radicals as children that they were somehow different, special, or apart from the majority of their contemporaries, and often from much of the surrounding community. This issue continues during early adolescence in the form of fears of being especially sinful, especially lonely, and especially wrong. As the individual moves toward becoming a radical, this same theme remains important, but it is now transvalued into a positive sense of special rightness, of special belonging, and of participation in a special movement that constitutes a small minority of all Americans. Yet here, as in other areas, change is also present, for while the sense of specialness remains, feelings of loneliness, isolation, and sinfulness are largely dissipated by participation in a movement of other principled people.

Other continuities will be apparent as we consider the process of radicalization and the "post-radical" careers of these young men and women. To anticipate only a few of these, the pleasure-denying asceticism of early adolescence has almost completely disappeared, but some of the same underlying impulse is still expressed indirectly in their capacity for dedication, organization, hard work, and the acceptance of responsibility. Another enduring theme is the continuing identification of almost all young radicals with the side of their fathers that is idealistic, effective, and actively principled. Still another theme is the continuing ambivalence of most young radicals toward the "merely academic," an ambivalence that has its precursors in maternal pressures for visible academic achievement, as in their perception of their fathers as being highly principled *but* inactive. Finally, and perhaps most crucial to the understanding of these young radicals and their work, their lives show a continuing concern with the issue of aggression, hostility, and violence, a concern that often begins in their earliest memories and continues throughout life until it is finally interwoven with their work to promote peace.

In emphasizing here the personal, familial, and psychological continuities in radical development, I do not mean to neglect the equally important sense of historical continuity, of involvement with an honorable radical tradition, that has been evolved by most of these young men and women. Despite their many doubts about the particular ideologies and tactics of older forms of radicalism, many of these young radicals have identified themselves, from a very early age, with some tradition of radical protest against injustice. I have already quoted the young man who refers to his basically "theological rhetoric," and who likens himself to the seventeenth-century New England preachers. Others found in their own families individuals or values that they identified with radical protest long before they came to think of themselves as radicals. The earliest fantasies of another involved a pact with the poor whereby he would use his own abilities and social position to improve their condition. And still another recalls in early childhood attending with an admired relative a meeting of the editorial board of an Old Left journal.

Many young men and women have had such fantasies and such identifications in their childhood, but what distinguishes these particular individuals is that in late adolescence and adulthood they began to pattern their emerging identities on such fantasies and identifications. Yet one feels, at least in retrospect, that when these young men and women made a pact with the poor in early childhood, they in some way "meant it" more than most children do, and that their continual allusions to early "radical" experiences and ideas are more than the retroactive search for continuity, although they obviously are that, too. In any case, as young adults, these men and women had found or created roots for their own radicalism that transcended the merely familial, and that linked them to a historical tradition wherein the well-born, the privileged, and the advantaged seek to correct the injustices and corruptions of society.

In stressing the many underlying continuities in the development of these young radicals, I do not wish to minimize the many areas of discontinuity and change. My earlier discussion of psychological issues in the early lives of these young radicals gives some intimation of the important changes in their lives, for example, the rejection of that aspect of the father and of the family tradition seen as ineffectual, inadequate, or "merely intellectual"; the repudiation of academic performance as a criterion of personal achievement and work; the abandonment of asceticism and defensive intellectualization; the rejection of the Establishment options that each radical was clearly expected to seize. But the most important change, upon which this study was focused, was the change from not being a radical to thinking of oneself as one. It is this change that will concern us for the rest of this chapter.

The "naturalness" of commitment

In considering the process of radicalization, "joining" must be distinguished from becoming committed to the Movement, just as becoming committed must be distinguished from staying committed. The kind of commitment we find in these young men and women almost invariably evolved *after* they first "joined" some radical organization; in some cases, there was a lag of years between joining and feeling oneself to be a radical. Most of those interviewed had belonged to (and sometimes led) reformist, liberal, or even radical groups in secondary school and the early college years. But few considered themselves "radicals" in any self-conscious sense at this point.

I have already discussed the gradual but growing sense of nearing the end of the line that plagued most of these young radicals in the years before they became involved with the New Left. Out of this sense of stagnation, gradually, slowly, and unreflectedly, they "found themselves" more and more involved with radical activities. Many commented that at the time they were not aware of the direction they were taking, and that if they had been aware, they might not have taken it. For example, one young woman, in recalling a summer job that led directly to her increasing engagement with the Movement, said:

Now that I look back on that job, if I had known what I was accepting, I probably would not have done it, because of the insecurities and what seemed to be so many threatening things and so many insecure things. [K. K.: Was it a rough time, then?] No, it was great. I was totally absorbed in the work. [K. K.: You mean that now, you would do it again, but at the time, if you had known, you wouldn't have done it?] Yes, that's what I'm saying. I think that one of the valuable things was that I was open. I was looking. . . . At that point I wasn't certain in my own values. It's nice to come home and not live in the slums. But how much money do you really need to be happy? How many closets full of clothes do you need? When you make a decision like this, you're not at all certain of what it is you're choosing.

For some, Vietnam Summer itself was an important part of the radicalizing process. One young man, at the beginning of the summer, explained that he was different from many others in the office and did not consider himself a "radical." After the summer, he wrote as follows:

Little did I realize the "natural" steps that already had been taken. In the fall [of 1967], when I attended the Graduate Students' Conference, I could not keep myself from organizing people around the Vietnam issue. I ended up helping draft a statement calling for withdrawal, radical reorientation in U.S. foreign policy, and support for draft resistance. Surprisingly, two-thirds of those present signed; I then went to New York and got press releases to papers and magazines. If someone had suggested a year ago that I would be doing this, I should have laughed at them. . . . What I'm trying to say is that although I didn't realize it at the time, working for Vietnam Summer was the biggest and perhaps the most crucial natural step for me—a step whose importance I realized fully only after the summer was over.

And one young woman, asked about the "decisions" that led to her involvement in the New Left, replied:

I'm probably not the best person for you to interview. [Laughs] I have a very funny way of making decisions. In a way it seems very casual. But I operate on the assumption that you do what you have to do. And it was fun, it was good. Even though it was agonizing. . . . I remember once, I sat on a sea wall in Ocean City, and I sat and talked to Rick Cowell about what we were going to do. It was there, the job was there to be done. I could do it, and there was no one else at the time.

That was another thing that all of us felt. All of us, from the very beginning, you know, thought that we were not the people to do this. There were other, brighter, more intellectual, more political people, who could have done it and could have done a much better job at it. We resented that fact in a way, that we didn't feel adequate for it and yet we were doing it. And we probably felt that other people knew that we weren't adequate for it. That was a hard kind of thing for us. But it was there. I can't discuss it, really, at all.

Again and again, young radicals used similar phrases to characterize what to an outside observer would seem a decision or a choice. Psychologically, the perceived importance and rightness of Movement work removed the need for conscious choice. Such a sense of acting "naturally" bespeaks a powerful fusion of conscious and unconscious motives in the service of the developing identity of the radical. Specifically, it suggests that for these highly principled young men and women, a new harmony was being established between will and conscience, between ego and superego, between self and principle.

Reunions with old friends who no longer understood or sympathized with them were among the factors that made these young radicals aware of the changes they were undergoing. One interviewee, who had tried very hard to preserve her ties to her old friends, commented that, nevertheless, "Once I jumped into the circle it was a complete jump." And another young radical spoke similarly of meetings with former friends:

I always felt very acutely the fact that I was leaving people behind [when I got involved in the Movement], and that was not an easy thing for me to do. Like when I was really becoming involved in civil rights, I knew that there were some friends that I had been close to who did not understand. I never liked that to happen. I never wanted to be different—that was the thing. I had worked so hard *not* to be different, especially in high school and college, that it was not an easy thing to be different again on my own.

For others, who came from militantly liberal or radical family backgrounds, the awareness of becoming a radical was essentially a realization of reconnection with one's roots:

> You know, with all my background . . . I never really felt a part of it on my own until last year. . . . Then, for the first time, I really began to feel a part of the Movement. . . . I began to be able to trace my own roots in terms of being able to feel actually *of* it, not only in it. . . . I saw that the type of work that was being done, the types of people that were being involved, and the goals that were being put forward—I began to feel that I was *of* these, that in terms of my background, that this was the thing *from which I had sprung*. That was a really good feeling. I began to feel, for the first time, that there was a kind of continuity in my whole political development. . . . The continuity was always there, but me being able to appreciate it, being able to use it, in terms of being aware of it and what it meant politically, and being able to call on certain things from my own background—that came later. I began to be able to apply things that I already knew, had experienced with parents, uncles, and relatives. I began to be able to think about them and juggle them in my mind and apply them to a situation.

In only one individual was there a single event that dramatically summarized his entry into the Movement:

> I'm one of those people who was in a way trying to get into the System, but really couldn't make it for a whole series of reasons. . . . I had this idea that change was going to come about by the natural course of things. I mean, for example, there was going to be a Civil Rights Movement and it was going to get stronger. And I believed that it was important for people like myself, who were well educated and well connected, to get into positions of power so they could help facilitate things. . . . But all of this presupposed that our society in general and the government in particular would be open to things like this.

> Well, my hypothesis was really destroyed. It all hinged on whether or not the United States was going to get out of Vietnam. I was really convinced that Johnson would. The bombings of February, 1965, were a real shake-up for me. I went to bed for two days. It seemed to me to utterly close that door. . . . I had been working for the government before then, and I had taken two weeks off from my government job. . . . I realized that the only thing to do . . . in effect was to burn some bridges behind me. I was willing to do that, but there was a lot of reluctance. I mean it was a gradual process before I decided that I would become a full-time worker. . . . It took me four months before I realized that I would never pursue my academic studies.

Yet for this young man, even more than for many of his fellows, the actual "decision" to enter the Movement was built upon an identification with radicalism that dated from his earliest years, and that had been repeatedly recognized both by himself and by his intimates.

Although the actual process of entry into the Movement, and the concurrent development of a sense of oneself as a radical, was unself-conscious and "natural," it is possible to disentangle a series of more or less typical experiences and reactions that will help us understand what was experienced at the time as a natural process of development. Such an analytic separation of the components of radicalization, of course, does violence to the experience itself, inasmuch as it dissects an experience in which each of these components was inextricably related to all of the others. Nevertheless, in most of these interviewed, a process is visible that involves a confrontation with heretofore unexperienced aspects of American life, a growing disenchantment with existing institutions for social change, the development of a new interpretation of American life, a feeling of personal responsibility for social and political change, a complex process of self-modeling, and an engagement with the Movement.

How these factors are experientially interwoven can be seen in the following account by one young radical of an experience at an activist summer camp:

In the summer of 1964, I went out to the Camp for Social Responsibility. . . . And it really turned me on. I had always been very socially conscious, but after that I became a real activist. Before, I had done specific things. I had participated in picketing, and gone on a peace march. . . . The other thing was that I was getting older, I was seeing things more clearly. [K. K.: Like what?] Myself, my values. And I liked a lot of the people I was meeting. I thought I was understanding myself a lot more than I ever had before. Like in grade school, I guess I had always been fairly alienated in part, because my values were not shared, nor my family's values. So when I got into high school, I started making new friends from other parts of town. I started understanding myself much more. And I understood that I felt very responsible for things. Like in Birmingham, I just felt that I had to go down there and do something. People were getting killed, and there were the dogs, and I had to do something. I didn't know what I could do, but I felt responsible. . . . Part of it was that I felt more and more personally involved. Like before, when I heard about segregation in the South, it was esthetically repellent, but I didn't feel a part of it.

[K. K.: Let's take that feeling of being a part of it. How did that evolve?] I don't know. It seemed like I already had done the reading. I was a bright young kid who had done all the reading and knew about what was going on, but I had an intellectual remoteness and a feeling of objectivity. Somehow—I guess maybe it was the Camp or around that time—at the Camp there were all these kids right there from the South that had been in the Movement, SNCC kids, kids that had got shot at, kids that were really working. And older people who had been through the McCarthy period and had lost their jobs. It began to be brought home to me much more. It began to seem much more real.

The confrontation with inequity

Although the fundamental values of these young radicals had not changed since their earlier years, their perception and interpretation of American social and political life had changed profoundly. Even before their entry into the Movement, most had been inarticulately dissatisfied with the options open to them, but they had lacked the vocabulary and, indeed, the perceptions necessary to formulate their dissatisfactions. Perhaps even more than most young Americans of their talent and social advantage, they had been initially inclined to interpret their dissatisfactions in psychological terms, blaming themselves rather than the surrounding society for their "hang-ups." In understanding the sense of disillusion and outrage with which they reacted to the concrete recognition of inequity in American life, their relative affluence, privilege, and fortunate backgrounds are crucial, for in their own lives they had had little immediate experience with poverty, deprivation, discrimination, or oppression. Even more than most young middle-class Americans, these young men and women, while they had "done the reading," were not psychologically prepared for a personal and concrete confrontation with injustice, social repression, and discrimination.

The shock of confrontation—For such young men and women, privileged and idealistic, the confrontation with social inequity—the first personal meeting with poverty, injustice, political manipulation, and institutional dishonesty—may have a disproportionate impact. As relatively empathic and compassionate young men and women, when concretely confronted with the toll of American society, they quickly lost their "intellectual remoteness and feeling of objectivity," and felt "personally responsible" for doing something to change things. One young woman, for example, contrasted her early peripheral involvement to the shock of confrontation with the poverty that surrounded her graduate school:

> I was only peripherally involved in college: I was going through a whole lot of personal things and I wasn't really that active. The only thing I did was I went on a kind of peace march. . . . [In graduate school] that was really different from college, because it was right in the middle of the slums, and you were immediately faced with the kinds of issues, with the things you were learning . . . I suddenly realized what poverty was, and it wasn't in the books. All of a sudden it became very real. It hit me. . . .

Another young radical comments similarly on the impact of a series of early meetings with civil rights activists:

> This was the first time I had any sense at all of what had been going on in the Negro community, of the extreme deprivation and repression of Negroes in the South. . . . I was very much impressed by the intensity of the people there. They said they were going to open downtown Atlanta, and they meant it.

Similar illustrations could be multiplied almost indefinitely. Whether it was working with the unemployed in the inner city, in voter-registration drives in the South, with Negro families in the slums, or in a detailed study in American policies in Vietnam, these young radicals were forced into an immediate personal confrontation with the injustices of American life and policies.

The failure of the system—The traditional American political vision does not deny the existence of inequity, injustice, and unfairness in our society. But the liberal vision maintains that institutions *already* exist by which such inequities can be relieved; and it proposes that the discontented channel his efforts for social change into these institutions. In most cases, the first impulse of the incipient radical was to do precisely that: to seek amongst existing institutions channels for the remedy of injustice. Yet just as these individuals found the vocational options open to them in conventional American life unsatisfactory, so they were almost uniformly disillusioned in their efforts to work within the System. It might be argued that those who are on the way to becoming radicals may need to create confrontations in which their efforts to work through the Establishment will prove ineffectual. But this explanation, while perhaps partly true, hardly seems adequate to explain all of the incidents they recounted. What is most impressive is not their secret motivation to have the System fail, but their naïve hope that it would succeed, and the extent of their depression and disillusion when their early reformist hopes were frustrated.

In some instances, these early efforts involved working with existing poverty programs, as in the following incident:

In the summer, by a fluke, someone called me up from Washington and said that they had heard about our school, would we start one? I didn't know what OEO was, but I began to talk to people. Then I got that very official letter that said, "Please submit for a proposal immediately." . . . So we wrote a proposal up very quickly, and we got several thousand dollars to run a school. The school was really beautiful. There were only two white people, everyone else was black, and none of them had been to school. We started out with sixty kids and ended up with eighty. We were understaffed, and the money wasn't anywhere nearly enough, we realized afterwards. It was a place where teen-agers came and made toys for the kids, the parents came and planned the program, and it was very well worked out. The curriculum was planned each week for the next week by the parents. And the parents started getting very concerned about what the public schools were doing. . . . They started going into the classroom and they told us what we should do.

The next year we tried to get a new proposal to try to run this school full time, and I think we wrote a very good one. But it was refused. I had gone to a lot of poverty meetings and talked about parent-run schools: that's what it said we should do in the law. But the proposal was jumped on all over the place for having sub-professionals running the schools, because how could they do it when they don't know anything? Also, our buildings were not licensed. It was refused and they said the reason was "too many sub-professionals in decision-making positions," so we couldn't have the money. . . . It really destroyed that organization. If we hadn't spent months preparing our proposal it would have been all right. But the school sort of fell apart. . . . I was discouraged, but I felt closer to the parents, so that was important. I was really upset, and I didn't work for a couple of months. . . .

Another, who had for many years contemplated entering church educational work, faced a similar disillusion:

I began to feel that [all of the church curricula] were irrelevant. . . . They weren't conservative politically, but they were conservative religiously, and that had bad overtones in politics. . . .

Another thing that happened was that there was this minister from Africa, he came from Rhodesia. And he was supported by one of the large town churches that had missionaries there. But he was not admitted into membership in that church. That really shook me up a little bit about the church. Basically, you know, I got all my instincts from my religious background. I really believed what the church had taught me all along; I took it for its face value. And then I was disconcerted to find that it didn't work, or that the church itself did not accept it. But all of my values first came from my religious background.

Finally, disillusion with the American government played a major role in the radicalization of others:

I went to Washington because I wanted to be relevant, I wanted to do things, and I felt that just being a student was not that. I wanted to try to be part of the world. So I went to Washington and I spent six very frustrating months trying to be relevant to a situation where I was intrinsically irrelevant. . . . I read books and made phone calls and got information and wrote chapters. But it was very unsatisfying. First, because in retrospect the stuff I wrote was just terrible. . . . It was couched in this Washington rhetoric that assumed that everybody was interested in the topic and wanted to do the right things. . . . I'd sit there in the office all day long and really think I was saying important things. . . . But then it began to dawn on me that even that wasn't really possible, because nobody really gave a shit. There wasn't going to be any change. And the person I was working for could tolerate only a minimal kind of critical analysis. I had to say more than I felt he wanted to say at that point. . . . I had very basic feelings and angers about the society, and I was in a position where I couldn't do anything about that. It was very, very bad. . . . But I was just determined to try to do this. I didn't let myself think about other things very much. It was only when I finally dropped it that I realized what a heavy burden it had been for me.

All of these anecdotes indicate that the first impulse of most young radicals was to attempt to work within the System; and it was often only after the apparent failure of such efforts, and only with the developing conviction that the System could not be trusted to remedy its injustices, that they turned toward a Movement that stressed the need for *new* institutions.

The radical reinterpretation—Concretely confronted with inequity and disillusioned with the System, the emerging radical tends to move toward a reinterpretation of the social and political world. To some, it initially appeared that American society was not rationally intelligible at all: its prime characteristics seemed to be aimlessness, random movement, and lack of any clear direction. In a paradoxical acceptance-and-critique of the prevalent academic views about consensus and the interplay of pressure groups in American society, some young radicals concluded that the policies and direction of the United States were largely determined by a kind of random crashing together of pressure groups, lobbies, and powerful corporations, individuals, and influences, so that the future was no more predictable than an individual molecule in a gas chamber.

But this minimal analysis did not last long, and most of those interviewed had come to accept some variant of a "radical" interpretation of American life and politics. Although these young radicals rarely discussed their formal interpretations of American society at any length in our interviews, they tended to agree that American society is dominated by a loose combine of industrial, corporate, and military interests, a "power elite" that is economically and militarily imperialistic and more concerned with maintaining its own power and containing the "Communist menace" than with implementing the creedal values of our society. This interpretation has the double advantage of explaining the imperviousness and unwieldiness of the System, while at the same time indicating the groups that the Movement must vigorously oppose.

A corollary of the radical reinterpretation of society is a progressive sense of *estrangement from the mainstream.* Although these radicals' fidelity to most of the creedal values of American society remained firm, their sense of connection to the institutions and practices of our society became attenuated. As the young radical begins to reinterpret American society, he also redefines his own relationship to it. Radical work intensifies his awareness of oppression by throwing him into daily contact with those for whom the American dream is an illusion. As he identifies with the oppressed, and as his initial efforts to work within the System seem futile, he loses his early hope that his reformist efforts will "make a difference." Having reinterpreted the System, he can no longer define himself as a part of it.

Yet the extent of change should not be exaggerated: these young men and women had always considered themselves in some sense different, and despite their relative success within the System, they had never accepted it unquestioningly. The redefinition of relationship to the System, then, was in part an extension of a position they had held long before becoming radicals. Estrangement from the mainstream was further qualified because, despite their growing feeling of disillusion and disconnection, these young radicals did not feel compelled to break all ties with American life. Unlike a few other radicals whose estrangement has led them to leave the country, these remained, and have continued to be involved with colleges, graduate schools, political organizations, and even (in earlier years) government agencies that they considered useful in their personal and political development.

The radical reinterpretation of American society, while it requires that the radical redefine his relationship to society and disconnect himself from the liberal vision of social change, led to an only partial estrangement. On the one hand, these radicals no longer believed they could count upon existing institutions to effect the changes they sought. But on the other hand, the radical commitment is a commitment *to* a vague vision of a more just, more participatory, and less violent America.

Outrage, deprivation, and guilt—In some accounts of the motivation of left-wing radicals, guilt over social privilege, affluence, and prestige is said to play a major role. It is therefore noteworthy that, despite their middle-class backgrounds, these young men and women felt indignation, disillusion, and anger far more intensely than guilt. Only one spontaneously mentioned guilt, and then it was in a stereotyped aside: "I suppose I must have felt guilty because my own life had been so good." The others stressed their shock upon realizing concretely that their own good fortune was not shared, their disillusion when the social myths they had believed began to seem false, and their indignation when they "really" understood that the benefits they had experienced had not been extended to others.

In explaining the preponderance of shock, disillusion, and indignation over guilt, we must recall that all of these young men and women grew up in an affluent, post–World War II world. Although their unusual talents and family backgrounds had often given them special opportunities and privileges, their social situation was not fundamentally different from that of the majority of their fellows. They grew up in a society where the poor and the disadvantaged were a minority, and they usually lived in areas and went to schools where the concrete facts of poverty and injustice were screened away from them. Thus, as they had experienced it, theirs had not been a "privileged" position at all; and the "discovery" of inequity and the unwieldiness of existing institutions for social reform could hardly have made them feel guilty because of advantages and social position that did not seem in any way unusual to them. Put differently, these young men and women took affluence and opportunity for granted, so it rarely occurred to them to feel guilty about something that had always been a fact of their lives.

The fact that these radicals do not come from impoverished, deprived, and disadvantaged backgrounds is not surprising, for it is a cliché that revolutionaries are rarely found in the most oppressed strata of any society. But it is often argued that expectations that rise more rapidly than the opportunities for their fulfillment provide a powerful motive force behind radical and revolutionary activities; that is, that the radical is in a state of "relative deprivation." Whatever the applicability of this thesis to other groups and to other nations, it does not seem to apply to the young radicals I interviewed. For them, economic security was a matter of course. Nor was this in any way a politically oppressed group. While many had been arrested *after* their radicalization for some form of civil disobedience, none had experienced more than minor inconvenience because of his political beliefs before becoming a radical. And later, when they were arrested, it was because they chose to be arrested in order to demonstrate their convictions. In these young radicals, then, identification with *others* who are oppressed is a far more important motivating force than any sense of personal deprivation. If these radicals can be said to have been "deprived" relative to their own aspirations, it is only insofar as these aspirations include high principles involving the extension to others of the benefits they had experienced. But to define "relative deprivation" as having high social and political principles is to deprive the term of meaning; and it can safely be said that this hypothesis about revolutionary discontent does not apply to these particular young men and women.

Activation and engagement

The process of confrontation, disillusion, and reinterpretation that I have so far emphasized is obviously not sufficient to "make" a radical. Many Americans share "radical" perceptions, disillusions, and interpretations of our society, but are embittered, soured, alienated, or apathetic: they are "curdled idealists," but not active radicals. Such individuals can at most be considered latent radicals, for they lack a commitment to action and a sense of engagement with others who seek to change society.

A further process of activation and engagement is therefore essential in the making of a radical. Not only must the individual perceive social reality in a certain light, but he must come to feel personally responsible for effecting change, he must acquire models of commitment and action, and he must somehow deal with the issue of his effectiveness as a radical political actor. No doubt the great majority of latent radicals are prevented from radicalism because they lack these further qualities: they feel no personal responsibility for remedying the injustices they perceive, they possess no models for action, or they have little hope that their efforts will be effective, resigning themselves with "What is the use?"

The extension of responsibility—I have already discussed at some length the issue of personal responsibility in these young radicals. Their accounts of their parents in their early experiences point to a family emphasis on responsibility and "stick-to-itiveness," and to the early acquisition of these qualities in childhood. In each instance, the origins of a sense of personal responsibility are complex and different. But the development of the following young man is not unusual. His family was highly involved politically. He learned from an early age to expect that adults like his parents and most of their friends would be actively engaged in the local community. But equally important, great responsibility for the care of a difficult sibling fell upon this young man during his early adolescence:

> [My sister] always felt she could call on me, and in many situations that has been the case. Even when my father can't talk to her, I've been able to. What I'm trying to say is that in terms of people and situations, I was forced into developing a kind of a sense of responsibility a hell of a lot earlier. I mean . . . when she ran away from home, I was the one who went to get her. . . .

His reaction to this responsibility was ambivalent. On the one hand, he was sometimes pleased and flattered, but on the other hand:

> I reacted very violently. . . . I just got furious. . . . [My parents and I] had these tremendous shouting matches, just *pure* shouting matches, as just where responsibility lay. . . . I was feeling very rejected and very unattended to. But my parents understood that, they knew it very well. . . .

It was later, in his early adulthood, that this same young man felt responsible enough for what was happening to Negro Americans to become intensely involved with civil rights work. And when I asked him how he had been able to persist so long in community organizing work, he said:

> One of the reasons is because I have this thing, this personal thing, about trying to finish things. I have a hang-up, you might say, ever since high school. . . . I felt it was necessary for people who believe that certain kinds of organizing had to be done—for those

people to stay on and to try to help that along. I don't know, it may just be a kind of stick-to-itiveness. Maybe that's a family trait. I just did.

The sense of responsibility has an equally complex history in most of those interviewed. For some, one source lay in the parental expectation that they would be precociously responsible even as children. For others, the tendency to take responsibility was seen in early political activities, especially in high school, when many were leaders of activist groups. From an early age, most of these young men and women had grown accustomed to accepting responsibility. So when they were concretely confronted with injustices in American society, it was not a major step to feel "naturally" responsible for taking action. Without such a readiness, the most likely reaction to inequity that affects others is a defensive withdrawal into one's own private life.

The finding of models—Even given a pre-existing sense of responsibility and a series of catalysts that extend this feeling of responsibility to the social scene, the incipient radical must learn how to act. And in this process, the availability of individuals who could serve as models of radical commitment, tactics, and ideology was crucial. To be of genuine assistance in the process of activation, such individuals had to be physically available to the incipient radical: for no matter how important his identification with distant or historical figures, the latter rarely can substitute for real people whom he actually knows. In the early stages of radicalization, such real people serve to concretize the meaning of radicalism, to relieve the sense of aloneness, to focus vague discontent into a new interpretation of American society, to provide specific ideas, tactics, and models of effective action, and to enable the fledgling to begin to identify himself as a part of the Movement. When such models are not available in the immediate environment of the individual, the potential radical, no matter how personally responsible he may feel, is likely to become a lonely and frustrated eccentric operating in quixotic solitude.

In the early radical experience of those I interviewed, slightly older and more experienced New Left figures had great importance. In some instances, these older radical leaders (generally those now considered part of the old New Left) had already been physically "available" to the novice for some time; but he only seized upon them as exemplars when his sense of personal stagnation and aimlessness increased, and he began semiconsciously to search for alternatives to the Establishment options. For example, one girl who was becoming disillusioned with graduate school met a group of young men and women working in a local community action project:

> I began to meet new people, and there was a graduate chapter of SDS that got started. I really liked these people. [K. K.: What was it about them?] I can tell you the names and then describe it. The first person I met was Steve Green. . . . He's about the most turned-on person that I've ever met. He's really excited about everything. I was going through such a slump, feeling, "This is crappy; I don't want to be in graduate school, and I'm not learning anything." . . . It was this group that provided the kind of thing that I had really wanted to get out of graduate school. . . . The thing about those people was they really wanted to learn, and learn in a way that I felt was very relevant. Because I could go out from school and see that they were talking about real things . . . so that group was a really important group for me. . . . I spent less and less time thinking about school. The courses were so bad, I would just take my exams and somehow pass them.

The qualities of these Movement models that most impressed the interviewees seem to have been three: commitment, human warmth, and intellectual relevance. Their relative importance varied with each individual, according to what he personally seems to have been looking for. One interviewee, for example, describes himself before his involvement in the New Left as "forcing myself to be on my own, forcing myself to be hostile and mistrusting of all people." He reacted positively to the warmth of the members of the first New Left group he belonged to:

> I was very impressed with them. Really, the isolated life is not very pleasant. At least it wasn't for me. . . . There happened to be,

luckily, some very fine individuals who were completely the opposite from the way I was. They assumed everybody was good until proven otherwise. I was impressed by that. You know, they were nice to me, and I would never have been nice to them. I was accepted, I was new, I was an outsider. I liked that, working together. Here was a group I could throw my chips in with and say, "Ha-ha, I will identify with this group. I will allow my name to be associated with this group and with other people. So that a condemnation of one is leveled at all. One is attacked, the other comes to his defense. . . ." I said, "Okay, these guys are all right. I'll throw my chips in and work with them."

This same young man was also impressed with the intellectual relevance of this group:

There was a lot of intellectual stuff going on too . . . we had some good internal education. . . . I was impressed by the kids who were involved. They were smart, they knew their cookies. I was impressed by the fact that the kind of learning—the way they were approaching intellectual problems—was vital to them, because these were real problems. They were not hypothetical or theoretical quandaries to be solved; they were not things you get aesthetic pleasure from working out. You got immediate pleasure because it was a vital thing, a pressing need. It spoke to their lifework. It was associated with what they were doing. You know, there were a lot of things in academia that turned me off. I thought the best part of the university life was the student's life. I wouldn't, at this stage of the game, want to be purely a professor and spend my time in the library piling up file cards for my next book. There has to be some vitality to it or I just wouldn't do it. I just don't work well unless I'm motivated, because I go off to the other courses and get C's.

For others, the qualities of kindness, warmth, and even saintliness of some of the Movement figures they met early in their careers were crucial. One young woman, for example, spoke at length of her admiration for a well-known civil rights leader:

I became fairly close to Bill Washington that year, and really had an awful lot of respect for him, and liked him a lot. There was a big demonstration downtown one day, and eight of us were sitting in a church after it was over. There had been a lot of intimidation by young white thugs from the lower-income part of town: they had

> been hitting the demonstrators, hitting the girls, getting them caught in doors and pushing them, and the police weren't doing very much about it. We were sitting in the church afterwards, and about six of these young white guys walked into the back of the church. I couldn't believe they had enough gall to do that, and I said, "I don't believe those hoodlums have the audacity to do that." And Bill looked at me and with all seriousness he said, "Don't you dare call those people hoodlums. They're human beings like us and it's not their fault that they're that way." That really got next to me. There was blood all over the floor of the church, and he had been beaten time and time again. I just couldn't believe that anyone could be that good, could say that sort of thing after what happened that day. It made a very deep impression on me.

But whatever the particular characteristics most underlined in these early Movement models, the interviewees' encounter with them was fateful because it came at the right time. One young woman, for example, described her state of mind on graduating from college:

> I didn't like working in an office. I've worked in offices before, and I wanted to be with academic or intellectual people, but in a non-academic atmosphere. This was a very vague kind of thing. I didn't really know what options were open to me. . . . I knew that having a house or car wasn't important. But I didn't know whether there was any other place, any other focus point. It was a very conscious effort to try to grab a hold of new roots, to try to look for them. . . .

She was offered several jobs, one of which involved a summer peace training institute. She described her first reaction as follows:

> I looked into this summer program, and they really wanted me. . . . My concern for peace was a very, very honest thing. But I wasn't really a pacifist. I didn't even know what pacifism really was. . . . Anyway, as soon as I met the person who was in charge of the program, I was very, very impressed with him. He was really a marvelous guy—not intellectual, but very nice. . . . And as soon as I went to the Training Institute, the people I met who were participants in the workshop—some of them were very intelligent, very political people. That whole week was something like I was living twenty-four hours a day. Before, I had been the only one on

campus. But these weren't kooky people, these were solid American people. . . .

The whole summer was very much an authenticizing process. It was in the first day, in fact, that I decided I wanted to take part in the program. I had talked to enough people to find out what was involved. Then I decided that *that* was what I was going to do. [K. K.: It sounds like you found kindred spirits.] It wasn't that I found kindred spirits, it was really that even though I didn't have these values, these were the kinds I wanted to acquire.

In connecting the effect of the summer institute with her search for "new roots," and in denying that she found "kindred spirits," this young woman makes explicit feelings common to many other young radicals. The young activist tends to seek out and accept Movement models only when he is unconsciously or consciously looking for a "focus point" or commitment. And he does not find his models among those who share his feelings of aimlessness, stagnation, and frustration. Rather, he is drawn to those who seem to possess conviction, commitment, human kindness, and intellectual relevance—qualities whose absence in himself increasingly troubles him.

Like all of the developments I have described in this chapter, the finding of models of radicalism amongst one's contemporaries and those slightly older was neither self-conscious nor deliberate. Yet in retrospect, the process seems psychologically meaningful. For those whom these incipient young radicals took as models had a special *charisma of commitment* that spoke directly to their own search for a way out of personal stagnation and vaguely articulated guilt over the seeming meaninglessness of their futures. The models possessed the qualities these young men and women felt to be most lacking in themselves: passionate moral conviction and dedication to principle, personal kindness, openness and warmth, and intellectual strength combined with relevance. By identifying with such committed radicals, the novice does not identify with those who are like him, but with those whom he seeks to be like. Yet at the same time, his capacity to do so expresses a side of him that has not yet found expression.

The process of modeling one's self upon others was usually

transient. Upon acquiring independent stature in the Movement, after learning skills, developing positions, and gaining a reputation of their own, the young men and women I interviewed often reconfronted their earlier models as peers and contemporaries—sometimes as friends and sometimes as adversaries. This process also contributed to their awareness of their own radicalization: to realize that they knew more than their former heroes, to know that they were more effective than those who had once served as exemplars, was both saddening and deeply gratifying. To most, it signified that they were no longer merely in the Movement, but *of* it.

The role of models in the development of almost all of these young radicals serves to underline the obvious importance of social and historical events in the process of radicalization. None of those I interviewed can be counted among the "founders" of the New Left. Although they have contributed to its development, the opposite is equally true: their radicalization was assisted by the fact that a Movement was already there, in contrast to the situation a decade ago. In the 1950's, when committed radicals were few in number and largely invisible, they were obviously far less available to activate the latent radical. But once the Movement began, and especially as it grew and was publicized, there were more and more potential models to assist the incipient radical in his own development. In order to become a radical, one must generally be able to find, within one's own personal experience, exemplars of the radical commitment.

The issue of effectiveness—Finally, the process of activation requires some resolution of the issue of effectiveness. Most of those I have called latent radicals—those who share the radical perception of American society—are never activated because they assume that effective action is (1) essential but (2) impossible. Given these assumptions, even the latent radical with a strong sense of personal responsibility, who has before him admirable models of radical commitment, is likely to conclude (with most of his fellow Americans) that any efforts on his part to change his society are doomed to failure, and that political action is therefore a waste of time. In a complex, rapidly changing, and confusingly governed society like our own, this feeling of personal and collective powerlessness is widespread, and prevents political action.

But if either of these two assumptions is undermined, political action becomes possible. If the individual concludes that political action can be effective, either now or in the distant future, *or* if he decides that success is not really important, then the likelihood of making an active commitment to radical work increases. When the potential radical convinces himself that success is possible or inevitable, or if he resolves that winning does not matter, he is armored against the continual frustration and discouragement that inevitably beset anyone who attempts to effect massive and revolutionary changes in his society and the world.

In response to this dilemma, many radical movements in the past have been premised upon the conviction that the success of radicalism is historically guaranteed, as, for example, among doctrinaire Communists and among many traditional Socialists. In the New Left, however, there is little belief in an inexorable historical dialectic that will guarantee the success of revolutionary efforts. To be sure, many new radicals derive support from the recent history of the non-industrialized world, and identify themselves strongly with the liberation movements and revolutionary struggles of the oppressed abroad. Yet this identification itself is not enough to yield a sense of inevitable success in America, given their awareness of the many differences between the formerly colonial nations and modern America.

With no conviction in the historical inevitability of success, then, today's New Leftists tend to alternate between hopes of effectiveness in the very long range, and the sometimes stated view that the essential rightness of the task makes the issue of ultimate success irrelevant. In the next chapter I will discuss the despair and weariness that inevitably beset the radical. Here, I will merely note that most of those who worked in the Vietnam Summer National Office had long ago lost any illusions about the possibility of early success for the New Left. On a day-to-day level, they were instead sustained by the satisfactions they derived from their work, from their associations with their friends in it, and from the deep, if usually unstated, conviction that what they were doing was politically and ethically important.

A more long-range response to the problem of the effectiveness of the Movement was a continual effort to increase their own effectiveness as people. The interviews already quoted give some indication of the deliberateness with which many of these young radicals were attempting to shape themselves into more effective Movement workers. Those who felt they lacked a sufficient intellectual basis generally planned to devote themselves to study; others planned to return or turn to community organizing in order to retain contact with the grass roots; and most judged their own continuing psychological development in the context of their effectiveness in the Movement. In all these deliberate efforts at self-change, the explicit issue of personal effectiveness was intertwined with the implicit issue of the long-range success of the Movement.

In fact, however, the question of long-run "success" was seldom discussed, either in interviews or in group meetings. When I raised this question in interviews, many of these young men and women dismissed it with a formula, turned to other topics, or discussed the short-range effectiveness of particular projects. Clearly, success *did* matter to them, and some gave hopeful examples of projects and movements—among them Vietnam Summer itself—that they considered effective. But many also voiced great gloom about the future of America, about the possibility of outbreaks of further domestic or international violence, and about the dim prospects for any mass radical movement. Yet they also seemed to resist the view that success did not matter, perhaps from an unstated awareness that the individual who has abandoned all hope of success and acts merely to express his own inner principles courts both moralistic self-righteousness and political failure.

The discomfort many young radicals feel about the issue of effectiveness may help explain other aspects of the new radicalism.

In the next chapter, I will consider the absence of a program and a clear vision of the future in the New Left. This non-programmatic outlook has many origins, but one reason for the heavy emphasis on immediate tactical questions, limited goals, and short-range effectiveness may be that this emphasis allows the radical to discuss the future without really confronting the issue of long-range success. Similarly, the characteristic vagueness of these New Leftists as to the specifics of their vision of a just, free, peaceful, participatory society may be related not only to their distrust of simple blueprints, but to the fact that contemplation of the distant future arouses feelings of frustration, discouragement, and despair that would undermine their effectiveness in short range. Even within Vietnam Summer, questions about the effectiveness of the summer were generally avoided. This was partly a result of the realistic difficulties in defining success, but partly it was because everyone realized from the start that ending American involvement in Southeast Asia, preventing any future interventions of this kind, allying America with the forces of "liberation" throughout the world, and radically transforming American society domestically was inconceivable as a result of one summer's efforts.

Engagement with the Movement—In discussing the effect upon these young men and women of their confrontation with inequity and the unwieldiness of existing institutions for social reform, I emphasized the radical's sense of estrangement from the main-streams of American society. As his activation as a radical proceeds, his estrangement from the mainstream is countered by his feeling of engagement with the Movement. His earlier feeling of stagnation is replaced by a greater sense of being in motion, his feeling of aimlessness by a new sense of direction, and, perhaps most important, his feeling of lonely isolation by a new solidarity with others moving and searching in the same ways. Little by little, there developed a feeling of being a part of something bigger than oneself, something linked not only to one's individual life but to the broader social and historical scene. By identifying with others, by coming to feel responsible with them for doing something about the perceived inequities of our society, these young men and women came to feel more a part of the world in which they lived.

One interviewee, for example, when talking about a singularly unsuccessful summer project, described her growing sense of participation:

> Everybody who has ever talked about that particular project has talked disparagingly. It was not the time. Definitely not. We should have realized that much earlier. And there were a lot of internal problems in the project. . . . It didn't have any effect at all. The thing that it did do, however, was to politicize Bill, myself, and those who were working on the project. We got to know what was going on in terms of the state-wide movement, and all across the country. . . . I became more aware of what was going on in the United States. . . . I felt more a part of that. I was not only watching it, I was a part of it. . . .

Insofar as the process of radicalization can be identified, isolated, and dissected, it seems characteristically to consist of two related changes. The first is a change in the perceptions of social reality, mediated through personal confrontation with social inequity, and leading through disillusion with existing institutions for social reform to the beginnings of a radical reinterpretation of socio-political reality. Concurrent with this articulation of a radical outlook, a process of personal activation and engagement occurs. The individual's pre-existing feelings of personal responsibility are extended to the oppressed and deprived; he seeks out and finds models of radical action from amongst radicals whose commitment gives them a special charisma; and he develops complex stratagems for dealing with the fear that none of his efforts can possibly be effective. The end product of this process is most commonly a growing awareness of the extent of one's radical commitment; a realization—sometimes slow and sometimes sudden—that one has changed; the common experience of "finding oneself" acting, reacting, thinking, and feeling in ways that at an earlier stage of life would have been inconceivable.

To analyze the process of becoming a radical into aspects, stages, preconditions and end products is, of course, to impose a conceptual framework upon an experience that is itself largely unanalyzed, whole, and in many respects highly idiosyncratic. A general account cannot convey how much radicalization drew upon underlying themes of special personal significance to each individual. In everyone I interviewed, the general issues I have underlined in this chapter were intertwined with factors that could only be understood through a detailed study of that one person. For example, I asked one young radical what it was that had attracted him to the first New Left organization he joined. His answer illustrates the mixture of the personal and the public in this single act:

> Well, I was able to develop a couple of friends. . . . [He talks about them.] Secondarily, I could say it was because of the idea that, in terms of my religious training, when you are committed to something, you have to do it, even if you'd like to do something else, even if you're tired. When you're picketing, you have to keep going. That's what you believe and you have to do it. . . . And they were a really interesting group of people. They were people I could talk with. . . . One of them had a beard which made it a very interesting thing to belong to that group. And a couple of the girls had long hair and sort of looked as if they were beatniks [laughs] . . . and then, it wasn't difficult for me within a month or a month and a half to take some kind of leadership there. Because I talked relatively easily, and I had some kind of experience, I just took charge of things.

In this young man, as in his co-workers in Vietnam Summer, the process of radicalization had been gradual, slow, and continuous. It was something that he experienced as "happening" to him, and it did not end with the realization that he was becoming a radical. For him, as for all of those interviewed, no matter how enduring and deep their commitment to the New Left, radicalization was still occurring, but increasingly now as a personal response to the social and historical facts with which the radical continually confronts himself. To an unusual degree, these young men and women had been historically conscious, socially aware, and politically involved from an early age: their lives and their most personal fantasies and thoughts were interwoven with the history of the post–World War II era. But with their radicalization, their sensitivity to the social, the political, and the historical increased still more, and their later development cannot be discussed except in the context of the tensions of Movement work.

5 The tensions of Movement work

The gradual awareness of becoming a radical was neither the end of a period of psychological change nor the beginning of a period of stability. Just as the consciousness of commitment to the New Left developed slowly, so it merged gradually with a shift of focus from questions of identity to questions of competence and effectiveness as a radical. Awareness of their commitment to the New Left in itself changed little, for by the time that awareness dawned upon these young men and women they were already deeply involved in Movement work.

In the one, two, or more years that had elapsed since the first beginning of a radical commitment, those I interviewed had undertaken a great variety of Movement and non-Movement activities: organizing work in the slums, interrupted and recontinued college careers and graduate studies, peace-education projects, teaching the children of migrant workers, organizing groups of Southern white students who support civil rights, "internal education" work within the New Left. They had experienced disappointments, defeats, and occasionally a rare success.

One young woman, for example, described several years of work in peace organizing:

> The first thing I wondered was why are there so many organizations when we are so small to begin with? I learned the whole

meaning of what it is to appeal to different kinds of constituency groups. . . . I got to know things like how to run a mimeograph, how to set up a teachers' program, how to take people around. We did a lot of work in non-violent workshops, in training people who work with demonstrations, but trying to give them a non-violent base. I was involved with a lot of mechanics, a lot of the recruitment, but I also participated myself. . . .

I came in as an outsider, beginning to question how it was you change or affect American society. . . . At first, I was very critical of what they were doing because I wasn't in that circle. But what I was doing those two years, and that I liked, was learning to be something of a catalyst, learning to lead discussion groups, learning an educational technique—how you go about teaching people, letting people begin to express their own concerns. It was only after the second year that I realized that I had really been politicized. I knew more of what this kind of program meant than my former teachers did. . . .

Another consequence of prolonged Movement work was growing sophistication about the "political implications" of radical organizing work. Another said:

Then there was the question of Red-baiting. We worked very closely with the Andrews of the Citizens' Action Project. They were doing the same kinds of things we were doing, and we didn't understand when people said, "You must not work with those people." After a year, we began to understand some of the political implications of it.

[K. K.: What were the implications?] Well, this group had always been disrespectable, in terms of being a Communist front or something like that. We didn't know anything about things like that then. All we knew was that there were adults who were with us when we needed them, who were willing to give us money to fund our first conferences, who were there. . . . The next year, the questioning became a very pressing one. . . . And then later, after our staff people went to New York, foundation people said, "What is this about your working with the Andrews?" And I said, "Yeah, I do." The whole thing was put into a bag of national politics we didn't understand then.

It caused very serious problems internally. For example, one of the people in the office said to me, "We've got to get that money, and if we don't get it the organization will fold and it will be your

> fault." He could have been right and I knew that—I knew we might not get the money and that we might fold, and that it might be my fault. We went through incredible internal struggles. . . . Finally, I resigned from the board of the Citizens' Action Project because the majority of the staff, in the end, asked me to do it. I refused to make that decision myself.

This incident is typical of the Movement experiences of these young radicals in that their psychological development became increasingly inseparable from the social, political, and organizational tensions with which they had to cope. From the initial impression that "there were adults who were with us when we needed them," this young radical came to realize that what she was doing was involved in a "bag of national politics we didn't understand," but about which she soon learned. This episode also illustrates the way issues of psychological importance (her loyalty to adults who helped her) were interwoven with tensions within her Movement group (the pressure upon her to resign from the board), and in turn with events on the national political scene (the unwillingness of foundations to support anyone who might be working with a Communist front).

Most of those I interviewed had been through tedious and frustrating periods of what they called "shit work"—running a mimeograph machine, canvassing, arranging publicity, raising funds, learning where to buy cheap mimeograph paper, and when long-distance telephone rates are lowest. During these years, they were picked out by more experienced Movement leaders as competent and able, and rapidly became immersed in a national network of loosely aligned New Leftists. They attended planning meetings and summer institutes; they traveled from Mississippi to New York and back to the West Coast; they went from campus to campus speaking and organizing; they worked in slums and migrant camps and middle-class neighborhoods. Little by little, they became learned in the sparse but growing literature of the New Left, developed tactical positions, and came to feel a growing disdain for "liberals" and "Old Leftists."

In the course of this continuing apprenticeship, these young radical leaders changed not only because of their inner needs, but because of the problems of the work they were doing. Work in the New Left characteristically involves a series of special tensions that result partly from the psychological make-up of those who become radicals, partly from the tactics, customs, forms, and values of the New Left, and partly from the conflicts of American society and the modern world. Learning to live and thrive amidst these tensions is no easy matter: the process of accommodation changes those who survive it, just as it leads many to drop out.

Encapsulation and solidarity

Vietnam Summer was the largest Movement organization any of those I interviewed had ever worked with—indeed, it was the largest organization ever developed in the New Left, where large-scale organizations are the exception. The "national offices" and "national co-ordinators" of most New Left groups generally serve as sources of funds and dispensers of requested services to local chapters, not as centers of initiative, program, or power. The principles of the New Left, which stress local autonomy and decision-making, are generally practiced, with the result that the Movement is unco-ordinated, fragmented, and disorganized at the national level. But Vietnam Summer, even though it defined itself largely as a co-ordinating and servicing organization, possessed a relatively large and talented national staff that attempted both to create new constituency groups and to provide program, initiative, funds, and sometimes even staff for local projects.

Yet even within the National Office of Vietnam Summer, most of the organizational forms characteristic of traditional bureaucracies were absent, and a studied effort was made to preserve group decision-making and intense group involvement at all levels. Within the National Office, a group of less than a dozen individuals eventually constituted the effective leadership of the project; and in the field, another dozen or so field organizers were the chief means of communication, co-ordination and stimulation of local projects. Despite its scope, Vietnam Summer tended to rely heavily on small face-to-face groups as the basis of its organization.

Reliance on small-group decision-making reflected both the values of the Movement and the previous experience of these New Left leaders. Whatever their previous Movement work, it had usually been carried out with a small group of other young radicals. Such groups generally consisted of three to twelve members who co-ordinated their activities, views, and tactical positions, avoiding hierarchical control or traditional patterns of leadership. Partly because these groups often worked in situations where they were viewed with suspicion or hostility by the surrounding community, they tended to focus inward upon themselves, and to develop the characteristic styles of interaction that are both the strength and the bane of the New Left.

One consequence of the inward focus of Movement groups—whether in Mississippi, the slums of Northern cities, or National Headquarters of Vietnam Summer—is the intensification of relationships between their members, and the development of *strong feelings of solidarity,* closeness, intimacy, and openness within the group. Many of these young radicals recalled with gratitude and warmth their co-workers on earlier projects:

> There was this small group of people who sat around talking about what could education do. That really kept me going for these two years. The same people who had been at that conference two years ago were still here at this one. They had had a whole lot of experience in the meanwhile. . . . The whole idea of having that group to come back to is a very important thing for me.

For others, reunions with co-workers in former groups brought nostalgia and sadness:

> I used to be able to know that when the group was operating, was really working, we were all working together. And that if we weren't, it was just a breakdown of communications. . . . I really

> enjoyed that, I considered that important, I worked much better then. [When we got together recently] it was just a great big reunion. And when we all get together, it's really just great. We'd go back and tell all the old stories and remember this person and remember that person, and "Boy, did we put it over on them."
>
> But it doesn't work together any longer. You start discussing politics or organization, and we get to fighting now. [He gives several examples of disagreement over tactics.] The differences are ideological now, but I think they're rooted in different experiences. I think that the personal problems in that group are much more significant than the political problems. . . .

In connecting political, ideological, and tactical disputes to the conflicts of group members with each other, this young man summarizes the experiences of most of his fellows.

One reason for the closeness within Movement groups is the practical difficulty in finding any kind of diversion, respite, or distraction in the surrounding community. Especially when working in hostile communities or when doing extremely frustrating work like community organizing in the inner city, members of the same group developed a mutual affection akin to that of soldiers who have survived the same battle. Even when opportunities for distraction and contacts in the surrounding community were realistically available, radicals seemed inclined to combine work, sociability, love, and recreation within the same group. To be sure, many fought against this tendency. But the frequency with which they told me that they had "successfully" resisted the pressure to become totally absorbed in the Movement indicated how strong was the temptation, inner and outer, to do so. One interviewee, for example, kept in her room an easel which, although she rarely used it, symbolized for her the artistic interests she had not completely lost during several years of Movement work. But even for her, Movement work had brought a progressive sense of estrangement from old friends and loyalties, and she now finds it hard to talk to old friends: "Once I made the jump into that circle, it was a complete jump." Given this immersion in the Movement group, it is not surprising that those interviewed had generally found their most important personal relationships with other young radicals, whether of the same sex or the opposite sex.

The strength of the feelings generated within Movement groups also led to a great intensification of *neurotic interaction and conflict.* In all intense groups, ordinary personality conflicts, struggles for leadership, and differences in outlook and style are magnified enormously, sometimes assuming life-and-death proportions. Especially when aggravated by frustration in the field or by racial differences within the group, intragroup conflicts took on nightmarish dimensions. One young man, describing a lengthy period of community organizing, said:

> Personal relationships are very surreal types of things. You are in a very artificial situation. When you were there, you know, you were forced to be together. There was a forced community. And there were forced subjects of conversation. It took a great effort to have a bull session just about philosophy, or theology, or history. Unfortunately, what happened was that most of the time it was only the white staff that did that. . . .

Intragroup tensions mount to particularly high levels during the "long winter months." In the winter, the enthusiastic support of students vanishes with their return to college, the momentum of Movement projects decreases, and both financial support and public interest are at a low ebb. One young radical described his winter experience in the South as follows:

> [The state leadership] were so interested in building a bridge from Birmingham to Washington that they forgot all about the local people. They said, "We have to do this because we have to get the press, and we have to get the excitement, and to get people behind us. And the way to do that is to have this kind of big campaign." . . . What happened was that with the passage of the Civil Rights Act and the beginning of its implementation, support immediately started to fall off from the North. It was harder to raise money, it was harder to raise bail, it was harder to get cars. Okay. That was one problem, and it caused people to say, "Jesus Christ, I'm down here right in the middle of it, and people aren't going to come through and back me up."

Number two was that Black Power was on the way, long before it was ever mentioned. It was there. There were quite a few black-white staff problems. You know, white kids with a lot of technical skills. Well, all the problems that had been written and rewritten about again and again. They were very, very present and very, very hard to deal with at the local level. We were living with guys day in and day out. You get drunk at night, and start to fight and things like that. . . .

I had some really rough times. Roger Demson and I had it out three or four times. Once, it was funny, it was an inverted argument about Black Power. He wanted me to go in and open up a new county. I said to him, "Look, Roger, at this stage of the game, they're going to send in a *white* civil rights worker to open in a new county, and build up the same kind of dependency and passive relationship upon me? No matter how good an organizer I might or I might not be, there's still that same old reaction: 'Now here's this powerful civil rights worker, and he can do it for us.' I won't do that. I won't go. Send someone else. I'll go in with someone else, as an assistant to a local person or someone black from this region. But I'm not going in there by myself." He said, "You *are* going to do that. I am the project director and I'm telling you." I said, "Kiss off!" He was about ready to throw me out of the project. But finally we sat down and had a long talk and worked the damn thing out. He finally did just that, he sent a local guy in who worked out tremendously well. But there were lots of problems.

Another spoke in similar terms of the tensions in an urban organizing project:

For a while I worked on the Inner City Project. The kids who worked there, some of them have been there for a year, now they will have been there for two years. They didn't get along at all well, and there were a lot of feuds. I got the impression that a lot of that was because they had been so completely unsuccessful. [K. K.: What kinds of feuds?] Personal feuds—somebody wouldn't wash the dishes. They never washed the dishes. A lot of them lived together in one apartment which was a bad deal—much too close, much too filthy. . . . They had gotten very discouraged and started being hesitant about going out and working. They would sleep late hours and waste a lot of time, and then they really felt bad because, "What the hell are we doing here?"

It wasn't a virtue in itself to be living in a slum. They had control of the local poverty board, but the local poverty board didn't have any money because their money was cut off from Washington. So what good was the control doing them? They couldn't do anything for the area, and they couldn't even show people that politics was the way to get anything for the area. . . .

During such periods of discouraged questioning, bickering, and squabbling, many workers tend to feel personally disorganized, to become cantankerous and difficult, and to turn to self-analysis and hostile analysis of their co-workers. In retrospect, much of the affection that springs up amongst survivors of the same group arises from just these moments of anguished analysis. Yet not everyone can tolerate such intensity: during such times, many Movement workers dropped out or were pushed out.

In the conflicts within Movement groups, personal and political controversies were often impossible to separate. One young radical discussed his co-workers in a small group as follows:

Some of them were people I didn't respect politically. One was an old Communist who was very heavy on ideology, a nice guy but who was out of tune with the way America was. He was in tune with the West Side of New York. . . . And there was another guy who used to refuse to write letters in which you used a capital "I," because that was too egotistical. . . . A real martyr but a real worker. So I was left all by myself. I didn't know how to be the regional co-ordinator of anything. The only thing I could do was to move toward where my inclinations went: that was toward some kind of community organizing. . . . I survived it because every once in a while when I was there, people I respected came into town.

Many commented on the *psychological boundaries* that surrounded Movement groups:

It was just that if you ever tried to step out for a second, you felt that that was a very different world, and that it didn't relate to anything inside of the Movement. The office was there, and it was concerned with these problems. People had almost two different lives. Leroy Aldridge, for example, had a life and a relationship

> with certain staff people in the office, but back home where he was from, he had something else that wasn't at all connected with us. Also, the conversations were just sometimes unbelievable, in terms of—well, people that you got to know outside, or that you knew from before, it just seemed that they were very different people, a different *kind* of people. Some people I knew from before—I knew them outside, and I knew them there—there was a lot of difference.

As this young man recounted it, the Movement project and the outside world were experienced as different worlds requiring "very different people."

The boundaries around Movement groups also created an *information barrier* between the group and the rest of the world. It sometimes becomes extremely difficult to send or receive accurate information between the group and those it is attempting to organize, to say nothing of other individuals, groups, the press, and so on. This barrier was defined as the "isolation of leadership" in Vietnam Summer, and studied efforts were made to overcome it. Staff workers deliberately involved themselves with the constituencies being organized. Some of the early members of the National Office staff were eventually "rotated" out into field assignments, and some of those who remained in uninterrupted staff work argued that they needed to return to grass-roots organizing the following year.

The barriers around Movement groups, of course, have positive functions as well. They serve as armor against the opposition of the surrounding community; they are a way of preserving group cohesiveness and enthusiasm despite the frustrations of Movement work; they help to prevent "dropping out." But whatever their uses, these barriers also encourage the elaboration of private "in-group" languages that make communication between Movement groups and others extremely difficult. Even more important, the encapsulation of Movement groups can subvert their major objective of producing change in the community. And these barriers make it difficult to form any realistic judgment of the effectiveness of Movement work and tactics. The tendency during times of frustration and weariness to confine contacts to other members of the group obviously means that at such times New Leftists tend to talk largely to each other.

Furthermore, evaluations of the success or failure of Movement efforts are often carried on in an atmosphere of empirical unreality. Movement projects often have trouble defining the criteria of success and failure, a difficulty that is inherent in the goal of "organizing the people" so as to express *their* needs. But in addition, when Movement workers become excessively encapsulated, accurate information from the "outside" is often quite lacking: a chance conversation with one person positively affected by Movement work can lead to an inflated sense of effectiveness, while a discouraging day can lead to a crushing feeling of failure. And when the chief source of information about the effectiveness of many New Left groups comes from other members of that group, realistic assessments of effectiveness are hard to separate from personal arguments or political disputes over tactics. Almost delusionary perceptions of the possibility of overwhelming success and equally extreme perceptions of utter ineffectuality or counterproductivity are difficult to correct with information from the outside world. All of this was less true of Vietnam Summer than of other groups in which these radicals had taken part: Vietnam Summer, of course, had no "long winter months," and its leaders made conscious efforts to prevent themselves from becoming encapsulated within their own Movement world.

Prolonged immersion in Movement primary groups also tends to increase further the radical's feelings of *estrangement from the mainstream* of American society. Living and working among those at the bottom of American society or identifying with peasants who are the "accidental victims" of American military involvement abroad—both tend to consolidate the radical perception and interpretation of American life. The story of the traffic light that the SDS-sponsored Newark Community Union Project attempted to obtain for slum dwellers illustrates the frustrations that underly this increasing estrangement. Despite what radical organizers saw as a clear need based on the safety of Newark children, and despite strong organized community pressure, Newark city officials delayed, demanded studies, and after many years have still not installed the traffic light. Confronted with such "failures," the radical inevitably becomes cynical. His is not the cynicism of a man without ideals, but the cynical "realism" of one who progressively learns how difficult it is to implement the nominal ideals of his society. His cynicism about the power structure inevitably pushes him farther away from traditional politics, toward more "radical" tactics (in particular, tactics of resistance and confrontation), and toward efforts to create a "power base" in the community that will eventually *force* the implementation of the principles that seem to him so unquestionably right.

Finally, Movement groups, like all enclosed groups, tend to generate *strong pressures toward unanimity*. Working twelve to sixteen hours a day with the same small group, and often living with them the rest of the day, requires that something approaching operational unanimity be achieved on important matters. When the group is not able to achieve working agreement, it tends to become polarized around conflicts that merge personal differences in style and outlook with political differences in tactics. When polarization occurs, communication between the polarized subgroups breaks down and massive misunderstandings and conflicts may eventually break the group apart. Several interviewees told of groups that had fallen apart in just this way. Even the development of intense affection or love between two members of the group sometimes proved intolerable to the group as a whole: within long-standing Movement groups, something akin to an incest taboo can develop to prevent pairing off. Others emphasized their personal difficulties in "submerging" their own viewpoints and interests in order to achieve a harmonious group. And their accounts of their Movement experience made clear that inability to "compromise" had been one of the major reasons that others had dropped out of Movement projects, and often out of the Movement itself. Dropping out tends to occur especially at those times when the individual feels that his own integrity and intactness is threatened by group pressures.

Movement groups are in many ways similar to training groups, sensitivity groups, and other intensely interacting taskless groups. Such groups tend to develop strong barriers on their outside boundaries, which impede communication and movement outside the group; they frequently exhibit an "anti-empirical" inability to use facts in order to counter emotion-based distortions and impressions; interaction within the group often has a quality of "surreality"; group members commonly find themselves behaving in unusually neurotic and emotional ways; and the group tends to become estranged from the "outside world." All such groups, if they are to endure, must develop a strong internal cohesion that militates against the formation of special love relationships within the group, but that also often threatens the individuality of the members. In all these respects, Movement groups exhibit the familiar problems of any small group.

Despite these problems, the young radicals I interviewed have prospered in the Movement, and generally viewed their past associations with affection. One consequence of encapsulation is solidarity: the sustaining function of intense group involvement, and the positive role of a "good group" in enabling its members to deal collectively with their shared and individual problems. The groups these radicals considered most effective were usually those that had a clearly defined and manageable task. A focus on a job to be done dissipated potentially disruptive group problems and gave group members a sense of achievement. For these particular young radicals, achievement was especially sustaining, given their long-standing motivation to do things well. Also, the history of the Movement during recent years is a history of growth: whatever the failures of the Movement, it has gathered membership and been much publicized during the past few years. This fact, too, has been sustaining.

But perhaps most important in enabling these particular young men and women to survive the problems of encapsulation is their own sense of individuality and specialness. If it is true that conflicts and dropping out occur in part because group members feel their individuality and basic convictions "compromised" by group pressures, then the possession of a strong sense of inviolable individuality may be a prerequisite for survival within Movement groups. The young radicals who led Vietnam Summer by and large possessed this inner conviction of individuality, built upon their early sense of specialness. Indeed, for many, one of the greatest rewards of Movement work was the relief, through solidarity with other special people, of their sense of isolation.

Participation and power

In the middle of Vietnam Summer, there occurred a "revolt of the secretaries," which can stand as introduction to the vexing problems of authority, participation, leadership, and power that continue to plague the New Left.

As Vietnam Summer was originally organized, the National Office was divided into two groups: the "political staff," concerned with questions of national organizing, co-ordination, programing, publicity, funding, and so on; and the "office staff," who addressed envelopes, typed, ran the mimeograph, and answered the telephone. This second group was largely recruited from among college girls and recent college graduates in the Boston area: it was a group of attractive and intelligent young women. As the summer progressed and members of the two staffs came to know each other, their roles began to blur and overlap. Some of the members of the political staff seemed embarrassed that, often for the first time in their Movement experience, they had others to do their "shit work" for them. Furthermore, the political staff realized that the office workers were not only unusually able, but that they had volunteered to work for subsistence wages because of their commitment to the goals of Vietnam Summer.

In the middle of the summer, the secretaries were "organized" by a few members of the political staff. Said one of the organizers:

> It was a classic organizing situation. . . . They were underemployed and dissatisfied with the work they were doing. And they

> had a lot of good ideas about what they should be doing. So it was just a matter of encouraging them to speak out.

The organized confrontation occurred, the political staff (which included both the exploiters and, in part, the organizers of the exploited) capitulated immediately, and the distinction between political and office workers was abolished. A major effort was made to integrate the ex-secretaries into the political staff and to give them political responsibilities. Girls who had been typing letters one week found themselves attempting to arrange concerts with Sol Hurok or co-ordinating Vietnam Summer activities in an entire state the next.

The completeness and success of the "revolt of the secretaries" should not be exaggerated. Not everyone on the political staff was equally enthusiastic about this redefinition of roles. After the summer, one wrote pointedly:

> After the revolt, overworked political staff people sometimes could not find a typist for material which needed excellent typing on the mimeo machine. This was because the former secretaries were now busy advising local projects. . . . Yet they knew very little about organizing, literature on Vietnam, etc. As a result they *listened* on the WATS line, offering little useful advice. How could they offer advice when they were talking to field secretaries with years of Movement experience, and yet they themselves had never rung a single doorbell? . . . What the revolt meant was that these girls . . . were now spending much of their time in the "glamor" roles of calling on the WATS line and arranging public concerts (none of which ever came off). Those who suffered most, undoubtedly, were the local projects.

In the end, the superior training and skills of the political staff meant that they had to continue to make most of the major decisions, but there was increasing participation from ex-office workers as their competence grew.

In the early part of the summer, an effort was made to reach decisions in large staff meetings that included both political and office staff. After the summer, one of the least radical of those I interviewed said of these general meetings:

> The prevailing tone and atmosphere was set by the most radical there, who spoke in such a way that those with less revolutionary views were made to feel like unprincipled compromisers if they expressed disagreement. It is often very difficult for those more "political" . . . to raise even tactical objections to the most radical. . . . When [the most radical] spoke this way, they did so with such sincerity, earnestness, and high principle that it seemed very difficult to disagree. . . . In the very radical atmosphere created at many staff meetings, it was almost impossible to make specific programmatic decisions.

Partly as a result of the unwieldiness of these large meetings, in mid-summer, a smaller group of eight to twelve people began to meet without the rest of the staff and, in effect, assumed the leadership of Vietnam Summer. The larger staff meetings became increasingly irrelevant to the actual planning of the summer's program and policies. Furthermore, faced with six hundred local projects across the nation that had to be contacted and serviced effectively, Vietnam Summer began to evolve a semblance of "bureaucratic" structure, involving clearer definitions of responsibility and better sharing of information within the National Office and between isolated field co-ordinators.

Toward the end of the summer, there occurred another incident that illustrates the discomfort most Vietnam Summer workers felt over their involvement in a "bureaucratic organization." One of those interviewed was semijokingly given a title to acknowledge the considerable responsibilities he had been carrying throughout the summer. He was then teased mercilessly by his friends. This teasing expressed both the affection they felt for him, and their (and his) embarrassment that he should have a position with "bureaucratic" implications. One interviewee commented after the summer:

> . . . Part of the joking stemmed from the feeling of some of us that he might in fact have been given large *new* powers of authority over us, and we felt threatened by this. By kidding him, we were, in an unconscious way, very serious—we were probing to be reassured that in fact our personal, equal relations with him would be just as they were before.

Because of its size and scope, Vietnam Summer in many respects had to be more "bureaucratic" than most New Left organizations. Also, unlike most Movement organizations, Vietnam Summer was in the beginning a "top-down" project that began without a base in local communities. One of the prime objectives of the summer's work was, of course, to create a community base, with the explicit hope that as the summer progressed, local organizations would increasingly take over direction from the bottom up. Yet two and a half months was hardly enough time for this to happen. By joining together to create an initially "top-down" organization, these young radicals had violated their own values of participatory democracy and grass-roots organizing, and there was not enough time to make this lapse good. To make matters worse, the National Office and the field workers had to deal with the anxieties of some local workers, who were afraid that the summer project was excessively dominated from what was called the "walled city of Cambridge" (the site of the National Headquarters). Other local workers questioned the source of Vietnam Summer funds (did they perhaps come from Bobby Kennedy's political machine?).

An incident at the Cleveland Training Institute in June illustrates these anxieties. CBS television cameramen filmed one of the plenary meetings of that institute, and one of the leaders of the summer joked to the audience, "We are making CBS finance the summer for us." The joke backfired, and it was later necessary to explain that funds did not come from national television networks, but from designated individuals and groups. Similarly, some of the more radical local workers were afraid that the "achievement" of the summer would simply be turned over to some existing political machine (again, Robert Kennedy's) for use in conventional party politics.

While the leaders of the summer had to reassure the more radical field workers that they were radical enough, they also had to defend their own radicalism against the National Steering Committee of Vietnam Summer. This group included a number of old New Leftists, now mostly in academic posts, plus representatives of traditional peace organizations. In arguments with the National Steering Committee, the National Office staff insisted that it was not interested in entering conventional political alignments, that its main interest was in multi-issue community organizing, and that it approved of, and wanted to support, such tactics as draft resistance. The National Office staff was thus in the position of simultaneously defending its own radical position from the somewhat less radical position of the National Steering Committee, and allaying the worries of those in the field that it was not radical enough.

While all of these issues were raised with singular intensity in Vietnam Summer, they illustrate a general tension between participation and power that plagues New Left organizations and young radicals. The incidents I have recounted point to the special discomfort felt by many young radicals when they are in a position of control over another person, especially if he is expected to do routine, boring, or unenjoyable work. For many of those interviewed, it was extremely difficult either to lead or to follow—especially when it entailed power, control, or domination. In their personal manner and values, these young men and women favor open, equal, and direct relationships with other people; they are psychologically and ideologically hostile to formally defined, inflexible roles and traditional bureaucratic patterns of power. Their organizational ideal is the face-to-face group of equals:

> Maybe it's just that I don't like to be too involved in organizations, where there is always a matter of adjustment—adjusting relationships very carefully so that things run well. For me that would be constantly tense. If it were really a good team, I could picture myself enjoying it for long periods—where everyone liked each other and everyone were more or less equal. But that rarely turns out to be the case for a very long time. . . .
>
> Sometimes it naturally happens that everyone is personally about equally strong, where different people have different strong points, as far as their abilities go. That was true for a while in college. There were a number of people who more or less had respect for each other and who were very, very close. That's really nice, I enjoyed that. . . .

This young man clearly states his ideal of "a good team": everyone is "personally about equally strong," people respect one another, and they are "very, very close" to each other.

Another interviewee, in the process of denying that he has any problems about the exercise of power, suggests the tension he feels over this issue:

> I don't have problems in terms of thinking that the exercise of power is illegitimate. . . . Well, sometimes I do, but I usually have a feeling of what I am doing. Of course I could be a little more effective if I could be more ruthless. I have a lot of psychological problems about that. . . . I mean you *can* be ruthless without being vicious. . . .

By first denying that he believes that "power is illegitimate," going on to admit that he sometimes does, and by connecting power with ruthlessness and then with viciousness, this young man indicates his underlying fears about what power might mean: what is frightening is that it *might* lead to ruthless, vicious, and sadistic domination of others.

For those with prolonged Movement experience, sensitivity to the issue of domination, ruthlessness, and viciousness often grew out of unhappy experience. One interviewee, for example, recounted leaving a project partly because of an "intimidating" coworker:

> The office was just beginning to get next to me. It was just awful. Offices are bad. We had added more staff, and personal tensions were terribly intense. [K. K.: What kinds of tensions?] Personality things, mostly. . . . There were eight people working in the office and they all were very independent. There was this whole question of whether the head of the organization should spend his day writing papers or whether he should run the mimeograph machine. We had one person who maintained that you had to do fifty per cent shit work and fifty per cent creative work. I maintained that you just didn't make people equal by the kind of work they did. . . .
>
> We had a guy in our office who I think was one of the most destructive people I've ever met because he intimidated people with that. He intimidated us to the point where we couldn't do good

> creative work. . . . I always said, "You're a totalitarian person. You really are totalitarian, even though you pose yourself as a democrat." And he would agree with that, but he wouldn't change.
>
> What he really did was inflict his demands on people, and insist they do the shit work, which was very intimidating. . . . He would say, "You won't do shit work, you just want to be a big cheese in the organization. She wants to answer correspondence because she gets some sort of sense of power out of it. Information is power." There was a lot of trouble in the office. But one thing was clear, he would tell everyone what everyone else was to do, and he had to know exactly what everyone was doing. Everyone had to share all their information. That was the first time that had happened. . . .
>
> We just broke away when that began to happen. . . . I had been working there for eighteen months, and I was tired, and I needed a change of scenery. . . . You have to leave after a while. . . . I just felt I needed to get away at that point, get away for a while.

Here again the good group of "very independent" equals is contrasted implicitly with the bad group in which a "totalitarian" individual "intimidates" the rest—in this instance, by a paradoxical appeal to their participatory values.

Another young radical, discussing conflicts between Movement groups, commented:

> I had a good deal of trouble getting involved in local power struggles. I mean having someone as my enemy and not feeling bad because he's been defeated. Take somebody like Herb. He doesn't mind if people don't like him. But I care a lot about people. I want people to like me.

Given such experiences, and in particular given the equation of power with viciousness, ruthlessness, intimidation, and unpopularity, the tendency to suppress leadership in Movement groups becomes more comprehensible. Even in Vietnam Summer, "bureaucratic" though it was considered to be, individuals who were not informed about the issues were sometimes included in policy-making discussions, while the "natural" leaders with the greatest experience, the best ideas, and the surest grasp of the facts sometimes deliberately refrained from voicing their opinions lest they appear to dominate. Indeed, the distinction between rational authority based on competence and the authoritarian exploitation of power sometimes seemed blurred. Similarly, power based on capacity and role sometimes seemed confused with sadistic control.

Closely related to the fear of intimidating and vicious power is the concern within the Movement over "manipulation." In keeping with their open and personalistic style, most young radicals seek, both in politics and personal relationships, a direct, unmanipulative, and honest encounter. For example, the organizational infighting that occurred during Vietnam Summer seemed to me extremely overt, with most disagreements openly stated and aboveboard. In their interviews with me, these young radicals expressed considerable affection for their co-workers, and often after stating a controversial view would add, "But you should talk to X—he will give you a very different picture." To be sure, in any large, hectic, and pressured office, a certain amount of manipulation occurs: this was inevitably commented upon in extremely negative terms by those I interviewed. For example, the midsummer move toward decision-making by a group of the most experienced leaders was interpreted by some as undemocratic and manipulative, despite considerable agreement that decision-making was impossible in the very large staff meetings. Or again, several of those I interviewed were viewed as "authoritarian" by others, despite recognition of their competence.

Stated differently, eagerness to be participatory, equal, and unmanipulative sometimes seemed to conflict with other goals of Vietnam Summer. If everyone is to be completely honest, open, and direct with everyone else, and if all are to have a full say regardless of experience and competence, decision-making is slow, especially in times of crisis. Decisions that might best be made by a small group of the best informed tend to be made by larger groups, to take longer to arrive at, to become fuzzy or blurred—or not to be made at all. All of this happened at times in Vietnam Summer. Yet when I shared my impression that those I interviewed were unmanipulative, reluctant to dominate and participatory to a fault, several commented that I simply did not understand the amount of behind-the-scenes manipulation and "operating" that was going on. Their comments may reflect the unusual intolerance of young radicals to *any* covert manipulation, rather than the unusual amount of it that occurred. For example, a young man who was often perceived as "authoritarian" by others, was the one who said:

> I don't want to . . . have to operate. I mean I want to be part of something where I don't have to worry about what I'm going to say and what I'm going to do, or about whether I have to keep things silent. . . . I don't enjoy it, it's too manipulative, it doesn't give me a sense of satisfaction. . . . I just don't like to get the feeling that I'm alone and I'm doing something to everybody else. . . . I want to feel that I have friends and that I'm in a spirit of comradeship with them. . . .

The desire to avoid manipulation also affected the political style of these radicals. Like those in conventional politics, Movement workers are often confronted with the problem of how to make people want what they do not want, but what the organizer feels they *should* want. In recent years, conventional American politics has partly "solved" this problem with public-relations techniques like "managing the image" of political candidates, selectively appealing to the anxieties of the electorate, and suppressing or selectively emphasizing certain crucial facts. All of these techniques are closed to the New Left by virtue of their own principles, and "playing to the media" or "flashiness"—though their value is sometimes acknowledged—are generally frowned upon as tactics. One interviewee, for example, clearly stated his opposition to "flashiness":

> I had always favored long-term intensive careful work, and gone less for flashy things than a lot of other people. I remember one discussion in our group [in college] . . . about what one of the guys had started calling the Brick Wall Theory of Social Change—that you should lead people against the brick wall and lead them to demand things of society that society wasn't going to give them. But I was in favor of organizing so as to achieve small victories at least, in order to build a movement. . . .

> I think it's a bad mistake on the part of the radicals in this country who are so wound up in radicalism that they expect defeat and don't mind. They're not in it in order to win. But the people that are being organized *do* want these things. . . .

Implicit in this critique of flashiness is the assumption that it involves a manipulation of the "people who are being organized." Flashiness, then, amounts to a form of exploitation. While intensive, long-haul, multi-issue, and "unflashy" community organizing has many arguments to recommend it, it especially appeals to the New Left because it seems the least "manipulative" tactic available.

The attitude of Vietnam Summer workers toward the National Conference for a New Politics (NCNP), held in Chicago at the end of the summer, further illustrates these young radicals' attitude toward manipulation. What was to happen at the Chicago conference, intended as a planning meeting of all "radical" political and social groups in the country to formulate plans for national action, was of considerable personal importance to many of those I interviewed. Some had been involved in planning NCNP, and still others imagined that they might later work in this effort to form a radical coalition. As the end of the summer neared, questions about what would become of Vietnam Summer were often coupled with discussions of the Chicago meeting. For example, either of the two main proposals advocated for the future of Vietnam Summer—a larger year-long anti-war project, or an effort to train a small group of dedicated and experienced field organizers—might have been an outgrowth of the Chicago meeting.

But despite the importance of NCNP, the National Office staff of Vietnam Summer made almost no prior effort, formal or informal, to influence the proceedings at NCNP. Before the meeting, many anticipated that the conference might be dominated by Old Left factions or by a coalition of Old Left and Black Power groups. The loosely defined voting rules at NCNP gave maximum voice to organizations with a strong community base: the existence of local projects was therefore crucial in determining voting power. Vietnam Summer was involved with more than six hundred local projects, and was therefore in a position to wield considerable power at NCNP. But three days before the opening of the Chicago meeting, several of those interviewed had not even tried to secure individual voting rights for themselves. It goes without saying that Old Left groups under the same circumstances would have made consistent efforts to control NCNP by exploiting the organizations they had helped create. Asked after the summer why Vietnam Summer made no effort to influence NCNP proceedings, one young radical answered:

> It couldn't have been done unless we were willing to become a very top-down organization. I remember we talked about that . . . about the issue of what would happen at NCNP. We tried to give people in the field some idea of where the people in the National Office stood—all the different points of view. That was about as far as we went. . . . The convention was wide open, and I suppose what happened could have been expected to happen. But I'm not saying that it should have been closed.

What happened at the tumultuous and confused Chicago meeting has been discussed at length elsewhere. Some days after the development of a "black caucus," which eventually obtained equal representation for the minority of Negroes present, a "radical caucus" was slowly organized, partly around a nucleus of Vietnam Summer staff and field workers. But this group grew up *after* the beginning of NCNP, as an *ad hoc* response to the crosscurrents within that meeting. Whether the confusion and the outcome of NCNP could have or should have been avoided will be debated within the New Left for many years. But what is clear is that, as individuals and as a group, the young radicals I interviewed are basically non-factional, unmanipulative, and, in the context of left-wing politics, anti-organizational and perhaps even ineffectual.

Indeed, although the importance of "power" is increasingly stressed in the rhetoric of the New Left, it seems conceivable that the tough talk of power may be partly a reaction against the anxieties it engenders. Many of these anxieties are obviously legitimate: fear of the abuse of power, of ruthless authority, vicious leadership, sadistic control, totalitarian intimidation, and exploitative manipulation is in many respects a rational reaction to a world where power, authority, and leadership are often used cruelly rather than benignly. It is also a reasonable response to an era of big bureaucracies that often dehumanize and manipulate their members. No matter how incomplete, the emerging styles that cluster around the concept of participatory democracy illustrate an important effort to devise new forms of organization and action that will humanize the organized and vitalize the actors.

The strengths and weaknesses of this concept are apparent in the revolt of the secretaries and the Vietnam Summer reaction to NCNP. On the one hand, a fidelity to basic principles was maintained; the secretaries *were* involved, educated, and, to some extent, politicized. Vietnam Summer as an organization refused to approach NCNP as a "top-down organization," and to a large extent the conference was "wide open." But on the other hand, the integration of political staff and office staff probably reduced the organizational effectiveness of Vietnam Summer; while at NCNP, the undisciplined, unorganized New Left was confronted with much smaller, tightly organized, and centrally controlled Old Left groups, which were able to exert a disproportionate influence. The extent to which it is possible to retain an unmanipulative and participatory style, and yet mount an effective program on a national scale, is one of the unresolved questions of the New Left.

These tensions around power and manipulation have important psychological roots. In considering the early lives of these young radicals, I have suggested that the experience with struggle accustomed them to conflict and yet inoculated them against it, teaching them how to cope with anger in themselves and in others, how to respond "rationally" to provocation, and how to avoid fruitless violence. Perhaps they are now so determined to create forms where the abuse of power will be impossible because they know so well from their own experience that the desire to control others can be angry, ruthless, and sadistic. In addition, their sense of specialness, coupled with their considerable talents, requires special restraint lest it lead to domination, exploitation, and manipulation. In recalling their experience in the Movement, several commented on how painfully they had had to learn to delegate responsibilities to others, to work co-operatively with other people, or to suppress their own tendency to "take over" groups with their articulateness. The fusion of will and conscience in these young radicals also requires restraint if it is not to become overbearing self-righteousness. Those I interviewed often had had to learn to hold themselves back in dealing with those they considered less competent, less experienced, or simply wrong. Another partial reason, then, for their tension around power and manipulation may be the need to suppress the tendency in themselves to feel more able and more right than others.

The suppression of leadership and control within Movement groups can also be seen as a compromise necessary when a group of talented, principled, individualistic, and articulate young men and women join in a common endeavor. One young radical, commenting on the leadership group that evolved in Vietnam Summer, noted:

> If in a group of this sort one is led by others, it somehow denies one's own special importance. . . . The need for one's own and others' recognition of his specialness is a crucial factor behind this distrust of authority. Part of the strain toward leadership, after all, is the need for recognition of one's specialness. To have others lead one in the special group one has tied one's identity to thus seems intolerable.

Put differently, the demand for full group participation can be seen as a compromise whereby everyone agrees to give up his own claim to special leadership in return for the promise that no one else will try to lead him.

The many unresolved tensions and discomforts that surround the problem of power and manipulation in the New Left can thus be seen as related simultaneously to psychological issues within young radicals themselves, to the requirements of small Movement groups, and to the effort to find alternatives to the viciousness, ruthlessness, manipulation, and "operating" that characterize much of modern life. The fear of power and manipulation is a fear with historical and social, as well as psychological, roots: it constitutes, understandably, a central theme in this group of young radicals who worked together for a summer to attempt to persuade their fellows to end violence.

Process and program

Almost all the radicals I interviewed commented apologetically at some point that they found too little time to read, in contrast to their earlier days when they had been voracious readers; they sometimes added that they were sorry that they had not read my book. Part of the motive behind such statements must be a polite yet faintly ironic commentary on my own position as a "merely academic" observer of a group of dedicated activists. Although I discussed with them the possibility that I would write about them and Vietnam Summer, these young radicals were too friendly to broach directly the question of my "using" them to advance my own academic career. But they did occasionally discuss in scathing terms the disadvantages of the "publish-or-perish mentality" and the "academic rat race," and they sometimes asked me if I found academic life stultifying or unreal. At the same time, many mentioned rather wistfully their abandoned or postponed plans to resume their academic careers, and commented on the problems of "keeping up" when in the midst of organizing work.

One part of this persistent contrast between action and reflection doubtless results from the relationship that developed between me—an intellectual, academic observer—and them—active, committed radicals. But the research relationship alone is not enough to explain the recurrence or the many ramifications of this issue. Again and again, the interviewees returned to it: doubts about the academic world were matched by doubts about the possibility of acting *without* "academic" knowledge; satisfaction over their active involvement in the process of organizing work was counterbalanced by a peculiar uneasiness about discussing the over-all program of the New Left. In reviewing the lives and plans of these radicals, I have noted their alternations between activity and contemplation, organizing work and intellectual work; similarly, in commenting upon the over-all views of the New Left, I have noted the strong emphasis on the process of organizing, on tactics and the short range, and the relative absence of long-range formulations and programs. These two tensions, between action and intellect and between process and program, are closely related.

Their relationship is illustrated by one young radical who described an early Movement project she helped to organize:

> We felt terribly inexperienced, of course, and all of us recognized it. We were inadequate for putting together an organization. None of us had any organizational experience. We didn't know a damn thing about politics. We were just babes in the woods. And yet there we were. . . .
>
> We knew what we wanted to do, as far as talking to kids and holding conferences. We knew that there needed to be a base built among people who could talk with each other. That whole idea of communication, vague as it was, was really the thing that pushed us. . . .
>
> We ended up a year later having three thousand people on our mailing list, communicating with each other, but us not being prepared to do anything with them. It was frightening. No programs, no action, nothing. We knew that we were inadequate, except that we didn't know what to do. That crippled us. We could have developed much better and done a lot more things. . . . I really don't know what held us together.

Here the emphasis on the process of communication was not enough to carry the organization along in the absence of a program.

On leaving this organization, she recalled:

> I wanted to sit down and reflect and start learning. I thought, "Well, what you need—you have all this identification with these people, so that what you need is to go and read about it for a while." So I went to the Center, under the plan that I would read,

which I did absolutely none of. . . . That was a discovery. I'm not the type to sit down with a book and read about radicalism. On the other hand, I used to read a lot, and I got out of the habit of reading during those times I was traveling. Now I'm beginning to make myself read again. I wish I could more. I should have used my time when I had it for that. I got angry at myself, that I had the time and I didn't do any reading.

Like most of her co-workers in Vietnam Summer, this young woman felt that her major inadequacy was in the area of interpretation, theory, and program. An experienced organizer, she bemoaned her own inability to read, yet when the opportunity arose, she found it difficult to do so.

Others spoke in similar terms. One young man, who had spent several years in organizing and administrative work in the Movement, described his activities after Vietnam Summer:

I'm spending a great deal of time in basic political writing and thinking about American class structure, the dynamics of the productive system. I feel that's a great lack of mine. I feel that I really have been operating without much of a theoretical understanding of what I am doing. . . . People used to ask me, "What are your politics?" I couldn't tell them. . . . Now I have to wade into the ideological struggles of the New Left. . . . I'm not going to take an administrative job or anything for a while. I plan to do a lot of reading, writing, speaking. Let other people do the organizational things. I have to begin to define the parameters, instead of accepting the parameters that other people have put together.

Another young radical said:

I need things that would give me more perspective to help me analyze what it is I've done and what it is I need to do. I need to know more about economics . . . I want to do more reading in history . . . I think if you have a radical perspective, you really should. I just don't have those things.

Another young radical, who did go back to graduate school for a time, stressed her need for perspective:

I got tired just being over a mimeograph machine. It's tiring, wondering, Is this what you're going to do for the rest of your life?

And I also very consciously knew I didn't have enough sense of what happened before I got into the activity. I didn't even know there were things like social protest schools. I'd taken history courses but I didn't really learn anything. I wanted to go back to school to learn about what I'd been doing. I was getting an education, but it was a very different kind of education. It gave me a completely different perspective on what real education should be. So I went back to graduate school then, being much less tolerant of what the kids were, what they were studying, the whole concern with exams and papers. . . .

Although they phrase the issue in largely personal terms, these young radicals point to a conflict between activity and process on the one hand and reflection and program on the other that is probably inevitable in any political movement. Anyone who tries to transform a complex and rapidly changing society, which is embedded in an even more unstable world, is inevitably confronted with a conflict between acting in order to change things and reflecting in order to know what to change. The radical seeking popular support should ideally know a great deal about his society, about the psychology of his constituency, and about the groups, institutions, and traditions that might support or impede his efforts. He also needs time to formulate a program—some vision of the desired future—that will inform the organizing process in which he is engaged. The many discussions about effectiveness and tactics that continued throughout Vietnam Summer usually required for their resolution (and even for their rational conduct) a considerable store of knowledge about American society and about the history of radical movements, an informed sense of the short-range and long-range trends of American opinion, and—perhaps most important—a set of priorities and goals for the New Left as a whole. But as these radicals recognized, their previous experience had given them greater strength in action, in tactics, and in the process of Movement work than in understanding, analysis, and the development of program.

As several of those interviewed pointed out, the problem is that there are only twenty-four hours in a day, at least a few of which must be spent sleeping. It is difficult to spend twelve hours a day in community organizing and still have time and energy left over to read books, much less to formulate lofty visions of the future. Also, the radical must struggle against a sense of historical fatalism that says history is controlled by forces beyond human control. Fatalism would obviously dispose him to study history rather than to attempt the futile task of changing it. To justify his work, he must believe that history is at least partly determined by human efforts, and his focus must be on the process of *making* history. Add to this a sharp sense of historical urgency, and many radicals understandably conclude that informing themselves, deepening their interpretations, and sharpening their vision of the future must await the accomplishment of more pressing political and social goals.

The tension between doing Movement work and defining a program that might help guide it is heightened in the New Left by the relative sparseness of "radical" analyses of American society and the world. The more doctrinaire Old Left found in Marxism a clear interpretation of society, politics, and history, a program for action, and a defined vision of the desirable future. The New Left, in contrast, finds much of traditional Marxist thought at best of limited use in understanding the modern world. Marxism may provide an important source of ideas, but it is not generally seen as an adequate interpretation, much less a program. Only with the coming of age in the last five years of the first generation of New Leftists has there appeared even a small body of analysis of American society and the world in harmony with the principles and perceptions of the new radicals. And even the authors of these radical works—some of them members of the National Steering Committee of Vietnam Summer—sometimes seemed suspect because of the "conservatism" brought on by increasing age or the excessive "sophistication" produced by involvement in the academic community.

Rejecting the doctrinaire intellectual radicalism of the past, the new radical must try to formulate a new interpretation of American reality, a new set of social and political programs, and a new vision of the desirable future—all while he is immersed in full-time Movement work. The repeated refrains "I never seem to have time (or energy) to read a book these days," and "I need more perspective on what I am doing" reflect both a universal dilemma of radical political action and the particular intellectual history (or lack thereof) of today's Movement.

But the particular way these refrains are phrased, like the effort to resolve the tensions they reflect, is given a special form by the personal needs of these young men and women. In discussing the personal roots of radicalism, I emphasized that academic achievement and excellence were relatively constant facts of their earlier lives, attained without great effort, rewarded and praised by their families. These are intelligent and intellectual young men and women, taught from an early age to seek "rational" solutions, to look before they leap, and to use their heads before their fists. Yet for many of them, academic performance was also associated with parental pressure, especially maternal pressure. And while most found academic success easy, they also found it largely irrelevant to their search for meaning and commitment: the sense that they were wasting their lives developed *despite* academic achievement. Thus, the life of intellectual performance, of theorizing and reflecting, had already demonstrated its irrelevance to them: they moved into the New Left *away* from the academic world. It is as if disengaged intellectual activity had become associated with nearing the end of the line, and perhaps ultimately with compliance to maternal wishes.

The connection of pure intellect with inadequacy was strengthened for many of those interviewed by their perceptions of their fathers. Recall that some of their fathers were at their strongest in discussions of political, social, and ethical principles. But when it came to action, whether in the domestic or the political arena, they sometimes proved ineffectual, acquiescent, or unable to implement their principles. A father who regales his son with accounts of his earlier radical activities and his theories of radicalism, but is unduly submissive in both his work and his marriage, is likely to create in his son a correlation between theorizing and ineffectuality. For one young man, the issue is even more complicated:

> [My father] has always pushed for academic and intellectual achievement, but has strongly derided the idea of my becoming an "academic," because it is so passive, inactive, and removed from the real world. If I wish to become less ineffectual than my father, who only talks a good line, how can I retreat to an academia even *he* despises for its passivity? Somehow, academia has always seemed very unmasculine for me, because it seems even farther away from the real world my father at least talked about.

Other young radicals derived the correlation of the "merely" theoretical with the ineffectual not so much from their own parents, but from their own analysis of the parental generation as a whole. The late childhood and early adolescence of these young men and women took place during the McCarthy era, and the parents of one or two were embarrassed or silenced because of their own past left-wing activities. But even for the majority whose parents were not personally affected during this period, the parental generation as a whole was sometimes perceived as ineffectual, frightened, cowed into silence. The McCarthy era was mentioned at some point by almost all of those interviewed; and some implied that their intellectually liberal parents might have been more politically active had it not been for the general atmosphere of fear symbolized by McCarthy. Failure to act, while professing high principles, is thus an indictment that extends to most of the liberals of the previous generation; it contributes to the frequently implied view that those who are "merely academic," whatever their political outlooks, are in some sense unmanned.

Yet ultimately most important in these young radicals' distrust of the purely intellectual was the defensive and life-denying use they themselves had made of the mind. Early and middle adolescence had been for many a period of defensive intellectualization, of extreme religiosity, of excessive scrupulosity. During this stage, intellect had been used to create a barrier of thought between themselves and their impulses, to dilute the betrayal and rage they felt when their parents did not live up to the principles they espoused; the mind even had been used to create an illusory world that countered, rather than complemented, the real world. Many of these radicals knew all too well from their own experience how effectively intellect could desiccate life rather than inform it: they understood what it means for life to become "sicklied o'er with the pale cast of thought." This personal experience with the use of the mind to deny life may help explain why their search for intellectual relevance is so strong.

In explaining the process-oriented, non-programmatic outlook of the New Left, the experiences and values of these young radicals must also be given full weight. In their accounts of college and graduate school, they commonly noted how few of their professors seemed responsibly involved with social and political issues, and how many appeared to be careerist publish-or-perish types. This impression can hardly be faulted: most American intellectuals take relatively little part in political life, and are indeed involved in narrowly academic interests. For young men and women searching for models of responsible commitment, the scarcity of such models on the faculties of their colleges was disappointing.

The explicit values and principles of the Movement are of even more importance in understanding the relative absence of program in the New Left. Although the young radicals I interviewed frequently stressed their need for more "perspective" on their work and the Movement, they did not express any need for "ideology." On the contrary, the term "ideology" was almost always used pejoratively. And in underlining the connection between the personal and the political, they spoke with some pride, as if to contrast arid ideological positions with honest personal views. Ideology to them seemed to suggest dogmatism, doctrinaire rigidity, lack of responsiveness to people and events, and, ultimately, the misuse of intellect. On the whole, these young men and women believe that doing things the right *way* may be more important than having neatly formulated but possibly unrealistic, irrelevant, or misleading programs and goals. Whatever its psychological meanings, the avoidance of long-range programs and "utopian" visions of the ideal future is not an unconscious symptom, but largely a deliberate position. The New Left is different from the Old Left in part *because* it emphasizes process rather than program, and *because* it seeks to avoid the doctrinaire interpretation of society, the rigid structuring of goals, and the inflexible definitions of the ideal of earlier radicalism.

The emphasis on process rather than program thus has meaning at many levels. It reflects accurately the psychology of this group of "unfinished" young men and women in an incomplete Movement: their lack of political program parallels their openness toward their personal futures. Distrust of the "merely academic" reflects their perception of the academic world, one side of their image of their fathers, and their personal experience with the defensive use of intellect. But though profoundly anti-academic, these particular young radicals are not anti-intellectual: without exception they recognize in themselves the need for more perspective and greater understanding. Their opposition to the academic was invariably coupled with efforts—not fully successful—to find new ways of invigorating action with thought.

But no matter how accurately the unprogrammatic and anti-academic emphasis of the New Left reflects the values and the psychology of its members, the question remains whether this orientation is adequate to the political requirements of the Movement. The emphasis on tactics rather than goals means that the responses of young radicals tend to be situational and short range, organized around particular crises rather than around a vision of the future. The absence of program means that the New Leftist is generally reacting *against* some flagrant abuse of his values, and less often working *for* the achievement of his goals. It therefore remains to be seen whether a movement that seeks political effectiveness and a mass base can achieve the necessary impetus, persuasiveness, and direction without clearer statements of goals, priorities, and positive program.

Cultural and political revolution

If the New Left lacks clear statements of programs and articulated visions of the future, it makes up for these lacks in part by continual discussion of tactics. I have already mentioned some of the conflicting tactical perspectives apparent within Vietnam Summer: the effectiveness of demonstrations, of electoral politics, of community organizing, and of resistance was continually argued. On the least radical end were one or two individuals with considerable doubt as to precisely how "radical" they were. At the other end were those two who said they were working for Vietnam Summer precisely because they expected it to fail, thereby demonstrating the validity of their own more militant position. And the most recurrent dispute within the National Office of Vietnam Summer, as amongst the far-flung participants within that project, was between those inclined toward organizing for political action, especially with middle-class groups, and those who favored long-range and less "political" organizing efforts, especially with the poor, the deprived, and the politically powerless. The first ("political") position generally favored a cluster of interrelated projects: supporting third-party candidates or running peace candidates in local primaries, attempting to mount large and publicly visible national projects to oppose the war, promoting anti-war-referendum campaigns, seeking maximum publicity for radical objectives, attempting to woo fence-sitting middle-class liberals. The second position favored long-range community organizing activities, rather than involvement in conventional electoral politics or direct efforts to influence national policies through existing political institutions. The objective was to build a viable community base for the New Left, starting especially with those who now lack political voice and power: Negroes, the poor, the deprived, and the disenfranchised. Only by politicizing these groups, by relieving their sense of powerlessness and helping them to voice their needs, can American society be transformed. I will call this second position the "cultural" position, inasmuch as it lays primary stress on transforming underlying values, attitudes, feelings, and ways of thought.

To contrast these two positions in their extreme form may suggest a polarization within Vietnam Summer that did not exist. All of those I interviewed were somewhere between the extremes: most favored some mixture of both tactics—efforts to work within existing electoral institutions, together with attempts to change the lives and attitudes of the poor and the excluded so that they may obtain more power. But although no sharp polarization existed, a continuum of differences between the political and the cultural perspective was apparent within Vietnam Summer, just as it is apparent within the whole New Left in America.

The two major proposals for the future of Vietnam Summer can be placed in this continuum. The more political proposal involved mounting a year-long national effort of far greater scope than Vietnam Summer. As one of its advocates wrote:

> A 1968 project must be much bigger and it must be completely new, for Vietnam Summer, too, has been guilty of limited thinking. . . . Based on what we accomplished, it is not at all unreasonable to suggest a 1968 project with a two-million-dollar budget, six thousand local projects, a newspaper with one million circulation, a vastly expanded program, and a far larger degree of accomplishment. New leadership must staff the project: a new grouping of organizations, bigger and more inclusive than what we accomplished, is essential. . . .

Although the author of this proposal also stresses the need for community-based projects, his main emphasis is on maintaining *political* thrust and impetus around the anti-war movement.

Others, arguing against this position, proposed that all available resources should be devoted to linking together the experienced radical organizers in the country, and to training as many new ones as possible. This second proposal emphasizes the "symptomatic" nature of the war in Vietnam:

> Unless we are willing to dig deeply into the issue of the war to discover how much what we are at home is reflected in what we do abroad, and unless we use these insights to go beyond the anti-war movement to include other problems, other priorities and other wrongs, there is nothing we can do together to end the war. . . . The only option open to us is to build alternative networks in all the places where the old networks hold strong. But the new networks must offer new ways of dealing with the day-to-day issues facing people—issues like welfare, schools, housing and job conditions. . . . Winning an initiative in every community across the country would not in itself affect the outcome of the war if the initiative campaign did not help you to raise and pursue fundamental questions beyond the war. . . . If we cannot bring ourselves to care deeply about what happens to us and our own people, there is nothing we can do for the Vietnamese.

The rhetoric of this statement differs from that of the first: the emphasis is on "digging deeply," going beyond the anti-war movement, dealing with "day-to-day issues facing people," raising and pursuing "fundamental questions beyond the war," and "caring deeply."

Still another Vietnam Summer leader, arguing against supporting a third-party presidential candidate, wrote:

> It is essential that local organizations feel some sense of power and control over their communities. . . . To build an organization that will speak to these needs is far more important than a temporary campaign with a great deal of action and excitement. . . . To proceed with it would show an insensitivity to the needs of most local organizations. . . . The focus of our organizing, then, must be local, stemming from the conditions that people are close to and understand. . . . Although [electoral activities] should be used wherever possible to put together loose coalitions that build local political bases, our emphasis must be on the construction of strong community-based organizations that fight with direct action as well as electoral action.

Here again, the cultural rhetoric predominates; the stress is on "feeling a sense of power and control," speaking to local needs, starting from conditions that "people are close to," fighting "with direct action."

While the differences between the two proposals are not extreme, they are nonetheless important. The "political" tactic lays primary stress on momentum, political viability, size, and scope. The cultural perspective emphasizes multi-issue organizing, the construction of "alternative networks," caring deeply, and, in the last analysis, helping individuals transform not only the policies of their government, but their lives. And the goal for the culturalist is not so much to elect an anti-war President in 1968, but to lay the basis for the long-range changes in the mood of the American people that might create a truly radical mass movement in ten, twenty, or fifty years.

Each of these positions is a variant on a theme familiar to radicals and revolutionaries the world over. The "cultural" position is related to the assumption that the only lasting changes are those that occur in men's minds and outlooks; meaningful change, therefore, cannot be achieved via "mere" political manipulations and changes. According to this view, institutions are admittedly unwieldy and unresponsive to the needs and demands of the people, but in order to change bad institutions, one must change the attitudes, outlooks, and values of those who now tolerate them or work in them. Put differently, any important and lasting change in the organization of society requires a prior change of heart: the apathetic must be politicized; the demoralized must gain new self-esteem; the disenfranchised must gain a voice; and the vast American middle class must confront the spiritual emptiness of its life. The radical's primary task is, in the words of one young radical, to "help people be people." His most enduring accomplishment will be the humanization of the lives of those with whom he works, and the rest—social, political, and institutional changes —can only be meaningful after this transformation. As long as individuals remain demoralized, apathetic, powerless, or unable to confront the problems in their own lives, political and institutional changes will be empty.

The "political" position is more optimistic about achieving meaningful reform within existing structures, and more pessimistic about changing the basic outlooks and attitudes of the disenfranchised, the powerless, and the oppressed. Meaningful social changes have occurred, it is argued, *without* profound transformations of psychology and outlook. For example, stopping the war in Vietnam would be a significant change in American policies that would not require a major change of heart in the American people, a plurality of whom are already convinced that becoming involved in Vietnam was a mistake in the first place. A sense of urgency also argues against "long-haul" organizing that aims at changing basic attitudes: if it be true, as some argue, that war with China is likely if escalation in Vietnam continues, then every effort must be made to bring the war to an immediate end—if this effort fails, anti-war work will become treason. Furthermore, the "political" argues that the hope that a radical movement can be based upon the poor and disenfranchised is an illusion: any viable American radicalism must rest on middle-class support, and must thus use the electoral and political tactics aimed at enlisting that support.

Stated in their extreme form, the cultural and the political tactics are thus connected to different interpretations of revolution. Of the two positions, the cultural position is clearly the most radical: it insists that nothing less than a transformation of outlooks, values, and perhaps even of human character is needed: what must change is the way men think of themselves, the way they lead their lives. In its most extreme form, this view is embodied in the thought of Mao Tse-tung, with his strong voluntaristic stress on the importance of revolutionary ferment after the Revolution, of continuing ideological reform, and of the value of "struggle" in creating a new socialist man. Another variant of this outlook is found in the writings of Frantz Fanon, who argues that revolutionary violence is necessary to politicize backward, oppressed, and disenfranchised peoples: the objective of violence is not only to create the revolutionary army that will destroy the enemy, but, equally important, to transform the culture and character of those who become involved in it.

The "political" position is better expressed in the tactical views of Khrushchev and his successors, with their revisionist willingness to compromise, to enter into coalitions, and to be satisfied, at least for a time, with effective control of governing institutions. Although today's Russian Communists theoretically share Mao's emphasis on the creation of a new "socialist man," their tactics emphasize a transformation of governing institutions that may permit a *later* change in men's outlooks and relationships with each other. Thus, disciplined political activity aimed at gaining control of governing institutions is given first priority. A similar position, stated in less radical terms, is taken for granted in the traditional American political scene: both major American political parties seek control of existing political institutions, but neither seriously attempts to transform the character or the values of the electorate.

In starkly contrasting the cultural and the political interpretations of revolution, I am not suggesting that anyone in Vietnam Summer held either of these positions in pure form. But the tactical positions held by those interviewed reflected a compromise between these two interpretations of radicalism. The more moderate were much interested in electoral politics, and extremely critical of what they termed the "romantic rush to the underclass" for support. There is an important distinction in America, the "politicals" argue, between "the class that is oppressed" and "the class that may make far-reaching change." In general, this political position seems to attract those who are most organizational in personal style, most analytic in outlook, and least angry and intense in their radicalism.

But to the advocates of organizing the poor, the political position seemed expedient, shortsighted, and even manipulative. To be sure, the poor are a minority, but they constitute the most potentially radical force in American life. In the long run, and in eventual alliance with the "new class" of middle-class professionals, they are the only basis for a viable radicalism in America. To focus all of one's efforts on a goal like ending the war in Vietnam would be to attack the symptom while ignoring the basic disease. This view was most attractive to the most anti-bureaucratic and personalistic among those interviewed; they occasionally argued that the only way to build radicalism in America was to begin working with children. It was also most attractive to those with prolonged experience in community organizing under difficult conditions.

Prolonged immersion in Movement work in general tends to push the radical toward emphasizing the need for "far-reaching changes in the power structure," to be accomplished by awakening and politicizing the oppressed. In community-organizing work, the radical's efforts to create "new institutions" tend to be frustrated by the fact that many of the poor are personally handicapped because of lifelong exposure to poverty and discrimination. Awareness of this in turn pushes the radical farther toward insisting that only building a dedicated radical movement, which grows from profound and revolutionary changes in outlook, can effect change, while "merely political" tactics are bound to fail.

Another factor that pushes the young radical toward the cultural tactic is his own experience of self-transformation. These are young men and women who have experienced major changes in the course of their adult lives. Without formal therapy, they have largely overcome the flatness, stagnation, or psychological symptoms of late adolescence: their own lives have been invigorated by their commitment to radicalism. The concept of personal change has immediate meaning to all those I interviewed. It therefore makes special sense to them that involvement in radical activities can be a powerful catalyst for personal change in others, and may be the requisite for a large radical movement. Indeed, some radicals within Vietnam Summer and the New Left show a tendency toward what Robert J. Lifton, commenting on the "cultural revolution" in China, has termed "psychism"—the view that psychological changes alone can produce political changes, the conviction that inner transformations and forces are more "real" than what happens outside the psyche.

The experience of prolonged Movement work and of their own personal growth, then, disposes many young radicals to emphasize the power of mind over matter, and to give priority to psychological change as against institutional and political change. But countering this voluntarism is a political realism born of long experience. Most of these young radicals are well aware that their own experience may not be generalizable. And most know that far from breaking totally with their personal roots, they have, to a large extent, changed because they were able to assimilate and use their past in their current work. Even amongst those who most strongly advocated the tactic of "long-haul organizing with the poor," there were few illusions that this would produce drastic transformations in the outlooks of large numbers of people within a short time: they spoke in terms of decades and generations. Conversely, even those committed to political tactics agreed with the over-all objective of changing many of the basic outlooks and attitudes of American society; they only disagreed over how this could best be accomplished.

The pull toward cultural radicalism was further decreased for these New Leftists by their own political and organizational effectiveness. The leaders of Vietnam Summer were non-messianic, anti-prophetic, and unutopian to a fault. Throughout their lives, they had been unusually successful in working with others in groups and organizations. Several had repeatedly been offered jobs in business and public agencies because of the presumption that they could, if they chose, work effectively in that context. Indeed, the considerable achievement of creating Vietnam Summer in six weeks, of organizing and co-ordinating six hundred projects involving more than twenty thousand part- or full-time workers, indicates considerable political effectiveness. And precisely because of their often frustrating encounters with the power structure, these young radicals knew full well that one word from the mayor, the local congressman, the police chief, or the President of the United States could in the short run accomplish far more than years of organizing work in Appalachia, Lowndes County, or Hough. In all these respects, these young radicals were eminently political beings, whatever their inner propensity toward psychism.

In the participants in Vietnam Summer, then, the tension between what I have termed the cultural and political concepts of revolution found an equilibrium somewhere between the two extreme poles. Yet this equilibrium seemed provisional; and in discussions over the policies and future of Vietnam Summer, those I interviewed seemed to be arguing not only against their co-workers, but against one side of themselves. Vietnam Summer, perhaps wisely, attempted to be both political and cultural: on the one hand, local groups were organized to mount pressure to end the war through existing political institutions, while on the other hand, the organizations formed were encouraged to become on-going, multi-issue, long-range groups that might radicalize their members.

My point here, as in discussing the other tensions in Movement work, is not to attempt to resolve the controversy between these two positions, but to underline their complexity and origins at many levels. A tension between political and cultural revolution is inherent in the position of anyone who attempts to promote revolutionary change; both positions can be reinforced by actual experience in radical organizing work; and both poles of the conflict find simultaneous echoes in the personal development of the radical. In Vietnam Summer, a middle position was taken, one that granted the importance of both institutional and personal change. In these young radicals who worked for Vietnam Summer, these two positions were in uneasy balance. Yet the tension clearly existed, and one suspects that it will continue to be a central and divisive issue in the New Left in years to come.

Group tension and personal change

In the preceding pages, I have argued that the tensions between encapsulation and solidarity, participation and power, process and program, and cultural and political revolution continually confront young radicals in their work in the New Left: in each instance, the nature of the New Left in the context of modern American society creates a dilemma with which the young radical worker must cope: this problem can be analyzed in terms of its sources in current history, ideology, and group process. But in each case, too, what the young radical brought by way of psychological strength and sensitivity from his own past colored the way he and his co-workers attempted to resolve a dilemma inherent in their work. For example, one factor that contributes to the encapsulation of Movement groups is the smallness of the radical movement in America; another factor is the tendency of all intensely interacting groups to become armored against the outside world; and still a third factor is the sense of specialness and estrangement from the mainstreams of American society of these young radicals themselves. I have tried to show that a similar analysis applies to each of the other tensions I have discussed: the particular form this tension takes is the product of historical, political, sociological, and psychological facts intertwined in the experience of the young radical. As with all events studied as they naturally occur, the ongoing history of the New Left cannot be explained with the concepts and theories of any one discipline. As these young men and women continually insist, the personal and the political, the social and the historical, are fused.

As these young radicals turned from discussing their early lives to narrating the events of the past few years, a subtle shift occurred in the way they described their experience. Recalling his earlier life, the young radical concentrated more on how he felt, on his inner world, on his thoughts, personal reactions, perceptions, and fantasies, and less on what he did and what actually happened. But as he became a radical and involved himself in the Movement, his narrative became more of a chronicle of events, other people, outward behavior, and actual achievements or failures. He first talked about what happened, and only later turned to how he felt about it; his inner life became increasingly fused with his actions.

This shift in emphasis points to a process of engagement with the world, a mobilizing of energies and resources, a living out of inner fantasies in activity, all of which characterize the further development of these radicals. The meaning of personal change had been redefined so that the locus for further psychological development was no longer the self-conscious world of introspection, self-awareness, and self-doubt, but the stage of the Movement itself. Personal growth is increasingly defined by these radicals in terms of the tensions of their work. To move ahead personally means to be able to tolerate the stresses of Movement groups without irrationality or despair, to participate without dominating, to be effective without being ruthless, to gain perspective while still staying engaged, and to acknowledge the simultaneous need for both personal and political development without neglecting either. The attempt to change as a person and the effort to create a radical movement can no longer be clearly distinguished.

6 The continuation of change

Even in the few months that have elapsed between the end of the summer and the completion of this book, these young radicals and their Movement have both changed: the Movement has changed toward greater emphasis on confrontation, resistance, and disruption; and these young radicals have become increasingly impatient and angry at the policies of their government. Since the summer of 1967, social and political events have gone badly from the radical's point of view. In early 1968, the war in Vietnam continued to escalate. Public opinion, moving during the summer toward negotiation or withdrawal, swung back toward a more bellicose outlook. The urban riots of the summer of 1967 increased the mood of militancy among black Americans and made it more difficult for white and black radicals to work together. The enormous demands of the war in Vietnam have siphoned off funds and energies from the domestic problems of American society, reducing the War on Poverty to a series of small skirmishes. Even the hope of establishing a unified radical movement in America was set back by the tumult of the National Conference for a New Politics in Chicago in the fall of 1967. Little of what these young men and women hoped to accomplish is being done. The tide, if anything, is moving against them.

But they have persisted since the summer, just as in the past they have endured the discouragements of Movement work. The fact of their persistence in itself makes these young radicals an unusual group. It attests to their ability not only to withstand the weariness, anger, and isolation of their work, but to prosper amidst these frustrations. They have learned to cope with the inevitable tensions of radical work; and they have, without exception, been able to maintain a sense of continuing personal growth and movement. In their own eyes, they have changed in ways they like since they first came to think of themselves as radicals. Becoming a radical was only the beginning of a continuing process of further radicalization, involving both the development of the skills required of the radical organizer and the continuing effort to articulate an outlook adequate to the radical perspective.

The demonstrated ability to persist and prosper amidst the tensions and frustrations of the New Left distinguishes these young men and women from many or most of those who think of themselves as radicals. An account of the despairs and rewards of radical work for these young men and women will help us understand why they persist, and what their work does for them.

Weariness, rage, and resistance

Disappointments such as those of the last part of 1967 are not new to these radicals. The history of the New Left from 1964 to 1967 was in many respects a history of growing frustration, discouragement, anger, and what Robert Coles has aptly called the "weariness of social struggle." This weariness cannot be understood without recalling how extensive are the changes proposed by the New Left: basic transformations in American institutions that would overturn what is seen as the military-corporate power structure and end deprivation, poverty, and discrimination; the granting to the individual of wider participation in making decisions that affect his life; a massive reversal of American foreign policy, focused on immediate withdrawal from Vietnam, but ultimately including the support of social revolution in the Third

World and an end to anti-Communism and economic exploitation overseas.

Given the revolutionary nature of these objectives, Movement work inevitably entails despair and failure. To attempt to change the attitudes and social structure of the American South in a summer or even in several years of civil rights work was to face almost inevitable frustration, whatever the real accomplishments of the Civil Rights Movement. To attempt to end not only the war in Vietnam but the possibility of any similar wars is a herculean task that none of the participants in Vietnam Summer expected to accomplish solely as a result of their summer's work. But conscious realism, whether with regard to community organizing, civil rights work, or peace work, cannot altogether erase the secret hope that somehow "total" success will be possible. One of the inevitable consequences of work in the New Left (or in any radical movement) is the continual dashing of private hopes of how much *might* be accomplished.

Another source of frustration is especially important for the community organizer—those whom he attempts to help find their own voice often prove indifferent, apathetic, or hostile to his efforts. In civil rights work in the South, one of the most common frustrations was the fear-filled apathy or hostility of large portions of the Negro community. In community organizing work in the inner city, young radicals must continually confront the defeatism, indifference, mistrust, and unreliability of the very people they are trying to help find self-esteem and power to control their own destinies. In peace-organizing work, the organizer faces the suspicion, indifference, or helplessness of even those who are opposed to the war. The radical finds himself attempting to persuade others that actions or attitudes that they currently fear or oppose would really be in their own best interests. Despite its consistent efforts to avoid condescension or domination, the New Left continually courts rejection from those with whom it is most closely identified.

Such rejection is the more telling because it destroys the naïve activist's romantic hope that he will find a new home, community, or sense of belonging amongst the poor, the disadvantaged, and the disenfranchised. At best, the middle-class, white, college-educated youth is perceived by the poor as another well-meaning "social worker" attempting to impose his alien values on them; at worst, he is seen as another representative of City Hall, to be exploited for handouts, jobs, and money. Especially today in black areas, he is likely to be seen as an enemy and subjected to continual testing. And although prolonged and dedicated work can sometimes enable the organizer to alter these perceptions, he always remains different in the eyes of the poor. Often willing to abandon his "home" in the American middle class, he must also learn to abandon any hope of finding another home among the deprived. The radical finds that he is now estranged not only from the mainstream, but from the excluded.

This exclusion is often difficult to bear for long, especially when support is not forthcoming from those on whom the radical has previously depended. One young man, for example, described the mood of depression that overcame civil rights workers in the South:

> It was right after the Voting Rights Act was passed during the summer. It was beginning to be implemented in the fall. But with the passage of the Voting Rights Act, there was a significant decrease in support from the North again. People really felt that it was all over, and that a great big federal victory had been won. The great federal forces of truth, justice, freedom, beauty, purity, and loveliness would come in there and prevail over the forces of feudalism in the capitalist South. They felt that we would have everything hunky-dory. . . . But it didn't work that way.

The "long winter months" that followed were a time of depression when many left the South. Those who remained were tense and strained as they reassessed their tactics and their relationships to each other. The results of this agonized reappraisal were eventually apparent in the emergence of the Black Power mood among black radicals, and in the virtual exclusion of white radical organizers from black areas.

One of the most difficult experiences for the radical, then, is his growing awareness that his own perspective, which seems so self-evident and right to him, is not shared by others. When support falls off, when it becomes impossible to find others who will share his burden, fundamental questions are raised about the meaning of radical work:

> It's terribly frustrating. I used to think, "God, we're never going to make it," and then six months later, I got out of the organization, quit working for it full time, and then I thought, "Well, I think we did probably work together better than most groups." Maybe it's because we did discuss all of these things together. It was a learning process for us. . . . And we all gave it more than one year. That was a very bad problem.
>
> We kept thinking, "Are we the only fifteen people . . . that think this way? Why can't we get more staff people? Why can't we get more people who will work full time like we have for twenty dollars a week? Why don't other people feel as committed as we do to this organization?"

Equally important in inspiring weariness are events on the national and international scene. The current angry mood of the peace movement, for example, obviously cannot be understood without attending to the direction of the war in Vietnam. Similarly, the increasingly militant and insurrectionist stance taken by some of the survivors of the Civil Rights Movement is related both to the falling off of support for civil rights workers and to the later collapse of the War on Poverty. Even such apparently unrelated events as the 1967 Arab-Israeli war indirectly affected the radical movement: some of those who had undertaken to contribute to Vietnam Summer gave money to Israel instead. And in the summer of 1967 this war was itself a highly divisive issue within the New Left. A disproportionate number of New Leftists are Jewish, and some of these tended to side with Israel. Other American radicals saw Israel as the aggressor in the war, and as a leading ally of American imperialism, and so supported the Arab cause. Still others argued that radicals should support neither side. Even superficially remote and unrelated events affect the mood of the Movement.

I have suggested that many young radicals attempt to cope with the fear of failure and ineffectuality in part by a focus on the short range, an emphasis on tactics as opposed to program, and a stress on *personal* effectiveness. But confronted, as the Movement was during the mid-sixties, with repeated failures despite increasing membership, other stratagems are required to deal with constant discouragement. Conflicts within radical groups, like their isolation from the outside world, naturally tend to increase during times of gloom and frustration. And at such times, anger, resentment, and rage inevitably increase as well, resulting in in-fighting and hostility, and sometimes in the splitting or breaking up of the group.

But in addition, weariness and anger are often connected to thoughts of "resistance," civil disobedience, creative disorder, provocative acts, or disruption. One young radical made the connection as follows:

> In this little group we had, we felt a very deep despair. We wrote a paper which was circulated to a number of different people . . . where we argued that the anti-war movement seemed to have lost its momentum. . . . The only thing to be done would be for people like ourselves to . . . organize a series of civil disobedience demonstrations in Washington. And through these confrontations, we hoped to give the anti-war movement a new drive, and force a lot of liberals, who were sort of hanging on, to say which side they were on, you know. But then I began to feel that we had misjudged the state of the anti-war movement. In fact, there were a lot of people who were willing to move if there was just something they could move on.

The stages through which this group went are typical. First, they experienced "deep despair" and a sense of "loss of momentum." The "motion in the Movement" had been lost. Next, the "only thing to be done" is to organize "civil disobedience" and "confrontations." Such confrontations have as a major aim to reachieve momentum and to force fence-sitters to take sides. The plan for confrontation is abandoned only when the despair lifts, only when the group begins to believe that "there were a lot of people who were willing to move." In other words, with the relief of a sense of stagnation, of going nowhere, resistance no longer becomes necessary.

The tactics of resistance, civil disobedience, confrontation, and disruption have many arguments to recommend them. But one reason resistance becomes more attractive during times of weariness may be because it is covertly provocative. Manifestly, the radical justifies resistance because it dramatizes the moral issues involved, forces fence-sitters to take sides, or even because it is way of "bringing the machine to a halt" by disrupting its operations. But it is a fact well known to all radicals that even nonviolent resistance tends to provoke the anger of those against whom it is directed. Civil disobedience, for example, has more generally elicited violence from those who oppose it than inspired them to reconsider their own positions. It may be, then, that one function of resistance as a tactic is to provoke in others a rage the radical feels but often cannot allow himself to express.

Equally important, resistance is a way of regaining momentum. One young radical, discussing a period of prolonged, boring, and unrewarding administrative work, noted his depression and discouragement. He went on to say:

> I had a kind of campaign of keeping up my spirits by traveling. I enjoyed speaking at chapters, going to conferences. That's one of the things that kept me going. Then in about January of that year . . . I was arrested and put in jail for a few weeks in University Town. . . . I did it because this was what I liked to do, and I was tired and bored with the City. But I also did it because I felt that this is what we should be doing. . . . I got arrested three or four times during a two-week period, for inciting to riot, trespassing, criminal disorder, assault and battery, anything you could think of. . . .

Here, traveling and getting arrested in street demonstrations, whatever their other justifications, also seem to have served the psychological need to restore motion after a period of inertia and boredom.

These examples suggest that the appeal of resistance and confrontation increases during times of depression. Whatever the rationale for these tactics, they are most likely to be employed at times of frustration, weariness, stagnation, and inertia. Psychologically, then, resistance is related to the anger and "flight into activity" that often accompany inertia and depression.

Yet here, as in all other areas, psychological, group, and historical factors cannot be neatly disentangled. Civil disobedience and resistance may indeed be effective tactics for mobilizing support and for dramatizing the moral issues involved: this argument finds confirmation in the experience of civil rights workers in the South. And if one believes that American policies in Vietnam are not qualitatively different from Nazi policies toward the Jews, and that conventional political tactics are ineffective, then resistance indeed may become the most "rational" tactic available. If those who remain silent and follow orders are involved in criminal complicity, then the only reasonable position is to try to stop the war with every resource available—if necessary by disruption, resistance, and insurrection.

The move within the New Left in the past year from dissent to resistance and increasingly to disruption is inspired *both* by weariness and frustration of efforts to stop the war by working within existing institutions, *and* by the growing conviction among many young radicals that the war is absolutely wrong, and even desperate measures are justified if they will help end it. It seems likely that if escalation of the war in Vietnam continues, the mood of resistance—among those who remain in the New Left—will increase. And just as yesterday's most radical tactics today seem routine, so tomorrow's resistance may give way to more open disruption.

Another factor that may move the New Left toward increasingly disruptive tactics is the difference between young radicals like those I interviewed and the "new New Left" now in college. One of the leaders of Vietnam Summer, commenting on student radicals perhaps five years younger than himself, said:

> Sometimes these are people whose politics are Cuban, urban guerrilla warfare, "We must organize a revolution," that kind of thing. These are people who have done a lot of reading of Old Left writing. They feel romantically attached not to the Southern Civil

Rights Movement, but to some vision of the IWW or Algeria. We in the older New Left came out of a relatively successful activity in our universities. Bill Williams was president of student government at State; Andy Garfield was vice-president of student government at Private. We had learned how to play that kind of politics pretty well. . . .

Secondly, we were all alone intellectually. For example, when you went into the political science department, you had to fight practically everything the department stood for if you wanted to develop a radical politics. Not only wasn't there anything happening in the country, but also the Lipsets, the Kornhausers, and the Bells were the dominant ideology. So we were really faced with the job of developing an alternative intellect. . . . You had to learn to be able to argue for five hours with the head of the sociology department that his view was wrong, and this view was right. It was a very rigorous intellectual training. . . .

Our organizational spurs were earned and our romantic ideals were attached to the Southern Civil Rights Movement and to Northern-ghetto community organizing. The emphasis was placed on virtues like stability, responsibility, continuation, subsuming your personality in your work, not becoming a leader. We felt that indeed it was possible to change the country, although it was going to take many, many years.

But now the kids that are coming up have a very different experience. They're coming onto campuses where they don't have to do the same kind of intellectual work. The Left groupings on most campuses are more ingrown than they used to be. More kids are coming into college really so disgusted by American life, so alienated as high-school kids, that they just stay very close together. Secondly, because the dominant mood in many colleges is radical, and because this kind of movement now has more legitimacy and a lot of professors kowtow to it, a new rhetoric predominates.

And finally, the kids who for instance are just going into colleges now—say who are freshmen in September—well, the war started when they were twelve years old. That is their entire political experience, the war in Vietnam. And it is a war in which the government in America is totally unresponsive to anything they can do. They face a political past of failure and irrelevance and lack of power. I think that has a lot to do with the new kinds of organizational forms and rhetoric that is emerging. . . . But there is an awful lot of bias in my view. I think that the new kids have a number of virtues that we didn't have.

If it is true that the new New Left is increasingly "Cuban" in outlook, the mood of the Movement will be increasingly angry and militant in coming years.

I have already noted the wide range of tactical views within Vietnam Summer. But the personal outlooks of almost all of those I interviewed were more "radical" than the official positions taken by Vietnam Summer. And at least three were in considerable sympathy with the "Cuban" positions described above. One of these commented about the radicalizing process:

> That process is one of frustration: frustration with societal institutions and in particular those institutions providing for the change of society, such as electoral politics. When these institutions fail them, those who want to change are, by definition, radicalized in the sense that they now know that more radical action must be taken to accomplish their goals. Whether or not they become more actively radical or give up and drop out as a result of this new consciousness is another question. Witness the peace movement in the last year. Many people have become discouraged with the possibility of ending the war and dropped out, while those who have remained active have become increasingly militant. . . . While we were working on Vietnam Summer, many of us were also working on projects which would have to fit us in the [more radical] Left.

The alternatives stated by this young man are important: persistence in the New Left generally involves increasing militancy, increasing radicalism, that is, a steady move toward resistance and disruption. Those who cannot tolerate this continuing radicalization tend to drop out.

None of those I interviewed were advocates of violence per se, either as an effective tactic or as a radicalizing force. While many felt great sympathy for the Black Power group, their own views were in a sense more "political." And as I have noted, members of the most radical, disruptive, or insurrectionist wing of the New Left were often unwilling to take part in Vietnam Summer, which seemed to them excessively "coalitionist." Nevertheless, this account should make clear the close connection between long Movement experience, an increasing sense of disengagement from American society, and a propensity to favor increasingly dramatic and militant tactics. The frustrations of radical organizing tend to "cool out" less committed (and less radical) workers, while the weariness, inertia, and rage engendered by prolonged immersion in the Movement tend to push the activist toward resistance and confrontation. It is worth recalling that Stokely Carmichael's most radical pronouncements followed the electoral failure of the Black Panther Party that he organized in Lowndes County. And the increasingly militant position of the Student Non-violent Coordinating Committee as a whole followed the slow disintegration of most of its community organizing and action projects in the South after the summer of 1964. Amongst those interviewed, both during the summer and particularly during the following fall, a movement toward increasingly disruptive tactics was evident. For others whom I did not interview, the step toward resistance had been taken long before the summer.

Despite the psychological and historical forces that are moving today's young radicals toward resistance, those interviewed are in no way a personally violent or psychologically aggressive group. Although the issues of struggle and conflict are central to their psychological development and historical position, their early experience disposed them to argue, persuade, and discuss, rather than coerce or attack. One young man, for example, in discussing his mother's influence, said:

> From [my mother] I got that strain of not wanting to hurt anything physically. Well, where I grew up, you're nobody if you don't play football. One year I actually made a break with it. I said, "You know, I'm not going to play football." But I just couldn't hold out. Also, that was inconsistent with a lot of other things, because I wasn't a pacifist and I did like to fight. But the only time I played football well was when I was seventeen and eighteen [in college], when I was much less hung up about hurting people. . . .

In this young man, the inhibition on physical violence was related to his mother's influence; though not a pacifist, he describes himself as "hung up about hurting people."

Others already quoted emphasized that as children *they* were the ones who seemed to be able to settle arguments without a fight, to bring reason into an angry discussion, or to use words rather than fists in order to resolve it. Psychologically, these young men and women are basically non-violent, and their "hang-ups" about hurting people or having them be hurt are among the factors that led them to work together to attempt to end the war in Vietnam. Indeed, to an outside observer, one of the more remarkable qualities of these young men and women is their capacity to have resisted so well the tendency to express in action the anger and rage inspired by their work.

Persistence and reward

Only a small proportion of those who join Movement organizations come to think of themselves as radicals. And of those who are committed enough to the Movement to devote themselves to it full time, only some are able to tolerate the tensions of Movement work. It is clear from their accounts that these young radicals—who joined, became committed, and have persisted—are among a minority of those who first joined with them. The great majority dropped out somewhere along the line. The reasons this minority persisted and thrived have to do with their psychological qualities and the rewards they derived from their work.

As these radicals talked about why others left and about the problems they themselves found hardest to cope with, a few central issues recurred. Perhaps most important was the feeling of isolation. One, recalling a period of civil rights work in the South, said:

> A lot of people didn't stick it out. A lot of people who had been there during the summer left. . . . They tried to stay, and they stayed three or four months after the summer. Then they just couldn't take it and got out. [K. K.: Why was that?] Well, there was the frustration. For example, in January—at the opening of Congress, that was—they tried to unseat the Mississippi delegation.

> People thought, "Well, we couldn't do it at the Democratic Convention, but the Congress won't fail us. It's illegal." Those kids really worked their tails off to get reams and reams of legal evidence. Everybody felt a great deal of confidence that this was going to happen. That's a good example of the kind of feeling . . . where people have been promised time and time again that the white folk in the North would come through. "The support will come through, the society will be able to provide for you," this is the same thing that [Martin Luther] King was saying. . . . Of course, it didn't happen that way. It caused a very serious setback to us all.

Movement work, especially in community organizing, tends to increase the young radical's feelings of estrangement from the mainstreams of American life. Sometimes separated even from sustaining relationships with other young radicals, living under extremely trying conditions, and involved in work whose frustrations more than equal its tangible rewards, the young radical feels himself drifting farther and farther away from the society of which he was once a successful part.

One of the personal qualities that contributes to persistence in Movement work is the ability to tolerate isolation and aloneness—to preserve a sense of self even when it is not buttressed or rewarded by the outside world. Most of those I interviewed had this quality. One, for example, commented on his reserve and his reluctance to confide his personal problems to others:

> I'm outwardly very friendly and open and all of those things, outgoing and the rest, but still I never talk to people about my problems. That has organizational repercussions, because I don't say that there *are* problems, and so people think that things are going better than they should. Secondly, people don't take responsibility off my shoulders, because I don't want to admit that there are problems.

Whatever the organizational problems created by this young man's inner reserve, his tolerance for isolation enabled him to endure prolonged periods of Movement work. In him, as in others, the loneliness of early adolescence had prepared him for the loneliness of some of his later work in the New Left.

The problems of group encapsulation were also hard to deal

with. The intensification of neurotic interaction, and tendencies toward polarization and conformity within Movement groups tended to "cool out" young radicals who could not maintain control and perspective on what they were doing. One young radical, recalling one group he had worked with, said:

> In some cases, there was a marked tendency on people's part to lower their own level of intellect. If I stepped back and looked, I could see myself doing that. Because you were so afraid of putting people down. You would stop in the middle of a sentence and change the words. . . .
>
> You were constantly trying, you were constantly making an effort to be relaxed, to stay cool, not to go absolutely out of your mind. It just changed the way you dealt with all sorts of situations. You know, they were things which might, in the outside context, really have upset you. But here you wouldn't let them upset you. You couldn't let them upset you. You didn't show any feeling about it. You just, well, stoically accepted it. It was a kind of enforced stoicism, because you had to be cool. Those people that didn't really just went "pow!" They had a lot of problems. They couldn't deal with it.

The demand for emotional control in enclosed Movement groups comes through in this recollection: keeping "relaxed," staying "cool," and not showing "any feeling" were essential in order not to go "pow!"

Another factor that makes some young radicals drop out of the Movement is their own intransigent ideological position. Given the pressures toward conformity within any small and isolated group, those who hold doctrinaire positions that they cannot compromise without feeling a loss of personal integrity are almost required to drop out. Some leave the Movement altogether, while others join more sectarian Old Left groups where their particular ideological commitments are shared by others. Only those who are "flexible" enough to yield to group pressure can go on working with others despite their disagreements.

Given the problems of prolonged work in the New Left, it is clear that individuals with special personal styles, defenses, outlooks, and talents are most likely to survive. Among the qualities that had enabled the young radicals who led Vietnam Summer to persist in the Movement were their capacity for detachment and emotional control, and their ability to tolerate loneliness and estrangement from the mainstream without feeling personally undermined or threatened. But perhaps the single most important requisite for persistence was a capacity to retain individuality and "separateness" even within a solidary and intensely interacting group, to keep distance and perspective, and to preserve private resources not totally dependent upon harmonious relations with others or on successful accomplishment of group objectives. Then, too, a capacity for a kind of gallows humor—an ability to crack a joke when the tension was greatest, to laugh when the going was worst—helped some of these radicals to survive moments of special conflict and tension. Perspective, a capacity for distance, and humor all presuppose a high degree of self-control with regard to anger and any inner propensity to violence. This capacity had made it possible for these young radicals, not to "act out" their clearly felt anger during intense group or community conflict, but to act so as to preserve the smooth functioning of the group.

Stated in another way, continuing commitment to Movement work seems to require the development of a *radical identity,* as contrasted with mere support for specific radical aims and tactics. Confronted by the endemic frustrations of the New Left, the radical must not stake his entire sense of self on the use of any particular tactic or the adoption of any special position. Only if he defines himself as "a radical" and keeps his underlying sense of integrity, despite the need to compromise and accept views to which he is sometimes opposed, can he tolerate the rigors of Movement work.

Other characteristics required for persistence in the New Left are willingness to work hard for low wages and few immediate rewards, plus a strong sense of responsibility. The young radicals who led Vietnam Summer had a considerable ability to undertake a job and carry it through to completion, and to accept hard, boring, and tedious work. What they called "shit work" is of course ubiquitous in all organizations. But it is a special problem in the small primary groups of the New Left, where the ordinary solution of hiring others to do menial work is usually unavailable for both ideological and financial reasons. A willingness on the part of highly intelligent and capable young men and women to do shit work is therefore crucial. On the blackboard in the office of one of the national co-directors of Vietnam Summer, his co-workers had chalked the wry motto, "even Mao does shit work," an allusion to the fact that he had someone to type for him. This capacity for hard work also served as an antidote to depression:

> There were several instances where I had been very down. But I had gotten over it by just throwing myself back into work, with twice as much energy as I would normally have done, burying myself in my work. [K. K.: What were you burying?] Well, a lot of uncertainties. [Pause] [K. K.: Do you mean personal uncertainties or political uncertainties?] More personal uncertainties than political ones. Not about "What am I doing? Is this the right thing I should do?" . . . It's not that. It's more a question of what I am, what I've done on my own, my abilities, that kind of thing.

Another tactic employed to counter the frustrations of the New Left was sheer physical mobility. At times of intense discouragement and anger, physical movement, travel, and a change of locale had often "saved" them. Some had held positions where lecturing, visiting local chapters of the organization they worked for, recruiting, or doing co-ordinating work were possible. Others had reached a point where they felt they had to allow themselves a vacation, a return "home" for a week or a month, or a visit to friends in another city to gain greater psychological distance. As a group, these young radicals are enormously mobile in their personal habits. At home with the complex technology of transportation and communication that interconnects American life, they can move with little sense of uprootedness from one end of the continent to the other. The term "Movement" as applied to the New Left also points to the mobility of the radical, the fact that his home is the Movement, and that he is at home with the fact of geographic movement as well.

The problems and frustrations of Movement work are many. And most of those who "enter" the Movement are pushed out or drop out because of these frustrations. Some seem to have dropped out partly because they were frightened by their sense of increasing estrangement from the System. Some left because of their own excessive emotional involvement in intragroup conflicts; others, because they could not tolerate the failure to achieve the goals of the New Left. Some were pushed out because their co-workers found them too abrasive and dominating: such individuals tended to become involved in violent struggles for leadership, or to feel personally humiliated and undermined when obliged to compromise. Sheer fatigue and weariness led others to become discouraged and leave; and the tug of the academic world seems to have drawn many others back to their formal studies. Still others found that Movement work, far from relieving their psychological problems and symptoms, merely exacerbated them. A few abandoned the New Left for the more factional Old Left. A number returned to the "Establishment options" they had temporarily abandoned, attempting to change the System from within rather than without. And some, wearied by the unavailing struggle of Movement work, became pessimistic about the possibilities of social change and turned to the far reaches of personal change through the psychedelic drugs.

Even for those who remained, like these young radicals, continuing involvement in the New Left exacts a price. It requires a high degree of psychological integration and self-control. It involves forgoing many of the conventional satisfactions available to other equally talented young Americans—a safe, sure, and well-remunerated career in a respected university, organization, or agency; continuing formal education; geographic settledness, and, for most, marriage and family. It is not only frustrating, but at times infuriating: it requires living without tangible success, accepting continual compromise and accommodation, renouncing the possibility of exercising power over one's co-workers, and confronting a community that, when not violently opposed to the radical, tends to be elusive or indifferent. The physiological price of Movement work is shown by the commonness of psychosomatic ulcers among Movement workers involved in prolonged work in hostile communities. It is a standard Movement joke that you can tell community organizers at a party, because they drink only milk. Although overstated, the joke points to the toll of organizing work: a certain suppression of feelings, an inhibition of rage, and the possibility that—for those who are physiologically predisposed—suppressed feelings may be translated into the heightened autonomic activity that can corrode the lining of the stomach.

But merely to emphasize persistence and survival is to state the radical commitment in a more negative way than any of those I interviewed would have done. What they themselves emphasize are the rewards of Movement work. Perhaps the greatest of these rewards is their *growing sense of rightness,* in both meanings of this ambiguous term. On the one hand, these young radicals feel that what they are doing is psychologically "right" for them—in accordance with their needs, responsive to their talents. At the same time, "rightness" means a feeling of ethical and political justification, a conviction that Movement work (though frustrating and difficult) is unquestionably in accord with their own principles.

This inner sense of rightness may help explain why these young radicals can approach the future with such apparent calm and openness. Just as their becoming radicals was the result of a series of "natural" and unreflective steps, so their continuing work in the New Left retains the same quality of naturalness and inevitability. One Vietnam Summer leader, for example, was offered a Poverty-Program job after the summer of 1967 that would have paid him over ten thousand dollars a year. He was amused and flattered by the offer, but he never seriously considered it—his present work earns him thirty dollars a week. The rightness of his work, the satisfactions of doing work in keeping with his basic principles and psychological needs, make Movement work more rewarding. Although these radicals often questioned their effectiveness and bemoaned their personal, intellectual, or political inadequacies, the rightness of their objectives was not at issue.

For example, I asked one young radical how he dealt with the many discouragements of his work. He answered:

> One thing is that sometimes you were involved in a political movement that was really successful, and you remember that. That keeps you going for a long time—the fact that it could have been done. . . .
>
> I mean I just wouldn't drop out. . . . If you keep reading or seeing the kind of the things that go on in the world or in this country—I would feel much too guilty to really drop out. I don't expect success to come very soon, so I'm sort of protected against that. . . . In the meanwhile, I have a good life, lots of friends. If you just don't decide to expect overwhelming success, you're okay.

This reply is premised on the essential rightness of what he is doing. He need only look at the world around him, and "I would feel much too guilty to drop out." He recalls the successes of the past, and consoles himself with "a good life, lots of friends." But what really keeps him going is his unquestioning sense that what he is doing is worth while.

Beyond this shared sense of rightness, each of those I interviewed gave his own reasons why his work in the New Left had been satisfying. One, for example, recalled an incident in the South:

> They had an all-night meeting on New Year's Eve, a night-watch meeting in the church, where they had singing and praying and preaching. There was a gospel group there, and as the evening wore on, one of the local civil rights leaders was talking. Up until then, we had been moving in and out of the county, not staying during the night, but just moving in during the day and leaving every night. We were now at the point where we were looking for families we could stay and work with in the county full time.
>
> All of a sudden that night there was this big commotion in the back of the church, and Bill said to me, "Hey, Rick, go tell those

> people to be quiet." These four women were arguing very heatedly about something. And I said, "Look, it's your church and you go tell them." And he said, "No, you go back and tell them." And do you know what they were arguing over? Who was going to put me up, and who was going to put up my friend, and who was going to put up my other friend. Here were these people who literally had nothing, and they were fighting for possession of us. It just blew my mind. It was such a great feeling.

Although this young man by no means found a permanent home among those he worked with, experiences like these helped to keep him going.

Asked what had enabled him to persist, this same radical first mentioned his conviction that the kind of organizing work he was doing "had to be done," so it was "necessary" for people to "stay on and to try to help that along." He continued:

> Then I also had very close personal relationships with a lot of the people I was working with. . . . There were several families I really felt just very, very close to. . . . There was Ma Jackson, she was a kind of second mother. She was somebody I could talk to about problems, and she really just understood. She was so sweet and so nice. She was real. A very strong and a very vital person. And there were others. . . . We could talk about things in general. It was just sort of being able to talk to people about things other than political and Movement problems.

His ability to find warm friends and even a "kind of second mother" outside the enclosed Movement world was a major source of the satisfaction he derived from his work.

Another, recalling two years of organizing work, said:

> It wasn't exciting particularly, but I was doing a job that I was interested in, that I got a reward from, in the sense that people thought I was important and people thought I was a significant person for doing these things. I love to do political things. Working in terms of radical political activities was a meaningful job, it was one that could give meaning to my life, and that's why I did it. I wasn't happy personally in the sense that I didn't enjoy every minute of what I was doing. Maybe I was generally *un*happy

> because I was working too hard. But it was a satisfying life generally when I look back on it. . . .

The rewards of Movement work for this young man involved his sense of being "important" and "significant," his "love" of doing political things, and, perhaps most important, the fact that radical political activities "could give meaning to my life."

Another, asked why he persisted, answered:

> Partly it's [pause] you have to do what you think. . . . If you're very sure about what you believe, you go ahead and do it. From early on, I was surer about the details than I've gotten to be since. Since then, I've questioned many of the things I'd learned when I was a child, although not the essence of it. I've become much more flexible, and it has involved more decision-making on my part as to what I thought. Then also, I've been active in order to be involved in a social group. This was something I could do. In high school, I was always miles ahead of other people in political sophistication.

In this statement, too, the rightness of Movement work is interwoven with other factors of idiosyncratic importance: his increased flexibility, his satisfaction at his involvement in a "social group," his having found a group of peers who are his equal in "political sophistication."

Another major reward of Movement work was the feeling of personal growth that had come from it. One young woman, summarizing her years of work in the Movement, said:

> I feel as though I had a very long maturation. But maybe it's been somewhat more critical, and given me a more solid foundation. I just don't know.

Others stressed in different ways the contribution of Movement work to their psychological growth. One, after commenting on the importance of sexual expression and love in his personal development, added:

> But politics and political struggle were my avenues toward some self-respect, without which loving someone else is pretty tough. . . .

For this young man, as for most of his peers in Vietnam Summer, the connection between the political and the personal, the sexual and the ideological, is very close, and one of the chief rewards of work in the New Left has been that it relieved him of a feeling of "self-destructive" stagnation and permitted him to begin to move again as a person.

But it would be wrong to emphasize only the ethical and psychological rewards of Movement work. Those who led Vietnam Summer enjoyed it. For all of their principled sense of responsibility, these young men and women, throughout the summer, were lighthearted and cheerful. One said of the Vietnam Summer political staff:

> This is the dancingest group of people that I know. In terms of the frug and the this and the that. . . . For instance, a party that is held is not the usual political party; everybody is dancing, and enjoying themselves and having fun. And, for example [at a recent party, people from the old New Left], generally, *they* were talking. But everybody from Vietnam Summer was dancing. I don't know what that means, but it is a significant sociological fact. Maybe it means that people are closer together, or that they are more tense.

No doubt both tension and closeness contributed to the good cheer that enveloped much of the summer. "When is the next party?" was a common conversation opener when Vietnam Summer workers met in the corridor of their headquarters. Although these young men and women possessed a great capacity for self-control, they were not joyless zealots. Along with their capacity for restraint went an ability for enjoyment, abandon, and zest. The planning and conduct of the frequent parties that interlaced the summer were matters of continual half-serious, half-joking discussion. More important, many of those I interviewed were involved in intense sexual relationships, and these relationships also constituted a major source of personal renewal and strength. Such relationships were almost always with other young radicals; and though not married, those I interviewed were basically "monogamous" and viewed their partners with a strong sense of love and responsibility. The Pill meant that marriage could await the desire to have children; and while the women interviewed were predictably more concerned with the issue of having a family, both men and women generally agreed that marriage and childbearing should be deferred.

Restraint and self-control, then, were balanced in most of those interviewed by an ability for abandon and passion, which gave this group a special quality of zest. In their own past lives, control had usually come first, epitomized by the asceticism of early adolescence. But out of this asceticism had come a lesson about the value of the senses that a few of those I interviewed were still struggling to let themselves live out: these few felt they were still too puritanical. But most were merely grateful that they had come so far from the guilt-ridden moralism of their earlier years.

The rewards of Movement work, then, are many and mixed. Perhaps most important is the sense that the work is important, right, and even necessary. In addition, these particular young radicals felt that their involvement in the Movement had contributed to their personal growth, assisting them in the resolution of older problems and making them "better" people. Despite the smallness of their Movement and the loneliness of much Movement work, they felt less isolated than before; their work gave them a sense of their own significance and of being amongst their peers; it gave meaning to their lives. And they had fun doing it.

One young man, after a lengthy discussion of the weaknesses of Vietnam Summer, concluded:

> But I think the whole summer was very good and very worth while, not only for me personally but from the point of view of the Movement. We got a lot of people feeling things and talking about things. [He talks about meeting with a group of eighty-five students who had been "recruited" through Vietnam Summer.] That's the kind of thing that doesn't get mentioned in the headlines. Those kids were fresh. Very few of them were faction-fighter types. And they were all very willing and eager to work. I found that really refreshing and good. . . .
>
> We had a Goddamn good staff. Not only the people there were smart, and knew how to organize things, to get people in motion, but they realized the necessity—most of them—for some kind of

continuity, some kind of regularity. Not only that but they were great people personally. We had a lot of fun working together. I've seen a lot of groups where political debates get very personal, where there are sparks of electricity flying for weeks on political grounds. But we didn't have that. We all worked out pretty well.

The continuation of change

Becoming a radical has not meant the cessation of change and personal development. On the contrary, change has, if anything, accelerated since these young men and women came to think of themselves as part of the Movement. To be sure, its context and quality are now different. Formerly, personal change was associated with introspection, self-analysis, and self-consciousness. As they became increasingly involved with the work of the New Left, these young radicals became less self-absorbed, more focused upon changing themselves in the context of their work. The goal of change also differs: they now seek not only to become "better people," but to acquire the skills necessary for their work. Their despairs are increasingly tied in with the loss of motion in the Movement; many of the rewards of Movement work also derive from the sense of personal and group development it yields. Even the fact that these young radicals have not committed themselves to occupation or family is related to their continuing desire to avoid being "tied down" to institutional obligations that might limit their freedom to change and to move.

When I commented to one young radical that he seemed to have overcome successfully many of the problems that concerned him in adolescence, he answered:

Yeah. Well, it was consciously done. I knew. I realized what I had to do. I went about doing it. . . . But I do that even now, in terms of things I see I have to do, or have to learn how to do. Maybe it'll take two or three years to learn to do them. In other words, I'm trying to change my personality all the time—as well as other things. But the first is a little more difficult. [Laughs]

In "trying to change my personality all the time—as well as other things," this young man underlines the importance for him of continuing personal and social change.

It is significant that these young men and women consider themselves part of a movement, rather than a party, an organization, a bureaucracy, an institution, a cadre, or a faction. The term "movement" suggests a spontaneous, natural, and non-institutional group; it again points to their feeling that they are in motion, changing, and developing. Moreover, theirs is a Movement *for* Social Change—one that attempts to alter social, political, and international history. Finally, "movement" summarizes the radical's perception of the modern world, a world itself in flux, unstable, continually changing.

The concepts of movement, process, and change are therefore central to understanding these radicals. As individuals, they have undergone an extremely complex psychological development that, despite many core continuities with the past, is nonetheless a history of continuing change. In their work, they emphasize process rather than program. They avoid fixed ideologies and dogmatic positions that would freeze them to a particular time or situation. They remain exceptionally open to the future, prepared to be moved by it even as they attempt to change it. Their responses to current events are often, for better or worse, situational, *ad hoc,* and based on the needs of the present. They have tied their psychological fates to the fate of a movement that seeks to create social change. And although they are estranged from most of the traditional structures of their society, they are nonetheless deeply identified with the rapidly changing world in which they live. Psychological change, the movement for social change, and the changing modern world are linked in them.

This linkage means that predictions about their future are extraordinarily difficult. Although they are psychological adults, they have not made the institutional commitments that give stability and predictability to the lives of most adults. Having chosen neither occupation nor family, they remain "free" to develop as most of their contemporaries are not. Yet paradoxically, by their involvement in a movement that is highly dependent on national and international history, they have put their personal fates more directly in the hands of politics and history than are the fates of most of their contemporaries. Furthermore, increasing age alone will mean that they cannot remain "young radicals" indefinitely, and the passage of years will require of them new adaptations. In all these respects, despite their openness to the future, their futures will be unusually tied to events over which they have no control.

But if little can be said about how they will change in the future, something can be said about the changes in their lives so far. I began this account of their personal development by presenting two hypotheses, which I called the radical-rebel hypothesis and the red-diaper-baby hypothesis. The first argues, in essence, that radicalism is a kind of displacement of feelings about family conflicts onto the wider social scene. The radical is intolerant of authority because he is rebelling against the authority of his family. The red-diaper-baby hypothesis, in contrast, posits complete continuity in values, actions, and outlook between the radical and his family. Radicals are simply chips off the old block, the new generation that lives out the values and repeats the actions of the old.

The preceding chapters should make clear how oversimplified both of these hypotheses are. The actual development of these particular young radicals is a dialectic of continuity in change, stability in transformation. As the red-diaper-baby hypothesis would have it, continuity is indeed important. Many of the central issues in their present lives were prefigured in their childhoods: their special sensitivity to principle, their early sense of specialness, their concern with the issues of struggle, conflict, and violence. While the stage on which these issues are enacted has changed, the underlying issues endure. Indeed, in one respect, becoming a radical meant a return, rather than a rebellion—a return to actualize the childhood sense of being different, a return to fidelity to the core principles of early life, a return to the issues of anger, rage, and violence in order to overcome them once again.

But change is equally present. Even in the three young radicals who come from radical families, their reconciliation with parental radicalism is far from complete, and it was accomplished only through inner conflict, turmoil, and outer rebellion. Indeed, these children of radicals were among those who rebelled *most* violently against their parents. And all three, though they accepted their parents' basic values, rejected their parents' inactivity, ineffectuality, or acquiescence, together with many of the specifics of their formal political ideology. Also, in discussing the adolescences of all these young radicals, I have noted two major discontinuities, one in early adolescence, one at the gates of adulthood. In the crisis of early adolescence, the psychological stability of childhood crumbled, and an abrupt reversal of feeling and behavior took place. Childhood specialness now became a frightening sense of inner difference; high childhood principles became moralistic self-condemnations; and early sensitivity to conflict became an adolescent fear of passion and an angry denunciation of parents.

In later adolescence, continuity with childhood was re-established—the pattern of intellectual achievement, leadership, and success was resumed. But this new equilibrium also proved provisional. Faced with imminent entry into adulthood, they faltered, turned their backs on the Establishment options, and little by little became immersed in the New Left. In one sense, these young radicals "rebelled" twice: first, against their parents and the inconsistencies of their immediate environments; second, against the options that society offered them as adults. Finding none of these options morally satisfying, they (and others of their generation) chose an option outside of the System—the identity of a radical.

Many commentators have connected radicalism with psychological problems about authority. But among those I interviewed, such problems did not seem especially important. Doubtless there are other young radicals to whom this explanation applies. In other contexts, I have interviewed young men and women (not radicals) for whom obedience to, or rejection of, authority was in fact a crucial issue. But in general, the young radicals who led

Vietnam Summer were characterized by an unusual insight into the connections between their personal lives and political lives, their pasts and their presents. And in neither their accounts nor my inferences did the issue of authority loom large. When these young men and women criticize the President of the United States, it is not so much because they cannot tolerate constituted authority, as because they consider the President's policies contrary to their own fundamental principles—which they take to be the principles of this country. When they distrust the pronouncements and promises of government officials, it is not so much that they are irrationally distrustful of those in positions of power, but that their own experience has given them reason to mistrust these pronouncements and promises. And the wariness of these young radicals toward some of their elders seemed less a rebellious projection of hatred of their fathers than a reflection of the very real differences in outlook and style that separate the generations. The early attempts of these young radicals to "work within the System" suggest that their first impulse was to trust authorities and authoritative agencies; it was through experience that they turned away.

It would be wrong, then, simply to call these young men and women rebels against authority. Their early adolescent rebellions were generally brief, and they have been largely resolved into a complex perception of their parents as people. And turning toward the New Left after late adolescence was not so much a rejection of the authority of their parents and society, as a dissatisfaction with themselves—a sense of their *own* inadequacy, of the "wastefulness" of the lives *they* were leading, of the "self-destructiveness" of *their* activities. The principals of their schools, the presidents of their colleges, and some of their potential employers clearly judged their behavior rebellious. But to these young men and women themselves, it felt more like a search. And the resolution of this search was not a simple break with their pasts or with society, but a complex rejoining of both. Part of what they re-established was connection with their own ethical sense, a fusion of action and principle, of will and moral sense, of superego and ego. They thus achieved a sense of being on good terms with their own consciences that is vouchsafed few of their contemporaries. And their repudiation of the Establishment options, their growing sense of estrangement from the mainstream, was also a commitment to the future of their society and an acceptance of the time-honored and traditional identity of the radical.

In all of these radicals there is also an underlying continuity between the non-political, personal, ethical values taught in their families as children, and the values they now seek to implement in their work. All of these young men and women agree that the *political* values of their parents are dated—the products of a different generation, irrelevant to the needs of modern America. But their parents' *personal* values—responsibility, seriousness, honesty, concern with people—have been largely accepted, and these personal values now underlie much of the radicals' commitment. Yet at the same time, a powerful motive for radicalism is not only the desire to implement the parents' principles, but is an equally powerful wish to *avoid* the ineffectuality, failure to act, or "compromises" of these same parents. Neither the radical-rebel hypothesis nor the red-diaper-baby theory in any way suggests this complex dialectic of continuity and movement.

Out of this complex dialectic of growth has come an unusual degree of psychological integration. Being radicals has enabled them to synthesize previously conflicting needs, to overcome earlier inhibitions, and to resolve many of the "hang-ups" of earlier adolescence. Obsessional symptoms vanished, leaving in their wake only an unusual capacity for single-minded dedication to a task. The leaden depressions of the past flattened into the milder and often quite realistic discouragements of the present. The fantasy world of knights and peasants was transmuted into the actual world of attempting to create a New Left in America. Those who came from a radical tradition became increasingly able to accept its full burden without being overwhelmed by it; those in manifestly violent rebellion against their fathers became more able to perceive the positive components in their identifications with them. So, too, the negative pole of specialness—the fear of being especially wrong, especially guilty, or especially unworthy—was transvalued. In its place, these young radicals are now able to see themselves as part of a group with special values, recognized by others as a part of that group and yet adequate, competent, and individual in themselves.

As individuals, the young radicals I interviewed possess many of the characteristics of high levels of psychological integration, flexibility, and "adaptive" functioning. They have been able to establish continuity with some aspects of their parental tradition, while repudiating, without excessive conflict, other aspects of this tradition. Their earlier symptoms have largely disappeared; and their aggravated conflicts with their parents have now become milder and less important. As a group, these are committed young men and women with a capacity for work, for love, and for play. They have learned to tolerate frustration, arduous work, and even defeat. Indeed, in the short run at least, "winning" is no longer necessary: what is important is the continuing effort to create new tactics, institutional forms, and intellectual formulations that can help transform the modern world. For these particular young radicals, then, the "identity" of a radical has thus far been integrative and satisfying; they are exemplars of one unusual but nonetheless highly successful form of personal development.

Yet merely to emphasize the high degree of adaptation, psychological synthesis, and resolution of past conflict in these young radicals is not enough. Although I have stressed the unusual psychological openness and insight of this group, the conflicts of the past are still often visible in the inner and outer tensions of their present lives. Some are troubled by these residues of the past; others are less conscious of them. But in each one, there is invariably some small or large unresolved conflict—the reaction against the inadequacy of a father, a heightened identification with the ambitions of a mother, or the only partially successful effort to overcome the sense of superiority that is one kind of specialness.

To call this a "conflict-free" group would be an overstatement; it would be more exact to say that these young radicals have been unusually able to find or create lives and a sense of themselves that enable them to live out their inner strengths, minimize their inner weakness, and reconcile their ambivalences.

The psychological fate and personal stability of these young radicals are unusually tied to the fate and stability of the Movement. Just as their entry into the New Left coincided with the "cure" of many of the anxieties, depressions, and other problems of earlier years, their continued well-being may be partly dependent upon the continuation of Movement work. Whatever their inner resources, these young men and women have many needs that may be hard to fulfill outside of their Movement. Among these are the central issues of their lives: specialness, concern with conflict and violence, a high devotion to principle, personal independence, and, perhaps most important, a desire to continue their own growth and development without becoming mired in some fixed position or personal form. After adolescence, all of our fates are increasingly tied to the fortunes of the individuals, groups, and institutions to which we become committed. But this is even more true of these young radicals: while they have avoided ties to conventional institutions, occupations, and even to families, their psychological well-being is paradoxically even more dependent than that of their "adjusted" contemporaries on the political future of their Movement, as well as on the future of American society and the world. It is safe to predict that the strength and stability of these young radicals will be tested repeatedly in the future, and that if their Movement fails to prosper, they too may falter.

From a clinical perspective, too, there is much in these young radicals that does not conform to our view of "typical" development after adolescence. These young men and women, while they have unusually strong commitments, have very few specific plans; their statements about their own futures are invariably vague and hedged about with conditions. Despite my frequent use of the term "identity" to characterize their sense of self, identity formation in these young men and women is far less complete than for most of their contemporaries. They do not view themselves as "finished"; they deliberately expose themselves to new experiences in efforts to create the conditions for personal change; they have not "settled down" like most of their age-mates. When asked how they visualize themselves twenty years from now, they turn to a discussion of the social and political future of America and the world. And they have neither regular occupations nor families of their own. From a diagnostic perspective, then, one might view these young radicals as suffering from a "protracted adolescence," still immersed during their mid-twenties in an "unresolved identity crisis."

Yet before such judgments with their pejorative connotations are sealed, we should recall the special involvement of these young men and women with social and historical changes that have yet to occur. "Leaders" in a Movement without leaders, "revolutionaries" who believe their revolution will take a generation or more to achieve, and people strongly identified with the changing historical process they seek to affect, they have linked their emerging identities to an emerging movement for social change that may never occur. Given this fusion of inner identity with ongoing historical process, it follows that their development *must* be more unfinished than that of their peers who have joined their selfhoods to more conventional and circumscribed tasks. It may be that the radical must "stretch" his development over a longer period than his adjusted contemporaries. Perhaps his identity can be achieved, if ever, only with the socio-political transformations he seeks.

In the end, how one judges the psychological development of such young men and women is not fully separable from how one judges their principles and their works. They exhibit many of the qualities we ordinarily associate with psychological integration, complexity, and effectiveness. Yet in their commitment to the New Left, as in the individual style each brings to it, one can invariably perceive the residues of childhood conflict, early assumptions, and parental precept. Those who consider the values and work of these young radicals as being without merit, unrealistic, or destructive will be able to find in this account evidence that they are merely "acting out" the conflicts of their childhoods in their present commitments.

To me, however, such a judgment would seem incomplete, for it overlooks the fact that throughout their lives all men and women live out the conflicts, assumptions, and precepts of their childhood. In this respect, the new radicals are no different from old radicals, new and old conservatives, liberals, or the simply apathetic. What matters is not the inevitable residue of childhood in the adult's life, but what becomes of that residue—whether it undermines or informs his life, whether it inhibits or invigorates, whether it promotes productivity and care or destructiveness and indifference. My own judgment should therefore be clear: whatever the continuing conflicts in these young radicals, they have so far shown an unusual capacity to integrate the issues of their childhoods into lives that are productive and concerned.

Accident, obedience, and history

A psychological study of a group of political activists may leave the impression that psychological factors, because they are most closely examined, provide an adequate account of these individuals. In psychological interviews, we perceive the world through the eyes of the subject, gaining some access to his inner world of motives, fantasies, and rationalizations. But with this method, we cannot see clearly how the subject affected those around him, when he misperceived or distorted what "really" happened to him, or how much of what really happened to him happened because he *made* it happen. In interviews, we can glimpse only that part of the social and historical scenery of which the individual himself was aware, or whose existence we can infer in the background of his observations. Both interviewer and interviewee tacitly agree to take for granted most of what the sociologist, the student of culture, the historian, or the political scientist would deem most interesting: the history of the Movement, the shifting and often contradictory values of the culture, the wider political scene, the social matrix. The power of this unspoken agreement was illustrated on several occasions when one of these young men and women apologized for comments on the social, historical, or political scene with, "Do you have time for this?" Although I invariably said I did, such apologies make clear how much was left out of these interviews.

Some of the omissions of my account so far deserve to be underscored. In emphasizing the psychological meaningfulness of the development of radicals, I have not adequately noted the importance of what, from a psychological point of view, appear to be "accidents." The development of these young radicals was often profoundly affected by things that "happened" to them through no plan, motive, or design of their own: a major family illness; the psychological problems of brothers or sisters; a chance move to another school in another city. No one can weigh exactly the impact of such events upon a developing individual: much depends on his stage of development and his sensitivities at the time. But neither can anyone deny that they have a powerful impact. In several instances, for example, major family upheavals in early adolescence deprived young radicals of parental attention, forcing them to become independent long before most adolescents do. In another case, the "accident" of going to a private school reinforced psychological tendencies that might not otherwise have been strengthened.

Also, I have largely accepted these young radicals' view that becoming radicals involved turning away from the Establishment options as they approached adulthood. But as these young men and women do not note, their radicalism is also a special kind of obedience. As a social phenomenon, today's radicalism is the obedient answer of a few members of the younger generation to the desperate plea of the older generation to "clean up the mess we have made." Radicalism is also a response to the perceived needs of American society, and to the traditional American ideology that has always made the aspirations and idealism of youth the source of social renewal. And more specifically, for these young men and women to become radicals was often to obey the implicit requests of crucial adults in their environment. They remain largely true to the core values of their childhood families. And many of them, in addition, complied with their parents' wishes that they enter public life—even though few of their parents had radicalism in mind.

Recall, too, the number of times these young men and women, long before they became radicals, were told that they were "too independent," "too cosmopolitan," and perhaps even "too idealistic" to fit into this or that conventional social role. Such characterizations provide a young man or woman with a provisional, if negative, identity. By later becoming a radical, he accepts and transvalues that identity, now affirming his independence, cosmopolitanism, or idealism in a group where these qualities are honored. Even more important, radicalism involves a profound fidelity to many of the fundamental values of American society. Although the changes in institutions and policies proposed by the New Left are often revolutionary, and the means proposed to attain them are sometimes disruptive, the essential values of the New Left are, after all, the traditional values of American democracy: peace, justice, freedom, participation, equality. And finally, as I have noted, the radical and a group of his contemporaries enter into a tradition of radicals and revolutionaries who were often without honor in their own times, but were revered by the generations that followed.

Radicalism, then, is more than a psychological matter. Or, put more precisely, the psychology of these radicals is the psychology of a group of young men and women whose lives and present identities are profoundly linked to their Movement, to American society, and to the history of the modern world. More self-consciously than most of their fellows, these young men and women are responsive to, identified with, and actors on the stage of history. They are joined with the age-old history of radicals and revolutionaries; but they are also the unique products of the modern world. The words to describe the development of these young radicals are the same words to describe the history of the post-war era—process, movement, change, growth, development, openness, and flux. We cannot understand these young radicals without attempting to understand the changing, affluent, and violent historical era in which they have lived.

7 Change, affluence, and violence

The young radicals I interviewed were born near the end of the Second World War, and their earliest memories date from the years just after it. Their parents were born around the time of the First World War; their grandparents are, without exception, the children of the nineteenth century. Their parents are thus members of the first modern generation to emerge from the Victorian era. And these young radicals are the first products of the post-war world, the first post-modern generation. In tracing the story of their lives, I have discussed the personal meaning of three central themes: change, affluence, and violence; in each, the psychological, the social, the political, and the historical are fused. And each of these issues was so much a part of the young radicals' lives that it is only by stepping aside to consider the historical ground on which they grew that we can perceive the impact on these lives of the history of the post-war era.

In the last chapter, I argued that the issue of change is pervasive in the development of these young men and women. Despite their underlying ties to their personal and familial pasts, their development has involved major alterations, reversals, and reassimilations of that past. As young adults, they remain acutely aware of how far they have come, of the differences between their generation and their parents'. More than that, they have in their own lives witnessed and experienced social and historical changes on an unprecedented scale, lived through the Cold War, the McCarthy era, the Eisenhower period, the short administration of Kennedy and the long one of Johnson. By becoming involved with the New Left, they have linked themselves to a moving, changing movement of dissenting youth. And as individuals, even in their early adulthood, they remain open to the future, eager to change, "in motion."

Similarly, the fact of affluence is crucial to their lives. Not one of these young men and women comes from a background of deprivation, poverty, discrimination, or want. From their earliest years they have simply taken for granted that there would be enough—not only enough to survive, but enough for a vacation every year, a television set, a family car, and a good education. They grew up in a world where they and virtually everyone they knew took prosperity and the luxuries it provides most Americans totally for granted. Until they reached adolescence and social consciousness, few of them were immediately aware of the facts of poverty, discrimination, and hunger. Their affluence provided them not only with economic security, but with the preconditions for the independence they exhibit in later life: families generally free from acute anxiety over status, thoughtful and well-educated parents, schools and colleges that—whatever their limitations—exposed them to many of the riches of world tradition, and the extraordinary privilege of a lengthy adolescence and youth in which to grow, to become more complex, to arrive at a more separate selfhood.

The issue of violence, and of the fear and anger it inspired, starts with the earliest memories of many of these young radicals. Recall the young man whose first memory involves his backyard parade at the end of World War II, and whose second memory is of his hysterical terror at the encyclopedia pictures of an atomic-bomb explosion and an army tank. Remember the angry and menacing mob in one early memory, the jealous rage at a younger brother in another, the "gruesome" fights in the playground in still another. Such early memories, of course, mean many things. They point to themes of lifelong importance; they can serve as a "screen" for other less conscious issues—as symbolic alternatives to what is not remembered—and they indicate something about the fears of the dreamer both when he was small and as an adult. Taken with the rest of what we now know about these young radicals, these memories indicate a special sensitivity to the issue of violence—inner and outer—that continues as a central theme in their lives.

These young radicals, then, are members of the first post-modern generation, and their lives are permeated with the history of the past two decades. They, and I as their interviewer, took such changes completely for granted, and rarely felt compelled to note their occurrence and significance. Indeed, in the last third of the twentieth century, we all take for granted the revolutionarily changing world in which we have lived from birth. Yet to understand better what these radicals have done and are attempting to do, to comprehend the style they are creating, requires that we also examine the historical ground of their development.

Change and the credibility gap

The twentieth century, as a whole, has been a period of unprecedentedly rapid social, industrial, ideological, and political change. But during the post-war era, the pace of change has increased still further, transforming the world in a way that no one, twenty-five years ago, could have anticipated. These post-war years have brought to the more advanced nations of the world a kind of affluence rarely even dreamed of before. They have seen the often violent liberation of the majority of the world's population from colonial rule. They have been a time of extraordinary scientific and technological innovation that has profoundly transformed our physical, human, social, and cultural environment. And no one can foresee the end of change.

In the last two decades, it has become increasingly obvious that extremely rapid social change is endemic to the modern world. It is unnecessary to chronicle in detail the specific changes that have occurred. Suffice it to note that the material and technological changes that are easiest to pinpoint and discuss constitute but a small part of the over-all process of social change. Even more important have been the less tangible, more gradual, often unnoticed yet radical transformations in social institutions, in the ways men relate to each other and their society, in interpretations of the world and of history, and in the definitions of the goals of life itself. Increasingly, we take such changes for granted, welcoming them, accommodating ourselves to them as best we can, growing used to a world where nothing is permanent. Partly for this reason, we have barely begun to understand the human effects of rapid, continual social change. Especially for the post-war generation, who have always known a world of flux and transformation, change is so much a part of life that they seldom reflect on its meaning. It is like the grammar of our language, or the quality of the air, or the face of a family member: we seldom stand back to notice.

Yet the forces that affect us most profoundly are often those we never stop to notice. In *The Uncommitted* I have discussed at greater length some of the human effect of chronic social change. All of these effects are evident in the lives of the young radicals who led Vietnam Summer. Even in these young men and women, for example, we see a gap between the generations, such that each generation must reconsider and re-examine the values of its heritage for itself. The parents of these particular young radicals have been able to establish a continuity in what I have called core values between themselves and their children. In this respect, there is probably *less* of a generational gap in the families of these young radicals than in the families of most of their contemporaries. But this continuity is at the level of basic personal values like honesty and responsibility, rather than at the level of specific political programs and social creeds. Even the children of old radicals simply take it for granted that their political values and goals will be different from those of their parents. As far as formal values are concerned, then, the prime symptom of the generational gap is apparent: both generations take more or less for granted that the public philosophies of parents are largely irrelevant to their children. In a time of rapid value change, it may be that the only possible value continuities between the generations must involve core values so broad, general, and basic that they can remain relevant despite a radically transformed human and social world.

Another corollary of rapid social change is a focus on the present as contrasted with the past and future. As the pace in social change accelerates, the relevance of the past (and of those like parents who are a part of it) decreases; similarly, the predictability and stability of the future as an object of planning lessens. No traditional verity can be accepted without testing its continuing validity: the skills, styles, rules, and truths of the past become quickly old-fashioned. Since the rate of social change is continually accelerating, and since, in the past, most efforts to predict the future have been dismal failures, the possibility of making concrete plans for the future decreases steadily. Whatever its many other meanings, the focus on the short range and the tactical in the New Left reflects the consciousness of many of today's youths that long-range planning is virtually impossible, given the many imponderables that make the best laid plans go astray. And the absence of utopian visions of the future among young radicals may not reflect a failure of imagination as much as an awareness that the future is simply impossible to anticipate.

Another consequence of a rapidly changing world is the emphasis placed on such psychological qualities as flexibility, openness, adaptability, and personal change. Men always identify themselves with what they take to be the nature of the historical process in which they are immersed: in a time of rapid social and historical change, psychological changeability is therefore stressed. But flexibility is also a way of coping with the demands of the modern historical process. In a stable society, changing individuals must at each stage of their psychological development accommodate themselves to the same static society. But in a rapidly changing society, individuals must adapt themselves at each stage of their personal development to a constantly different physical, human, and social environment. Fixed positions—be they fixed character traits, rigid defenses, absolutely held dogmas, or tenaciously acquired skills—are a commitment to obsolescence. To "keep up with the times," men and women must be ready to change—often radically—throughout their lives. This readiness is, of course, a salient quality in young radicals.

Even the ambivalences of these young radicals toward their parents of the same sex, and the extreme selectivity of their identifications with these parents, are connected to the fact of social change. In an era when the life-situations of children differ so drastically from the environments of their parents as children, simple and "total" identification between generations is rarely possible. Children recognize intuitively that their parents are the products of a different social and historical matrix, and become more selective about following in their footsteps. Parents, in turn, also tend to acknowledge these generational differences, and no longer dare demand the same filial loyalty, obedience, or imitation. Children must learn to winnow the historical chaff from the grain in identifying with their parents, just as these young radicals chose a few core values as their inheritance, rejecting the rest. The particular content of parental identifications among young radicals has many special features, but the need to be selective in identifying is inherent in an era of rapid change.

The major transformations of the past decades also contribute to a widespread sensitivity of today's youth to the *discrepancy between principle and practice,* and may help explain why the charges of insincerity, manipulation, and dishonesty are today so often leveled by the young against the old. During a time when values change with each generation, the values most deeply embedded in parents and expressed in their behavior in times of crisis are often very different from the more "modern" principles, ideals, and values that parents profess and attempt to practice in bringing up their children. Filial perception of this discrepancy between parental practice and principle may help explain the very widespread sensitivity amongst contemporary youth to the "hypocrisy" of the previous generation. Among the young radicals interviewed, the schism in the parental image seems related not only to the idiosyncratic behavior of specific parents, but to this broader problem of transmission of values in a time of rapid change.

The grandparents of today's twenty-year-olds were generally brought up during the pre–World War I years, heirs of a Victorian tradition as yet unaffected by the value revolutions of the twentieth century. They reared their own children, the parents of today's youth, in families that emphasized respect, the control of impulse, obedience to authority, and the traditional "inner-directed" values of hard work, deferred gratification and self-restraint. Their children, born around the time of the First World War, were thus raised in families that remained largely Victorian in outlook.

During their lifetimes, however, these parents (and in particular the most intelligent, well educated, and privileged of them) were exposed to a great variety of new values that often changed their formal convictions. During their youths in the 1920's and 1930's, major changes in American behavior and American values took place. For example, the "emancipation of women" in the 1920's, marked by the achievement of suffrage for women, coincided with the last major change in actual sexual behavior in America: during this period, women started to become the equal partners of men, who no longer sought premarital sexual gratification solely with women of a lower class. More important, the 1920's and 1930's were an era when older Victorian values were challenged, attacked, and all but discredited, especially in educated middle-class families. Young men and women who went to college during this period were influenced by "progressive," "liberal," and even psychoanalytic ideas that contrasted sharply with the values of their childhood families. Moreover, during the 1930's, many of the parents of today's upper-middle-class youth were exposed to, or involved with, the ideals of the New Deal, and sometimes to more radical interpretations of man, society, and history. And in the 1940's and 1950's, when it came time to raise their own children, the parents to today's youth were strongly influenced by "permissive" views of child-rearing that again clashed with the techniques by which they themselves had been raised. Thus, many middle-class parents moved during their lifetimes from the Victorian ethos in which they had been brought up to the less moralistic, more humanitarian, and more "expressive" values of their own adulthoods.

But major changes in values, when they occur in adult life, are likely to be less than complete. To have grown up in a family where unquestioning obedience to parents was expected, but to rear one's own children in an atmosphere of "democratic" permissiveness and self-actualization—and never to revert to the practices of one's own childhood—requires a change of values more comprehensive than most adults can achieve. Furthermore, behavior that springs from values acquired in adulthood often appears somewhat forced, artificial, or insincere to the sensitive observer. Children, always the most perceptive observers of their own parents, are likely to sense a discrepancy between their parents' avowed and consciously held values and their "basic instincts," especially with regard to child-rearing. In addition, the parental tendency to "revert to form" is greatest in times of family crisis, which, of course, have the weightiest effect upon children. No matter how "genuinely" parents hold their "new" values, many of them, when the chips are down, fall back on the lessons of their own childhoods.

In a time of rapid social change, then, a *credibility gap* is likely to open between the generations. Children are likely to perceive a discrepancy between what the parents avow as their values and the actual assumptions from which parental behavior springs in times of crisis. In the young radicals interviewed, the focal issue of adolescent rebellion against parents seems to have been just this discrepancy: the children argued that their parents' endorsement of independence and self-determination for their children was "hypocritical" because it did not correspond with the parents' actual behavior when their children seized the independence offered them. Similar perceptions of "hypocrisy" occurred for others around racial matters: there were a few parents who supported racial and religious equality in principle, but became upset when their children dated someone of another race or religion. Around political activity similar issues arose, especially during the 1950's. For example, many of the parents of today's youth espoused in principle the cause of political freedom; but most were not involved in politics themselves and some opposed their children's involvement lest they "jeopardize their records."

Of course, in no society do parents (or anyone else) ever fully live up to their own professed ideals. In every society, there is a gap between creedal values and actual practices; and everywhere the recognition of this gap constitutes a powerful motor for social change. But in most societies, especially when social change is slow and social institutions are powerful and unchanged, there occurs what can be called the *institutionalization of hypocrisy.* Children and adolescents routinely learn when it is "reasonable" to expect that the values parents profess will be implemented in their behavior, and when it is not reasonable. There develops an elaborate system of exegesis and commentary upon the society's creedal values, excluding certain people or situations from the full weight of these values or "demonstrating" that apparent inconsistencies are not really inconsistencies at all. Thus, in almost all societies, a "sincere" man who "honestly" believes one set of values is frequently allowed to ignore them completely, for example, in the practice of his business, in his interpersonal relationships, in dealings with foreigners, in relationships of his children, and so on—all because these situations have been defined by social consensus as exempt from the application of his creedal values.

In a time of rapid social change and value change, however, the institutionalization of hypocrisy tends to break down. "New" values have been in existence for so brief a period that the exemptions to them have not yet been defined, the situations to be excluded have not yet been determined. The universal gap between principle and practice appears without disguise. Thus, the mere fact of a discrepancy between creedal values and practice is not at all unusual. But what is special about the present situation of rapid value change is, first, that parents themselves tend to have two conflicting sets of values, one related to the experience of their early childhood, the other to the ideologies and principles acquired in adulthood; and, second, that no stable institutions or rules for defining hypocrisy out of existence have yet been fully evolved. In such a situation, the young see the Emperor in all his nakedness, recognizing the value conflict within their parents and perceiving clearly the "hypocritical" gap between ideal and behavior.

This argument suggests that the post-modern youth may not be confronted with a gap between parental preaching and practice that is "objectively" any greater than that facing most generations. But they do confront an unusual internal ambivalence within the parental generation over the very values that parents successfully inculcated in their children, and they are "deprived" of a system of social interpretation that rationalizes the discrepancy between creed and deed. It seems likely, then, that today's youth may simply be able to perceive the universal gulf between principle and practice more clearly than previous generations have done.

This points to one of the central characteristics of today's youth in general and young radicals in particular: they insist on taking seriously a great variety of political, personal, and social principles that "no one in his right mind" ever before thought of attempting to extend to such situations as dealings with strangers, relations between the races, or international politics. For example, peaceable openness has long been a creedal virtue in our society, but it has rarely been extended to foreigners, particularly those with dark skins. Similarly, equality has long been preached, but the "American dilemma" has been resolved by a series of institutionalized hypocrisies that exempted Negroes from the application of this principle. Love has always been a formal value in Christian societies, but really to love one's enemies—to be generous to policemen, customers, criminals, servants, or foreigners—has been considered folly.

The fact of social change, then, is not only distantly perceived by those who are growing up, but immediately interwoven with the texture of their daily lives as they develop. Many of the seemingly "special" characteristics of this small group of young radicals are connected not only to the vicissitudes of their individual histories, but to the history of their generation and of the modern world. The tenacity with which these young men and women adhere to a small number of the core values from their early family lives, their short-range plans, their absence of political program and visions of the future, and their enormous emphasis on openness, change, and process is both a reflection of, and a response to, a world changing at a dizzying rate in a direction that no one can foresee.

And these speculations on the credibility gap and the "deinstitutionalization of hypocrisy" in a time of rapid change may help explain two further facts about young radicals: first, they frequently come from highly principled families with whose core principles they continue to agree, but they often see their parents as somehow ineffectual in the practice of these principles; second, they have the outrageous temerity to insist that individuals and societies live by the values they preach. And these speculations may also explain the frequent feeling of many who have worked intensively with today's dissenting youth that, apart from the "impracticality" of some of their views, these sometimes seem to be the only clear-eyed and sane people in a society and a world where most of us are systematically blind to the traditional gap between personal principle and practice, national creed and policy.

The advent of automatic affluence

To any American who has grown up since the Second World War, one of the most important facts of life has been the continually increasing affluence around him. For all middle- and upper-class young Americans, as for increasing numbers of working-class youth, the fact of affluence is simply taken for granted—prosperity has become automatic. For example, although one or two of the young radicals who led Vietnam Summer came from lower-middle-class families and considered themselves "poor" during childhood, questions of income, security, social status, upward mobility, and finding a job were largely irrelevant when the time came for them to consider adult commitments. And when they realized during their adolescences that the affluence they so took for granted did not extend to all Americans—much less to the impoverished two-thirds of the world—they reacted with surprise, shock, and dismay. Material prosperity alone has made a difference in the development of this generation. The "luxuries" of an affluent age—electronic communications, rapid transport, good housing, physical comfort, readily available music, art, and literature, good health care and longevity—have helped give this generation its distinctive style. Without material affluence, the restlessness, mobility, and "wastefulness" of today's youth could hardly be understood.

But the impact of affluence extends considerably beyond its material benefits. "Affluence" can stand as shorthand for a variety of other changes in American institutions, the economy, family life, education, and the definition of the stages of life, all of which have affected the outlook of this generation. Material affluence is made possible by a system of production, innovation, and organization that defines the options open to today's young men and women, just as it has been the framework for their development to date. Affluence, in a broad sense, has both opened new doors and closed old ones.

Social criticism in the past decades has emphasized the destructive aspects of technology, bureaucracy, specialization, centralization, and bigness. Yet we have also begun to realize that these ambivalently viewed features of our society may be necessary conditions for the advantages of affluence. Our prosperity is built upon high technology, as upon complex and bureaucratic social organization. And both technology and differentiated social roles involve specialization and technical competence far beyond the basic requisites of literacy and fluency with numbers. Furthermore, in any highly specialized society, complex systems of co-ordination, social control, and communication must be developed to harmonize the work of specialized role-holders. Even sheer size sometimes increases affluence: centralization not only can permit industrial efficiencies, but sometimes facilitates administrative co-ordination. The advent of electronic communications and rapid transportation had made it increasingly possible for a small number of men to co-ordinate and control the activities of vast numbers of their fellows. For better and for worse, then, our affluent society is technological, specialized, bureaucratized, and complexly controlled. In such a society, most educated adults not only do highly specialized work, but are involved in complex networks of social co-ordination that they must accept if the System is to function smoothly.

All of these characteristics of modern society contribute to the malaise and reluctance of many of today's youth when they confront the System. Yet these same young men and women, like all of us, consider the many benefits of affluence as "givens" of modern life. They take for granted that just as the machine and factory production made possible the industrial revolution by multiplying each man's physical efforts a dozenfold, so now, in the technological era, the computer is increasingly freeing men from routine and repetitive mental work. Men and women need no longer work in the fields or factories from dawn to dusk to produce the requisites for survival. For affluent Americans (who are the majority), survival, subsistence, and starvation are no longer at issue. A small part of the population can produce the essentials of life, while the rest produce goods and services that, to previous generations, would have appeared unprecedented luxuries.

These "luxuries" include not only the material commodities that fill American life, but less tangible opportunities for education, the cultivation of the mind, and the fulfillment of psychological needs beyond the need for subsistence, security, and status. By vastly extending the power and reach of each individual, the affluent society both permits and requires men to be "unproductive" for many years of their lives. The labor of children, adolescents, and, increasingly, post-adolescents is no longer needed by the economy. On the contrary, keeping young men and women off the labor market is a net social gain because it allows fuller employment of their elders. In addition, an affluent society increasingly requires the young to stay off the labor market in order to learn the high technological skills required to maintain affluence. The result, of course, is the historically unprecedented situation of prolonged higher education, extending well into the twenties, for a larger and larger proportion of the American population.

The postponement of entry into the labor force has contributed to a redefinition of the life cycle, underlining the connection between social opportunity and developmental stage. Giving large numbers of young men and women the opportunity to have an adolescence is an achievement of industrial societies. In many preindustrial societies, even childhood was forcibly aborted by the requirement that children begin to work before puberty. When this happens, the full psychological experience of childhood as we define it in modern society is inevitably cut short: children are small adults—by our modern standards, old before their time. But even in those societies where psychological childhood continues until biological puberty, adolescence as a psychological experience is rarely permitted.

To be sure, the physiological changes that announce the possibility of an adolescent experience occur in every society, regardless of what the society chooses to make of these changes. But in most previous societies, only the extraordinarily wealthy, talented, or fortunate were allowed anything like an adolescence. Even the wellborn Romeo and Juliet were thirteen years old; in the Middle Ages, kings assumed their thrones in their teens; and most children of the common people began working in the fields (in later times, in factories) well before they reached puberty. Allowing the possibility of adolescent development is only one possible reaction to the approach of biological adulthood: historically it is a relatively rare reaction. Even today, in primitive societies, puberty rites more often serve to hasten the child toward adulthood than to permit him anything like the possibility of adolescent turmoil, emotional growth, and independence. Although from the beginnings of history, the old have deplored the irreverence of the young, adolescence as a distinctive stage of life that *should* be made available to all young men and women has only begun to be recognized during the past two centuries in advanced societies.

By creating a vast surplus of wealth, modern societies have freed first children and then teen-agers from the requirements of farm and factory labor. Even before the industrial revolution, of course, a small number of young men and women were allowed a deferment of full involvement in adult work. And a few of them—a few from among the pages and princes, novices and apprentices—were sometimes able to create for themselves what we now recognize as an adolescence. But most, lacking opportunity and social sanction, moved directly from childhood to adulthood. The industrial revolution, however, created a new bourgeoisie with a commitment to education as a pathway to success for their children. This new middle class also had the means to allow children freedom from labor after puberty. There began to develop—for the middle classes at least—a vague concept, at first, of a post-childhood, preadult stage of life, a stage of continuing education that was initially modeled after the apprenticeship. Little by little, however, it became clear that this stage of life had qualities of its own. The adolescent gradually emerged as something more than a cross between a child and an adult.

First for the upper middle class, then for the lower middle class, and then, increasingly, for the working-class youth, adolescence became routinely available. And although the precise definition of the expected qualities of the adolescent is sensitive to the particular values of each society, in most affluent societies today, adolescence is recognized as *sui generis,* as important for the fullest possible unfolding of human potentials, and as a right to be guaranteed through compulsory education and anti-child-labor laws.

We should not forget how recently all of this has taken place, nor how incomplete it still is. Some of Marx's most vehement strictures in the middle of the nineteenth century were directed against the use of children in factories. And in America, the child-labor laws were passed only in the twentieth century. For many young Americans, and for an even greater proportion of the young in other nations, the psychological experience of adolescence is still aborted by the failure of education or the assumption of major economic responsibilities in the mid-teens—years that by our modern reckoning are only the beginning of adolescence. For large numbers of the poor, the deprived, the undermotivated, the psychologically or intellectually handicapped, adolescence still does not take place.

Even if it has not yet been extended to all, making the experience of adolescence available to most young men and women in modern society must be counted among the achievements of affluence. The possibility of adolescence as a psychological experience is dependent on economic conditions that free adolescents from the need to work, as upon the development of new values that make child or adolescent labor seem "outrageous" to right-thinking men and women. Only when a society produces enough to liberate young men and women between the ages of twelve and eighteen from labor can it demand that they continue their educations and allow them to continue their psychological development; only then can abhorrence of the "exploitation" of adolescents develop.

Affluence has also permitted changes in the quality of family life, especially among better-educated Americans. During the twentieth century, growing numbers of men and women, responding to the opportunities and demands of industrial society, have at least begun college, with many completing it and continuing on for their Ph.D. Higher education changes the outlooks and styles of at least some of those who pass through it. Its impact is difficult to describe precisely, but at best it allows greater freedom to express underlying feelings and impulses, greater independence of outlook and thought, and increased sympathy for the underdog. Also, since the best educated are generally those who attain greatest affluence in their own lives, higher education indirectly gives its graduates an adult life that is more secure, freer from the struggle for subsistence and status, and more open to the pursuit of non-material, self-expressive goals. Educated parents who have attained professional and economic security are in turn able to develop a distinctive family style that has important effects upon children.

Although they themselves may have had to struggle out of poverty, today's well-educated and affluent parents have generally "arrived" by the time they raise their own children. Compared to their own parents, they are more likely to instill in their children the special values of self-actualization—independence, sensitivity to feelings, concern for others, free expression of emotion, openness, and spontaneity. And since such parents tend to have relatively few children, they are able to lavish on each child an enormous amount of individual attention. Upper-middle-class educated women need not work to support the family: most devote themselves entirely to bringing up their small children. Even those who do work are likely to feel restored by their work rather than depleted. All of this means that affluent mothers are increasingly free to devote themselves to their small brood of children. Such devotion can have the bad consequences we see in the familiar stereotype of "Momism." But its good consequences are equally important: in many affluent families, children grow up unusually well cared for emotionally and psychologically, the objects of thoughtful attention and informed devotion. Increasingly, affluent middle-class parents *educate* their children, rather than merely training them. And in some affluent families, one finds a parental devotion to the autonomy, self-determination, and dignity of children that is without precedent, even in American history.

Obviously, not all affluent middle-class families fit this rosy description: such families are clearly in a minority. A full account of the impact of affluence and education of the American family would have to discuss other parental responses, among them family styles that lead to filial apathy, alienation, neurosis, or conformity. But affluence means that families like those I am describing—devoted, principled, expressive, thoughtful, humanitarian, and permissive—are increasing in number. Whatever the other satisfactions they derive from their children, parents in these families genuinely desire them to be independent, thoughtful, honorable, and resourceful men and women. To be sure, in these as all families, parents are full of foibles, contradictions, inconsistencies, and faults. And as I have suggested, in a time of rapid value change, the values that parents attempt to apply in bringing up their children may contrast with the more "instinctive" values that have their roots in the parents' own upbringing.

Yet for all their characteristic faults, the families of the educated and affluent have freed a growing number of today's youth to concern themselves with the welfare of others and the wider society. Their security makes possible an identification with others who are insecure; their affluence permits them to worry about those who are poor; their freedom allows them to care about those who are enslaved. Families like the families of the radicals who led Vietnam Summer are impressively *good*. They have given their children great strength, integrity, and warmth. The devotion to family core values that we see in many young radicals derives from parents who have principles and care lovingly for their children. Even the ability of young radicals to be different from their parents may stem partly from their parents' genuine willingness to let them be different. These are children, then, who have been taught from an early age to value independence, to think for themselves, to seek rational solutions, and to believe that principles should be practiced. As Richard Flacks, one of the most astute observers of the contemporary New Left, has put it, these young men and women are members of a "liberated generation."

This argument suggests that in an affluent society, the psychological and social underpinnings of radicalism have begun to change. In non-affluent societies, radicals and revolutionaries—who almost invariably come from relatively privileged backgrounds—tend to react with guilt to the "discovery" of poverty, tyranny, and misery. Furthermore, many radical and revolutionary groups have in the past sought social and political changes that would improve their own position, giving them freedom, power, or benefits they did not possess. In a society like our own—where affluence, economic opportunity, and considerable political freedom are the rule—radicalism is less likely to be built upon personal feelings of deprivation or a desire to improve one's own position. Nor is the guilt of the wealthy when confronted with the poor as likely a motivation for the radical's commitments. While radical leaders of all eras have typically been men of high principle, the role of principle increases further in an affluent era. The radical's basic goal is not to achieve new freedoms, opportunities, or benefits for himself, but rather to extend to all the freedoms, opportunities, and benefits he himself has always experienced. In an affluent world, the radical feels indignation rather than guilt; outrage rather than oppression.

Violence: sadism and cataclysm

The focal issue in Vietnam Summer was ending American involvement in violence in Southeast Asia. And the issue of violence is central not only for young radicals, but for the modern world. Hanging over the lives of all men and women during the past decade has been the Bomb, and the terrifying possibilities of *technological death* it summarizes and symbolizes. These include not only holocaustal destruction by thermonuclear blast and radiation, but the equally gruesome possibilities of the deliberate spread of virulent man-perfected disease or the use of lethal chemicals to destroy the functioning of the human body.

Premature death has, of course, always been a fearful possibility in human life. But technological death is new in a variety of ways.

It is now realistic to imagine not only one's own unannounced death and perhaps the death of one's intimates through natural catastrophe, but to envision the "deliberate" destruction of all civilization, all human life, or, indeed, all living things on earth. Furthermore, technological death has a peculiar quality of impersonality, automaticity, and absurdity to it. Until the relatively recent past, most man-inflicted deaths have at least been personal acts: the jealous husband murders his wife's lover, the soldier shoots the enemy on the battlefield, the cannibal kills the member of a neighboring tribe, the sadist butchers his victim. Technological death, in contrast, requires no contact between man and man. One well-intentioned bureaucrat (who means no harm, is only following orders and is doing his duty for his country) can press a button and set in motion a chain of events that could mean the burning, maiming, and death of most of those now alive. Paradoxically, malice, anger, and hostility are no longer necessary to create a cataclysm beyond the imaginings of the darkest sadist. It only takes an understandable inability to visualize the human meaning of a "megadeath."

The technology of death has hung like a sword over the lives of this post-modern generation. Recall, once again, how in the early memories of these young radicals, the violence of the outside world found echo and counterpart in the violence of inner feelings: on the one hand, the atomic bomb, the menacing mob, the gruesome playground fights; on the other hand, rage, fear, and anger. The word "violence" itself suggests both of these possibilities: the *psychological* violence of sadism, exploitation, and aggression, and the *historical* violence of war, cataclysm, and holocaust. In the lives of these young radicals, as in much of their generation, the threats of inner and outer violence are fused, each exciting the other. To summarize a complex thesis in a few words: *the issue of violence is to this generation what the issue of sex was to the Victorian world.*

The context of development for the post-war generation must again be recalled. These young men and women were born near the end of the most savage, wanton, and destructive war in the history of the world. Perhaps 100,000,000 men, women, and children, most of them "non-combatants," were killed, maimed, or wounded. All of Europe and large parts of Asia and North Africa were laid waste. The lessons of that war for this generation are summarized in the names of three cities: Auschwitz, Hiroshima, Nuremberg. At Auschwitz and the other Nazi concentration camps, more than six million Jews were systematically exterminated. Although their executioners were sometimes brutal sadists, acts of personal cruelty were the least momentous part of the extermination of European Jewry. Even more impressive are the numbers of "decent," well-educated Germans (who loved their wives, children, and dogs) who learned to take part in, or blind themselves to, this genocide. Murder became depersonalized and dissociated, performed by a System of cold, efficient precision whose members were only following orders in doing a distasteful job well. Bureaucracy, technology, and science were linked in the service of death. Evil became "banal," in Hannah Arendt's words; it was impersonal, dissociated from its human perpetrators, and institutionalized in an efficient and "scientific" organization. It became clear that science and civilization, far from deterring technological death, were its preconditions.

The Second World War ended not with the discovery of the Nazi concentration camps, but with the American use of atomic bombs on the cities of Hiroshima and Nagasaki. This act, which in retrospect hardly seems to have been necessary, helped define the nightmare of the past two decades. Just as the experience of the concentration camp showed that the apparently civilized and "advanced" nations of the world could perform barbarities more cruel than any heretofore imagined, so the atomic bomb and its even more frightening thermonuclear successors provided the concrete imagery for the collective terror of the world. Germany had shown that civilized nations could do the unthinkable; Hiroshima demonstrated how simple, clean, and easy (from the point of view of the perpetrator) doing the unthinkable could be.

In Nuremberg after the war, the German leaders were tried and convicted for their crimes. Here the principle was enunciated and affirmed that there is a law above national interest, an ethic above national purpose, and an accountability above obedience to national leaders. Policies that have the full support of national law may be, nonetheless, criminal and illegal. Confronted with such policies, it is the duty of an ethical man to resist. The principle of collective responsibility was also proposed, and many maintained that the German people, by silence, acquiescence, or deliberate ignorance, had assented to and facilitated the crimes of Nazism.

Auschwitz, Hiroshima, and Nuremberg are the birth pangs of the post-war generation, and their lessons—the bureaucratization of genocide, the clean ease of the unthinkable, and the ethic above nationality—have marked post-modern youth. But despite the nightmare of retaliation that has so far deterred men from the use of their most destructive weapons, the post-war years have not been calm or peaceful. On the contrary, these have been decades of constant international unrest, of continual wars of containment, civil violence, and revolutionary liberation. Since the war, the oppressed two-thirds of the world have largely achieved independence, often through strife, violence, and cruelty. Millions were killed in the civil war that followed the partition of India; more millions in the victory of the Communist revolution in China; and the struggles for independence in nations like Algeria, Kenya, and Vietnam were cruel and violent. American involvement first in Korea and then in Vietnam, the American "military presence" in dozens of nations across the world, our national policies of "massive retaliation" premised upon city-annihilating thermonuclear weapons, the continually unsuccessful attempt to prevent, limit or control the manufacture of atomic, biological, and chemical weapons—these have been the context for this generation's growth. The marvels of electronic communication have brought these violent realities of the post-war world into the living rooms of almost every young American, concretizing and making emotionally immediate—at least to those who are capable of identification—the absurd violence of the modern world, and the even more frightening possibilities of world-wide cataclysm.

In the lives of young radicals and of their generation, the threat of outer violence has been not only a backdrop, but a constant fact of life. It is reflected not only in childhood terrors of the Bomb, but in the routine experience of air-raid drills in school, in constant exposure to discussions of fallout shelters, preventive warfare, ballistic missiles, and anti-missile defenses, and sometimes in a compulsive fascination with the technology of destruction. The Bomb and what it symbolizes has set the tone for this generation, even for the majority who make a semideliberate point of trying not to think about it. There are relatively few young Americans who, upon hearing a distant explosion, seeing a bright flash of light, or hearing a faraway sound of jets overhead at night, have not wondered for a brief instant whether this might not be "It." And there are a surprising number who have thought, often with horror and dismay, that they wished "It" were over so they would no longer live in fear. Most thoughtful members of the post-war generation have had elaborate fantasies—usually wishful fantasies of survival and rebirth—about what would become of them if "It" happened. All of this points to a great investment of energy, attention, and thought around the issue of violence, although most find the issue too painful to discuss or even to think about.

Continual confrontation with the fact and possibility of violence in the world has activated and become joined with the universal human potential for aggression, anger, and rage: the psychological and historical possibilities of violence have come to strengthen each other. Witnessing the acting out of violence on a scale more gigantic than ever before, or imaginatively participating in holocaust—both activate the fear of inner violence; while heightened awareness of the inner potential for rage, anger, and destructiveness in turn increases sensitivity to violence in the world. It therefore does not require an assumption of increased biological aggression to account for the importance of violence to post-war youth. Starting with the Second World War, we have witnessed violence and imagined violence on a scale more frightening than ever before. Like the angry children in a violent home who fear that their rage will destroy the warring adults around them, we have become vastly more fearful of our inner angers. In fact, we live in a world where even the mildest irritation, multiplied a billionfold by modern technology, might destroy all civilization.

The fear of violence has led to a fascination with it that further surrounds us with its symptoms. Our society is preoccupied with the violence of organized crime, the violence of urban rioting, the violence of an assassinated President and the televised murder of his alleged murderer, the violence of madmen, the oppressed and the rage-filled. And to have been an American child in the past two decades is, as many have noted, to have watched the violence of television, both as it reports the bloodshed of the American and non-American world, and as it skillfully elaborates in repetitive dramas the potential for brutality and aggression in each of us. We have been repeatedly reminded in the past decade that our society, despite its claims to peaceableness and justice, is in fact one of the most violent societies in the history of the world.

In the Victorian era, what was most deeply repressed, rejected, feared, controlled, projected onto others, or compulsively acted out was related to the issue of sex. The personal and social symptomatology of that era—the hysterical ladies who consulted Freud, the repressive moralism of middle-class life, and the sordid underlife of the "other Victorians"—can only be understood in the context of the preoccupation of the Victorian era with human sexuality. The post-war generation, in contrast, is freer, more open, less guilt- and anxiety-ridden about sex. Sex obviously remains important, as befits one of the primary human drives. But increasing numbers of post-modern youth, like these young radicals, have been able to overcome even the asceticism and puritanism of their own adolescences and to move toward a sexuality that is less obsessional, less dissociated, less driven, more integrated with other human experiences and relationships. Inner and outer violence is replacing sex as a prime object of fear, terror, projection, displacement, repression, suppression, acting out, and efforts at control.

At the same time, the symptomatology of violence and repressed violence is becoming more visible. In the complex and highly organized modern world, open displays of rage, anger, and fury are increasingly tabooed: they are considered "irrational"; they threaten to disrupt the finely tuned system in which we live out our working lives; we consider them "childish" or "dangerous." Driven underground, our inevitable angers sometimes seek less direct forms of expression: they heighten autonomic activity to the point of psychosomatic illness; they are turned against the self, producing angry depression; and they are expressed interpersonally in subtle undercutting, backbiting, viciousness, and pettiness. The repression of inner violence makes us eager consumers of the packaged violence of television and the trashy novel. Equally important, our suppressed aggression is projected onto others. We grossly exaggerate the violence of the oppressed, of our enemies, and even of those to whom our society has given good grounds for anger. Consider, for example, the white fear of black violence. Until the summers of 1966 and 1967, it was the Negroes and their friends whose churches were bombed, who were shot, beaten, and injured by whites, and rarely, if ever, vice versa. And even in the urban rioting of 1966 and 1967, the number of black men killed by white men far outweighed the toll of whites. Yet it is the fear of *black* violence that preoccupies the white public.

To connect the fear of black violence, or the war in Vietnam, or the assassination of a President, or the violence of television solely to the threat of technological death would be a gross oversimplification. My argument here is simply that we live in an unusually violent society, in an unprecedentedly violent world. In our society—as in others—the fears and facts of violence are self-stimulating. The greater the outer reality of violence, the more the inner fear of it, and for many, the greater the need to create or find external situations in which violence can be experienced vicariously outside themselves. The way men react to constant confrontation with violence in the world of course differs: some tolerate it; others develop symptoms related to their inability to confront directly their own inner anger; others project their inner aggression onto others; still others develop a "neurotic" preoccupation with the possibilities of world holocaust. And, most dangerous of all, some need to act violently in order to discharge their own excited rage. If we are to choose one issue as central to our own time, one danger as most frightening, one possibility as most to be avoided and yet most fascinating, one psychological issue that both rationally and irrationally preoccupies us, it is the issue of violence.

In tracing the development of the young radicals who led Vietnam Summer, I have underlined the related themes that center on the concept of violence. Many of their earliest memories involve conflict, outer anger, and inner fear. They were, throughout their childhoods, especially sensitive to the issue of struggle within their families and communities. Although in behavior most of these young radicals were rather *less* violent than their contemporaries, this was not because they were indifferent to the issue, but because their early experience and family values had taught them how to control, modulate, oppose, and avoid violence. Verbal aggression took the place of physical attack. They learned to argue, to compromise, and to make peace when confronted with conflict. So, too, although their adolescent experience was full of inner conflict, they acted on their often violent feelings only during a brief period of indignant rebellion against the inconsistencies of their parents. These young radicals are unusual in their sensitivity to violence, as in their need and ability to oppose it.

I have mentioned the many tensions—psychological, interpersonal, and organizational—that are related to this issue in their work. The avoidance and control of violence, whether in international warfare, political organizations, small groups, or face-to-face personal relations, is a central goal and a key psychological orientation in the New Left. Many of the problems of the Movement are related to the zealous effort to avoid actions and relations in which inner aggression or outer conflict may be evoked. Recall, for example, the extraordinary efforts made to avoid domination within the Movement, the distrust of "totalitarian intimidation," the suppression of leadership lest it lead to manipulation, the avoidance of "flashiness" that might exploit the organized. Remember, too, the deliberate efforts of many of these young men and women to overcome their own angers, their capacity to stay "cool" when provoked, their initial preference for "non-violent" forms of protest, and their largely successful struggle to overcome in themselves any vestige of sadism, cruelty, domination, or power-seeking in human relationships.

I do not mean to suggest that young radicals in particular, or their generation in general, are rage-filled deniers of their own inner angers. On the contrary, amongst these young radicals, exuberance and zest are the rule rather than the exception. Nor are these young radicals incapable of anger and resentment—although they find these emotions easiest to tolerate when, as in their adolescent rebellions, they can be buttressed by a sense of outraged principle. But young radicals, even more than most young men and women of their generation, learned early in their lives the fruitlessness of conflict; and this lesson, in later years, was among the many forces that went into their decision to work for Vietnam Summer.

The position of the psychologically non-violent revolutionary in opposition to a violent world is paradoxical. On the one hand, he seeks to minimize violence, but, on the other, his efforts often elicit violence from others. He works toward a vague vision of a peaceful world, but he must confront more directly than most of his peers the warfare of the world. The frustrations of his work repetitively reawaken his rage, which must continually be redirected into peaceful paths. Combating destructiveness and exploitation in others, his own destructiveness and desire to exploit are inevitably aroused. Furthermore, he is a citizen of a nation whose international policies seem to him only slightly less barbarous than the policies of the Nazis toward the Jews. He has been recently reminded that, with the support of world opinion, the State of

Israel executed Adolf Eichmann because of his complicity in the extermination of the Jews (despite his plea that he was only following orders). Rather than be an accomplice in a comparable enterprise, should the radical not move toward the violent resistance that the world would have preferred from Eichmann? For all his efforts to control violence, cataclysm, and sadism, the young radical continually runs the danger of identifying himself with what he seeks to control, and through a militant struggle against violence, creating more violence than he overcomes. The issue of violence is not resolved for these young men and women. Nor can it be.

8 Youth and history

Like these young radicals, we are all the creatures and the creators of our ongoing history. Social change, affluence, and violence is the ground on which they and we have grown; it is also the stuff of our current lives. It would be wrong to see in these radicals a historical role and reaction that is not present in others. What is articulate and visible in these young men and women is also in all men and women. The difference is only a difference in awareness, not in kind: history is the fabric we are all made of.

One young radical, after reading an earlier version of some of these pages, commented:

> I enjoyed being cast as a world historical being. And it probably is valid within the context of Vietnam Summer. But Vietnam Summer was an extremely intense experience. I was working an average of twelve hours a day; eating, sleeping, living politics; we all were. So it was easy to start seeing ourselves purely in terms of our political concerns, to make the jump from seeing our fate tied up with that of humanity, to seeing ourselves as part of a world historical process. One way to maintain a separate consciousness, a multidimensionality, was, as you mentioned, keeping an easel next to one's bed.
>
> For me, however, the fact that I was more than a world historical being was constantly brought home to me by all the problems I had, primarily as a result of the strains of my work, with the girl I was living with, who also worked in the office. . . . You tended to

romanticize us, much as we romantics tended to do to ourselves. . . .

His caution is well taken. This book about a small and accidental group of young radicals who happened to lead Vietnam Summer in 1967 is largely an account of what makes these young men and women different from others—their elders, the great mass of their less radical contemporaries, the small group of their more radical friends in the New Left. I have traced the development of their commitment to the New Left from its personal roots in childhood and adolescence, through their coming to think of themselves as radicals, to their immersion in the tensions, weariness, and rewards of their changing Movement. In emphasizing what distinguishes them from most other Americans, I have noted the unusual features of their psychological development, social position, and historical role. And I have stressed that these youths self-consciously seek to continue their personal and political development as do only a few of their age-mates. In all of this, I have largely accepted their view of themselves as "special."

But in turning from their lives and work to the impact on them of the history of their times, I turn from what is special to what is universal. To be a "world historical being" is not, as my correspondent assumes, a special attribute of the New Left, but a simple fact of life. Nor, indeed, did these young radicals present themselves as possessing any "special" connection to history. To be sure, political, social, and historical events were closer to the forefront of their consciousness and daily concern than they are for most of us. Yet they had little personal sense of special historical mission: they are too tactical, too unideological, too pragmatic. If there is any romanticism in these young radicals, it is in their hope that their ill-defined Movement (rather than they as individuals) will make an impact on American life. And only time, together with their efforts, will tell whether this hope is romantic wishfulness or a sound assessment of the future.

Precisely because they share their historical involvement with their generation, the experience of these young radicals can be a starting point for speculations about the impact of post-modern history on youth. Although their response to the social and historical events of the past decades is in many respects special, it points to trends and pressures with which we all must come to terms, each in his own special way. Specifically, their curious position between adolescence and adulthood suggests that post-modern society is offering growing numbers of young men and women a heretofore unrecognized stage of life—the stage of youth. Their approach to the world—fluid, personalistic, anti-technological, and non-violent—suggests the emergence of what I will term a post-modern style. And their search for new forms and formulations adequate to the post-modern world points to problems we are all called upon to solve.

"Young radical": a temporary identity

The end of adolescence is usually defined in modern societies as the beginning of adulthood. Psychologically, adolescence is characterized by an absence of enduring commitments, by a continuing focus on questions of philosophy, morality and ideology, by a lack of readiness for work and intimacy with others, and, above all, by a preoccupation with questions of identity, inner intactness, and wholeness. Adolescence is the stage when childhood ties to parents are being outgrown, before the individual becomes independent and responsible in his own right. It is a time of turmoil, fluctuations, and experimentation, when passing moods and enthusiasms follow each other with dizzying speed. The adolescent has little lasting sense of solidarity with others or with a tradition, and little ability to repudiate people and ideas that are foreign to his commitments. In contrast, the psychological adult is usually defined as ready to embark on committed and productive work, to enter into enduring and mutually satisfying heterosexual relationships, to be concerned for the welfare of the next generation. Sociologically, the adolescent in modern societies is defined by his non-involvement in adult institutions, in particular, the institutions of occupation and family. He is not accorded the same status or expected to behave in the same way as the adult. The adult, in contrast, has a role in interlocking social institutions like his occupation and his family: he has the rights and responsibilities of full membership in the society.

If we apply these definitions of adolescence and adulthood to the young radicals who led Vietnam Summer, they fulfill most of the psychological criteria of adulthood, but none of the sociological ones. They have passed through the "identity crisis" of late adolescence. They have developed a sense of *inner identity;* they have a demonstrated capacity to *work, love,* and *play;* they have *commitment* to their Movement; they have a sense of *solidarity* with others; they feel joined to a radical *tradition;* and they have more of an *ideology* in the broad sense than do most adults in America. By such psychological criteria, then, they must be considered adults. Yet by more sociological standards, they seem less than adult. Although capable of extended intimacy, they rarely have spouses or children. Although they work, and work hard, they have avoided all occupational commitments and possess few of the academic degrees or technical skills required by the professions for which their talents suit them. Although committed to a movement, they remain deliberately uninvolved with the institutions, guilds, and organizations of their society. In a word, they lack the prime sociological characteristic of adulthood: "integration" into the institutional structures of society.

It is, of course, possible to think of the New Left as an "institution," deeming those who are committed to the Movement occupiers of "deviant" roles—adults in the same sense as occupiers of other deviant roles, like those of criminal, drug-pusher, and artist. Yet this analysis overlooks the fact that being a young radical, unlike being a criminal, is temporary. The New Left is almost entirely a Movement of *young* men and women. While few young radicals would take literally Mario Savio's statement, "Don't trust anyone over thirty," clear lines separate the old New

Left (generally over thirty) from the New Left and the new New Left. As I have noted, the New Left has a high dropout rate, and most young radicals have left active Movement work before they reach the age of thirty. From those who wish to persist, organizing work generally demands an acceptance of subsistence wages and geographic mobility that is hard to combine with job and family. Those who make firm work and family commitments generally leave active organizing work, often to enter academic life. Their perspective and style changes, and they sometimes become commentators on the New Left rather than actors in it. Furthermore, increasing age and experience alone tend to alter an individual's outlook. Finally, there are major generational differences between those who are twenty-five and those who are thirty-five. The thirty-five-year-old is a child of the mid-Depression; the twenty-five-year-old is a child of the post-war era. These recurring generational differences alone make for major distinctions between older and younger radicals that tend eventually to exclude the older. The New Left has yet to find ways for those who become involved in the conventional institutions of society to retain their active commitment to the Movement.

Even marriage, as contrasted to intense but not binding love relationships, seems extraordinarily difficult within the New Left, No one knows what the actual rate of marriage failure is in the Movement, but the figure of fifty per cent was often cited. In discussions of this topic, several young radicals ventured that "people with stable politics have stable marriages." They less often noted that many of the Movement marriages cited as most successful involved older New Leftists who were also committed to some stable occupation—usually academic work. Given the life of the young radical, it is easy to see why marriage presents special problems. His physical mobility, his lack of a "stable" occupation or profession, his minimal income, his lack of definite plans for the next month, year, or decade, his sense that he should be available, flexible, and open to change—all preclude setting up the permanent household that is the usual basis for married life in America.

Furthermore, Movement jobs rarely come in pairs: the married radical is often faced with the difficult decision of whether to place his wife or his radical work first. For all of these reasons, marriage, family life, and an established occupation do not mix well with active Movement work; and many, if not most, of the old New Leftists who survived the weariness of the Movement have now made major commitments outside the New Left.

The determination and optimism of these young radicals about their continuing commitment to the New Left, however sincere and deeply felt, may not be a realistic judgment of the difficulties that lie ahead for them. In five years, if they do not drop out, most of them will be old radicals. Even if they do not shift their primary commitments to jobs and/or families, and even if they do not drop out for some other reason, the passage of time will inevitably alter the way they are seen by others. A young man or woman who persists as an organizer for five or ten years is considered by others to have become a "professional" organizer, whatever he thinks of himself. A young man who, despite one or more intense long-range affairs, does not marry (or if he marries, does not have children) is considered by others to be a "bachelor" (or "childless"). To do the same thing for a number of years commits one not only to a personal calling, but to a "profession," and increasingly affects one's view of one's self. And to be considered a professional organizer or a bachelor is to have achieved a "finished" identity and defined social role of a kind that these young men and women at present deliberately avoid.

It seems likely, therefore, that many of these young men and women will in the next years face another crisis similar to the crisis that occurred at the end of their adolescences. And it also seems likely that out of this next period of self-examination and self-redefinition will come a "natural" decision (like those of the past) concerning whether to remain as a "professional" radical or whether to become a "part-time" radical with primary commitments elsewhere. Indeed, the beginnings of such a crisis were already apparent in some of those I interviewed, especially those who were beginning to consider marriage or to think about whether to go back to school to earn a union card in one of the professions. For these young men and women, the question of how to remain a radical while at least formally entering the System was pressing and unresolved.

The young radicals who led Vietnam Summer are, in most respects, psychological adults but sociological adolescents. They occupy an uncharted stage of life that intervenes between the "normal" resolution of most adolescent issues and the "normal" assumption of adult roles in the institutions of the wider society. They have long since settled most of the basic questions that preoccupy the adolescent, yet they have not made the further commitment to occupation or to a lasting relationship with one other person that is said to be characteristic of adulthood. A similar stage of life, observed in others, has sometimes been called a "protracted adolescence," or a "prolonged psychosocial moratorium." But neither of these concepts is adequately descriptive, for both refer to states that are supposed to *end* with precisely the kinds of psychological, political, group, and historical commitments these young men and women have already developed. In addition, both concepts suggest a limbo-like waiting period of withdrawal, preparation, and continuing self-exploration. But with these young radicals, while self-exploration is important, waiting and withdrawal are not. And if theirs is a protraction of adolescence or a prolonged moratorium on adulthood, it is one that is increasingly taken by others and one that often lasts a decade. And it is preceded, rather than concluded, by the development of a basic outlook on the world and sense of oneself.

It seems more descriptive to argue that in the experience of these young men and women, and of others like them, we can discern an *emergent stage of life that intervenes between adolescence and adulthood,* a stage of life made possible by the affluence of the post-modern world, and made necessary by the ambivalence that world inspires in the most talented, thoughtful, principled, sensitive, or disturbed of those who have an adolescence. For lack of a better name, I will call this period *the stage of youth,* using this ancient but vague term to refer not to all those who are young, but only to those who after adolescence and before adulthood enter a further stage of development.

Youth as a stage of life

Just as making a later stage of adolescence available to large numbers of children was an achievement of industrial society, so a post-adolescent stage of youth is beginning to be made available by post-industrial society. In discussing the relationship of affluence and adolescence, I argued that industrial society had freed children from the need to work at the same time that it demanded skills teachable only through post-childhood education. These changes went hand in hand with new social attitudes that eventually made it seem desirable for most children to experience a post-childhood, preadult stage of continuing psychological growth.

In the last third of the twentieth century, comparable changes in the economy, education, and social attitudes are slowly beginning to permit growing numbers of young men and women the possibility of a post-adolescent, preadult stage of psychological development. The productivity of the machine and the factory has been further multiplied by the computer and automation, with economic results that are apparent in increasing individual output, a shortening workweek, and a decreasing need for young workers in the labor force. Technological society also demands increasingly complex and difficult-to-acquire technical and intellectual skills. In America, this demand is reflected each decade in the addition of one year to the average number of years of school completed, as in the numbers of young men and women who prolong their educations into the middle or late twenties. What industrial society did for the years between twelve and eighteen, post-industrial society is beginning to do for the years between eighteen and twenty-six. For the most talented and privileged, deferred entry into the economic system because of continuing higher education is not only possible, but highly desirable. And the high unemployment rate among non-college youth suggests that even the less talented and privileged are being forced to postpone entry into the adult labor force.

Concurrently, attitudes toward postponing job and marriage commitments are becoming more permissive. Upper-middle-class families in particular do not consider it alarming for their children to remain unemployed and unmarried until the age of thirty—as long as they are in school. Indeed, training for many professions is now so protracted that full citizenship in the profession is impossible before the late twenties. And although the average age of marriage has dropped in recent decades, this drop reflects the affluence that requires fewer to postpone marriage solely for financial reasons. Instead, we increasingly permit wide individual latitude in the age of marriage, and consider "psychological unreadiness" a valid reason to defer family commitments. This social sanction for the postponement of "adult" commitments goes with an increasing expectation that post-teen-age youth—especially from upper-middle-class families—may continue experimentation, search, and self-exploration for a number of years before taking "the final plunge" into adulthood.

Such economic, educational, and attitudinal changes are beginning to make the stage of youth possible. But like adolescence, youth is an option that society can only make possible: it is up to individuals whether they accept or refuse this option. Other characteristics of modern society help motivate more and more post-adolescents to desire a deferral of adult social involvement. I have argued that affluence is producing more and more families who bring up their children to be idealistic, responsible, and serious about the creedal values of our society—children who are therefore dismayed and outraged when they discover the societal lapses between principle and practice. Social change erodes the institutionalized hypocrisies that in other eras helped conceal this gap between social creeds and deeds. The bigness and impersonality of modern society make it particularly unattractive to the children of affluent families whose core values include independence, personal fulfillment, and rounded human development. The immanence of violence in the technological era makes many of today's youth question involvement in a System that created but cannot control the instruments of destruction. And finally, in a society changing at an accelerating rate, the longest possible delay before taking the leap into some specific social role may simply be the better part of wisdom. A prolonged survey of the social scene provides that much more time to see how things are shaping up before placing a bet on the future. For all these reasons, some of those who reach the end of adolescence actively seek to postpone entry into the System.

I have said that the stage of youth is emergent. By this I mean that youth as a separate phase of life is only now becoming visible, is rarely recognized as such, is frequently deplored or called by other names, and is available only to a small though growing minority of post-adolescents. Adolescence, in contrast, is today a majority phenomenon, clearly recognized, sanctioned, and institutionalized in the many variants of "teen-age" culture. But the chance to have a youth is only available to the most talented, well-educated, rich, determined, sensitive, or lucky in our society. And that opportunity is only accepted by a minority of this minority—those whose personal sensitivities and social positions inspire in them the greatest reluctance to enter the System. The great majority still move straight from adolescence to adulthood.

But although the stage of youth is neither recognized nor institutionalized, we can nevertheless discern its beginnings. In a small number of institutions like the Peace Corps or Vista, increasing numbers of post-adolescent young men and women defer their entry into established society, examine their relationship to it, and continue the process of personal change. In the New Left, as in the hippie movement, other young men and women similarly continue their personal development and redefine their relationship to the Establishment options. And in American higher education, the phenomenon of the "developmental dropout" is increasingly visible: this is the young man or woman in good academic standing who leaves college or graduate school to "find himself" outside an institutional context. Characteristically, such youths consider higher education unrewarding, stagnating, or stifling, question their connection to colleges, graduate schools, and established professions, and seek time and freedom to observe their society "from the outside." Their only psychological symptom is their feeling of being trapped against their will in the machinery of higher education that automatically ejects them without their consent into the Establishment.

Finally, there are others who make of higher education itself a search for a viable relationship with the society at large. In every graduate school and many professional schools, there are a few who, although they are psychologically well past adolescence, use continuing education as a means of deferring "final" entry into sociological adulthood. Such students usually must go through the motions of learning the techniques of a profession—be it legal, academic, or medical. But they are inwardly far from identified with that profession, its techniques, or the role for which they are ostensibly preparing. Their major psychological energies are involved in the effort to define their basic relationship to the existing Society, deciding how, where, and whether they will enter it.

Like adolescence, youth is defined neither by a fixed span of years nor by membership in any specific group, but by a state of mind, a set of questions, and a trajectory of psychological change. Just as there are chronological teen-agers and members of teen-age gangs who are not yet psychological adolescents, so many of those in the New Left, the hippie movement, or the Peace Corps, in graduate schools and professional schools, or among the legions of dropouts in America are not psychological youths. Many, and perhaps most, college dropouts, for example, are primarily concerned with adolescent problems; in graduate and professional schools, the vast majority are basically adolescent or adult apprentices to the System, rather than youthful doubters of their relationship to it. Furthermore, since youth is not a socially recognized or accepted stage in development, those who are in this stage must either risk social disapproval—as do New Leftists, hippies, and dropouts—or, like some graduate students, conceal their youthful disconnection from the System by going through the motions of preprofessional training. Most youths exist in a limbo of social marginality or conceal their youth by pretending to commitments they do not feel.

Though neither formally acknowledged nor socially sanctioned, youth is a stage with characteristics of its own. First, youth follows the resolution of what are usually called "adolescent" problems. The basic contours of the individual's fundamental outlook on the world have usually been arrived at. He has effectively emancipated himself from his emotional dependency upon his family. He has come to terms with his own sexuality, and has established a lasting pattern of sexual adjustment. Although he has not entered into permanent relationship with another person, he is usually capable of intimacy and mutuality with the opposite sex. He has passed through the phase of adolescent rebellion against his parents. He knows his strengths and weaknesses relatively well, and has a sense of his own psychological intactness and capacity to cope. Put differently, he by and large knows what kind of person he is, what he is potentially good at, who he is potentially good for. Like the young radicals who led Vietnam Summer, he may even possess an unusually strong sense of vocation. What Erikson terms the issues of "inner (or ego) identity" have generally been resolved.

Yet such men and women are unwilling to move directly into adulthood. Although many doors are open to them, they lack the will to enter any of them, fearing that once inside they will be trapped and robbed of their freedom to change and be themselves. Despite the dazzling vista of jobs, life-styles, mates, ideologies, recreations, and avocations before them, they question them all, fearing fixity. Some have an inner calling so strong that they can find no niche in society where they can follow it. Others have no calling and are unwilling to settle for a job; although they may possess many skills, talents, and interests, they are unwilling to stake their selves on any one or any set of them. Usually hard put to define precisely why they falter, they nevertheless hesitate and turn away from the lures of the existing society. Some reject it, others withdraw from it, others, like young radicals, seek to change it. All question their connection to it. The focal issue for youth is the issue of social role, of the *individual's relationship to the structures of the established society.*

Like adolescence, youth is of indeterminate length. Characteristically, this stage is marked by the assumption of a meaningful yet temporally limited identity: graduate student, dropout, Peace Corps volunteer, young radical, hippie, and so on. Although temporary in that they cannot outlast youth, such identities often endure many years, inspiring deep commitment and loyalty; and in this respect, they differ from the shallower, fluctuating enthusiasms of adolescence. The temporary identities of youth provide vantage points outside the existing System, where the individual can test his relationship to his society as a whole. "Unintegrated" into the conventional structure of adult social roles, he can explore and evaluate them, testing them against himself and himself against them. During this phase, his stance toward his society is likely to be ambivalent and changing, reflected in his position of outsider looking in. Not yet ready to take a "professional" position either of operator within the Establishment or of opponent to it, youth is a little of both.

What happens during youth, then, is that the individual clarifies the relationship of self and society. The task of youth is to find or create some congruence, in a broad sense, between the individual and existing institutions. An almost limitless number of solutions to this task are possible. They include efforts to change society to bring it more in line with the individual's principles and needs, as among young radicals. Or the youth may devote this phase of life to changing himself so as to be able to fit better into the existing system of rewards, demands, and opportunities. Others search for some obscure niche in society where they can preserve, strengthen, or protect what they value most in themselves. Still others create new roles or new styles of life that will permit a fuller expression of personal needs in a societal framework. Many, during youth, redefine the hierarchy of "reality," deciding, for example, that what "really" matters is inner life, so that social role is irrelevant. Others decide the opposite, and seek with uncompromising vigor a social involvement in which individuality can be totally expressed.

Both self and society are infinitely complex, variegated, ambiguous, and changing: there can be no such thing as perfect congruence between them while each retains separate existence. Only the automaton who loses his self in total social obedience and the psychotic who creates a pseudosociety out of his own fantasies "fit" perfectly. There is, therefore, no single answer to the central question of youth, no one path to social connection.

The achievement of youth is an enduring ability to acknowledge both self and society, personality and social process, without denying the claims of either. Men and women sometimes achieve with each other a mutuality in which the individuality of each is the precondition for loving the other and being able to join together. So in youth, acknowledging the independent reality and the separate claims of both self and society is a precondition for achieving a defined relationship in which both coexist as separate yet interlocked entities. There is no precise word to describe this achievement: *individuation* comes closest. Nor is there an adequate vocabulary to define the failure of youth. But the essence of youthful failure is a kind of alienation either from self or society—a denial of the reality and importance of the self, or a repudiation of the existence and importance of social reality; an abandonment of personal principle, integrity, and aspiration in favor of social success via conformity or, conversely, a denial of existing social organization in uncompromising zealotry or a "let the world perish" insistence on absolute moral purity. The exemplars of these contrasting failures are Babbitt and Don Quixote. Following the paradigm of polarities that Erik Erikson has taught us to use, we might summarize the tension of youth as *individuation vs. alienation.*

Youth ends when the individual moves into a more enduring social role, whether because of a clear choice, or because of the passage of time that transforms the youthful amateur into an adult professional doing much the same thing but now "permanently" committed to it. As youth ends, the individual accepts or is forced by age into a social role that hereafter is likely to define his relationship to society. This role, of course, may be "deviant"—revolutionary, criminal, mental patient, crank, innovator, and so on. But when youth ends, it is no longer necessary for the individual to proclaim repeatedly that he will not abandon his youthful commitments—that fact (or its falsity) is obvious in his social position. With the successful resolution of youth, a man or woman is more able to compromise without feeling compromised and, conversely, to stand alone on principle without feeling isolated. With the end of youth, too, the future becomes less open, and the individual establishes a more-or-less enduring mode of relationship to his society—be he critic or executive, revolutionary or yeoman, radical or apologist, apathetic or indignant.

For some, the ending of youth may be a period of turmoil and crisis. Abandoning the openness and fluidity of youth in favor of a defined position vis-à-vis society may entail a feeling of "selling out," being "fixed" to a set of social categories, becoming "bogged down" in an institution, losing the possibility of further growth, and gaining only entanglement and limitations. But for others, youth ends with the discovery or creation of a role in society through which the individual can preserve his youthful commitments and express what he is. But whether slowly or gradually resolved, and whether its end entails mourning or relief, youth does always end. Only an adult can be a "professional youth."

If it is true that technological society is opening the possibility of youth as a separate stage of life to growing numbers of young men and women, then we will need to rethink many of our views of adolescence and early adulthood. For example, we will need to re-examine concepts like "youth culture," now applied to phenomena as disparate as early teen-age infatuation with rock-and-roll and the New Left. Increasingly, there are important differences in age, functions, and style between truly adolescent cultures and the cultures of what I have called "youth"—differences recognized in the conversational distinction between "teen-agers" and "older youth." We may also need to reconsider our definitions of adolescence itself, and we may find that some of the characteristics ascribed to the "late adolescent" or "young adult" are more properly described as phenomena of youth. And we may have to examine again the connection between identity and social role, perhaps allowing that for some in post-modern societies the development of inner identity may precede by many years the acceptance of social role.

Finally, the social usefulness of allowing a stage of youth will need to be considered. To be sure, those who have had a youth—who have seriously questioned their relationship to the community that exists, who have a self and a set of commitments independent of their social role—are never likely to be simple patriots, unquestioning conformists, or blind loyalists to the *status quo*. Witness the fact that much of the most vigorous dissent from our society today comes from those whom I have called youth. Perhaps we may learn as a society to question the merits of unexamined patriotism, unquestioned conformity, and blind loyalty. Moreover, the graduates of a youth will not automatically "adjust" to what their society offers them. Their involvement cannot be taken for granted: they will have to be persuaded by the evidence of their own experience that their society is worth joining or at least trying to save. But it may be that post-modern societies especially need these men and women—and not merely as gadflies or jesters, but as the essential basis for social change. Indeed, as we look back across history, we may discover that those men and women whom we now remember because their lives transcended their particular time and place were often those granted the opportunity for a youth.

The post-modern style

I have argued that rapid social change, automatic abundance, and a preoccupation with the issue of violence define the terms of discourse for the generation born since the end of the Second World War. The technological, post-modern world is beginning to open to larger numbers of post-adolescent young men and women the possibility of a youth as a separate stage of life. And although only a few have seized the option of youth—increasingly available to the well-born, talented and privileged in post-modern societies—enough have done so to permit the preliminary definition of the distinctive style of post-modern youth. In part, this style reflects the characteristics of youth itself—the concern with developing a "personal" position vis-à-vis the wider society, the combination of psychological adulthood with unreadiness to become involved in the structures of occupation and family. But in part the post-modern style reflects the constants of the historical situation of this generation.

Only with caution can we generalize from a small group of young radicals and others like them to the concept of a post-modern style.* Those who enter a stage of youth are clearly an elite—psychologically, socially, and economically privileged, and often possessed of unusual talent and vitality. Moreover, my comments here will be based on observations of American youth, members of the most advanced technological nation in the world, a nation of unprecedented prosperity, but, also, in 1968, a nation of malaise, inner divisions, and domestic and international violence. Furthermore, even today, most young men and women, if they have an adolescence at all, move directly from adolescence to adulthood. Most are not radicals, not dissenters, hippies, dropouts, protesters, or activists. Here, as in other nations, most young men and women accept the "Establishment options" with greater or lesser enthusiasm, generally support the policies of their government, and have no articulate criticisms of the structures, roles, and institutions of their society. And in America, even more than in most nations, most young men and women remain primarily concerned with their jobs and their families, and are relatively uninterested in the wider world.

Yet there are other factors that may justify the effort to define

* My speculations in this section are much influenced by Robert J. Lifton's concept of Protean Man.

a "post-modern style." In America, as in other nations, new styles of youthful dissent, protest, social action, and relationship to the wider society have begun to emerge. And there is reason to believe that a post-modern style may extend increasingly beyond national boundaries to the youth of other nations. America is ambivalently emulated throughout the world. More important, the historical situation of American youth is similar to that of youth in other nations. Despite the national traditions, cultural inheritances, and historical facts that continue to distinguish the youth of each nation, the modern world is united by the same facts that press most intensely on American youth. In all nations, massive and often bewilderingly rapid social change is the rule; all youth are linked by their common vulnerability to technological death. Even the affluence of the advanced nations affects the youth of the non-affluent world by inspiring their hope, envy, anger, or admiration. Modern communications make the events of one continent reverberate in the next a second later. Increasingly, our destinies are tied to those of our three billion fellow humans; increasingly, we are moving toward a world where there is only one history—world history.

The two most visible and influential variants of the post-modern style in America in 1967 are found in the hippie world and the New Left. Although their combined "membership" numbers but a few per cent of all young Americans, both movements have begun to evolve styles that are already giving their imprint to their generation. Both groups share a visible discomfort with the existing society and an often agonized search for ways to change or escape this society. Furthermore, most hippies and young radicals tend to be drawn from similar backgrounds: upper-middle-class, politically liberal, secular families, excellent educations and attendance at prestigious colleges—in short, the kind of background that makes a stage of youth most possible.

I have elsewhere discussed at length the important psychological differences between alienated hippies and activist radicals. (See Appendices B and C.) Radicals and hippies differ profoundly in the stance they take toward the society: radicals systematically attempt to reform and change their society, whereas hippies turn their backs on society in their effort to find meaning through an intensification of personal experience. Beyond these differences, however, a comparison of the two groups reveals similarities in style that reflect the response of historically conscious, talented, and, in some cases, disturbed youth to the shared psychohistorical matrix of this generation.

In emphasizing "style" rather than ideology, objectives, positions, or traits, I mean to suggest that the similarities in post-modern youth are to be found in the *way* they approach the world, rather than in actual behavior, formal beliefs, or goals. A focus on process rather than on program is perhaps the prime characteristic of the post-modern style, reflecting a world where flux and change are more apparent than direction, purpose, or future. As I will suggest, post-modern youth, at least in America, is itself very much in process, unfinished in its development, psychologically open to a historically open future. In such a revolutionary world, where ideologies come and go and radical change is the rule, a style, a *way* of doing things, becomes more tenable and more important than any fixed goals, ideologies, programs, institutions, or psychological traits.

Fluidity, flux, change, movement—Post-modern youth is open, flexible, in motion. Although throughout these observations I have spoken of a "radical identity," the term "identity" as ordinarily used suggests a greater fixity, stability, and "closure" than most radicals or post-modern youth possess. Put differently, identity itself is tied to a changing world and to the process of psychological change. For post-modern youth, psychological change, flux, and mobility continue long past the time when, in earlier eras, they "should" have stopped. Psychological closure—shutting doors and burning bridges—becomes impossible. Just as the concept of the "lifework" recedes before the unpredictability of the future, so the effort to change oneself, redefine oneself, and reform oneself continues long past adolescence. In post-modern youth, furthermore, the effort to continue psychological change is self-conscious and deliberate. I have stressed the importance to young radicals of continuing to move and to change as people. Among hippies, efforts at self-transformation through the use of drugs, through interpersonal relations, or through spiritual exercises are even more deliberate. Even many college and graduate-school dropouts conceive of their absence from higher education as a deliberate attempt to alter their personalities.

This fluidity, movement, and openness extend through all areas of life. In particular, it affects youth's relationship to ideology and dogma. Post-modern youth are non-dogmatic, anti-ideological, and intensely hostile to doctrine and formulas. In the New Left, the focus is on tactics rather than program; amongst hippies, on simple direct acts of love, expression, and communication. In neither group does one find hard-and-fast adherence to a fixed and unmodifiable system of beliefs. In both groups, youth seeks to preserve the capacity to change beliefs with changing circumstances; the goal is to remain responsive to a changing environment, even if it means altering apparently fundamental beliefs.

Openness and flexibility extend, above all, to the future. The stage of youth itself is of indeterminate length; as long as the individual remains in this stage, his future is by definition open. His focus is on the short range—on the next day, week, month, or year. The distant future is considered unpredictable and possibly inconceivable: indeed, given youth's awareness of the constant possibility of unannounced technological death, whether there *is* a distant future at all is often said to depend upon what men do today or tomorrow. And since the social and historical future is unstable and unpredictable (yet will profoundly affect the future course of psychological development), personality must remain fluid in order to undergo continuing transformations in response to the transformations of the historical world.

The fluidity of the post-modern style and the flux of the modern world are thus closely connected. The post-modern emphasis on process involves a simultaneous identification with, and effort to deal with, historical change. On the one hand, post-modern youth floats with the tide, remains open to the changing world, is alterable and malleable by the changes of the social and political environment. In this respect, the emphasis on change reflects the flux of the modern world. But on the other hand, each variant of the post-modern style involves an effort to find an anchor in the cross-tides of modern history. For the young radical, mastery consists of an effort to give direction to social change, creating a meaningful future more in accord with his own basic principles and needs. For the hippie, in contrast, the continual flux of the historical world is dealt with by de-emphasis. What matters is not the irredeemable social and political order, but the more controllable world of inner life, experience, and intimate relationships. It is this world that is most "real"; the rest is a "game." The hippie masters the flux of the modern world by defining it as irrelevant.

Generational identification, inclusion—The major conscious identifications of post-modern youth are with others of the same generation, rather than with elders, leaders, and heroes. Such young men and women do not consider themselves part of organizations or traditions, but rather of movements. And as I have noted, the term "movement" points not only to the absence of traditional patterns of hierarchy and leadership, but to the physical mobility, fluidity, and openness of post-modern youth. Among young radicals, for example, the absence of heroes and older leaders is impressive: even those five years older are viewed with suspicion or amusement. Although young radicals and hippies alike are often well-read in the literature of radicalism or of interior change, no one person or set of people is essential to their style of life. And although they live together in groups, these groups have no leaders.

Identification with a generational movement, rather than a cross-generation organization or non-generational ideology, distinguishes post-modern youth from its parents and from earlier generations. It also creates "generational" distinctions involving five years and less. Within the New Left, recall the age-related contrasts made between the old New Left, the New Left, and the new New Left or "young kids." Generations, then, are separated by a very brief span: the individual's own phase of youthful usefulness—whether as radical, hippie, graduate student, or dropout—is limited to a few years. Generations succeed each other quickly: whatever is to be done in and by youth must be done soon.

Generational consciousness entails a feeling of psychological disconnection from previous generations, their life situation, and their ideologies. Young radicals, for example, often state that older ideologies and institutions are exhausted or irrelevant. None of the formal values of the previous generation can be accepted before testing its relevance to the contemporary world. And whatever the ties of affection that link young radicals to their parents, the young are intensely scornful of the doctrinaire disputes of the Old Left and the ineffectuality of "old liberals"—that is, of their parents' formal beliefs. Among hippies, the irrelevance of tradition and the cultural past is even more complete. If there is any source of insight and understanding, it is the experience of today or the timeless wisdom of the East, not the traditions of the West or the ideologies of the previous generation. The most important values are those created in the present, by youth.

The post-modern style is highly inclusive, especially as regards the contemporary: incorporation and openness to the alien are cardinal principles. Today's youth attempt to include within their personalities and their movements every opposite, every possibility, and every person, no matter how apparently alien. Psychologically, inclusiveness involves an effort to be open to all of one's feelings, impulses, and fantasies, to synthesize and integrate rather than repress and disassociate, never to reject, deny, or exclude any part of one's personality. Interpersonally, inclusiveness means a capacity for identification, involvement and collaboration with those who are apparently alien: peasants in Vietnam, the non-white, the deprived, and the deformed. One way of explaining the reaction of post-modern youth to the war in Vietnam is through their inclusiveness: these young men and women react to events in Southeast Asia much as if they occurred in Newton, Massachusetts or Berkeley, California: they make little distinction in their reactions to fellow Americans and to those overseas. Indeed, so great is the desire to include the alien—especially among hippies—that the alien is often treated with greater respect than the familiar. Thus, the respect accorded people and ideas that are distant and strange is not always accorded those that are similar—for example, one's own parents and their middle-class values.

A corollary of generational identification and inclusiveness is interracialism and internationalism. It matters little to hippies or young radicals where a person comes from. Nor does the nationality of ideas matter: Zen Buddhism, American pragmatism, French existentialism, Indian mysticism, or Yugoslav Marxism are accorded equal hearings. Similarly, the traditional barriers between races and nations are minimized. Today's youth is interracial, and the ultimate expressions of unity between the races—sexual relationships and marriage—are considered natural and normal, whatever the social problems they currently entail. In post-modern youth, then, relationships and values are no longer parochial, national, or racial: increasingly, the reference group is the world, and the artificial subspeciation of mankind is rejected.

Personalism, participation—Despite the personal and intellectual inclusiveness in post-modern youth, almost all youth would agree in attempting to exclude from their lives the artificial, the non-genuine, the manipulative, and the hypocritical. Conversely, what are prized are direct, personal, I-thou encounters between two unique individuals. All values, roles, and organizations that impede or subvert person-to-person relationships are anathema. Among hippies, personalism usually also entails privatism—withdrawal from efforts to be involved in or change the wider social world, a focus on the immediate and at hand to the exclusion of the public world. Among young radicals, personalism is joined to efforts to change the world so as to make person-to-person relationships the rule rather than the exception. But despite this difference, both movements share a desire to create intimate, open, and trusting relationships between small groups of people. Writers who condemn the "depersonalization" of the modern world, who expose the artificiality, falseness, or manipulation of non-reciprocal "games" and "role-playing" find a ready audience. The ultimate judge of a man's life is the quality of his personal relationships; the greatest sin is to be unable to "relate" to others in a direct, open, trusting, and one-to-one way.

A part of personalism is a faith that all men and women have a self that transcends, but is often hidden by, their social roles. The hippie utopia of each man "doing his thing" is a utopia of self-expression regardless of traditional social role. And the radical's effort to "help people be people" by throwing off the social stereotypes, stigmas, and self-characterizations that rigidify and routinize his behavior also presupposes a "real self" waiting to be actualized beneath social roles. What is demanded for everyone, then, is self-expression and self-actualization, an ability to transcend or avoid artificial, stereotyped role-playing, and a willingness to be oneself. All conventions, prejudices, institutions, stereotypes, and habits of thought that interfere with "people being people" are strenuously condemned.

The other side of personalism among post-modern youth is the discomfort created by "objectified," professionalized, or, above all, exploitative relationships. Manipulation, power relationships, superordination, subordination, control, and domination are at violent odds with the I-thou mystique. Failure to treat others as fully human, inability to enter into "genuine" personal relationships with them, is viewed with dismay in others and with guilt in oneself. Even with opponents, the ultimate goal is to establish confrontations in which the issues can be openly discussed. When opponents refuse to meet with young radicals, this produces anger and frequently more violent confrontations. For example, the Harvard SDS obstructed former Defense Secretary Robert MacNamara's departure from Harvard after being refused an opportunity to meet with him to discuss American foreign policies. And the hippie "put-on"—a deliberately exaggerated misrepresentation—is an effort to expose through parody the false and manipulative relationships that prevail in modern society.

Among post-modern youth, then, the most profound source of personal guilt are the "hang-ups" that make intimacy, openness, and love impossible. Freely expressed love and sexuality in the context of "genuine" relationships are an important criterion of personal worth. The sexual freedom of the hippie world has been much discussed, exaggerated, and criticized in the mass media. One finds a similar sexual and expressive freedom among many young radicals, although it is less demonstratively provocative. Although many young radicals and hippies have emerged from an adolescent period of asceticism, they have reacted to puritanism with systematic efforts to move beyond inhibition to expression, freedom, intimacy, and pleasure.

In the era of the Pill, responsible sexual expression becomes increasingly possible outside marriage, at the same time that sexuality itself becomes less laden with fear, prohibition, and guilt. Among post-modern youth, as asceticism has been overcome, promiscuity has not followed. The personalism of post-modern youth requires that sexual expression occur in the context of a good relationship—of intimacy and mutuality. If the older morality that makes sexual expression outside marriage illicit has disappeared, it has been replaced by a new morality of "meaningful relationships"—relationships in which, as one young radical put it, "people are good to each other." Marriage is increasingly seen as primarily an institution for having children, while sex is the normal concomitant of close friendship or love between the sexes. What is morally important is not sexual activity itself, but the context in which it occurs: sharing, mutuality, "helping each other," is the sanctioning context, while exploitation, deception, or "using each other" are taboo in this area as in all others.

Another corollary of personalism is participation. The New Left's creed of participatory democracy involves a commitment to collective decision-making in small groups. A more general radical objective is to create "new institutions" that permit men to take active part in making decisions that will affect their lives. Such institutions, by maximizing participation, attempt to humanize and strengthen, rather than dehumanize, their members. The ideal is the face-to-face group of equals who meet in an atmosphere of trust and mutual respect. Similarly, in small hippie "tribes," there is a comparable stress on self-criticism, awareness of group interaction, and the continuing growth of each group member. Even outside the radical and hippie movements, the same participatory values are seen in the widespread enthusiasms for "sensitivity-training" groups and even in the use of groups as therapeutic instruments. All such participatory groups attempt to create styles of interaction that contribute to the personal development and self-respect of those who participate in them.

Ambivalence toward technology—Post-modern youth has grave reservations about many of the technological aspects of the contemporary world. The depersonalization of life, commercialism, bureaucratization, impersonality, regimentation, and conformity of modern society seem destructive and unnecessary to these young men and women. Bigness, impersonality, stratification, fixed roles, and hierarchy are all rejected, as is any involvement with the furtherance of purely technological values. Efficiency, quantity, the measurement of human beings—anything that interferes with the unique personality of each man and woman—are strongly opposed. In its place, post-modern youth seeks simplicity, naturalness, individuality, the avoidance of fixed social roles, and even voluntary poverty.

But a revolt against the effects of technology is of course only possible in a technological society, and to be effective it must inevitably exploit the technology it opposes. Thus, in post-modern youth, the fruits of technology—synthetic hallucinogens in the hippie subculture, the modern technology of communication among young radicals—and the extraordinary affluence made possible by a technological society are the preconditions for the post-modern style. The demonstrative poverty of the hippie would be less meaningful in a society where poverty was routine; and for the radical to work for subsistence wages as a matter of choice is to *have* a choice not available in most parts of the world. Furthermore, to "organize" against the pernicious aspects of the technological era requires of young radicals high skill in the use of the modern technologies of communication: the long-distance telephone, television, films, the use of the electronic media, high-speed travel.

Finally, in all post-modern youth, there is a mocking yet also genuine identification with the very technologies that are also opposed. The hippie, for example, applies to himself and his inner state a vocabulary derived from the electronic media. "Turn on," "turn off," "tune out," "flip out," "blow your mind," are terms that suggest a profound identification of the self with the electronic machine. Even the use of synthetic hallucinogens may point to an underlying image of the body as a complex chemical system (or computer) to be manipulated from the outside. Other examples abound: the electronic music and mixed media of the psychedelic world, the coiled cables of the WATS line in the headquarters of Vietnam Summer, even the suggestion (quickly rejected) by one Vietnam Summer leader that future national organizing efforts should use computers to process the masses of information needed.

In the end, then, it is not so much the material as the spiritual consequences of modern technology that are deplored—not so much technology as technologism. Only a few in the New Left, the hippie community, or the dropout world have any very strong personal objection to the material products and prosperity of the technological world. What they do reject, however, is the contamination of life with the spirit of technological organization, measurement, efficiency, and standardization. With greater or lesser articulateness, they seek ways of retaining the benefits of technology without dehumanizing, desiccating, and depersonalizing the citizens of technological society.

Related to this ambivalence toward technology, these young men and women reject the "merely academic" and the "merely vocational" aspects of American education, seeing them as irrelevant, mechanical, impersonal, and at times as actively destructive of human individuality. Knowledge, to be worthy of the name, must be relevant, personally meaningful, and a guide to action. Most of what is taught in schools, colleges, and universities, according to this view, is an indirect apology for the existing System, technical training that "adjusts" people to become good workers in the System, or aridly disconnected from the "really important" questions of man's nature, destiny, and relationship to society. It would be wrong simply to label this criticism "anti-intellectual," for most new radicals and not a few hippies are themselves intellectual people, actively engaged in a pursuit of "relevant" knowledge. What is demanded is that intelligence be engaged with the world, just as action should be informed by knowledge.

To post-modern youth, knowledge that does not grow out of or feed back into personal experience and action hardly seems worth knowing. In the prevailing epistemology of technological society, "objective" and "scientific" knowledge has a higher epistemological priority than knowledge that is "merely" personal. But post-modern youth questions this concept of "objective" knowledge, especially as it applies to the understanding of man and society. Pointing to the existence of unconscious assumption, historical presupposition, and motivated self-interest in many purportedly "objective" analyses, the post-modern mood reverses the conventional epistemological priority, placing the personally relevant, immediate, and experiential above the "objective" and "scientific."

Yet none of this means that post-modern youth rejects outright technology, the epistemology of scientific objectivity, or the knowledge of the past. Ambivalence—simultaneous attraction and revulsion, turning toward and away—is the essence of the post-modern stance toward the technological system, its epistemological assumptions, and its educational forms. Post-modern youth is the product of the technological world, and as such, is permeated with its assumptions, preconditions, and products. In reacting against technology, those who oppose it must use the same technology or else be relegated to utter ineffectuality. In all eras, those who question their relationship to society must simultaneously exploit, be identified with, and oppose the very technologies whose consequences they question.

Non-violence—Finally, post-modern youth of all persuasions meet on the ground of non-violence. For hippies, the avoidance and calming of violence is a central objective, symbolized by gifts of flowers to policemen and the slogan "Make love, not war." And although non-violence as an absolute philosophical principle has lost its power in the New Left, non-violence as a psychological orientation is a crucial—perhaps *the* crucial—issue. By nature and by conviction open to the shifting currents of the world around them, identified not with community, nation, party, or organization, but with their entire generation across the world, inclusive, interracial and international, valuing others as persons unique and irreplaceable, profoundly ambivalent about the technology that allows them their youth, skeptical and convinced only by the evidence of personal experience—today's youth is oriented to violence, sadism, and warfare as the greatest of all dangers.

Their non-violence should not be confused with pacifism. These are not young men and women who believe in turning the other cheek, or who are systematically opposed to fighting for what they believe in. But their basic style and psychological orientation is profoundly opposed to warfare, destruction, the exploitation of man by man, and to violence whether interpersonal or international. Their goals, more often sought than achieved, are goals of trust, openness, human responsiveness, and recognition of each man for who he is. Their aim, for themselves and for others, is a world where men can grow and develop, each at his own rate and in his own way, where people have learned to "be people," where each man can "do his thing." For any of this, peace is essential.

The search for new forms

The post-modern style both mirrors and opposes the contemporary world. It reflects modern history in its fluidity, change, and openness. It reacts against the impersonality of technological society with personalism, against irrelevant tradition with generational identification, against technologism, and above all, against violence. But more than either reflection or reaction, the style of post-modern youth is a search—a search for new values, for institutional forms, and intellectual formulations that are adequate to life in the last third of the twentieth century. And in no group is that search more deliberate and intense than in the New Left.

It is very easy to find good grounds to criticize the young radicals. Their outlooks are incomplete, changeable, hard to pin down. They seem "unrealistic" in their firm adherence to principle in the face of social and historical actualities that appear to demand compromise. They are anti-institutional, even anarchistic, in their fondness for the small scale, the participatory, and the face-to-face. They lack any detailed program of specific reforms. They are romantic in their identification with those who are superficially unlike them, as in their assumption that every man has a real self waiting to be actualized beneath his social role. They place great faith in the personal, the at-hand, and the subjective, yet seek a political effectiveness that requires dealing in public images and persuasions. They consider themselves involved in politics, yet shy away from the exercise of power.

As obvious and correct as all these criticisms are, they somehow miss the point. To criticize the New Left for not being an efficient political organization or a complete philosophical system is to criticize it for not being what it tries hard not to be. Its political goals are not to win the next election, or the one after, but to increase the social and political consciousness of the American people. And it deliberately avoids a finished philosophy and political program in its conviction that the way the political process operates, the spirit of its participants may be more important than the rhetoric of platforms and promises. The New Left grew out of dissatisfaction with the political forms of the old liberalism and the overly complete formulations of the old radicalism. In the new radical's view, liberal political institutions, however well organized and efficient, have failed to solve the problems of racism, poverty, and foreign policy. And the older radicalism, despite its coherence as a philosophy, is seen as largely irrelevant to the problems of political action and thought in an affluent, changing, middle-class society. From its first beginnings, the New Left deliberately defined its task as the search for new forms and formulations—a search that few young radicals believe is more than half begun.

Recall the facets of this search among the young radicals whose lives we have surveyed.

These young men and women seek new *forms of adulthood,* in which the principled dedication of youth to the betterment of society can be continued in adult work that does not require blind acceptance of the established System, but permits continuing commitment to social change. This search is age-old, but in a society that teaches its young to take ideals seriously, it takes on new importance and urgency.

They seek a new *orientation to the future,* one that avoids the fixed tasks and defined lifeworks of the past in favor of an openness and acceptance of flux and uncertainty. In their openness, they stress not ends but means, not goals but style, not program but process, not the attainment of utopia but a *way* of doing things.

They seek new *pathways of personal development* wherein the openness of youth, its fluidity, growth, and change, its responsiveness to inner life and historical need, can be maintained throughout life. Fearful of finished fixity, they look for means of combining social role and personal change so that human development does not slow or cease with entry into society.

They seek new *values for living,* values that will fill the spiritual emptiness created by material affluence. The first generation with no need to strive to subsist, to achieve security, or to augment their status, they turn toward goals of self-expression, fulfillment, and service, attempting to learn how to live wisely and well with the unprecedented abundance their generation takes for granted.

They seek new *styles of human interaction* from which the participants grow in dignity and strength. Repelled by the impersonality, cruelty, and dehumanization of many modern transactions between man and man, they are looking for ways for people to remain people and to confront each other in trust and respect in their daily lives.

They seek new *ways of knowing,* ways that combine intense personal conviction with relevance and enduring adequacy to the facts. In a world where the self-evident truths of one generation become the fallacies of the next, they want an epistemology that avoids rigidity, dogma, and claims to eternal verity, that permits responsiveness to personal and historical flux, but that creates the conceptual consistencies by which they can orient themselves to a world in flux.

They seek new *kinds of learning,* learning that maximizes the involvement of the intellect in the individual's experience, instead of divorcing the two. The "merely academic" is eschewed because it gives so little weight to either inner life or personal experience. What is sought is a means of connecting the knowledge of the past to the experience of the present so that together they inform life and action.

They seek new *concepts of man in society,* concepts that acknowledge the unique individuality of each human being without denying man's social embeddedness, that stress social involvement without neglecting the special potential that is often covered by social role. Unwilling to define man as either an existential isolate or a social cog, they would find a way to recognize both his specialness and his sociability.

They seek new *formulations of the world,* formulations that give adequate weight to the movement and change that is ubiquitous in their experience. Inheritors of an intellectual tradition that sees stasis as the rule, they search for alternate views that put the flux and process of post-modern life at the center of their views of man, society, and history.

They seek new *types of social organization,* institutional forms that include rather than exclude. Appalled by an immensely affluent society that excludes the black and the poor from its prosperity, angry at self-righteous "help" that devitalizes its recipients, they are trying to create new institutions that will activate, humanize, and strengthen those they touch.

They seek new *tactics of political action* that increase the awareness of those who take part in them and of those whom they affect. Opposing commercialization and manipulation in political life, they propose a politics of dialogue, participation, and confrontation that starts from what is near and immediate, gradually making men more aware of their unavoidable political involvement and responsibility.

They seek new *patterns of international relations,* patterns within which men of diverse nations can respect both their common humanity and their cultural uniqueness. Dismayed by foreign policies that suppress popular demands and oppose the reform of injustice, unafraid of the specter of "Communism," they would allow each people to shape its own destiny free from interference.

Perhaps most important, they seek new *controls on violence,* whether between man and man or between nation and nation. Products of the violence-ridden post-modern world, more aware of man's inner potential for violence than any previous generation, their most constant effort has been to put an end to the violence men do to each other, whether by racist oppression, hidden manipulation, or open war.

No one—and especially not these young radicals themselves—would argue that they have found adequate answers to any of the problems they confront. Most Americans will judge their efforts unrealistic, inconsistent, naïve, misguided, or even dangerous. And many will consider it impertinent of such young men and women to dare to advise their elders so insistently about matters that have puzzled older and perhaps wiser heads for a generation.

However we judge the young radicals, to describe their search is to enumerate the problems of our changing, affluent, and violent society, a society that has barely begun to catch up with the dilemmas it has created. The new radicals are right when they argue that our problems lie deeper than a particular election result or a particular war in Southeast Asia. Ours are in fact the problems of a new kind of society trying to find its way in a new kind of world where cataclysm is only a button away. Few of us know how to live wisely and well in such a world: that fact is reflected in the deep malaise, violence, and inner divisions of America and the world. The new radicals are at least confronting the central issues of our time, and confronting them more directly than most of us can afford to. They are asking the basic questions, making the mistakes, and perhaps moving toward some of the answers we all desperately need.

For this reason we should wish these young radicals success in their search. And more important, we should ourselves join in this search. For on its outcome rests not only the future quality of human life, but our very survival.

Appendix A A note on research involvement

Those familiar with the methods of research in the social sciences will realize that in making these observations on young radicals, I have not been able to avail myself of the ordinary "controls" by which the psychologist commonly attempts to control subjectivity and bias in his observations. Such methods, sometimes quantitative and statistical, sometimes embodied into the design of experiments, are an effort to check the general human tendency to perceive selectively whatever is most consonant with previous assumptions—neglecting, rejecting, or simply "failing to notice" the rest. A further goal of "scientific method" in the social sciences is to facilitate the task of assigning causal priority: for example, the use of "control groups" in experimental research often aims to distinguish the effects of experimental manipulations from changes that would have occurred in any event.

In a study such as this, involving a controversial group of young men and women involved in a program rejected by most of their fellow countrymen, the problem of subjective bias is even greater. As is clear throughout these observations, I myself became involved with those I was studying, found them an unusually likable group of young men and women, and was in sympathy with their over-all goals. I doubt that it is possible to study any human phenomenon without confronting the problem of the researcher's own involvement in his research and his research subjects. Even in the most rigorously controlled experimental research, a similar involvement is often apparent, and can affect the collection, description, and interpretation of data. But in observational research like this, the issue of personal involvement, though not qualitatively different, is far more obvious, and should be discussed as such.

In my view, to seek "total objectivity" in a study like this is pointless. My own involvement was crucial; without it, I would not have undertaken this study, or could I have carried it through. My personal reactions to these young radicals constituted a major part of the "data" upon which I base these observations. The assumptions and past experience in psychological research I brought to this study not only "biased" my perceptions, but informed them. To a very considerable extent, in observational studies like this, the researcher himself is his own microscope, and it is incumbent upon him to say something of what he brought to his perceptions of his subject matter. Thus, because it does not seem to me legitimate to claim "objectivity" for a study such as this, it is necessary to provide some statement as to what I brought to these observations, and how the process of making them affected me.

For the past years, I have been interested in the phenomenon of youth's relationship to the wider society, and in particular in youthful dissent and deviance. Furthermore, as a political science major in college, but a psychologist by later training, I had long been interested in the connection between individual life, society, politics, and history, a connection that seems to me both more intimate and more complex than is generally understood. Moreover, although I am academic by background, temperament, and training, I have always tended to study phenomena that seemed relevant to the understanding of the contemporary world. This choice of "topical" subjects may reflect a compromise between my adolescent thoughts of entering the world as a political actor and my adult decision to live in it as an academic. Not an activist myself, despite my occasional participation in petition-signing, marching, and other "academic" forms of political action, I respect those who are. All these factors influenced my decision to join in a study of "some aspect of Vietnam Summer."

Several previous research experiences were relevant to my observations of young radicals. For a number of years, I had been involved in intensive studies of individuals as they progressed through college, focusing in particular upon issues of alienation from, and commitment to, American society. Subsequently, I had studied or evaluated several different groups of students and young adults: voluntary college dropouts as they were leaving college or after they returned to it, student drug-users, and students who had elected to interrupt their college careers to work in the developing nations. These diverse groups, along with other individuals I have interviewed intensively, have given me some understanding of the "normal" development of talented youth during late adolescence, youth, and early adulthood, and provided me with several "comparison groups." The most important comparison was between these New Leftists and "alienated" and drug-using students I had studied in the past.

I approached the interviews with a series of hypotheses concerning the psychological development of radicals: these hypotheses are made explicit in Appendix B, a discussion of "activism" written before I embarked upon the study reported here. Some of my expectations proved incorrect. Specifically, I had expected a far greater involvement with and identification with maternal humanitarianism and liberalism; I had not anticipated the pre-eminent importance of relationships with fathers among young male radicals, or the extent of ambivalence toward the paternal inheritance. These incorrect initial hypotheses were inspired, in part, by a reading of the occasional studies of radicals that have been previously reported. But they also grew out of an assumption that young radicals were in some way "alienated," albeit in a different way from the "uncommitted" students I had earlier studied, and that maternal influence was crucial in all varieties of alienation. Thus, although I had previously written about the differences between activism and alienation, I had not fully realized how great these differences were.

My personal reactions as I conducted this study are relevant to placing it in perspective. I have already noted my incorrect fear that psychological interviews might be perceived as threatening and undermining by at least some of those I approached. This expectation was based in part upon previous interviewing experience, and in part on a fear that political radicals might be especially suspicious—or even "paranoid"—about "outsiders" within their midst. In retrospect, this fear showed an insufficient understanding on my part of the differences between the old, more secretive and factional Left and the style and outlook of the New Left.

A second personal reaction is, I trust, obvious throughout this book: I found almost all of those I interviewed engaging, interesting, and likable. I enjoyed conducting the interviews, did not begrudge the time "lost" from other activities, or the distances I had to travel. I was somewhat surprised by how positive my reactions were; and since I do not always react this way, I felt justified in attributing my reactions, in part, to the characteristics of these young radicals.

After I had conducted the first half-dozen interviews with the leaders of Vietnam Summer, I began to detect in myself a note of apology as I listened afterward to the recordings of our conversations. I realized that I felt considerable admiration and some guilt; admiration of their single-minded dedication to a set of principles in which they firmly believed, guilt because I myself was not similarly involved. This issue was related, I came to believe, not only to psychological issues in my own life, but to the characteristics of those interviewed. Once again, these feelings are not similarly evoked in me in other interviewing situations, so I concluded that they pointed to a certain quality in these young radicals that I have discussed as a "special sense of rightness." This quality, of course, need not evoke admiration or guilt: avoidance or anger are equally possible reactions to it.

As the interviews progressed, I found myself asking, "Why did I not become a radical?" In the early stages of interviewing, I identified with Vietnam Summer participants, found many aspects of my own early life similar to theirs and wondered why I, at a comparable age, had not become similarly committed to active efforts to change society. My attempt to answer this question led me to a sharper awareness that there were also important differences in my own development and theirs, and thus indirectly contributed to a formulation of the major psychological themes in their lives. Furthermore, this reflection increased my awareness of the importance of the social and historical setting on the development of radicals. To give but one obvious example, in my own early twenties, between 1950 and 1955, there was no "Movement" to become part of.

My interviewing schedule led me to complete most of the first interviews before beginning any of the second. My over-all impressions were different after completing each set of interviews. The initial interviews left me with a picture of the extremely adaptive, sensible, open, and intense current lives of these young radicals. But the second interviews, concentrating upon their earlier lives, gave a contrasting picture of the earlier turmoil, anxieties, and psychological conflicts through which they had passed. The contrast between these two sets of impressions increased my understanding of the amount of personal and interpersonal conflict that had been overcome, resolved, integrated, and synthesized in the development of a radical identity.

The need to travel from New Haven to Cambridge to conduct these interviews meant that I sometimes interviewed as many as six people in one long day. After such a day, I frequently felt that "ordinary" people were unusually two-dimensional, flat, and uninteresting in comparison to these young radicals. For example, I sometimes had to wait for some time at the Boston airport after a day of interviewing: I would find myself viewing my fellow passengers as pasteboard figures upon a painted landscape, contrasting them unfavorably with the more three-dimensional radicals I had come from. This impression, I came to believe, reflected in part the actual vividness, intensity, and high degree of mobilization of energy that occurred in Vietnam Summer, together with what one young radical called the "surreality" of Movement groups. I have discussed some of these issues in considering the tensions of work in the New Left.

Soon after the summer, I began to put down on paper some of my impressions of the young radicals I had interviewed. Rather to my surprise, I found that I soon had a draft of over one hundred pages. I dispatched this draft to those I had interviewed, and to a number of others familiar with the New Left or interested in youth and politics. Their reactions encouraged me to revise and complete it, and made me more aware of my own continuing involvement with those I had interviewed. For example, several correspondents noted that although I had emphasized the general issue of violence, I had minimized the specific attractiveness of (sometimes violent) "resistance" to radicals. In part, this underemphasis was due to the fact that the New Left had moved steadily toward greater militancy in the three months since my interviews had been conducted. But in part, I came to realize, it reflected my own preference for a non-violent style, which had led me to equate psychological non-violence with the choice of non-violent tactics.

Many of my correspondents, including the young radicals I interviewed, also raised the question of the "representativeness" of the leaders of Vietnam Summer. I have discussed this issue at some length in the Introduction, and have taken into account many of my correspondents' comments on the earlier draft. It has become even clearer to me as time progressed that no unified characterization can do justice to the enormous variety of outlooks, styles, and personalities that are joined together in the New Left.

But perhaps the major change in my own involvement with the subjects of this book came simply as a result of trying to formulate generalizations sufficiently inclusive to describe most of them, yet sufficiently precise to give a sense of their distinctiveness. Rereading the transcripts of my interviews with these young radicals itself helped give me greater distance, just as the written record is more distant than the spoken word. And as I attempted to connect these young radicals with social forces and historical trends that affect us all, I gained greater perspective on what was indeed "special" about them, as on what seemed related in an important way to the post-modern world. As my immediate identification with these young men and women diminished, my liking for them remained, but I increasingly questioned whether their style—to me a very attractive one—could carry them to the extensive and revolutionary social changes they propose. In all these ways, I felt that the immediacy of my own involvement diminished in the process of writing this book.

Yet my initially positive reaction to these young radicals and to their Movement has continued. Working with, and writing about, the leaders of Vietnam Summer was in some respects a "radicalizing" experience for me: I find myself more ready to understand, sympathize with and support many of their actions than I was before the summer. I had not expected to find these young men and women as open, insightful, intelligent, realistic, zestful, and dedicated as I did. Although I had argued in earlier writings against the "peacenik" stereotype (part hippie and part radical rebel), I was nevertheless surprised. A desire to share the impressions that surprised me was one of the prime factors that led me to write this book. And the hope that a better understanding of these young men and women—of who they are, what they object to in our society, and what they propose for it—might contribute to understanding our common desperate predicament led me to seek early publication for this book, despite my awareness of its many limitations.

Appendix B The sources of student dissent*

The apparent upsurge of dissent among American college students is one of the more puzzling phenomena in recent American history. Less than a decade ago, commencement orators were decrying the "silence" of college students in the face of urgent national and international issues; but in the past two or three years, the same speakers have warned graduating classes across the country against the dangers of unreflective protest, irresponsible action, and unselective dissent. Rarely in history has apparent apathy been replaced so rapidly by publicized activism, silence by strident dissent.

This "wave" of dissent among American college students has been much discussed. Especially in the mass media—popular magazines, newspapers, and television—articles of interpretation, explanation, deprecation, and occasionally applause have appeared in enormous numbers. More important, from the first beginnings of the student civil rights movement, social scientists have been regular participant-observers and investigators of student dissent. There now exists a considerable body of research that deals with the characteristics and settings of student dissent (see Lipset and Altbach, 1966; Block, Haan, and Smith, forthcoming; Katz, 1967; Peterson, 1968 for summaries of this research). To be sure, most of these studies are topical (centered around a particular protest or demonstration), and some of the more extensive studies are still in varying stages of incompletion. Yet enough evidence has already been gathered to permit tentative generalizations about the varieties, origins, and future of student dissent in the 1960's.

---

* From *The Journal of Social Issues* (1967), 23: 108–137.

In the remarks to follow, I will attempt to gather together this evidence (along with my own research and informal observations) to provide tentative answers to three questions about student dissent today. First, What is the nature of student dissent in American colleges? Second, What are the sources of the recent "wave of protest" by college students? And third, What can we predict about the future of student dissent?

Two varieties of dissent

Dissent is by no means the dominant mood of American college students. Every responsible study or survey shows apathy and privatism far more dominant than dissent (see, for example, *Newsweek,* 1965; Katz, 1965; Reed, 1966; Peterson, 1966; Block, Haan, and Smith, forthcoming). On most of our twenty-two hundred campuses, student protest, student alienation, and student unrest are something that happens elsewhere, or that characterizes a mere handful of "kooks" on the local campus. However we define "dissent," overt dissent is relatively infrequent and tends to be concentrated largely at the more selective, "progressive," and "academic" colleges and universities in America. Thus, Peterson's study of student protests (1966) finds political demonstrations concentrated in the larger universities and institutions of higher academic caliber, and almost totally absent at teachers colleges, technical institutes, and non-academic denominational colleges. And even at the colleges that gather together the greatest number of dissenters, the vast majority of students—generally well over ninety-five per cent—remain interested onlookers or opponents rather than active dissenters. Thus, whatever we say about student dissenters is said about a very small minority of America's six million college students. At most colleges, dissent is not visible at all.

Partly because the vast majority of American students remain largely uncritical of the wider society, fundamentally conformist in behavior and outlook, and basically "adjusted" to the prevailing collegiate, national, and international order, the small minority of dissenting students is highly visible to the mass media. As I will argue later, such students are often distinctively talented; they "use" the mass media effectively; and they generally succeed in their goal of making themselves and their causes highly visible. Equally important, student dissenters of all types arouse deep and ambivalent feelings in non-dissenting students and adults—envy, resentment, admiration, repulsion, nostalgia, and guilt. Such feelings contribute both to the selective overattention dissenters receive and to the often distorted perceptions and interpretations of them and their activities. Thus, there has developed through the mass media and the imaginings of adults a more or less stereotyped—and generally incorrect—image of the student dissenter.

The "stereotypical" dissenter as popularly portrayed is both a Bohemian and a political activist. Bearded, be-Levi-ed, long-haired, dirty, and unkempt, he is seen as profoundly disaffected from his society, often influenced by "radical" (Marxist, Communist, Maoist, or Castroite) ideas, as experimenter in sex and drugs, unconventional in his daily behavior. Frustrated and unhappy, often deeply maladjusted as a person, he is a "failure" (or as one U.S. Senator put it, a "reject"). Certain academic communities like Berkeley are said to act as "magnets" for dissenters, who selectively attend colleges with a reputation as protest centers. Furthermore, dropouts or "non-students" who have failed in college cluster in large numbers around the fringes of such colleges, actively seeking pretexts for protest, refusing all compromise, and impatient with ordinary democratic processes.

According to such popular analyses, the sources of dissent are to be found in the loss of certain traditional American virtues. The "breakdown" of American family life, high rates of divorce, the "softness" of American living, inadequate parents, and, above all, overindulgence and "spoiling" contribute to the prevalence of dissent. Brought up in undisciplined homes by parents unsure of their own values and standards, dissenters channel their frustration and anger against the older generation, against all authority, and against established institutions.

Similar themes are sometimes found in the interpretations of more scholarly commentators. "Generational conflict" is said to underlie the motivation to dissent, and a profound "alienation" from American society is seen as a factor of major importance in producing protests. Then, too, such factors as the poor quality and impersonality of American college education, the large size and lack of close student-faculty contact in the "multiversity" are sometimes seen as the latent or precipitating factors in student protests, regardless of the manifest issues around which students are organized. And still other scholarly analysts, usually men now disillusioned by the radicalism of the 1930's, have expressed fear of the dogmatism, rigidity, and "authoritarianism of the Left" of today's student activists.

These stereotyped views are, I believe, incorrect in a variety of ways. They confuse two distinct varieties of student dissent; equally important, they fuse dissent with maladjustment. There are, of course, as many forms of dissent as there are individual dissenters; and any effort to counter the popular stereotype of the dissenter by pointing to the existence of distinct "types" of dissenters runs the risk of oversimplifying at a lower level of abstraction. Nonetheless, it seems to me useful to suggest that student dissenters generally fall somewhere along a continuum that runs between two ideal types—first, the political activist or protester, and second, the withdrawn, culturally alienated student.

The activist—The defining characteristic of the "new" activist is his participation in a student demonstration or group activity that concerns itself with some matter of general political, social, or ethical principle. Characteristically, the activist feels that some injustice has been done, and attempts to "take a stand," "demonstrate," or in some fashion express his convictions. The specific issues in question range from protest against a paternalistic college administration's actions to disagreement with American Vietnam policies, from indignation at the exploitation of the poor to anger at the firing of a devoted teacher, from opposition to the Selective Service laws which exempt him but not the poor, to—most important—outrage at the deprivation of the civil rights of other Americans.

The initial concern of the protester is almost always immediate, *ad hoc,* and local. To be sure, the student who protests about one issue is likely to feel inclined or obliged to demonstrate his convictions on other issues as well (Heist, 1966). But whatever the issue, the protester rarely demonstrates because his *own* interests are jeopardized, but rather because he perceives injustices being done to *others* less fortunate than himself. For example, one of the apparent paradoxes about protests against current draft policies is that the protesting students are selectively drawn from the subgroup *most* likely to receive student deferments for graduate work. The basis of protest is a general sense that the selective service rules and the war in Vietnam are unjust to others with whom the student is identified, but whose fate he does not share. If one runs down the list of "causes" taken up by student activists, in rare cases are demonstrations directed at improving the lot of the protesters themselves; identification with the oppressed is a more important motivating factor than an actual sense of immediate personal oppression.

The anti-ideological stance of today's activists has been noted by many commentators. This distrust of formal ideologies (and at times of articulate thought) makes it difficult to pinpoint the positive social and political values of student protesters. Clearly, many current American political institutions like *de facto* segregation are opposed;

clearly, too, most students of the New Left reject careerism and familism as personal values. In this sense, we might think of the activist as (politically) "alienated." But this label seems to me more misleading than illuminating, for it overlooks the more basic *commitment* of most student activists to other ancient, traditional, and creedal American values like free speech, citizen's participation in decision-making, equal opportunity and justice. Insofar as the activist rejects all or part of "the power structure," it is because current political realities fall so far short of the ideals he sees as central to the American creed. And insofar as he repudiates careerism and familism, it is because of his implicit allegiance to other human goals he sees, once again, as more crucial to American life. Thus, to emphasize the "alienation" of activists is to neglect their more basic allegiance to creedal American ideals.

One of these ideals is, of course, a belief in the desirability of political and social action. Sustained in good measure by the successes of the student civil rights movement, the protester is usually convinced that demonstrations are effective in mobilizing public opinion, bringing moral or political pressure to bear, demonstrating the existence of his opinions, or, at times, in "bringing the machine to a halt." In this sense, then, despite his criticisms of existing political practices and social institutions, he is a political optimist. Moreover, the protester must believe in at least minimal organization and group activity; otherwise, he would find it impossible to take part, as he does, in any organized demonstrations or activities. Despite their search for more truly "democratic" forms of organization and action (*e.g.*, participatory democracy), activists agree that group action is more effective than purely individual acts. To be sure, a belief in the value and efficacy of political action is not equivalent to endorsement of prevalent political institutions or forms of action. Thus, one characteristic of activists is their search for new forms of social action, protest, and political organization (community organization, sit-ins, participatory democracy) that will be more effective and less oppressive than traditional political institutions.

The culturally alienated—In contrast to the politically optimistic, active, and socially concerned protester, the culturally alienated student is far too pessimistic and too firmly opposed to "the System" to wish to demonstrate his disapproval in any organized public way.* His

* The following paragraphs are based on the study of culturally alienated students described in *The Uncommitted* (1965). For a more extensive discussion of the overwhelmingly anti-political stance

demonstrations of dissent are private: through non-conformity of behavior, ideology, and dress, through personal experimentation and, above all, through efforts to intensify his own subjective experience, he shows his distaste and disinterest in politics and society. The activist attempts to change the world around him, but the alienated student is convinced that meaningful change of the social and political world is impossible; instead, he considers "dropping out" the only real option.

Alienated students tend to be drawn from the same general social strata and colleges as protesters. But psychologically and ideologically, their backgrounds are often very different. Alienated students are more likely to be disturbed psychologically; and although they are often highly talented and artistically gifted, they are less committed to academic values and intellectual achievement than are protesters. The alienated student's real campus is the school of the absurd, and he has more affinity for pessimistic existentialist ontology than for traditional American activism. Furthermore, such students usually find it psychologically and ideologically impossible to take part in organized group activities for any length of time, particularly when they are expected to assume responsibilities for leadership. Thus, on the rare occasions when they become involved in demonstrations, they usually prefer peripheral roles, avoid responsibilities, and are considered a nuisance by serious activists (Draper, 1965).

Whereas the protesting student is likely to accept the basic political and social values of his parents, the alienated student almost always rejects his parents' values. In particular, he is likely to see his father as a man who has "sold out" to the pressures for success and status in American society: he is determined to avoid the fate that overtook his father. Toward their mothers, however, alienated students usually express a very special sympathy and identification. These mothers, far from encouraging their sons toward independence and achievement, generally seem to have been over-solicitous and limiting. The most common family environment of the alienated-student-to-be consists of a parental schism supplemented by a special mother-son alliance of mutual understanding and maternal control and depreciation of the father (Keniston, 1965a).

In many colleges, alienated students often constitute a kind of hidden underground, disorganized and shifting in membership, in

---

of these students, see Appendix C, and also Rigney and Smith (1961), Allen and Silverstein (1967), Watts and Whittaker (1967), and Whittaker and Watts (1966).

which students can temporarily or permanently withdraw from the ordinary pressures of college life. The alienated are especially attracted to the hallucinogenic drugs like marijuana, mescaline, and LSD, precisely because these agents combine withdrawal from ordinary social life with the promise of greatly intensified subjectivity and perception. To the confirmed "acid-head," what matters is intense, drug-assisted perception; the rest—including politics, social action and student demonstrations—is usually seen as "role-playing."*

The recent and much-publicized emergence of "hippie" subcultures in several major cities and increasingly on the campuses of many selective and progressive colleges illustrates the overwhelmingly apolitical stance of alienated youth. For although hippies oppose war and believe in interracial living, few have been willing or able to engage in anything beyond occasional peace marches or apolitical "human be-ins." Indeed, the hippie's emphasis on immediacy, "love," and "turning-on," together with his basic rejection of the traditional values of American life, inoculates him against involvement in long-range activist endeavors like education or community organization, and even against the sustained effort needed to plan and execute demonstrations

* The presence among student dissenters of a group of "non-students" —that is, dropouts from college or graduate school who congregate or remain near some academic center—has been much noted. In fact, however, student protesters seem somewhat *less* likely to drop out of college than do non-participants in demonstrations (Heist, 1966), and there is no evidence that dropping out of college is in any way related to dissent from American society (Keniston and Helmreich, 1965). On the contrary, several studies suggest that the academically gifted and psychologically intact student who drops out of college voluntarily has few distinctive discontents about his college or about American society (Suczek and Alfort, 1966; Pervin *et al.*, 1966; Wright, 1966). If he is dissatisfied at all, it is with himself, usually for failing to take advantage of the "rich educational opportunities" he sees in his college. The motivations of students dropping out of college are complex and varied, but such motivations more often seem related to personal questions of self-definition and parental identification or to a desire to escape relentless academic pressures, than to any explicit dissent from the Great Society. Thus, although a handful of students have chosen to drop out of college for a period in order to devote themselves to political and societal protest activities, there seems little reason in general to associate the dropout with the dissenter, whether he be a protester or an alienated student. The opposite is nearer the truth.

or marches. For the alienated hippie, American society is beyond redemption (or not worth trying to redeem); but the activist, no matter how intense his rejection of specific American policies and practices, retains a conviction that his society can and should be changed. Thus, despite occasional agreement in principle between the alienated and the activists, co-operation in practice has been rare, and usually ends with activists accusing the alienated of "irresponsibility," while the alienated are confirmed in their view of activists as moralistic, "up-tight," and "un-cool."

Obviously, no description of a type ever fits an individual perfectly. But by this rough typology, I mean to suggest that popular stereotypes which present a unified portrait of student dissent are gravely oversimplified. More specifically, they confuse the politically pessimistic and socially uncommitted alienated student with the politically hopeful and socially committed activist. To be sure, there are many students who fall between these two extremes, and some of them alternate between passionate search for intensified subjectivity and equally passionate efforts to remedy social and political injustices. And as I will later suggest, even within the student movement, one of the central tensions is between political activism and cultural alienation. Nonetheless, even to understand this tension we must first distinguish between the varieties of dissent apparent on American campuses.

Furthermore, the distinction between activists and alienated students as psychological types suggests the incompleteness of scholarly analyses that see social and historical factors as the only forces that "push" a student toward one or the other of these forms of dissent. To be sure, social and cultural factors are of immense importance in providing channels for the expression (or suppression) of dissent, and in determining *which* kinds of dissenters receive publicity, censure, support, or ostracism in any historical period. But these factors cannot, in general, change a hippie into a committed activist, or a SNCC field worker into a full-time "acid-head." Thus, the prototypical activist of 1966 is not the "same" student as the prototypical student Bohemian of 1956, but is rather the politically aware but frustrated, academically oriented "privatist" of that era. Similarly, as I will argue below, the most compelling alternative to most activists is not the search for kicks or sentience but the quest for scholarly competence. And if culturally sanctioned opportunities for the expression of alienation were to disappear, most alienated students would turn to private psychopathology rather than to public activism.

Stated more generally, historical forces do not ordinarily transform radically the character, values, and inclinations of an adult in later life. Rather, they thrust certain groups forward in some eras and discourage or suppress other groups. The recent alteration in styles of student dissent in America is therefore not to be explained so much by the malleability of individual character as by the power of society to bring activists into the limelight, providing them with the intellectual and moral instruments for action. Only a minority of potential dissenters fall close enough to the mid-point between alienation and activism so that they can constitute a "swing vote" acutely responsive to social and cultural pressures and styles. The rest, the majority, are characterologically committed to one or another style of dissent.

The sources of activism

What I have termed "alienated" students are by no means a new phenomenon in American life, or for that matter in industrialized societies. Bohemians, "beatniks," and artistically inclined undergraduates who rejected middle-class values have long been a part of the American student scene, especially at more selective colleges; they constituted the most visible form of dissent during the relative political "silence" of American students in the 1950's. What is distinctive about student dissent in recent years is the unexpected emergence of a vocal minority of politically and socially active students.* Much is now known about the characteristics of such students, and the circumstances under which protests are likely to be mounted. At the same time, many areas of ignorance remain. In the account to follow, I will attempt to formulate a series of general hypotheses concerning the sources of student activism.†

* Student activism, albeit of a rather different nature, was also found in the 1930's. For a discussion and contrast of student protest today and after the Depression, see Lipset (1966a).

† Throughout the following, I will use the terms "protester" and activist" interchangeably, although I am aware that some activists are not involved in protests. Furthermore, the category of "activist" is an embracing one, comprising at least three subclasses. First, those who might be termed *reformers,* that is, students involved in community-organization work, the Peace Corps, tutoring programs, Vista, et cetera, but not generally affiliated with any of the "New Left" organizations. Second, the group of *activists proper,* most of whom are or have been affiliated with organizations like the Free Speech Movement at Berkeley, Students for a Democratic Society, the Student Non-violent Coordinating Committee, the Congress of Racial Equality,

It is abundantly clear that no single factor will suffice to explain the increase of politically motivated activities and protests on American campuses. Even if we define an activist narrowly, as a student who (a) acts together with others in a group, (b) is concerned with some ethical, social, ideological, or political issue, and (c) holds liberal or "radical" views, the sources of student activism and protest are complex and interrelated. At least four kinds of factors seem involved in any given protest. First, the individuals involved must be suitably predisposed by their personal backgrounds, values, and motivations. Second, the likelihood of protest is far greater in certain kinds of educational and social settings. Third, socially directed protests require a special cultural climate, that is, certain distinctive values and views about the effectiveness and meaning of demonstrations, and about the wider society. And finally, some historical situations are especially conducive to protests.

The protest-prone personality

A large and still growing number of studies, conducted under different auspices, at different times, and about different students, present a remarkably consistent picture of the protest-prone individual (Aiken, Demerath, and Marwell, 1966; Flacks, 1967; Gastwirth, 1965; Heist, 1965, 1966; Lyonns, 1965; Somers, 1965; Watts and Whittaker, 1966; Westby and Braungart, 1966; Katz, 1967; and Paulus, 1968). For one, student protesters are generally outstanding students; the higher the student's grade average, the more outstanding his academic achievements, the more likely it is that he will become involved in any given political demonstration. Similarly, student activists come from families with liberal political values; a disproportionate number report that their parents hold views essentially similar to their own, and accept or support their activities. Thus, among the parents of protesters we find large numbers of liberal Democrats, plus an unusually large scattering of pacifists, socialists, et cetera. A disproportionate number of protesters come from Jewish families; and if the parents of activists are religious, they tend to be concentrated in the more liberal denominations—Re-

---

or the Vietnam Summer Project. Finally, there is a much-publicized handful of students who might be considered *extremists,* who belong to doctrinaire Marxist and Trotskyite organizations like the now-defunct May Second Movement. No empirical study with which I am acquainted has investigated the differences between students in these three subgroups. Most studies have concentrated on the "activist proper," and my remarks will be based on a reading of their data.

form Judaism, Unitarianism, the Society of Friends, et cetera. Such parents are reported to have high ethical and political standards, regardless of their actual religious convictions.

As might be expected of a group of politically liberal and academically talented students, a disproportionate number are drawn from professional and intellectual families of upper-middle-class status. For example, compared with active student conservatives, members of protest groups tend to have higher parental incomes, more parental education, and less anxiety about social status (Westby and Braungart, 1966). Another study finds that high levels of education distinguish the activist's family even in the grandparental generation (Flacks, 1967). In brief, activists are not drawn from disadvantaged, status-anxious, underprivileged, or uneducated groups; on the contrary, they are selectively recruited from among those young Americans who have had the most socially fortunate upbringings.

The basic value commitments of the activist tend to be academic and non-vocational. Such students are rarely found among engineers, future teachers at teachers colleges, or students of business administration (see Trent and Craise, 1967). Their over-all educational goals are those of a liberal education for its own sake, rather than specifically technical, vocational, or professional preparation. Rejecting careerist and familist goals, activists espouse humanitarian, expressive, and self-actualizing values. Perhaps because of these values, they delay career choice longer than their classmates (Flacks, 1967). Nor are such students distinctively dogmatic, rigid, or authoritarian. Quite the contrary, the substance and style of their beliefs and activities tends to be open, flexible, and highly liberal. Their fields of academic specialization are non-vocational—the social sciences and the humanities. Once in college, they not only do well academically, but tend to persist in their academic commitments, dropping out *less* frequently than most of their classmates. As might be expected, a disproportionate number receive a B.A. within four years and continue on to graduate school, preparing themselves for academic careers.

Survey data also suggest that the activist is not distinctively dissatisfied with his college education. As will be noted below, activists generally attend colleges that provide the best, rather than the worst, undergraduate education available today. Objectively then, activists probably have less to complain about in their undergraduate educations than most other students. And, subjectively as well, surveys show most activists, like most other American undergraduates, to be relatively well satisfied with their undergraduate educations (Somers,

1965; Kornhauser, 1967). Thus, dissatisfaction with educational failings of the "impersonal multiversity," however important as a rallying cry, does not appear to be a distinctive cause of activism.

In contrast to their relative satisfaction with the quality of their educations, however, activists *are* distinctively dissatisfied with what might be termed the "civil-libertarian" defects of their college administrations. While no doubt a great many American undergraduates distrust "University Hall," this distrust is especially pronounced amongst student protesters (Kornhauser, 1967; Paulus, 1968). Furthermore, activists tend to be more responsive than other students to deprivations of civil rights on campus as well as off campus, particularly when political pressures seem to motivate on-campus policies they consider unjust. The same responsiveness increasingly extends to issues of "student power": *i.e.,* student participation and decisions affecting campus life. Thus, bans on controversial speakers, censorship of student publications, and limitations on off-campus political or social action are likely to incense the activist, as is arbitrary "administration without the consent of the administered." But it is primarily perceived injustice or the denial of student rights by the administration—rather than poor educational quality, neglect by the faculty, or the impersonality of the multiversity—that agitates the activist.

Most studies of activists have concentrated on variables that are relatively easy to measure: social class, academic achievements, explicit values, and satisfaction with college. But these factors alone will not explain activism: more students possess the demographic and attitudinal characteristics of the protest-prone personality than are actually involved in protests and social-action programs. Situational, institutional, cultural, and historical factors (discussed below), obviously contribute to "catalyzing" a protest-prone personality into an actual activist. But it also seems that, within the broad demographic group so far defined, more specific psychodynamic factors contribute to activism.

In speculating about such factors, we leave the ground of established fact and enter the terrain of speculation, for only a few studies have explored the personality dynamics and family constellation of the activist; and most of these studies are impressionistic and clinical (*e.g.,* Coles, 1967; Ehle, 1965; Draper, 1965; Fishman and Solomon, n.d., 1964; Gastwirth, 1965; Newfield, 1966; Schneider, 1966; Solomon and Fishman, 1963, 1964; Zinn 1965). But certain facts are clear. As noted, activists are *not,* on the whole, repudiating or rebelling against explicit parental values and ideologies. On the contrary, there is some evidence that such students are living out their parents' values in practice; and one study suggests that activists may be somewhat *closer* to their parents' values than non-activists (Flacks, 1967). Thus, any simple concept of "generational conflict" or "rebellion against parental authority" is clearly oversimplified as applied to the motivations of most protesters.

It does seem probable, however, that many activists are concerned with *living out expressed but unimplemented parental values.* Solomon and Fishman (1963, 1964), studying civil rights activists and peace marchers, argue that many demonstrators are "acting out" in their demonstrations the values that their parents explicitly believed, but did not have the courage or opportunity to practice or fight for. Similarly, when protesters criticize their fathers, it is usually over their fathers' failure to practice what they have preached to their children throughout their lives. Thus, in the personal background of the protester there is occasionally a suggestion that his father is less than "sincere" (and even at times "hypocritical") in his professions of political liberalism. In particular, both careerism and familism in parents are the objects of activist criticisms, the more so because these implicit goals often conflict with explicit parental values. And it may be that protesters receive both covert and overt support from their parents because the latter are secretly proud of their children's eagerness to implement the ideals they as parents have only given lip service to. But whatever the ambivalences that bind parents with their activist children, it would be wrong to over-emphasize them: what is most impressive is the solidarity of older and younger generations.

While no empirical study has tested this hypothesis, it seems probable that in many activist-producing families, the mother will have a dominant psychological influence on her son's development. I have already noted that the protester's cause is rarely himself, but rather alleviating the oppression of others. As a group, activists seem to possess an unusual *capacity for nurturant identification*—that is, for empathy and sympathy with the underdog, the oppressed, and the needy. Such a capacity can have many origins, but its most likely source in upper-middle-class professional families is identification with an active mother whose own work embodies nurturant concern for others. Flacks's finding that the mothers of activists are likely to be employed, often in professional or service roles like teaching and social work, is consistent with this hypothesis. In general, in American society, middle-class women have greater social and financial freedom to work in jobs that are idealistically "fulfilling," as opposed to merely lucrative or prestigious. As a rule, then, in middle-class families, it is the mother who actively embodies in her life and work the humanitarian, social, and political ideals that the father may share in principle but does not or cannot implement in his career.

Given what we know about the general characteristics of the families of protest-prone students, it also seems probable that the dominant ethos of their families is unusually equalitarian, permissive, "democratic," and highly individuated. More specifically, we might expect that these will be families where children talk back to their parents at the dinner table, where free dialogue and discussion of feelings is encouraged, and where "rational" solutions are sought to everyday family problems and conflicts. We would also expect that such families would place a high premium on self-expression and intellectual independence, encouraging their children to make up their own minds and to stand firm against group pressures. Once again, the mother seems the most likely carrier and epitome of these values, given her relative freedom from professional and financial pressures.

The contrast between such protest-prompting families and alienating families should be underlined. In both, the son's deepest emotional ties are often to his mother. But in the alienating family, the mother-son relationship is characterized by maternal control and intrusiveness, whereas in the protest-prompting family, the mother is a highly individuating force in her son's life, pushing him to independence and autonomy. Furthermore, the alienated student is determined to avoid the fate that befell his father, whereas the protesting student wants merely to live out the values that his father has not always worked hard enough to practice. Finally, the egalitarian, permissive, democratic, and individuating environment of the entire family of the protester contrasts with the overcontrolling, oversolicitous attitude of the mother in the alienating family, where the father is usually excluded from major emotional life within the family.

These hypotheses about the family background and psychodynamics of the protester are speculative, and future research may prove their invalidity. But regardless of whether *these* particular speculations are correct, it seems clear that. in addition to the general social, demographic, and attitudinal factors mentioned in most research, more specific familial and psychodynamic influences contribute to protest-proneness.

The protest-promoting institution

However we define his characteristics, one activist alone cannot make a protest: the characteristics of the college or university he attends have much to do with whether his protest-proneness will ever be mobilized into actual activism. Politically, socially, and ideologically motivated demonstrations and activities are most likely to occur at certain types of colleges; they are almost unknown at a majority of campuses. The effects of institutional characteristics on protests have been studied by Cowan (1966) and Peterson (1966).

In order for an organized protest or related activities to occur, there must obviously be sufficient *numbers* of protest-prone students to form a group, these students must have an opportunity for *interaction* with each other, and there must be *leaders* to initiate and mount the protest. Thus, we might expect—and we indeed find—that protest is associated with institutional size, and particularly with the congregation of large numbers of protest-prone students in close proximity to each other. More important than sheer size alone, however, is the "image" of the institution: certain institutions selectively recruit students with protest-prone characteristics. Specifically, a reputation for academic excellence and freedom, coupled with highly selective admissions policies, will tend to congregate large numbers of potentially protesting students on one campus. Thus, certain institutions do act as "magnets" for potential activists, but not so much because of their reputations for political radicalism as because they are noted for their academic excellence. Among such institutions are some of the most selective and "progressive" private liberal-arts colleges, major state universities (like Michigan, California at Berkeley, and Wisconsin) that have long traditions of vivid undergraduate teaching and high admissions standards (Lipset and Altbach, 1966), and many of the more prestigious private universities.

Once protest-prone students are on campus, they must have an opportunity to interact, to support one another, to develop common outlooks and shared policies—in short, to form an *activist subculture* with sufficient mass and potency to generate a demonstration or action program. Establishing "honors colleges" for talented and academically motivated students is one particularly effective way of creating a "critical mass" of protest-prone students. Similarly, inadequate on-campus housing indirectly results in the development of off-campus protest-prone subcultures (*e.g.,* co-op houses) in residences where student activists can develop a high degree of ideological solidarity and organizational cohesion.

But even the presence of a critical mass of protest-prone undergraduates in an activist subculture is not enough to make a protest without leaders and issues. And, in general, the most effective protest leaders have not been undergraduates, but teaching assistants. The presence of large numbers of exploited, underpaid, disgruntled and frustrated teacher assistants (or other equivalent graduate students and younger faculty members) is almost essential for organized and persistent protest. For one, advanced students tend to be more liberal politically and more sensitive to political issues than are most undergraduates—partly because education seems to have a liberalizing effect, and partly because students who persist into graduate school tend to be more liberal to start than those who drop out or go elsewhere. Furthermore, the frustrations of graduate students, especially at very large public universities, make them particularly sensitive to general problems of injustice, exploitation, and oppression. Teaching assistants, graduate students, and young faculty members also tend to be in daily and prolonged contact with students, are close enough to them in age to sense their mood, and are therefore in an excellent position to lead and organize student protests. Particularly at institutions which command little institutional allegiance from large numbers of highly capable graduate students (Lipset and Altbach, 1966) will such students be found among the leaders of the protest movement.

Finally, issues are a necessity. In many cases, these issues are provided by historical developments on the national or international scene, a point to which I will return. But in some instances, as at Berkeley, "on-campus" issues are the focus of protest. And in other cases, off-campus and on-campus issues are fused, as in the recent protests at institutional co-operation with draft-board policies considered unjust by demonstrating students. In providing such on-campus issues, the attitude of the university administration is central. Skillful handling of student complaints, the maintenance of open channels of communication between student leaders and faculty members, and administrative willingness to resist public and political pressures in order to protect the rights of students—all minimize the likelihood of organized protest. Conversely, a university administration that shows itself unduly sensitive to political, legislative, or public pressures, that treats students arrogantly, ineptly, condescendingly, hypocritically, or, above all, dishonestly, is asking for a demonstration.

Thus, one reason for the relative absence of on-campus student protests and demonstrations on the campuses of private, non-denominational "academic" colleges and universities (which recruit many protest-prone students) probably lies in the liberal policies of the administrations. As Cowan (1966) notes, liberal students generally attend non-restrictive and "libertarian" colleges. Given an administration and faculty that support or tolerate activism and student rights, student activists must generally find their issues off-campus. The same students, confronting an administration unduly sensitive to political pressures from a conservative board of regents or state legislature, might engage in active on-campus protests. There is also some evidence that clever administrative manipulation of student complaints, even in the absence of genuine concern with student rights, can serve to dissipate the potentialities of protest (Keene, 1966).

Among the institutional factors often cited as motivating student protest is the largeness, impersonality, atomization, "multiversitification," et cetera, of the university. I have already noted that student protests do not seem distinctively dissatisfied with their educations. Furthermore, the outstanding academic achievements and intellectual motivations of activists concentrate them, within any college, in the courses and programs that provide the most "personal" attention: honors programs, individual instruction, advanced seminars, and so on. Thus, they probably receive relatively *more* individual attention and a *higher* caliber of instruction than do non-protesters. Furthermore, protesters generally tend to occur at the best, rather than the worst, colleges, judged from the point of view of the quality of undergraduate instruction. Thus, despite the popularity of student slogans dealing with the impersonality and irrelevance of the multiversity, the absolute level of educational opportunities seems, if anything, positively related to the occurrence of protest: the better the institution, the more likely demonstrations are.

Nor can today's student activism be attributed in any direct way to mounting academic pressures. To be sure, activism is most manifest at those selective colleges where the "pressure to perform" (Keniston, 1965b) is greatest, where standards are highest, and where anxieties about being admitted to a "good" graduate or professional school are most pronounced. But, contrary to the argument of Lipset and Altbach (1966), the impact of academic pressure on activism seems negative rather than positive. Protest-prone students, with their superior academic attainments and strong intellectual commitments, seem especially vulnerable to a kind of academic professionalism that, because of the enormous demands it makes upon the student's energies, serves to cancel or preclude activism. Student demonstrations rarely take place during exam periods, and protests concerned with educational quality almost invariably seek an improvement of quality, rather than a lessening of pressure. Thus, though the pressure to perform doubtless affects *all* American students, it probably acts as a deterrent rather than a stimulus to student activism.

What probably does matter, however, is the *relative* deprivation of student expectations (see Brown, 1967). A college that recruits large numbers of academically motivated and capable students into a less than first-rate education program, one that oversells entering freshmen on the virtues of the college, or one that reneges on implicit or explicit promises about the quality and freedom of education may well produce an "academic backlash" that will take the form of student protests over the quality of education. Even more important is the gap between expectations and actualities regarding freedom of student expression. Stern (1966) has demonstrated that most entering freshmen have extremely high hopes regarding the freedom of speech and action they will be able to exercise during college: most learn the real facts quickly, and graduate thoroughly disabused of their illusions. But since activists, as I have argued above, are particularly responsive to these issues, they are apt to tolerate disillusion less lightly, and to take up arms to concretize their dashed hopes. Compared to the frustration engendered by disillusionment regarding educational quality, the relative deprivation of civil libertarian hopes seems a more potent source of protests. And with regard to both issues, it must be recalled that protests have been *fewest* at institutions of low educational quality and little freedom for student expression. Thus, it is not the absolute level either of educational quality or of student freedom that matters, but the gap between student hopes and institutional facts.

The protest-prompting cultural climate

Even if a critical mass of interacting protest-prone students forms in an institution that provides leadership and issues, student protests are by no means inevitable, as the quiescence of American students during the 1950's suggests. For protests to occur, other more broadly cultural factors, attitudes, and values must be present. Protest activities must be seen as meaningful acts, either in an instrumental or an expressive sense; and activists must be convinced that the consequences of activism and protest will not be overwhelmingly damaging to them. During the 1950's, one much-discussed factor that may have militated against student activism was the conviction that the consequences of protest (black-listing, FBI investigations, problems in obtaining security clearance, difficulties in getting jobs) were both harmful to the individual and yet extremely likely. Even more important was the sense on the part of many politically conscious students that participation in left-wing causes would merely show their naïveté, gullibility, and political innocence without furthering any worthy cause. The prevailing climate was such that protest was rarely seen as an act of any meaning or usefulness.

Today, in contrast, student protesters are not only criticized and excoriated by a large segment of the general public, but—more crucial—actively defended, encouraged, lionized, praised, publicized, photographed, interviewed, and studied by a portion of the academic community. Since the primary reference group of most activists is not the general public, but rather that liberal segment of the academic world most sympathetic to protest, academic support has a disproportionate impact on protest-prone students' perception of their own activities. In addition, the active participation of admired faculty members in protests, teach-ins, and peace marches, acts as a further incentive to students (Kelman, 1966). Thus, in a minority of American colleges, subcultures have arisen where protest is felt to be both an important existential act—a dignified way of "standing up to be counted"—and an effective way of "bringing the machine to a halt," sometimes by disruptive acts (sit-ins, strikes, et cetera), more often by calling public attention to injustice.

An equally important if less tangible "cultural" factor is the broad climate of social criticism in American society. As Parsons (1951, 1960), White (1961), and others have noted, one of the enduring themes of American society is the pressure toward "universalism," that is, an increasing extension of principles like equality, equal opportunity, and fair protection of the law to all groups within the society (and in recent years, to all groups in the world). As affluence has increased in American society, impatience at the slow "progress" of non-affluent minority groups has also increased, not only among students, but among other segments of the population. Even before the advent of the student civil rights movement, support for racial segregation was diminishing. Similarly, the current student concern for the "forgotten fifth" was not so much initiated by student activists as it was taken up by them. In this regard, student activists are both caught up in and in the vanguard of a new wave of extension of universalism in American society. Although the demands of student activists usually go far beyond the national consensus, they nonetheless reflect (at the same time that they have helped advance) one of the continuing trends in American social change.

A contrasting but equally enduring theme in American social criticism is a more fundamental revulsion against the premises of industrial—and now technological—society. Universalistic-liberal criticism blames our society because it has not yet extended its principles, privileges, and benefits to all: the complaint is injustice and the goal is to complete our unfinished business. But alienated-romantic criticism questions the validity and importance of these same principles, privileges, and benefits—the complaint is materialism and the goal is spiritual, aesthetic, or expressive fulfillment. The tradition of revulsion against conformist, anti-aesthetic, materialistic, ugly, middle-class America runs through American writing from Melville through the "lost generation" to the "beat generation," and has been expressed concretely in the Bohemian subcultures that have flourished in a few large American cities since the turn of the century. But today the power of the romantic-alienated position has increased: one response to prosperity has been a more searching examination of the technological assumptions upon which prosperity has been based. Especially for the children of the upper middle class, affluence is simply taken for granted, and the drive "to get ahead in the world" no longer makes sense for students who start out ahead. The meanings of life must be sought elsewhere, in art, sentience, philosophy, love, service to others, intensified experience, adventure—in short, in the broadly aesthetic or expressive realm.

Since neither the universalistic nor the romantic critique of modern society is new, these critiques affect the current student generation not only directly but indirectly, in that they have influenced the way many of today's college students were raised. Thus, a few of today's activists are children of the "radicals of the 1930's" (Lipset and Altbach, 1966); and Flacks comments on the growing number of intellectual, professional upper-middle-class families who have adopted "deviant" views of traditional American life and embodied these views in the practices by which they brought up their children. Thus, some of today's activists are the children of Bohemians, college professors, et cetera. But, in general, the explanation from parental "deviance" does not seem fully convincing. To be sure, the backgrounds of activists are "atypical" in a statistical sense, and thus might be termed empirically "deviant." It may indeed turn out that the parents of activists are distinguished by their emphasis on humanitarianism, intellectualism, and romanticism, and by their lack of stress on moralism (Flacks, 1967). But it is not obvious that such parental values can be termed "deviant" in any but a statistical sense. "Concern with the plight of others," "desire to realize intellectual capacities," and "lack of concern about the importance of strictly controlling personal impulses"—all these values might be thought of as more normative than deviant in upper-middle-class suburban American society in 1966. Even "sensitivity to beauty and art" is becoming increasingly acceptable. Nor can the socio-economic facts of affluence, freedom from status anxiety, high educational levels, permissiveness with children, training for independence, et cetera, be considered normatively deviant in middle-class America. Thus, the sense in which activists are the deviant offspring of subculturally deviant parents remains to be clarified.

Another explanation seems equally plausible, at least as applied to some student activists—namely, that their activism is closely related to the social and cultural conditions that promote high levels of psychological flexibility, complexity, and integration. As Bay (1967) has argued, social scientists may be too reluctant to entertain the possibility that some political and social outlooks or activities are symptomatic of psychological "health," while others indicate "disturbance." In fact, many of the personal characteristics of activists—empathy, superior intellectual attainments, capacity for group involvement, strong humanitarian values, emphasis on self-realization, et cetera—are consistent with the hypothesis that, as a group, they are unusually "healthy" psychologically. (See also Heist, 1966, and Trent and Craise, 1967). Similarly, the personal antecedents of activism—economic security, committed parents, humanitarian, liberal, and permissive home environments, good education, et cetera—are those that would seem to promote unusually high levels of psychological functioning. If this be correct, then former SDS president Tom Hayden's words (1966) may be a valid commentary on the cultural setting of activism:

> Most of the active student radicals today come from middle to upper middle-class professional homes. They were born with status and affluence as facts of life, not goals to be striven for. In their upbringing, their parents stressed the right of children to question and make judgments, producing perhaps the first generation of young people both affluent and independent of mind.

In agreeing with Bay (1967) that activists may be more psychologically "healthy" as a group than non-activists, I am aware of the many difficulties entailed by this hypothesis. First, complexity, flexibility, integration, high levels of functioning, et cetera, are by no means easy to define, and the criteria for "positive mental health" remain vague and elusive. (See Jahoda, 1958). Second, there are obviously many individuals of great psychological strength, flexibility, complexity, and integration who are not activists; and within the group of activists, there are many individuals with definite psychopathologies. In any social movement, a variety of individuals of highly diverse talents and motivations are bound to be involved, and global descriptions are certain to be oversimplified. Third, the explanation from "psychological health" and the explanation from "parental deviance" are not necessarily opposed.

On the contrary, these two arguments become identical if we assume that the preconditions for high levels of psychological functioning are both statistically and normatively deviant in modern American society. This assumption seems quite plausible.

Whatever the most plausible explanation of the socio-cultural sources of activism, the importance of prevailing attitudes toward student protest and of the climate of social criticism in America seems clear. In the past five years a conviction has arisen, at least among a minority of American college students, that protest and social action are effective and honorable. Furthermore, changes in American society, especially in middle-class child-rearing practices, mean that American students are increasingly responsive to both the universalistic and romantic critique of our society. Both strands of social criticism have been picked up by student activists in a rhetoric of protest that combines a major theme of impatience at the slow fulfillment of the creedal ideals of American society with a more muted minor theme of aesthetic revulsion at technological society itself. By and large, activists respond most affirmatively to the first theme, and alienated students to the second; but even within the student protest movement, these two themes coexist in uneasy tension.

The protest-producing historical situation

To separate what I have called the "cultural climate" from the "historical situation" is largely arbitrary. But by this latter term I hope to point to the special sensitivity of today's student activists to historical events and trends that do not immediately impinge upon their own lives. In other nations, and in the past, student protest movements seem to have been more closely related to immediate student frustrations than they are in America today. The "transformationist" (utopian, Marxist, universalistic, or democratic) aspirations of activist youth in rapidly developing nations often seem closely related to their personal frustrations under oppressive regimes or at "feudal" practices in their societies; the "restorationist" (romantic, alienated) youth movements that have appeared in later stages of industrialization seem closely connected to a personal sense of the loss of a feudal, maternal, and "organic" past. (See Lifton, 1960, 1963, 1964.) Furthermore, both universalistic and romantic youth movements in other nations have traditionally been highly ideological, committed either to concepts of universal democracy and economic justice or to particularistic values of brotherhood, loyalty, feeling, and nation.

Today's activists, in contrast, are rarely concerned with improving their own conditions and are highly motivated by identification with the oppressions of others. The anti-ideological bias of today's student activists has been underlined by virtually every commentator. Furthermore, as Flacks notes, the historical conditions that have produced protest elsewhere are largely absent in modern America; and the student "movement" in this country differs in important ways from student movements elsewhere. In many respects, then, today's American activists have no historical precedent, and only time will tell to what extent the appearance of organized student dissent in the 1960's is a product of locally American conditions, of the psychosocial effects of a technological affluence that will soon characterize other advanced nations, or of widespread changes in identity and style produced by psychohistorical factors that affect youth of all nations (thermonuclear warfare, increased culture contact, rapid communications, et cetera).

But whatever the historical roots of protest, today's student protester seems uniquely sensitive to historical trends and events. In interviewing student activists I have been impressed with how often they mention some world-historical event as the catalyst for their activism—in some cases, witnessing via television of the Little Rock demonstrations over school integration, in another case watching rioting Zengakuren students in Japan protesting the arrival of President Eisenhower, in other cases, particularly among Negro students, a strong identification with the rising black nationalism of recently independent African nations.

Several factors help explain this sensitivity to world events. For one, modern means of communication make the historical world more psychologically "available" to youth. Students today are exposed to world events and world trends with a speed and intensity that has no historical precedent. Revolutions, trends, fashions, and fads are now world-wide; it takes but two or three years for fashions to spread from Carnaby Street to New York, New Delhi, Tokyo, Warsaw, Lagos, and Lima. In particular, students who have been brought up in a tradition that makes them unusually empathic, humanitarian, and universalistic in values may react more intensely to exposure via television to student demonstrations in Japan than to social pressures from their fellow seniors in Centerville High. Finally, this broadening of empathy is, I believe, part of a general modern trend toward the *internationalization of identity*. Hastened by modern communications and consolidated by the world-wide threat of nuclear warfare, this trend involves, in vanguard groups in many nations, a loosening of parochial and national allegiances in favor of a more inclusive sense of affinity with one's peers (and non-peers) from all nations. In this respect, American student activists are both participants and leaders in the reorganization of psycho-social identity and ideology that is gradually emerging from the unique historical conditions of the twentieth century (Lifton, 1968).

A small but growing number of American students, then, exhibit a peculiar responsiveness to world-historical events—a responsiveness based partly on their own broad identification with others like them throughout the world, and partly on the availability of information about world events via the mass media. The impact of historical events, be they the world-wide revolution for human dignity and esteem, the rising aspirations of the developing nations, or the war in Vietnam, is greatly magnified upon such students; their primary identification is not their unreflective national identity, but their sense of affinity for Vietnamese peasants, Negro sharecroppers, demonstrating Zengakuren activists, exploited migrant workers, and the oppressed everywhere. One of the consequences of security, affluence, and education is a growing sense of personal involvement with those who are insecure, non-affluent and uneducated.

The future of student activism

I have argued that no single factor can explain or help us predict the future of the student protest movement in America: active expressions of dissent have become more prevalent because of an *interaction* of individual, institutional, cultural, and historical factors. Affluence and education have changed the environment within which middle-class children are raised, in turn producing a minority of students with special sensitivity to the oppressed and the dissenting everywhere. At the same time, technological innovations like television have made available to these students abundant imagery of oppression and dissent in America and in other nations. And each of these factors exerts a potentiating influence on the others.

Given some understanding of the interaction of these factors, general questions about the probable future of student activism in America can now be broken down into four more specific questions: Are we likely to produce (a) more protest-prone personalities? (b) more institutional settings in which protests are likely? (c) a cultural climate that sanctions and encourages activism? and (d) a historical situation that facilitates activism? To three of the questions (a, b, and d), I think the answer is a qualified yes; I would therefore expect that in the future, if the cultural climate remains the same, student activism and protest would continue to be visible features on the American social landscape.

Consider first the factors that promote protest-prone personalities. In the coming generation there will be more and more students who come from the upper middle class, highly educated, politically liberal, professional backgrounds from which protesters are selectively recruited (Michael, 1965). Furthermore, we can expect that a significant and perhaps growing proportion of these families will have the universalistic, humanitarian, equalitarian, and individualistic values found in the families of protesters. Finally, the expressive, permissive, democratic, and autonomy-promoting atmosphere of these families seems to be the emerging trend of middle-class America: older patterns of "entrepreneurial-authoritarian" control are slowly giving way to more "bureaucratic-democratic" techniques of socialization (Miller and Swanson, 1958). Such secular changes in the American family would produce a growing proportion of students with protest-prone personalities.

Institutional factors, I have argued, are of primary importance insofar as they bring together a critical mass of suitably protest-predisposed students in an atmosphere where they can interact, create their own subculture, develop leadership, and find issues. The growing size of major American universities, their increasing academic and intellectual selectivity, and the emphasis on "quality" education (honors programs, individual instruction, greater student freedom)—all seem to promote the continuing development of activist subcultures in a minority of American institutions. The increasing use of graduate-student teaching assistants in major universities points to the growing availability of large numbers of potential "leaders" for student protests. Admittedly, a sudden increase in the administrative wisdom in college deans and presidents could reduce the number of available "on-campus" issues; but such a growth in wisdom does not seem imminent.

In sharp contrast, a maintenance of the cultural climate required for continuation of activism during the coming years seems far more problematical. Much depends on the future course of the war in Vietnam. Continuing escalation of the war in Southeast Asia will convince many student activists that their efforts are doomed to ineffectuality. For as of mid-1967, anti-war activism has become the primary common cause of student protesters. The increasing militancy and exclusivity of the Negro student civil rights movement, its emphasis on "Black Power" and on grass-roots community-organization work (to be done by Negroes) is rapidly pushing white activists out of civil rights work, thus depriving them of the issue upon which the current mood of student activism was built. This fact, coupled with the downgrading of the War on Poverty, the decline of public enthusiasm for civil rights, and the increasing scarcity of public and private financing for work with the underprivileged sectors of American society, has already begun to turn activists away from domestic issues toward an increasingly single-minded focus on the war in Vietnam. Yet at the same time, increasing numbers of activists overtly or covertly despair of the efficacy of student attempts to mobilize public opinion against the war, much less to influence directly American foreign policies. Continuing escalation in Southeast Asia has also begun to create a more repressive atmosphere toward student (and other) protesters of the war, exemplified by the question, "Dissent or Treason?" Already a movement of activists back to full-time academic work is apparent.

Thus, the war in Vietnam, coupled by the "rejection" of white middle-class students by the vestigial black Civil Rights Movement is producing a crisis among activists, manifest by a "search for issues" and intense disagreement over strategy and tactics. At the same time, the diminution of support for student activism tends to exert a "radicalizing" effect upon those who remain committed activists—partly because frustration itself tends to radicalize the frustrated, and partly because many of the less dedicated and committed activists have dropped away from the movement. Furthermore, most activists find it difficult to turn from civil rights or peace work toward "organizing the middle class" along lines suggested by alienated-romantic criticisms of technological society. On the whole, activists remain more responsive to universalistic issues like peace and civil rights than to primarily expressive or aesthetic criticisms of American society. Furthermore, the practical and organizational problems of "organizing the middle class" are overwhelming. Were the student movement to be forced to turn away from universalistic issues like civil rights and peace to a romantic critique of the "quality of middle-class life," my argument here implies that its following and efficacy would diminish considerably. Were this to happen, observations based on student activism of a more "universalistic" variety would have to be modified to take account of a more radical and yet more alienated membership. Thus, escalation or even continuation of the war in Vietnam, particularly over a long period, will reduce the likelihood of student activism.

Yet there are other, probably more permanent, trends in American culture that argue for a continuation of activism. The further extension of affluence in America will probably mean growing impatience over our society's failure to include the "forgotten fifth" in its prosperity: as the excluded and underprivileged become fewer in number, pressures to include them in American society will grow. Similarly, as more young Americans are brought up in affluent homes and subcultures, many will undoubtedly turn to question the value of monetary, familistic, and careerist goals, looking instead toward expressive, romantic, experiential, humanitarian, and self-actualizing pursuits to give their lives meaning. Thus, in the next decades, barring a major world conflagration, criticisms of American society will probably continue and intensify on two grounds: first, that it has excluded a significant minority from its prosperity, and, second, that affluence alone is empty without humanitarian, aesthetic, or expressive fulfillment. Both of these trends would strengthen the climate conducive to continuing activism.

Finally, protest-promoting pressures from the rest of the world will doubtless increase in the coming years. The esteem revolution in developing nations, the rise of aspirations in the impoverished two-thirds of the world, and the spread of universalistic principles to other nations—all of these trends portend a growing international unrest, especially in the developing nations. If young Americans continue to be unusually responsive to the unfulfilled aspirations of those abroad, international trends will touch a minority of them deeply, inspiring them to overseas activities like the Peace Corps, to efforts to "internationalize" American foreign policies, and to an acute sensitivity to the frustrated aspirations of other Americans. Similarly, continuation of current American policies of supporting anti-Communist, but often repressive, regimes in developing nations (particularly regimes anathema to student activists abroad) will tend to agitate American students as well. Thus, pressures from the probable world situation will support the continuance of student protests in American society.

In the next decades, then, I believe we can foresee the continuation, with short-range ebbs and falls, of activism in American society. Only if activists were to become convinced that protests were ineffectual or social action impossible is this trend likely to be fundamentally reversed. None of this will mean that protesters will become a majority among American students; but we can anticipate a slowly growing minority of the most talented, empathic, and intellectually independent of our students who will take up arms against injustice both here and abroad.

Throughout this discussion, I have emphasized the contrast between two types of students, two types of family backgrounds, and two sets of values that inspire dissent from the Great Society. On the one hand, I have discussed students I have termed alienated, whose values are apolitical, romantic, and aesthetic. These students are most responsive to "romantic" themes of social criticism; that is, they reject our society because of its dehumanizing effects, its lack of aesthetic quality, and its failure to provide "spiritual" fulfillment to its members. And they are relatively impervious to appeals to social, economic, or political justice. On the other hand, I have discussed activists, who are politically involved, humanitarian, and universalistic in values. These students object to our society not because they oppose its basic principles, but because it fails to implement these principles fully at home and abroad.

In the future, the tension between the romantic-alienated and the universalistic-activist styles of dissent will probably increase. I would anticipate a growing polarization between those students and student groups who turn to highly personal and experiential pursuits like drugs, sex, art, and intimacy, and those students who redouble their efforts to change American society. In the past five years, activists have been in the ascendant, and the alienated have been little involved in organized political protests. But a variety of possible events could reverse this ascendancy. A sense of ineffectuality, especially if coupled with repression of organized dissent, would obviously dishearten many activists. More important, the inability of the student protest movement to define its own long-range objectives, coupled with its intransigent hostility to ideology and efficient organization, means that *ad hoc* protests are too rarely linked to the explicit intellectual, political, and social goals that alone can sustain prolonged efforts to change society. Without some shared sustaining vision of the society and world they are working to promote, and frustrated by the enormous obstacles that beset any social reformer, student activists would be likely to return to the library.

How and whether this tension between alienation and activism is resolved seems to me of the greatest importance. If a growing number of activists, frustrated by political ineffectuality or a mounting war in Southeast Asia, withdraw from active social concern into a narrowly academic quest for professional competence, then a considerable reservoir of the most talented young Americans will have been lost to our society and the world. The field of dissent would be left to the alienated, whose intense quest for *personal* salvation, meaning, creativity, and revelation dulls their perception of the public world and inhibits attempts to better the lot of others. If, in contrast, tomorrow's potential activists can feel that their demonstrations and actions are effective in molding public opinion and more important, in effecting needed social change, then the possibilities for constructive change in post-industrial American society are virtually without limit.

Appendix C Alienation in American youth*

In the past few years, the term "alienation" has become a catchword, a slogan, and a battle cry for that small segment of American students who are actively engaged in protest against some injustice in the prevailing system. The precise meanings of the term are seldom made clear—but from articulate student leaders, from their adult sympathizers, and even from many impartial commentators on the American student scene, we are told that a new tide of alienation is sweeping across American campuses. In context, this sense of "alienation" appears to involve many distinct things—a sense of disillusionment with traditional politics, dislike of University Hall, opposition to the war in Vietnam, impatience of the slowness of emancipation of Negro Americans, or, in a few cases, simple frustration at the visiting hours in women's dormitories.

I will here summarize several aspects of a research study that attempted to explore the characteristics of alienated students and the psychological origins of their alienation in an elite college population. I should make clear from the start, that I studied only *one* kind of alienation. The sense in which I have used the term alienation is the same sense in which we speak of "the alienated intellectual." That is, I have been interested in college students who took a critical or repudiative attitude toward their surrounding culture, and have defined alienation as "an explicit rejection of what are seen as the dominant values of American culture."

---

* Address to the Division of Personality and Social Psychology, American Psychological Association, New York, September, 1966. The research summarized here was supported in part by USPHS grants Nos. M–1287 and MH–8508.

The study I will discuss was conducted at Harvard College from 1957 to 1962. It was conducted with the guidance of Dr. Henry A. Murray, with the assistance of my colleagues Dr. Alden Wessman of Dartmouth, Dr. David Ricks of Teachers College, Dr. Arthur Couch of Harvard, and a variety of others. The study began from earlier work on alienation done by Murray and Anthony Davids. Essentially, our research had three parts. First, operational measures of alienation were developed and the correlates of these measures were studied systematically in personality tests, in background factors, in fantasy, and in interpersonal behavior. This aspect of the research, which extended over several years and involved approximately two thousand subjects in all, yielded a consistent picture of the characteristics of alienated students in the population studied. The second aspect of the study consisted of intensive clinical and long-range studies of extremely alienated students. And, finally, the understanding of individual alienation also requires, I believe, a more speculative inquiry into the social and historical factors which cooperate with psychological factors to produce cultural alienation in some, but not most, young Americans. In this report I will concentrate my remarks on the intensive clinical aspects of the study.

The alienation syndrome

In order to study alienated individuals, we first had to find a reliable way of identifying them. Over a period of several years, my colleagues and I developed a series of highly intercorrelated attitude scales. These attitudes constitute a kind of empirical cluster or "alienation syndrome"—a term borrowed from Murray and Davids.

The following scales were developed: (1) Distrust ("Expect the worst of others and you will avoid disappointment"); (2) Pessimism ("There is little chance of ever finding real happiness"); (3) Avowed Hostility ("At times, some people make you feel like killing them"); (4) Interpersonal Alienation ("Emotional commitments to others are usually the prelude to disappointment"); (5) Social Alienation ("Teamwork is the last refuge of mediocrity"); (6) Cultural Alienation ("The idea of trying to adjust to society as it is now constituted fills me with horror"); (7) Self-Contempt ("Any man who really knows himself has good cause to be horrified"); (8) Vacillation ("I make few commitments without some reservation about the wisdom of undertaking them"); (9) Subspection ("First impressions cannot be relied upon; what lies beneath the surface is often utterly different"); (10) Outsider ("I feel strongly how different I am from most people"); (11) Unstructured Universe ("The notion that man and nature are governed by regular laws is an illusion"). Together, these scales constitute an operational definition of the "alienation syndrome." To give a rough notion of the coherence of this syndrome, the mean scale-to-scale correlation is $+.47$, and the mean correlation of Distrust with all other alienation scales is $+.58$, in the population we studied.

The development of these scales enabled us to select a small group of students for intensive clinical study. A large group of Harvard College sophomores were given these alienation scales and, on the basis of their scores, three groups of a dozen students each were selected for intensive clinical study: (1) A highly alienated group, (2) a highly non-alienated group, and (3) a third "comparison" group. The modal alienated student was in the most-alienated eight per cent of the college population; the modal non-alienated student was in the least-alienated eight per cent; and the members of the comparison group stood very near the middle.

All of these undergraduates took part in at least one year of the research study and most of them were studied throughout the last three years of their college careers. During this time, they gave approximately two hours a week to the research, for which they were paid. The research ranged over a wide variety of topics. All students wrote a lengthy autobiography and a detailed statement of their basic values and beliefs. All were repeatedly interviewed about matters autobiographical, ideological, vocational, ethical, and experimental. All took the Thematic Apperception Test (T.A.T.) in a variety of familiar and unfamiliar versions. In addition, all took part in a great variety of other specific psychological experiments. By the end of the three-year period, large amounts of information had been collected about almost every aspect of the individual's life.

The clinical study of alienation focused on the following questions.

1. What is the ideology of alienation as seen in these students?
2. What common characteristics of behavior and life-style do these alienated students possess?
3. What aspects of past life (infancy, family characteristics, childhood, adolescence) do these alienated students share?
4. What are the central features of the fantasy life of alienated students?
5. What hypotheses can be advanced that might explain the psychological origins of alienation?

In an attempt to answer these questions, the case records of each student were first studied independently. Then, alienated students were systematically contrasted with the non-alienated, and with the comparison group. In certain respects, of course, all three groups were similar, for example, all students in all three groups were intelligent and academically oriented, and most were from middle-class social backgrounds. But in the account to follow, I will emphasize only those characteristics of the alienated students which were *not* found to the same degree among the non-alienated or the comparison group.

The ideology of alienation

Statistical studies had suggested that distrust was a primary variable in the alienation syndrome. Clinical investigations confirmed this finding. For alienated students, distrust extends far beyond a low view of human nature; they also believe that intimacy ends in disillusion, that attachment to a group entails the loss of individuality, and that all appearances are untrustworthy. Nor can American culture be trusted: it is mechanical, boring, trashy, cheap, conformist, and dull. Any kind of positive commitment is viewed negatively.

In addition, most alienated students are native existentialists. Few of them, when they began the research study, had read existentialist philosophers; yet they had often spontaneously arrived at a view of the world close to that of the most pessimistic existentialists like Sartre. From middle adolescence on, alienated students had become increasingly aware of the darkness, isolation, and meaninglessness of life. The universe itself is dead, lacking in structure, inherently unpredictable and random. Individual life, too, is devoid of purpose and preordained form. Consequently, any meaning or truth that an individual finds is inevitably subjective and solipsistic. Morality, too, is seen as egocentric, arbitrary, and individualistic. Given the unpredictability of the future, long-range ethical idealism is impossible; the present becomes overwhelmingly important.

Alienated undergraduates do not react stoically to this view of the universe. On the contrary, their response is scorn, bitterness, and anger. Love and hate, they insist, are inseparable. Their own hostilities are close to awareness, and their scorn is especially intense when they confront other students who are not alienated. Indeed, their anger is so corrosive that it extends even to themselves. True to the logic of their position, they maintain that the consequence of self-knowledge is self-contempt, and are quick to admit their own self-revulsion. Similarly, their resentment is expressed in their conviction that all men inevitably use each other for their own purposes.

Another distinctive outlook of these students is a profound pessimism about, and distaste for, politics and political action. One student, asked about world affairs, wrote, "I leave speculations about world affairs to our politicians . . . political activity is like the games children play . . . whatever happens will not affect my thinking." Another, discussing atomic warfare, notes, "Since the race is doomed to die someday, I can't see that it makes much difference." And still another, predicting a nuclear war "very eventually," says, "I'll let it bother me then." These are not, then, students who believe in the efficacy or value of political action.

Much of the explicit philosophy of these students is negative. They are, like Nietzsche (one of their favorite writers), philosophers with hammers, whose favorite intellectual sport is exposing the hypocrisy of others. They distrust all Positive Thinking and therefore find it almost impossible to agree with any questionnaire statement that clearly expresses an affirmative view. But despite the negative cast of their *explicit* views, the alienated share an *implicit* positive search in a common direction. Implicitly their philosophies emphasize the positive value of passion and feeling, the search for awareness, contact, intensity, the cultivation of responsiveness, the importance of solitude, and the need somehow to express their experience of life. Their positive values are therefore "expressive" or aesthetic, in that their main focus is the present, their main source is the self, and their main aim is the development of awareness, responsiveness, and sentience. Rejecting the traditional American values of success, self-control, and achievement, they maintain that passion, feeling, and awareness are the truest forces at man's disposal. For most of them, the primary objective in life is to attain and maintain openness to experience, contact with the world and spontaneity of feeling. Anything that might fetter or restrain their responsiveness and openness is opposed: the goal, as one student puts it, is "circumscribing my life as little as possible."

These alienated outlooks, of course, contrast sharply with "traditional" American views about the self, life, others, society, and the universe. Indeed, each alienated view is a rejection of some conventional wisdom of our society. Thus, the unifying theme in the ideology of alienation is the rejection of what are seen as dominant American values, an unwillingness to accept the trusting, optimistic, sociocentric, affiliative, interpersonally oriented, and culturally accepting values which are, or were in less troubled times, the foundations of the American world view.

Alienation as a style of life

When we turn from alienated views of the world to the everyday life of alienated students, we find much less surface distinctiveness. Formal socio-economic and demographic variables do not distinguish these students from their classmates, nor does a casual search through college records, high school records, or even police records. But if we examine not *what* they do, but *how* they do it, we soon discover that the alienated have a characteristic life-style.

One crucial feature of this style of life is intellectual passion. They pursue their intellectual interests with such single-minded dedication that they almost completely disregard the conventional distinction between "work" and "goofing off," made by most of their classmates. When they are challenged in their work, and above all when their assignments strike some deep personal or symbolic chord, they can become totally absorbed in intellectual work.

When they become involved in extra-curricular activities, alienated students are naturally drawn to those that allow them to express their artistic and "aesthetic" interests. And in whatever they do, the style of their participation characteristically involves a preference for the role of the detached observer. As a group, they avoid positions of responsibility or, when accorded them, repudiate them immediately. One student, elected to an important national position, confounded everyone from his parents to his classmates by dropping out of college on the eve of assuming his new office. Since the alienated see all groups as destructive of individuality, they distrusted even the beatnik groups that, during the years they were studied, flourished around the college: they found beatniks conformists, "not serious," and a phony creation of the Luce publications.

Their favored stance as detached observers led these students into systematic wanderings. Whenever they were confronted with a problem or conflict, they were likely to "take off," sometimes for a long walk at night, sometimes for a few years out of college. In all of these wanderings, they seem to be searching not so much to escape as to immerse themselves in intense experience. Sometimes they found such experience. In their interviews and autobiographies, there are occasional mentions of epiphanies, mystical experiences, and revelations of Everything in the garish pennants of a filling station, in the way the light of the setting sun falls through an archway, or in the smell of burning leaves.

But despite their outward appearance of detachment from others, alienated undergraduates are inwardly highly (though ambivalently) involved with them. They are often simultaneously attracted to, and somewhat fearful of, an admired person—tempted to emulate him, but afraid that emulation might mean the sacrifice of their inner integrity. Given such ambivalence, it is understandable that these students tend to ruminate, often obsessively, about all close personal relationships. No friendship escapes detailed analysis from every point of view. This ambivalent examination is especially pronounced with girls. Almost invariably, when they do become close to a girl, it is either to one who is described as passive, dependent, and subservient, or to one who is so totally unacceptable to their parents as to precipitate a complete break between the student and his family, as with the eldest son of a religious Jewish family who became enamored of a girl of Arab descent. In these relationships with girls, as in most of their relationships with other people, they combine an agonizing desire for closeness with a great fear of it.

In interviews, as on questionnaires, alienated students are quick to admit their confusions, angers, anxieties, and problems. Given a list of neurotic symptoms, they check them all, describing themselves as socially undesirable, confused, depressed, angry, neurotic, hostile, and impulsive. Yet the inference that these students are grossly disturbed can only be made with reservations. For one, they reject the value assumptions upon which most questionnaire measures of "maturity," "ego strength," and "good mental health" are based. Furthermore, they make a great effort to undermine any so-called "defenses" that might protect them from unpleasant feelings. For most of these students, openness to their own problems and failings is a cardinal virtue; and they make a further point of loudly proclaiming their own inadequacies.

But after we have made due allowance for the tendency of alienated students to exaggerate their own failings, many of them are, in fact, confused, disoriented, and depressed. In interviews, their public face of contempt often gives way to private admissions of unhappiness and apprehension. Secretly, some harbor fears that this unhappiness may be of their own making, rather than merely a consequence of the human condition. Their sense of themselves seems precarious and disunified; they often doubt their own continuing capacity to cope; they have little positive sense of relatedness to other people; the boundaries of their own egos are diffuse and porous. Strong in opposition, these students are weak in affirmation; unable to articulate what they stand for, they have little sense of self to stand on. As a group, then, they are not characterized by happiness, optimism, tranquillity or calm; they are more notable for the intensity of their convictions, the vehemence of their scorn, the passion behind their search for meaning.

Alienation and the personal past

An examination of what alienated students tell us about their families and their earlier lives shows a remarkable consistency in their reports. When discussing their mothers, for example, they frequently emphasize the renunciations and sacrifices their mothers have made. To their sons, these women appear to have been talented, artistic, intense, and intelligent girls who gave up promise and fulfillment for marriage. They also seem to their sons vivid, sensuous, and magnetic; and alienated students often wonder aloud "whether marriage was worth it" to their mothers. Throughout, these students express their special sympathy for and identification with their mothers, and their sadness at their mothers' lack of fulfillment.

But the mothers of alienated sons have another set of common characteristics—dominance, possessiveness, excessive involvement with their sons, oversolicitude. The typical alienated student tells of his mother's intrusiveness, of her attempts to limit, supervise, and restrict his independence and initiative. And although few of the alienated admit that their mothers have been successful in controlling *them,* they do on the whole believe that their mothers have succeeded in controlling their fathers. Thus, it was Mother who paid Dad's way through college, it was Mother who made Dad's mind up to marry her, it is Mother who somehow decides how things are done in the family. Seen through her son's eyes, she emerges as a woman who has turned her considerable energies to the domination of her family.

About their fathers, alienated students volunteer less information than do most undergraduates. We already know that fathers are usually seen as dominated by mothers. Fathers are also described as men who, often despite notable public success, are "failures in their own eyes," "apostates," disappointed, frustrated, and disillusioned men. But often, in addition, their college-age sons portray them as having *once* had youthful dreams, which they were unable to fulfill, as idealists whose idealism has been destroyed by life. The precise agent of this destruction varies: sometimes it was Mother; sometimes it was the father's own weakness, particularly his inability to stand up against pressures for social success and recognition. So despite their frequent scorn for their dominated fathers, alienated students retain some sympathy for the same fathers as they *might* have been—a kind of covert identification with the fantasy of a youthful idealistic father.

In characterizing their fathers at present, however. the alienated again and again emphasize qualities like detachment, reserve, inability to express affection, loneliness, and withdrawal from the center of the family. Contrasted with the expressive, emotional, controlling, and dynamic mother, the father appears weak, inactive, detached, and uninterested.

In their earliest memories, alienated students make unusually frequent references to "oral" themes, that is, to issues of consuming, being nurtured and cared for, to food aversions, feeding problems, and, in one student, to the assumption that his voracious nursing produced breast cancer in his mother. In these memories, women are always present; men are striking by their absence. Especially impressive are idyllic recollections of happy times alone with Mother on vacations, or family expeditions when Father was away from home. All of these memories suggest an unusually intense attachment between mother and son in early life.

In primary and secondary school, alienated students, like most undergraduates at Harvard College, were capable intellectually and interested in their schoolwork. But they differ from many of their classmates in that they seem consistently to have preferred imagination, thought, and staying at home to outgoing activities with others; they speak less than most students of group activities and "running with the gang"; they usually describe themselves as quiet, homebound, unrebellious, and obedient children.

But during adolescence, alienated students seem to have undergone even greater turmoil than most of their classmates. The symptoms of this turmoil are extremely varied: intense asceticism, tentative delinquency, vociferous rebellion, speeding, drinking, and, in one case, a half-hearted suicide attempt. From other evidence, it seems that the arrival of adult sexuality was especially disturbing to these young men. In discussing their sexual fantasies as college students, they emphasize to an unusual degree their enduring desire for passivity, oblivion, and tranquillity, and often mention difficulties about being initiating and "aggressive" with women. Only a few alienated students have found sexual relationships fully satisfying, and many mention strong feelings of anxiety, discomfort, or apprehension connected with sex. All of this suggests that one of the major problems in adolescence was great anxiety about assuming the traditional male sex role.

Surprisingly, at least to me, there was no mention of overt alienation in the life histories of these students until mid-adolescence—about the age of sixteen. At this age, we hear accounts of growing feelings of cynicism, distance, estrangement and scorn—initially for school classmates, later for parents and teachers, finally for all of society. In most cases, these feelings appeared spontaneously, though sometimes they were precipitated by the views of a friend, a trip abroad, or some other specific event. This growing sense of alienation usually contrasted sharply with continuing academic and social success; and the contrast between inner alienation and outer success led to increasing feelings of estrangement from all those who accepted them merely at face value. Their alienation usually developed in isolation and spontaneously; it was usually only *after* they became alienated that these students sought out books, ideas, and people that would confirm and support them in their views. Among the students studied, alienation could *not* be explained as the result of identification with an alienated parent; on the contrary, it always seemed to involve a sharp repudiation of perceived parental values.

Alienation in fantasy

The fantasies of alienated students, especially as seen on the T.A.T., are different from the fantasies of other students both in style and in content. Stylistically, alienated fantasies are rich, vivid, imaginative, anti-social, unconventional, and often bizarre. Thematically, the typical alienated fantasy involves an inferior or unusually sensitive hero who becomes involved in a difficult relationship with another person. The relationship goes from bad to worse, leading to great resentment and enduring hurt, especially on the hero's side. This plot format contrasts sharply with the typical stories of extremely non-alienated students, whose competent and superior heroes enter into positive and enduring relationships from which all concerned profit and grow.

Within this general format, the alienated characteristically tells stories reflecting one or both of two major themes. The first of these is the *loss of Eden*. Alienated fantasies are distinctively concerned with the loss of supplies, with starvation, with forcible estrangement, and a yearning to return to bliss. Sometimes these fantasies involve isolated heroes who die of starvation; more often, they entail a hero who seeks to regain his union with a lost loved one, usually a woman. Alienated fantasies are a catalogue of yearnings for the past: undertakers enamored of their female subjects, ghoulish grave robbers, heroes obsessed with the recovery of the lost gods, grief-stricken husbands who crawl into their wives' graves, detectives searching for missing persons, lovers mourning the dead, husbands who kill themselves on their wives' coffins.

The same theme of reunion with a lost love is reflected in other stories where the hero loses himself in some warm, fluid, or embracing maternal medium. Some heroes are lured to their deaths by warm and friendly voices speaking from the sea or calling from the air. Other fantasies involve heroes who dive to the bottom of the ocean, never to return. Developmentally, these often archaic and weird stories seem to refer to an unconscious obsession with the lost early relationship with the mother.

A second important motif in alienated fantasy is the theme of a *Pyrrhic Oedipal victory*. Many college students, when given the Thematic Apperception Test, are at some pains to avoid stories which involve competitive rivalrous triangles: rivalry between men is usually minimized, and struggles between two men for the love of a woman are especially avoided. The alienated, in contrast, take rivalrous triangles for granted, often importing them into stories where the picture in no way suggests this theme. Even more striking is the peculiar form and outcome of such fantasies. Again and again, it is the younger man who defeats the older man, but only to be overcome himself by some extraneous force. Attacks on fathers and father figures are almost inevitably successful: the father dies, the Minister of Internal Affairs is assassinated, the boss who has propositioned the hero's wife is killed. Or, in the many stories of political revolution told by these apolitical students, the established regime is seen as weak, corrupt, and easily overthrown. Traditional male authority topples at the first push.

Yet these stories of rebellion, rivalry, and revolution are, paradoxically, cautionary tales. The revolution succeeds, but it is followed by a disaster: the revolutionary murderer is assassinated by his own men; the revolutionary regime turns into a despotism worse than that which it overthrew, the avenged cuckold is killed in an automobile accident. These fantasies suggest that although traditional male authority is weak, its destruction leads to a new and worse tyranny.

Such fantasies are consistent with the hypothesis that the rebellious son unconsciously believes that he indeed succeeded in deposing his father, but that this deposition was followed by a new maternal tyranny. The real victor was neither father nor son, but mother, who now dominates them both. Supporting this hypothesis is the fact that most alienated fantasies portray adult women as active, controlling, and possessive. In particular, they restrain men's sexuality, aggressiveness, and non-conformity: they try to keep their sons from going out with girls; they keep men from fighting; they try to make their husbands settle down and conform—and, almost invariably, they succeed.

The dominant theme of relations between the sexes, then, is not love and intimacy, but the control of men by women. When intimacy begins to seem possible, the story usually ends disastrously. Also, women are not only seen as controlling and possessive, but, on occasion, as murderous and destructive: as lizard goddesses who eat their victims, as apparently lovable ladies who murder their husbands, as emasculating and destructive figures. Fathers and older men, in contrast, are almost always portrayed as weak, corruptible, absent, or damaged. Men are controlled by women, and even men who initially appear strong eventually turn out to be fraudulent and weak.

Hypotheses about the psychological sources of alienation

The themes of ideology, life-style, past history, and fantasy summarized here are, of course, open to many different interpretations. In some respects, the psychological origins of alienation are different for each alienated individual, and no composite account can hope to do justice to the uniqueness of each person. Nonetheless, the existence of many shared strands of belief, present feeling, past experience, and imagination suggests that, insofar as we can take these students' accounts as an adequate basis for an explanation, general hypotheses about the psychological origins of alienation are possible.

One of the most striking findings of this study is the great similarity in the families of alienated students. Both parents seem to have been frustrated and dissatisfied. The mother's talents and emotionality found little expression within her marriage; the father's idealism and youthful dreams were crushed by the realities of his adult life. The mothers of alienated students seem to have turned their drive and perhaps their own frustrated needs for love onto their sons, almost invariably oldest or preferred sons. Often, these mothers explicitly deprecated or disparaged their husbands. And confronted with this deprecation, the fathers of alienated students seem to have withdrawn from the family, becoming detached, embittered, and distant. Forced to choose between their families and their work, they almost to a man turned their energies outside the family, leaving mother and son locked in a special alliance of mutual understanding and maternal control.

This basic family constellation is reflected and elaborated in fantasy. Unconsciously, alienated students seem to believe that they defeated their fathers, who are now seen as weak and inadequate models of male adulthood. Probably, like most small boys, they attempted a "revolution" within the family in order to overthrow the tyrannical father and gain the exclusive love of the mother. But, unlike most boys, these boys believe that their revolution *succeeded* in destroying male authority. Yet, paradoxically, their apparent victory did not win them maternal love but maternal control, possessiveness, and oversolicitude. Furthermore, by displacing their fathers, they lost the right of every boy to a father he can admire. The son thus gained something very different from what he had wanted. At least in fantasy, he found himself saddled with a possessive and intrusive mother, and he lost the youthful idealistic father he could respect.

If these speculations are correct, they may help us to explain some of the other characteristics of these alienated students. For such a childhood experience would clearly leave a college student with the unconscious assumption that apparently admirable men were really weak and impotent; and that apparently nurturing and loving women were really controlling, possessive, and even emasculating. Conventional adulthood, as epitomized by the father, would also seem unattractive and have to be rejected. Adult closeness with women would be frightening, as it would evoke fears of being dominated, controlled, and limited. Similarly, competition and rivalry would be avoided in everyday behavior, not out of the fear of failure, but from a fear of another Pyrrhic victory. The apparent inability of our subjects' mothers to love them as sons, coupled with the sudden change in the sons' image of the mother from that of a nurturer to an emasculator might help explain the persistence into early adulthood of recurrent fantasies about fusion with the maternal presence.

The psychological factors that predisposed these students toward alienation are thus complex and interrelated. The sense and the stance of alienation are partially reflections of the unconscious conviction of these subjects that they are outcasts from a lost Eden, alienated forever from their mothers' early love. Then, too, the repudiation of conventional adulthood, of the dominant values of American society, is closely related to their unconscious determination not to let what happened to their fathers happen to them, and to covert identification with the fantasy of a youthful, idealistic father before he was "broken" by life. Similarly, the centrality of distrust in the emotional lives and ideologies of alienated students is probably in part a reflection of an early family situation in which neither parent turned out to be what he or she had promised to be. In a variety of ways, then, these students were prepared by their past experience and by the fantasies through which they interpreted this experience to be alienated from American culture.

Limitations and implications

The kind of clinical research I have described has many problems and limitations. The use of comparison groups provides a control only in the loosest sense of the word; and, in the last analysis, the possibilities of misinterpretation, false hypotheses, and excessive speculation cannot be eliminated. Above all, the interpretation of clinical data offers the psychologist a marvelous opportunity for projection; here I can only note that my research in this area has convinced me that, compared to the students I studied, I myself am not really alienated at all. I might also add that these clinical speculations are fully consistent with "harder" data derived from correlational and experimental studies.

It is also obvious that one cannot simply generalize about American students, or even alienated American students, from this small sample of a dozen Harvard undergraduates. How generalizable the findings of this study may be remains to be seen; my own estimate is that extremely alienated students like those I have described are concentrated largely at highly selective and academic liberal-arts colleges, particularly at those with a "progressive" reputation. Even on such campuses, I would imagine that they constitute a very small minority of all undergraduates—at most, five to ten per cent.

Let me underline the inadequacies of any purely psychological account of alienation, and the special inadequacies of this particular account. A psychological account of any complex ideological and intellectual viewpoint invariably tends to be seen as a "reductive" account. It may suggest that alienation is "nothing but" a reflection of an unfortunate family constellation or a particular psychodynamic pattern. Such an inference is very alien to my own thinking. On the contrary, the childhood events and fantasies I have discussed here could equally well be viewed as the fortunate and enabling factors that permitted these students to be aware of very real deficiencies in their society.

And, even on its own terms, this psychological account is far from complete. It seems likely that the factors I have outlined will dispose a young man to *some* kind of hesitancy about conventional adulthood. But they will not suffice to explain why this hesitancy took the particular form of cultural alienation. To explain this channeling of hesitancy into alienation we would need to consider in far greater detail the early propensity of these students to solve problems with their imaginations rather than their fists, their privileged social backgrounds, their very high talent, intelligence, imagination, and sensitivity, and the particular institutional and cultural climate of the college they attended.

Another dimension omitted from my account seems to me even more crucial. It is the social and historical context in which these students lived—the historical era in which they were studied. Alienation of the sort I have described is, of course, not an exclusively contemporary phenomenon: especially during the past two centuries, many of the most creative men and women in the Western world have been alienated from their cultures. But the precise forms, manifestations, and content of cultural alienation are given by the surrounding society—in this instance, by the late Eisenhower era, by the symbols of the beat generation, by the much discussed "silence" of American college students during the fifties, by the absence of available social channels for the constructive organized expression of dissent. For example, I suspect that had these same students been in college today, a disproportionate number of them would have turned to the psychedelic or hallucinogenic drugs, which promise a heightening of the sentience, subjectivity, intensity, passion, feeling, and perception that is so central among alienated students' goals.

Alienation is, of course, a reaction *to* and *against* certain aspects of American society: it is a transaction between an individual and his culture, and we cannot understand it without examining the characteristics of the wider society as they impinge upon young Americans. While it is not enough to attribute alienation *solely* to the characteristics of modern technological society (this would make it impossible for us to understand why most Americans are not alienated), it would be equally misleading to see alienation purely as an expression of individual psychology. Like most outlooks, alienation is a product of the inner world and the outer world as they continually interact in the developing individual's experience.

Finally, let me return briefly to the theme from which I began—the much touted "alienation" of the American college student, and the characterization of student protesters and student protest movements as evidence of this alienation. For one, even if student protest *were* a barometer of alienation, it is becoming increasingly clear that the number of active protesters is extremely small—zero per cent on most American campuses, and probably nowhere more than ten per cent. But even more important to my theme, I doubt that culturally alienated students are much interested in political protest. It is suggestive that among the thirty or so students studied intensively, only one was actively involved in the peace movement in the late fifties. But he was *not* alienated; on the contrary, he was in the extremely *non*-alienated group. Other, statistical, evidence tentatively supports this same conclusion. In the samples we studied, alienation was by no means associated with the liberal political outlooks found among protesters. On the contrary, it tended to have a slightly positive relationship to authoritarianism, and a significantly negative relationship with equalitarianism, both as measured by the Bales-Couch Value Profile. Similarly, our initial assumption that alienation from American culture would be associated with concern over social, political, and economic injustices proved false: the scales we devised to measure such concerns correlated negatively with alienation. Furthermore, the political pessimism, distrust, lack of interest in group activities, and scorn for politics and politicians of the alienated would seem to inure them from any prolonged participation in a protest movement.

It is always possible, like Humpty Dumpty, to make words mean what one chooses them to mean. And so it is always possible to define "alienation" in such a way that the civil rights marcher, the peace demonstrator, or the Berkeley activists are, by definition, "alienated." But after having worked for several years with a group of undergraduates who *are* intensely repudiative of American culture, I am inclined to see most student protest not as a manifestation of alienation (as I have used the term), but rather of *commitment* to the very values that alienated students reject. Furthermore, the psychodynamics of the activist seem to me, at least impressionistically, quite different from those of the alienated student: to oversimplify a relationship that is always complex and ambivalent, the activist seems determined to implement and live out his parents' values, whereas the alienated student is determined to repudiate them and find alternative values. I might also note that most activists seem to me to possess an optimism, faith in human nature, belief in the efficacy of human action, and a capacity for co-operative endeavors that few alienated students manifest. Thus, on the whole, alienation as I have studied it, and the current phenomenon of student protest seem to me two quite distinct, if not opposed, phenomena.

For reasons I have discussed elsewhere, I suspect that youthful alienation of the sort I have studied will be a continuing, if not an increasingly prevalant, phenomenon. The kinds of families these students came from, while not statistically typical, seem to me sufficiently close to the emergent norm of the American family so that we can expect at least some of their offspring to be predisposed to alienation in the coming decades. The simultaneous emergence of a similar family type in the etiology of male homosexuality, adolescent male schizophrenia, and intense identity diffusion, as well as its appearance of this same family type in a great number of current novels and plays, suggests that the alienating family may become an increasingly common variant in middle-class American society. As our society becomes ever more technological, more specialized, more highly organized, it seems to me likely that a continuing group of the most talented, sensitive, and suitably predisposed of our youth will be repelled by our society, and will experience a transient and, in many cases, an enduring phase of alienation. As Donald N. Michael has recently put it in his study of the prospects ahead for American youth, "A growing group . . . of the most talented, sensitive, and searching of young adults and adolescents will be repelled by what they interpret as politicking, commercialism, high-pressure bureaucracy, and the 'big' society, and by logic-chopping, 'dehumanized' and 'hemmed in' experience of the devoted scientist." Cultural alienation among a segment of our most talented and sensitive youth is, I think, an almost inevitable consequence of the kind of society we live in. And it is important that we understand its psychological, social, cultural, and historical origins. For one, to understand alienation is to be better able to understand some of our most perceptive students—not in order to "cure" them, for alienation is a condition that in itself neither seeks nor needs cure, but in order to help them find personally meaningful and culturally productive ways of focusing and expressing their alienation. More important, in 1966 in America, I suspect that *most* reflective men and women are somewhat alienated from our society and our culture—some of us more, most of us less, alienated than these college students. By trying to understand what it is in our modern world that contributes to the alienation of such young men, we may be led indirectly to an understanding of what is most dehumanizing, unjust, cruel, ugly, and corrupt in our society. And here understanding is a prerequisite to whatever cures we can create.

Reference Notes

Introduction: Vietnam Summer and the New Left

A growing number of books are concerned with the New Left. Two useful collections of documents and essays are Cohen and Hale (1967) and Jacobs and Landau (1966). Newfield's *A Prophetic Minority* (1966) gives a laudatory history of the New Left as of two years ago.

The Free Speech Movement that emerged in Berkeley in late 1964 is the subject of at least four books: Lipset and Wolin (1965), Draper (1965), Katope and Zolbrod (1966), and Miller and Gilmore (1965). Horowitz (1962) discusses earlier events at Berkeley. Zinn (1965), Ehle (1965), and Coles (1963, 1964, 1967) describe aspects of the Civil Rights Movement. Mallery (1966) discusses the general phenomenon of student activism on several campuses.

No one journal adequately reflects the diversity of opinion in the New Left. In the early 1960's, *New University Thought, New Left Review,* and *Studies on the Left* provided informative articles. More recently, *Our Generation, New Politics, The Activist,* and *Ramparts* give a sampling of New Left thought. Articles in *Liberation, Dissent, The New Republic,* and *The New York Review of Books* are good sources of commentary, usually sympathetic, on the New Left.

A number of journals have in recent years devoted special issues to student dissent, protest, and social action. See, for example, the 1964 and 1967 issues of the *Journal of Social Issues* on "Youth and Social Action" and "Stirrings Out of Apathy: Student Activism and a Decade of Protest"; the June, 1966, issue of *Comparative Education Review* on "Student Politics" (S. M. Lipset, ed.); the Winter, 1968, issue of *Daedalus* on "Students and Politics" (S. M. Lipset, ed.); the 1965 issue of *The Atlantic,* "The Troubled Campus" (republished by Editors of *The Atlantic,* 1966); and the Autumn, 1967, issue of *The American Scholar.* A selected bibliography on "Student Politics and Higher Education in the United States" has been prepared by Philip G. Altbach (1967).

Most of the empirical studies of student activists and radicals that have appeared in recent years are summarized in Appendix B of this book. Other summaries are to be found in Lipset and Altbach (1966), Peterson (1968), Block, Haan, and Smith (forthcoming). Among the several studies of activists and radicals that remain to be fully reported are those by Brewster Smith and his associates at the University of California at Berkeley, Paulus at Michigan State, Nevitt Sanford and Joseph Katz at Stanford, and Richard Flacks at the University of Chicago.

The representativeness of the radicals studied in this book obviously cannot be judged on the basis of one study alone. As I note in the Introduction, Vietnam Summer leaders seem "representative" of radicals described in other studies with regard to class and educational background, family value orientation, academic achievement, personal values and aspirations, et cetera. But given the amorphousness and changing nature of the New Left, and the wide variety of individuals and ideological positions represented within it, no one group can be truly "representative" of the whole. Among the factors that distinguish Vietnam Summer leaders from other radicals are (1) the length of their commitment to the New Left (averaging more than two years since they came to think of themselves as "radicals"); (2) their position as leaders in a movement where most are members; (3) their support for community-organizing tactics; (4) their willingness to take part in a relatively "bureaucratic" organization like Vietnam Summer; (5) their average age of twenty-three (which makes them two or more years older than the average undergraduate radical); and (6) the fact that most of the young radicals discussed in this study come from east of the Mississippi and have often lived much of their lives near the Eastern Seaboard.

Many of those I interviewed distinguished among East Coast, Midwestern, and Western radical styles, as among different age groups within the New Left. Furthermore, distinctions should be made among those who are only peripherally involved in the New Left, those who are intensely involved in it, and those who become leaders. The ongoing studies of Smith and his co-workers at Berkeley make explicit distinctions between "constructivists," "broad-spectrum activists," and "dissenters." Recent research by Kerpelman (1968) suggests that at least some of the characteristics assigned to left-wing activists are actually those of *all* political activists, regardless of ideology, while other characteristics distinguish right-wing from left-wing students regardless of degree of activism.

1 *The radical commitment*

The ability to talk "psychologically" about oneself is obviously not the same as useful insight: that these young radicals were articulate about their psychological lives is not in itself adequate evidence of good psychological functioning. Indeed, in the post-Freudian world, increasing numbers of young men and women are able to discuss intelligently the very psychological problems that they can do nothing about. With these particular young radicals, however, *other* evidence suggests that their self-understanding had been useful to them. Very few displayed major psychological symptoms that impaired their lives. For most, growing understanding of their motives and feelings had been accompanied by meaningful changes in behavior and interpersonal relationships. It seems justified, then, to speak of something like "genuine insight" in most of these young men and women.

Despite the important ideological and stylistic differences between the Old Left and the New Left, a cursory survey of the biographies and autobiographies of older radical and revolutionary leaders suggests that many in their youth were at least superficially similar to the young radicals interviewed in Vietnam Summer. Thus, such factors as a relatively privileged background, a highly principled family, early exposure to conflict, an early sense of being different from one's peers, an unusually tumultuous adolescence, and heightened ambivalence toward one's father may characterize the backgrounds of other radical leaders in other eras. See, for example, Shub on Lenin (1967), Schram on Mao (1967), Trotsky (1930), and Gandhi (1957).

These similarities, however, should not obscure the important differences in outlook and style between old and new radicals. Among these differences, the New Left's opposition to dogma and doctrine, its rejection of central organizational control, its absence of clear programs, and its emphasis on participatory democracy stand out.

Radicalism and alienation—Given the frequent equation of youthful radicalism with some form of alienation, it may be useful, in the notes to this and the following chapters, to contrast the young radicals who led Vietnam Summer with the group of "alienated" students on whom *The Uncommitted* (Keniston, 1965) was based. There are certain similarities between these two groups, but the differences are even more impressive.

The criteria by which subjects were included in these two studies were different, and some of the differences between the groups result from this fact. Alienated students were selected on *psychological* criteria: personality tests were the basis for inclusion in the study, and guaranteed a relatively high degree of psychological similarity among these students, who otherwise formed part of no identifiable social group and possessed no common self-characterization. On the basis of selection criteria alone, one would therefore predict that alienated students would show a relatively high degree of psychological similarity, together with variability in actual behavior. The young radicals upon whom the present book is based were self-selected by virtue of their holding "leadership roles" in Vietnam Summer. The only selectivity imposed by me was to limit this report to those whose commitment to the New Left was evidenced by at least one year of full-time involvement with the New Left and by a characterization of self as a "radical." Thus, the young radicals described here were selected primarily on the basis of *organizational* (group membership) criteria, with no prior knowledge of their psychological characteristics. For this reason alone, one would expect the far greater psychological diversity one finds in this group.

Another difference between the two groups is age. Alienated students were studied while they were college undergraduates, that is, between the ages of eighteen and twenty-two. The age range of young radicals was far greater, from nineteen to twenty-seven, with an average age of twenty-three. The fact that radicals were as a group two years older than alienated students when they graduated from college would lead us to expect that they would be somewhat farther along in their psychological development. But the differences found between the two groups do not seem to me accounted for by the slightly greater average age of radicals.

Stated in most general terms, the young radicals who led Vietnam Summer were a highly committed group of young men and women. They were firmly committed to a basic set of beliefs, to a "movement," to a style of behavior and interaction, to certain broad social and political objectives, and to other people. In this regard, they contrast sharply with the uncommitted alienated, who were engaged in a largely unsuccessful search for a satisfactory form of engagement with the world. The commitments of the radicals studied were largely social, political, and interpersonal; but alienated students were searching in a quite different area—in aesthetic, expressive, artistic, and subjective endeavors. As I suggest in Appendix C, there are many reasons why it is unlikely that an extremely alienated student would become actively involved in sustained political action.

Another related difference between these groups is the contrast between the alienated preference for withdrawal or introspective encapsulation and the radical preference for action and change. Both groups, of course, have major criticisms of many dominant American values. But alienated students are far more global in their criticisms, since they reject not only the patterns of careerism, familism, and materialism that are also rejected by the radical, but the validity or meaningfulness of a great many of the basic American values that radicals accept, *e.g.*, responsibility, trust in others, optimism, outgoingness, and social involvement. Alienated students are extremely pessimistic about human nature and the possibilities of affecting social changes, whereas radicals have a considerable faith in human nature and are far more optimistic—though hardly sanguine—about the possibilities of meaningful social change.

Both groups possess an unusual psychological openness and apparent insight into their motives. But alienated students are inclined to exaggerate their own negative feelings and take particular delight in recounting fantasies, wishes, and motives that are socially unacceptable. The self-presentations of radicals are more balanced in this regard. The alienated have a much higher degree of aesthetic responsiveness and appreciation than do radicals. As a group, the alienated seem more gifted artistically, more attuned to subtleties and nuances in meaning and perception, more likely to make a literary or artistic contribution. They are far less able or willing to "compromise" by joining with others in any group action; in this regard, the misanthropy of the alienated contrasts very sharply with the strong group orientation of the radical.

With regard to their conceptions of time, alienated students are firmly planted in the present, portraying the past (at least consciously) as dismal and black, and the future as utterly unpredictable. Radicals emphasize and even exaggerate the ties of continuity with their own personal pasts, as well as with their cultural pasts, and while they have little clear picture of their future plans, they see themselves as "in motion" and open toward an indeterminate future.

In their basic values, radicals are highly liberal (anti-authoritarian) and strongly equalitarian. They are idealists: they believe in, and readily articulate, a set of basic moral values that they feel applies to all behavior. Alienated subjects, in contrast, are anti-equalitarian, emphasizing the many differences between people; they are neutral with regard to liberalism-authoritarianism, seeing authoritarian control as necessary for other people, but as extremely objectionable when applied to them; they are anti-idealistic and extremely situational in their view of moral values. Both radicals and the alienated are highly individualistic. But the radical tends to be oriented toward serving others and effecting beneficial changes in the society, whereas the alienated student is generally egocentric, focused upon inducing personal and subjective changes in himself.

2 *Personal roots: struggle and specialness*

The study of how those involved in political action acquire their characteristic attitudes and styles is relatively recent. Psychoanalysis played a major role in inspiring hypotheses concerning the psychological roots of political behavior and conviction. Among pioneering works are Lasswell (1930), Fromm (1941), and Reich (1946).

More recent works in the psychology of politics include Adorno *et al.* (1950), Christie and Jahoda (1954), Smith, Bruner, and White (1960). In recent years, a growing number of increasingly sophisticated studies that make major use of psychosocial perspectives in the study of politics have appeared. See, for example, Riesman (1950, 1952), Lipset (1960), Lane (1959, 1962), and Greenstein (1965). Hyman (1959) provides a useful overview of studies in "political socialization." See also Levinson (1958, 1959, forthcoming), Greenstein (1967), and Sigel (1965).

The fields of political biography and autobiography are closely related. Here, the works of Erik Erikson have set a model for others. See, for example, his studies of Hitler's youth (1950), of Martin Luther (1958), and his ongoing study of Gandhi. For one political biography that makes especially good use of psychological materials, see Rogow (1964). Wolfenstein (1967) in a recent study of Lenin, Trotsky, and Gandhi stresses the issue of authority in the psychology of revolutionary leaders. The Freud-Bullitt study of Woodrow Wilson (1967) is a good example of psychoanalytic political biography in a highly reductive vein, as a review by Erikson (1967) points out.

The psychology of right-wing politics has been more thoroughly studied than that of the left-wing. The above-mentioned works by Reich, Fromm, Adorno *et al.*, and Christie and Jahoda all deal with right-wing politics. See also Lowenthal and Gutterman (1949), Bell (1955), and Schiff (1964). Two books dealing with the psychology of fanaticism and dogmatism, regardless of left-right distinctions, are Hoffer (1951) and Rokeach (1960). Systematic studies of left-wing radicals are infrequent. Almond (1954) remains the most authoritative summary. Current empirical and theoretical studies of the New Left are summarized in this book in Appendix B.

Greenstein's pioneering work, *Children and Politics* (1965), is virtually the only major study of the relationship between early socialization and political views. His work contains useful references to previous studies in this area. Longitudinal studies of the relationship of family dynamics, political conceptions, and general values in childhood with later political commitment and action remain to be undertaken.

Radicalism and alienation—Some of the differences in the childhood experience and family constellation of alienated students and young radicals should be emphasized. Among both the alienated and young radicals, there is evidence of an unusually strong tie to the *mother* in early childhood. But for the alienated, this tie seems both more intense and less adequately resolved. Those who become alienated describe a mother-son relationship that is intrusive, overprotective, and close-binding: the mother frequently involves the son in an alliance against the father. Furthermore, alienated students usually describe their mothers as sensuous and/or neurotic. These qualities are far less frequently ascribed to their mothers by radicals. Radicals describe their mothers as especially encouraging of achievement, independence, and initiative: these qualities are rarely reported in mothers of the alienated. And male radicals as a group seem more genuinely fond of, and grateful to, their mothers than do the alienated. Above all, young radicals generally appreciate their mothers' educating and individuating influences.

It is in their attitudes toward their *fathers* that the alienated and young radicals differ most drastically. Despite the variability in radicals' attitude toward their fathers, a majority expressed a kind of affection for their fathers that was extremely rare among alienated students. All radicals indicated that whatever their fathers' weaknesses, their fathers had important strengths, especially in the areas of values, principles, and convictions. Conscious ambivalence toward their fathers was the rule for activists, in contrast to the negative alienated perception of fathers as weak, detached, absent, distant, remote, and sometimes as totally uninvolved in the upbringing of their children. Radicals more often described their fathers as expressive, warm, sympathetic, and highly involved.

The *parental relationships* described by these two groups also differed. The prevailing pattern in alienating families involved a schism between the parents, coupled with a mother-son alliance against the father. This alliance often led the son to believe or suspect that the mother preferred him to her husband. The predominant pattern in radical families, however, is a parental "united front" vis-à-vis children. Even in those radical families where parents were in conflict, a mother-son alliance did not develop, apparently because the mother was not seductive toward her son.

The *family culture* or value milieu of the two types of families also differs. Both radical and alienating families were generally highly permissive with their children. But in radical families, permissiveness was combined with extremely high standards and expectations, and with strong support for the son's individuality and autonomy. In alienating families, permissiveness was more often combined with considerable parental confusion over principles and with reluctance—especially on the mother's part—to see the son become autonomous and independent of his family. Alienating families were most often oriented toward conventional goals of success and social status, while radical families emphasized values like responsibility, independence, societal involvement, expression of feelings, service to others, and self-fulfillment.

The reported *childhood experience* of these two groups also differs. Alienated students tell of greater involvement with parents throughout childhood, of considerably more preadolescent isolation, and of less participation with peer groups and community. Even in childhood, their characteristic reaction to stress seemed to be a withdrawal into inner life. Radicals, in contrast, reported more active involvement in the life of their schools and local communities, an involvement generally strongly supported by their parents. Radicals also reported an earlier moral and political sensitivity than did alienated students. Both groups were precocious intellectually, but radicals more often occupied leadership positions with their peers.

Both groups were exposed to considerable *childhood conflict*. For alienated students, however, this conflict was almost entirely within their own homes—between their parents—while for many young radicals conflict was outside the immediate family, in the larger community. Alienated students were almost always personally immersed in family conflicts, usually in alliance with their mothers. Radicals, however, tended to experience family conflicts from some distance, without being personally allied with either disputing parent. Furthermore, when parental quarrels occurred in radical families, the parents generally tried to conceal them from their children—an effort that is consistent with a general family emphasis on the inhibition of anger and the minimization of conflict. Alienated students, in contrast, reported that their parents (usually their mothers) confided frequently in their sons the sources of parental conflict and maternal discontent.

3 *Personal roots: turmoil, success, and the end of the line*

For early psychoanalytic accounts of adolescence, see S. Freud (1938), A. Freud (1946, 1958), and Fenichel (1945). More recent accounts of adolescence include Blos (1962), Erik Erikson (see especially his "Reflections on the American Identity" in *Childhood and Society* [1950], and "The Problem of Ego Identity" in *Identity and the Life Cycle* [1959]), Lidz (forthcoming), and Douvan and Adelson (1966). This last work, based on an intensive survey of a large sample of American teen-agers, suggests that most young Americans do *not* pass through an adolescence as defined by classical psychoanalytic theory.

There are few studies of the relationship of psychological development and political commitment during early adolescence. A number of the studies of political activists, however, offer useful speculations on the relationship between developmental stage and late adolescent political behavior. See the works by Solomon and Fishman (1963, 1964) and Fishman and Solomon (n.d., 1964), Flacks (1967), Block, Haan, and Smith (forthcoming), and Katz (1967), among others.

With the particular young radicals studied here, however, distinction must be made between adolescent political development and a post-adolescent commitment to radicalism. As I note in the text, "becoming a radical" seems more a characteristic of the post-adolescent period than of adolescence itself.

Radicalism and alienation—The adolescent experience of the alienated and radical youth again differs considerably. With both groups, there is considerable evidence of adolescent turmoil. And in both groups, as in many other early adolescents, a considerable portion of this turmoil was centered around issues of sexuality. But the alienated group seemed distinctively concerned with avoiding the active, initiating role required of men in sexual relationships, while the distress of young radicals seemed more connected to their early adolescent moral scrupulosity and to their problem in reconciling their own moral codes with the activities—often sexual—of their peer groups. Also, in the alienated group, incestuous fears and anxieties appear to have been more central than in the radical group, although they were present in both groups.

In many ways the mid-adolescent rebelliousness of radicals was more overt, vehement, and focally directed against parents than was the rebellion of the alienated, which took the form of a more pervasive rejection of the values of middle-class American society. Alienated students less often had confronted their parents directly with their complaints against them; in particular, they were less able to turn the parents' principles against the parents, since the parents themselves often appeared confused as to their own basic values. Perhaps as a result, the rebellion of the alienated, though less overt, was in many ways far more pervasive and long-lasting. Unlike radicals, alienated students rarely had been willing to assume positions of leadership and initiative in late adolescence. At the time they were studied, their major focus of interest was aesthetic and literary, and their preferred style was that of the detached and isolated wanderer and observer. All of this may be partly because their feeling of responsibility to others was far less pronounced than in the radical group.

4 *Becoming a radical*

There are undoubtedly other ways into political action than that described here. Schiff's work (1964), for example, suggests that among right-wing activists a process of "conversion" may be more frequent. Other writers have often noted a pattern of precipitous change from radical views on the right to those on the left, and vice versa. In the group studied here, there were no such changes, and the psychological characteristics of those interviewed make it seem unlikely that any of them will experience sudden changes in political conviction in the future. All of this once again indicates that any generalizations from this particular group must be extremely tentative. The way these young men and women became radicals is clearly only *one* of the ways people become involved in intense political commitments.

Sutherland's anthology, *Letters from Mississippi* (1966), however, suggests that many of the volunteers in Mississippi Summer in 1964 may have undergone a similar process of radicalization. The Aiken, Demerath, and Marwell (1966) study of the participants in Mississippi Summer suggests that their general characteristics were very similar to those of other activist groups and to those of the leaders of Vietnam Summer. It seems likely, then, that the pathway to radicalism encountered in the leaders of Vietnam Summer may be a pathway taken by a number of other contemporary Americans within recent years. In particular, the impact upon the children of affluence of a concrete confrontation with the inequities of American society clearly has the effect of pushing at least some of them toward efforts to do something to remedy these inequities. Others, of course, respond with despair or with a return to more private concerns. A study of the subsequent fates of the volunteers of the 1964 Mississippi Summer would help in a preliminary description of these and other reactions to Movement work.

My argument here implies that secular changes in the structure of the American family and its ways of rearing children make it likely that something like the radicalism found in the leaders of Vietnam Summer will be a continuing (and probably a growing) phenomenon among American youth in the future (see Michael, 1965). Increasing affluence will create a larger minority of each age group ready to be "shocked" by a confrontation with inequity; in those families where social responsibility and active political participation are valued, the likelihood of filial involvement in movements for social change will increase. But as I note in Appendix B, psychological readiness is only one of several factors involved in radicalism as a social movement. Even though the pool of potential radicals may increase, institutional, cultural, and historical factors play a crucial role in the actual process of becoming a radical, as in the formation of a radical movement. See my discussion of some of those factors in Chapters 7 and 8, and Flacks (1967).

Radicalism and alienation—No experience in the lives of the alienated comparable to becoming a radical can be defined. Among the alienated, adolescent development involves fewer changes in self-conception. Thus, while both the radicals and the alienated experienced an unusually tumultuous early adolescence, the alienated emerged from this phase into alienation, usually beginning at the age of fifteen or sixteen. Thereafter, their development was marked by an extension and elaboration of their alienation, but not by other major changes in outlook or commitment.

Radicals, in contrast, turned in mid-adolescence toward "successful" involvement in academic matters and peer activities. Only one of the fourteen radicals could in any way have been considered "culturally alienated" during high school, while only two of the fourteen had even begun to think of themselves as "radicals" during this period (both were the sons of radical families). For the remainder, a commitment to the New Left emerged after a number of years of "success," followed by what I have termed a sense of "nearing the end of the line." As a group, radicals have often changed considerably in their commitments and self-definitions since mid-adolescence; whereas the alienated have changed but little.

5 *The tensions of Movement work*

The major impact upon young radicals of their experience within the New Left suggests the limitations of any view of political action that considers only the impact of pre-adolescent experience on political behavior. Many of the political views, styles, and activities of the young radicals who led Vietnam Summer could only be understood as a reflection of their previous experience in the Movement. Even an account of their psychological development would be impossible without considering the deep psychological effects of political commitment and action upon them.

Yet relatively little has been written about the effects upon personality of political involvement: most writings assume that the relationship is only one way. The dearth of writings on this subject undoubtedly reflects the more general tendency to minimize the importance of post-adolescent experience on personality. (But see Bettelheim, 1960, and Erikson, 1950, 1959, 1964.) Political biographies suggest that other radical leaders, in other nations and eras, have been similarly influenced by their adult political experiences.

Within the New Left, there is relatively little formal discussion of psychosocial problems of Movement work. Most often, discussions center on alternative views of tactics, on descriptions of "model" projects, or on the more general principles of the New Left. The anthologies by Jacobs and Landau (1966) and Cohen and Hale (1967) both contain articles that touch upon the problems and effects of participation in the New Left; see especially "SNCC: An Overview Two Years Later" by Bruce Payne in Cohen and Hale (1967), Zinn (1965), Coles (1964), and Sutherland (1966). Recent issues of New Left journals (see notes to Introduction) often contain anecdotal accounts of specific Movement projects from which some of the characteristic tensions thereof can be inferred. But most of the considerable knowledge of the problems of working in the New Left exists only in the heads of the more experienced radicals, who pass it on verbally to others.

The parallels between the problems of small New Left groups and sensitivity-training or therapy groups are many. For differing accounts of the characteristics of the latter groups, see Mills (1964), Slater (1966), and Bion (1961). Movement groups differ from most sensitivity-training groups in at least two respects: first, they rarely have a recognized "leader" whose task is to assist the group in understanding its own interactions; second, they generally possess a defined task that transcends the understanding of group process or the facilitation of development of group members. In practice, however, many Movement groups tend to oscillate between the extragroup task (*e.g.,* organizing) and intragroup work aimed at increasing trust, co-operation, understanding, and individuality within the group. Whatever "paranoia" exists within the New Left seems to me primarily a result of the frequent encapsulation of Movement groups, rather than a consequence of the psychodynamics of most young radicals.

It is important to distinguish between those characteristics of a movement that result from the modal psychologies of its participants, and those that emerge from the style, process, structure, and organization of the movement. To give but one example, it is possible for relatively trusting and unsuspicious individuals in a highly encapsulated group to become "paranoid" about the out-group world because of the isolation of the group and the strong barriers that prevent communication across its boundaries. Similarly, it is possible for individuals whose personal psychologies are highly authoritarian to become involved in "participatory" or "democratic" groups in which their authoritarianism will be suppressed. A certain congruence generally exists between group structure and culture on the one hand and the modal personality structure and values of group members on the other. But this congruence is always less than complete, and any adequate account of a political (or other) movement must simultaneously consider the role of both psychological and organizational factors.

For two sympathetic accounts of the NCNP convention in September, 1967, see Waskow (1967) and Kopkind (1967). The quotations in this chapter advocating varying tactics for the New Left after Vietnam Summer are taken from *Vietnam Summer News,* Vol. I, Issue 6. My discussion of "political and cultural revolution" has been assisted by conversations with Robert J. Lifton on the meaning of the cultural revolution in China. His book *Revolutionary Immortality: Mao Tse-tung and the Chinese Cultural Revolution* will be published by Random House.

6 *The continuation of change*

The best brief analysis of the frustrations of work in the New Left is Coles's discussion, "Social Struggle and Weariness" (1964). My discussion in this chapter is essentially an argument that group and historical factors are more crucial in understanding the move toward resistance, disruption, and even insurrection among young radicals than are psychological factors. Stated differently, these young radicals are characterized psychologically by a strong inhibition on the direct expression of aggression. Insofar as they are representative, the talk of "violence" in the New Left arises more from a perception of social and historical needs than from the underlying psychological aggressiveness. (For one discussion of the political rationale of "resistance," see Chomsky [1967]). And while thoughts of taking action that might evoke violence are most common in times of depression, the depressed mood of New Leftists seems more a function of the political frustrations of their work than of their basic character structure. But in this regard, as in all others, there is enormous individual variability.

Another source of militancy in the white New Left, not discussed in the text, is the identification of white New Leftists with their black radical counterparts. The "rejection" of white activists by groups like SNCC and CORE has led to remarkably little counterrejection by white radicals. On the contrary, white radicals seem to be making an effort—conscious and unconscious—to keep their own rhetoric consistent with that of black radicals.

For an illuminating discussion of the issues of continuity and change in Japanese political activists, see Lifton (1964) and Wyatt (1965). On the general issue of relation of past and present in individual psychology, see Wyatt (1963).

In arguing that the issue of authority is not the central issue for most of the radicals I studied, I depart from many interpretations of radicalism. See, for example, Wolfenstein (1967) for an account of problems with authority in three revolutionary leaders. Many readers of an early draft of this book argued that among the young radicals *they* knew, hostility to authority was indeed a focal issue. And in *The Authoritarian Personality* (1950), Adorno *et al.* distinguish a variety of "liberal" types, some of which have major problems with authority. Doubtless all of these types are present within the New Left. My own observation that issues of hostility to parental and societal authority were not crucial for the New Leftists who led Vietnam Summer is therefore open to several differing interpretations: (1) the leadership of Vietnam Summer may be distinctive or atypical of the New Left as a whole in this respect; (2) my own biases may have led me to neglect what is actually a crucial issue for them; (3) other observers of radicals may exaggerate the importance of irrational opposition to authority in their explanations of the motives of New Leftists. This last possibility would be in keeping with a general tendency of those in positions of authority to view criticisms of them as reflecting the psychological problem of the critics rather than the manifest issues of the critique.

Throughout this account, I have emphasized psychological and historical aspects of the new radicalism, and have neglected many issues that would appear central to a sociologist. For example, I have not analyzed the "role" of the young radical—a role that is outside established institutions, but that is acquiring increasingly clear definition. From one perspective, becoming a radical could be seen as learning how to behave within the confines of this role. Nor have I stressed the "recognition" and "labeling" of the radical by others even before he came to think of himself as a radical. As with many other "deviant" roles, that of a "young radical" reflects not only the inner predisposition of the radical himself, but his reactions to the expectations of others in his environment. As I note in discussing "portents of later radicalism" in Chapter 3, most of these radicals were picked out by others in their environment as "cosmopolitan," "radical," "unwilling to take orders," et cetera, long before they came to think of themselves as members of the New Left. For expositions of the transactional view of deviance, see Becker (1963), and K. T. Erikson (1967).

I have also neglected that level of analysis that would see the New Left as a whole as an emerging innovative institution within the wider society. Such an analysis might examine in more detail the close relationship between the values of the New Left and the creedal values of American society. The new radicalism, in this context, can be seen as an *expression* of traditional American values like activism, social responsibility, individual involvement in politics, equality, "democracy," and so forth, rather than as a movement of opposition. In fact, of course, *all* protest movements similarly seize upon creedal cultural values in order to point out institutional practices that violate them. See Parsons (1951, 1960, 1963). For critiques of the structural-functional view of social change, see I. L. Horowitz (1964) and Dahrendorf (1968).

Radicalism and alienation—The contrast between the psychological functioning of alienated students and radicals is again marked. Many of the prime energies of the alienated are involved in working out internal conflicts—in particular, in attempting to deal with their longing for a simpler, more "direct" relationship with others like that which characterized their first relationships with their mothers. As a group, alienated students tend to be considerably more prone to actions that express symbolically themes and conflicts that date from childhood. For the young radicals I studied, however, more energy appeared to be in the service of the ego, as of the superego. Put in less technical terms, radicals seem more free to act in the service of their own principles and to possess a better grasp of reality. Alienated students as a group are far more depressed and rebellious than are radicals; in the alienated, there is often a general inhibition of all relationships, a withdrawal from potentially gratifying social and work involvements, and an active emphasis on inner life. With young radicals, focus on inner life is more than balanced by immersion into activity.

Also absent in radicals is the strong if diffuse hostility of the alienated. On personality tests, alienated students score very high on measures of neuroticism and direct hostility. While no personality tests were given to the young radicals studied, it seems likely that they would report less of both. Stated in somewhat oversimplified fashion, the alienated students I have studied had more than their share of psychological problems, although they were a highly creative and aesthetically imaginative group. Radicals, while they sometimes *have* had major psychological problems in the past, in general seemed to have been able to resolve their psychological conflicts in a relatively satisfactory way and to have turned their major energies toward changing the outer world rather than their own psychologies.

7 *Change, affluence, and violence*

Many of the ideas in this and the following chapter were influenced by conversations with Erik H. Erikson, Robert J. Lifton, Frederick Wyatt, and Christopher Jencks. Erikson's discussion of his current work on Gandhi at the 1967 meeting of the Group for the Study of Psycho-Historical Process contributed to my understanding of the issue of violence in young radicals. Robert J. Lifton's work on the survivors of Hiroshima (1968) also helped sharpen my awareness of the importance of technological death on American youth. For a thoughtful impact of the psychological problems of violent war, see Frank (1968); and on the impact upon children of the threat of nuclear warfare, see Escalona (1962).

Frederick Wyatt's discussion of the generational roots of superego conflict in today's college students (at the Group for the Study of Psycho-Historical Process) coincided with my own observations and helped me to formulate them. Conversations with Christopher Jencks about the relationships between radicals and their families also contributed to my discussion of the "credibility gap." For a brief exposition of Jencks's views, see his "Limits of the New Left" (1967). The impact of rapid social change upon individual personality is, in my view, a pervasive one, and the "credibility gap" is only one of the psychosocial consequences of continual historical transformation. For a more extended discussion of other psychological effects of "chronic" social change, see Keniston (1963, 1965a [especially Chapter 8]). Eisenstadt (1956) and Parsons (1951, 1960, 1963) also consider in detail the problem of cross-generational value transmission. Richard Flacks's emphasis on the importance of affluence to the new radicalism has also influenced my own interpretation (see Flacks, 1967).

In my discussion of the social facilitation of adolescence, I give more weight than do many accounts to the power of social factors not only to influence the course of adolescence, but to determine whether the opportunity for a full adolescence exists. Most accounts of adolescence (see reference notes to Chapter 3) are primarily based upon experience with middle-class youth in Western societies, and therefore take for granted the social and cultural facilities upon which the possibility of adolescence itself depends. But for a view that gives unusual weight to socio-cultural factors, see Group for the Advancement of Psychiatry (1966).

8 *Youth and history*

The study of the impact upon personality of historical forces has only begun to emerge as an area of special interest. The works of Erik Erikson and Robert Lifton occupy a central place in a small but growing literature. See also Mazlish (1963).

The problem of how to maintain a radical identity along with marital and professional commitments has been the topic of increasing discussion as the "first generation" of New Leftists reaches the age of thirty. A meeting of "radicals in the professions" in Ann Arbor, Michigan, in the summer of 1967 considered this problem. Some of the papers distributed at that meeting are printed in Steege *et al.* (1967). See in particular the article by the Habers. In suggesting in this chapter that the identity of "young radical" is temporary, I do not mean to impugn the sincerity of the radical commitment, much less to suggest that these young radicals will inevitably "outgrow" their radicalism. It seems possible that today's young radicals may begin to evolve new ways of combining a continuing commitment to social change with modification of marital and professional roles. Nevertheless, any identity in which youthfulness is crucial is by definition self-terminating.

The idea of a post-adolescent, preadult stage of life was first pointed out to me by Frederick Wyatt. In unpublished remarks, he has suggested that in other societies that allowed youth to postpone entry into adulthood for many years, such a stage has been recognized. He cites in particular the Greek concept of the ephebe.

The discussion of the "post-modern style" in this chapter has been strongly influenced by Robert Lifton's work "Protean Man" (1968). Lifton's concept of the Protean style is, however, somewhat more comprehensive than the ideas put forward here. And his observations are primarily based upon his research experience in the Far East, rather than in America. Nevertheless, the similarity between our findings suggests the validity of Lifton's central thesis—that the Protean style is a world-wide phenomenon, albeit with important cultural variations.

Bibliography

Adorno, Theodore W., Frenkel-Brunswik, E., Levinson, D. J., and Sanford, R. N. *The Authoritarian Personality*. New York: Harper, 1950.

Aiken, M., Demerath, N. J., and Marwell, G. "Conscience and Confrontation: Some Preliminary Findings on Summer Civil Rights Volunteers." University of Wisconsin (mimeo), 1966.

Allen, M., and Silverstein, H. "Progress Report: Creative Arts—Alienated Youth Project." New York: March, 1967.

Almond, Gabriel. *The Appeals of Communism*. Princeton: Princeton University Press, 1954.

Altbach, Philip G. (ed.). *Student Politics and Higher Education in the United States: A Select Bibliography*. Harvard University (Comparative National Development Project), preliminary edition (mimeo), 1967.

The Atlantic, the Editors of. *The Troubled Campus*. Boston: Little, Brown, 1966.

Bay, Christian. "Political and Apolitical Students: Facts in Search of Theory," *Journal of Social Issues* (1967), 23:76–91.

Becker, Howard. *Outsiders*. New York: Free Press, 1963.

Bell, Daniel (ed.). *The New American Right*. New York: Criterion Books, 1955.

Bernreuter, Robert G. "The College Student: He Is Thinking, Talking, Acting," *Penn State Alumni News* (July, 1966).

Bettelheim, Bruno. *The Informed Heart: Autonomy in a Mass Age*. Glencoe: Free Press, 1960.

Bion, W. R. *Experiences in Groups, and Other Papers*. New York: Basic Books, 1961.

Block, J., Haan, N., and Smith, M. B. "Activism and Apathy in Contemporary Adolescents," In J. F. Adams (ed.), *Contributions to the Understanding of Adolescence*. New York: Allyn and Bacon, forthcoming.

Blos, Peter. *On Adolescence.* Glencoe: Free Press, 1962.

Brown, Donald R. "Student Stress and the Institutional Environment," *J. Social Issues* (1967), 23:92–107.

Chomsky, Noam. "Resistance," *The New York Review of Books* (December 7, 1967).

Christie, Richard, and Jahoda, Marie (eds.). *Studies in the Scope and Method of "The Authoritarian Personality."* Glencoe: Free Press, 1954.

Cohen, Mitchell, and Hale, Dennis (eds.). *The New Student Left. An Anthology.* Boston: Beacon Press, 1967.

Coles, Robert. "Serpents and Doves: Non-violent Youth in the South." In E. H. Erikson (1963).

———. "Social Struggle and Weariness," *Psychiatry* (1964), 27:305–315.

———. *Children of Crisis.* Boston: Little, Brown, 1967.

Cowan, John Lewis. "Academic Freedom, Protest and University Environments." Paper read at American Psychological Association, New York, 1966.

Dahrendorf, Ralf. *Essays in the Theory of Society.* Stanford, California: Stanford University Press, 1968.

Davies, Alan F. *Private Politics.* Melbourne: Melbourne University Press, 1966.

Douvan, Elizabeth, and Adelson, Joseph. *The Adolescent Experience.* New York: John Wiley, 1966.

Draper, Hal. *Berkeley, The New Student Revolt.* New York: Grove, 1965.

Ehle, John. *The Free Men.* New York: Harper and Row, 1965.

Eisenstadt, S. M. *From Generation to Generation.* Glencoe: Free Press, 1956.

Erikson, Erik H. *Childhood and Society.* New York: Norton, 1950.

———. *Young Man Luther.* New York: Norton, 1958.

———. "Identity and the Life Cycle," *Psychological Issues* (1959), Vol. 1, No. 1.

———. (ed.). *Youth: Change and Challenge.* New York: Basic Books, 1963.

———. *Insight and Responsibility.* New York: Norton, 1964.

———. Review of Freud and Bullitt (1967), *International Journal of Psychoanalysis* (1967), 48:462–468.

Erikson, Kai T. *Wayward Puritans.* New York: Wiley, 1967.

Escalona, S. *Children and the Threat of Nuclear War.* New York: Child Study Association Publication, 1962.

Fenichel, Otto. *The Psychoanalytic Theory of Neurosis.* New York: Norton, 1945.

Fishman, Jacob R., and Solomon, Frederic. "Psychological Observations on the Student Sit-in Movement." Proceedings of the Third World Congress of Psychiatry, Toronto: University of Toronto/McGill, n.d.

———. "Youth and Social Action," *Journal of Social Issues* (1964), 20:1–28.

Flacks, Richard E. "The Liberated Generation: An Exploration of the Roots of Student Protest," *Journal of Social Issues* (1967), 23:52–75.

Frank, Jerome D. *Sanity and Survival. Psychological Aspects of War and Peace.* New York: Vintage, 1968.

Freud, Anna. "Adolescence," *Psychoanalytic Study of the Child.* Vol. 13. New York: International Universities Press, 1958.

———. *The Ego and the Mechanisms of Defense.* Translated from the German by Cecil Baines. New York: International Universities Press, 1946; reprinted 1962.

Freud, Sigmund. "Three Contributions to the Theory of Sex." (Part III: "The Transformations of Puberty.") In A. A. Brill (ed.), *The Basic Writings of Sigmund Freud,* New York: Modern Library, 1938.

Freud, Sigmund, and Bullitt, William C. *Thomas Woodrow Wilson: Twenty-eighth President of the United States.* Boston: Houghton Mifflin, 1967.

Fromm, Erich. *Escape from Freedom.* New York: Farrar and Rinehart, 1941.

Gandhi, Mohandas K. *Autobiography.* Boston: Beacon, 1957.

Gastwirth, D. "Why Students Protest." Unpublished paper, Yale University, 1965.

Greenstein, Fred J. *Children and Politics.* New Haven: Yale University Press, 1965.

———. "The Impact of Personality on Politics: An Attempt to Clear Away Underbrush," *American Political Science Review* (1967), 61:629–641.

Group for the Advancement of Psychiatry, Committee on Adolescence. *The Dynamics of Normal Adolescence.* Draft, November, 1966.

Haber, Allen and Barbara. "Getting By with a Little Help from Our Friends." In Steege, *et al.* (1967).

Hayden, T. Quoted in *Comparative Education Review* (1966), 10:187.

Heist, Paul. "Intellect and Commitment: The Faces of Discontent." In *Order and Freedom on the Campus*. Western Interstate Commission for Higher Education and the Center for the Study of Higher Education, 1965.

———. "The Dynamics of Student Discontent and Protest." Paper read at American Psychological Association, New York, 1966.

Hoffer, Eric. *The True Believer*. New York: Harper, 1951.

Horowitz, David. *Student*. New York: Ballantine Books, 1962.

Horowitz, Irving L. *The New Sociology*. New York: Oxford University Press, 1964.

Hyman, H. H. *Political Socialization: A Study in the Psychology of Politics*. Glencoe: Free Press, 1959.

Jacobs, Paul, and Landau, Saul. *The New Radicals: A Report with Documents*. New York: Vintage, 1966.

Jahoda, Marie. *Current Concepts of Positive Mental Health*. New York: Basic Books, 1958.

Jencks, Christopher. "Limits of the New Left." *The New Republic* (October 21, 1967).

Katope, Christopher G., and Zolbrod, Paul G. (eds.). *Beyond Berkeley: A Source Book in Student Values*. New York: World Publishing, 1966.

Katz, J. "The Learning Environment: Social Expectations and Influences." Paper presented at American Council of Education, Washington, D.C., 1965.

———. "The Student Activists: Rights, Needs and Powers of Undergraduates." Stanford: Institute for the Study of Human Problems, 1967.

Keene, S. "How One Big University Laid Unrest to Rest," *The American Student* (1966), 1:18–21.

Kelman, H. D. "Notes on Faculty Activism," *Letter to Michigan Alumni*, 1966.

Keniston, Kenneth. "American Students and the 'Political Revival,'" *The American Scholar* (1962), 32:40–64.

———. "Social Change in Youth in America," in E. H. Erikson (1963).

———. *The Uncommitted*. New York: Harcourt, Brace & World, 1965a.

———. "The Pressure to Perform," *The Intercollegian* (September, 1965b).

———. "The Faces in the Lecture Room." In R. S. Morison (ed.), *The American University*. Boston: Houghton Mifflin, 1966a.

———. "The Psychology of Alienated Students." Paper read at American Psychological Association, New York, 1966b.

Keniston, Kenneth, and Helmreich, R. "An Exploratory Study of Discontent and Potential Drop-outs at Yale." Yale University (mimeo), 1965.

Kerpelman, Larry C. "Student Political Activism and Ideology: Comparative Characteristics of Activists and Non-Activists." University of Massachusetts (mimeo), 1968.

Kopkind, Andrew. "The New Left: Chicago and After." *The New York Review of Books* (September 28, 1967).

Kornhauser, W. "Alienation and Participation in the Mass University." Paper read at American Ortho-Psychiatric Association, Washington, D.C., 1967.

Lane, Robert E. *Political Life*. Glencoe: Free Press, 1959.

———. *Political Ideology*. New York: Free Press, 1962.

Lasswell, Harold D. "Psychopathology and Politics" (1930), in *The Political Writings of Harold D. Lasswell*. Glencoe: Free Press, 1951.

Levinson, Daniel J. "The Relevance of Personality for Political Participation," *Public Opinion Quarterly* (1958), 22:3–10.

———. "Role, Personality, and Social Structure in the Organizational Setting," *Journal of Abnormal and Social Psychology* (1959), 58:170–180.

———. "Political Personality: II. Conservatism/Radicalism." In *The Encyclopedia of the Social Sciences*, forthcoming.

Lidz, Theodore. *The Person*. New York: Basic Books, forthcoming.

Lifton, Robert Jay. "Japanese Youth: The Search for the New and the Pure," *The American Scholar* (1960), 30:332–344.

———. *Thought Reform and the Psychology of Totalism*. New York: Norton, 1961.

———. "Youth and History: Individual Change in Post-War Japan." In Erikson (1963).

———. "Individual Patterns in Historical Change: Imagery of Japanese Youth," *Comparative Studies in Society and History* (1964), 6:369–383.

———. "Protean Man," *Partisan Review* (1968).

———. *Death in Life: Survivors of Hiroshima*. New York: Random House, 1968.

Lipset, Seymour M. *Political Man*. New York: Doubleday, 1960.

———. (ed.). Special Issue on Student Politics, *Comparative Education Review* (June, 1966).

———. "Student Opposition in the United States," *Government and Opposition* (1966a), 1:351–374.

———. "University Students and Politics in Underdeveloped Countries," *Comparative Education Review* (1966b), 10:132–162.

———. (ed.). *Student Politics*. New York: Basic Books, 1967.

Lipset, Seymour M, and Altbach, Philip G. "Student Politics and Higher Education in the United States," *Comparative Education Review* (1966), 10:320–349.

Lipset, Seymour M., and Wolin, S. S. (eds.). *The Berkeley Student Revolt*. Garden City, New York: Doubleday, 1965.

Lowenthal, L., and Gutterman, N. *Prophets of Deceit*. New York: Harper, 1949.

Luce, Phillip Abbott. *The New Left*. New York: David McKay, 1966.

Lyonns, G. "The Police Car Demonstration: A Survey of Participants." In Lipset and Wolin (1965).

Mallery, David. *Ferment on the Campus*. New York: Harper and Row, 1966.

Mazlish, Bruce (ed.). *Psychoanalysis and History*. Englewood Cliffs, New Jersey: Prentice-Hall, 1963.

Michael, Donald Nelson. *The Next Generation. The Prospects Ahead for the Youth of Today and Tomorrow*. New York: Vintage, 1965.

Miller, Daniel R., and Swanson, Guy E. *The Changing American Parent*. New York: Wiley, 1958.

Miller, Michael, and Gilmore, Susan (eds.). *Revolution at Berkeley*. New York: Dell, 1965.

Mills, Theodore. *Group Transformation: An Analysis of a Learning Group*. New York: Prentice-Hall, 1964.

Newfield, Jack. *A Prophetic Minority*. New York: Signet Books, 1966.

Newsweek. "Campus, 1965" (March 22, 1965).

Parsons, Talcott. *The Social System*. Glencoe: Free Press, 1951.

———. *Structure and Process in Modern Societies*. Glencoe: Free Press, 1960.

———. "Youth in the Context of American Society." In E. H. Erikson (1963).

Paulus, G. "A Multivariate Analysis Study of Student Activist Leaders, Student Government Leaders, and Non-Activists." Cited in Peterson (1968).

Pervin, Lawrence A., Reik, L. E., and Dalrymple, W. (eds.). *The College Drop-out and the Utilization of Talent*. Princeton: Princeton University Press, 1966.

Peterson, Richard E. *The Scope of Organized Student Protest in 1964–65*. Princeton: Educational Testing Service, 1966.

———. "The Student Left in American Higher Education," *Daedalus* (1968), 97:293–317.

Reed, M. "Student Non-Politics, or How to Make Irrelevancy a Virtue," *The American Student* (1966), 1:7–10.

Reich, Wilhelm. *The Mass Psychology of Fascism*. New York: Orgone Institute Press, 1946.

Riesman, David. *The Lonely Crowd*. New Haven: Yale University Press, 1950.

———. *Faces in the Crowd*. New Haven: Yale University Press, 1952.

Rigney, Francis J., and Smith, L. D. *The Real Bohemia*. New York: Basic Books, 1961.

Rogow, Arnold A. *James T. Forrestal: A Study of Personality, Politics, and Policy*. New York: Macmillan, 1964.

Rokeach, Milton. *The Open and Closed Mind*. New York: Basic Books, 1960.

Schiff, L. F. "The Obedient Rebels: A Study of College Conversions to Conservatism," *Journal of Social Issues* (1964), 20:74–96.

Schneider, Patricia. "A Study of Members of SDS and YD at Harvard." Unpublished B.A. thesis, Wellesley College, 1966.

Schram, Stuart, R. *Mao Tse-Tung*. Baltimore: Penguin Books, 1967.

Shub, David. *Lenin: A Biography*. Baltimore: Penguin Books, 1967.

Sigel, Roberta (ed.). "Political Socialization: Its Role in the Political Process." Issue of the *Annals of the American Academy of Political and Social Science* (1965).

Slater, P. E. *Microcosm*. New York: Wiley, 1966.

Smith, M. Brewster, Bruner, Jerome S., and White, Robert W. *Opinions and Personality*. New York: Wiley, 1960.

Solomon, Frederic, and Fishman, Jacob R. "Perspectives on the Student Sit-in Movement," *American Journal of Ortho-Psychiatry* (1963), 33:873–874.

———. "Youth and Peace: A Psycho-social Study of Student Peace Demonstrators in Washington, D.C.," *Journal of Social Issues* (1964), 20:54–73.

Somers, R. H. "The Mainsprings of the Rebellion: A Survey of Berkeley Students in November, 1964." In Lipset and Wolin (1965).

Steege, Ted, *et al.* "Radicals and the Professions," *Our Generation* (1967), 5:2:48–101.

Stern, G. "Myth and Reality in the American College," *AAUP Bulletin* (Winter, 1966), 408–414.

Suczek, Robert Francis, and Alfert, E. "Personality Characteristic of College Drop-outs." University of California (mimeo), 1966.

Sutherland, Elizabeth (ed.). *Letters from Mississippi*. New York: Signet Books, 1966.

Trent, James W. and Craise, Judith L. "Commitment and Conformity in the American College," *J. Social Issues* (1967), 23:34–51.

Trotsky, Leon. *My Life*. New York: Grosset and Dunlap, 1930.

Trow, Martin. "Some Lessons from Berkeley." Paper presented to American Council of Education, Washington, D.C., 1965.

Waskow, Arthur I. "Notes on Chicago." Washington, D.C.: Institute for Policy Studies (mimeo), 1967.

Watts, William Arthur, and Whittaker, D. "Some Socio-psychological Differences between Highly Committed Members of the Free Speech Movement and the Student Population at Berkeley," *Applied Behavioral Science* (1966), 2:41–62.

———. "Socio-psychological Characteristics of Intellectually Oriented, Alienated Youth: A Study of the Berkeley Nonstudent." University of California (Berkeley) (mimeo), 1967.

Westby, D., and Braungart, R. "Class and Politics in the Family Backgrounds of Student Political Activists," *American Sociological Review* (1966), 31:690–692.

White, Winston. *Beyond Conformity*. Glencoe: Free Press, 1961.

Whittaker, D., and Watts, W. A. "Personality and Value Attitudes of Intellectually Disposed, Alienated Youth." Paper presented at American Psychological Association, New York, 1966.

Wolfenstein, E. *Revolutionary Personality: Lenin, Trotsky, and Gandhi*. Princeton, New Jersey: Princeton University Press, 1967.

Wright, E. O. "Student Leaves of Absence from Harvard College: A Personality and Social System Approach." Unpublished paper, Harvard University, 1966.

Wyatt, Frederick R. "The Reconstruction of the Individual and of the Collective Past." In R. W. White (ed.); *The Study of Lives*. New York: Atherton Press, 1963.

———. "In Quest of Change," *Comparative Studies in Society and History* (1965), 7:384–392.

Zinn, Howard. *SNCC: The New Abolitionists*. Boston: Beacon, 1965.